P9-DND-056

RAVES FOR

babytalk

FROM THE EXPERTS . . .

"We read *Babytalk* magazine with each of our eight babies, and we've been writing for *Babytalk* for more than twenty-five years. Millions of children throughout the world are better off because of the terrific resource this magazine is for new moms. Keep talking, *Babytalk*!"
—**WILLIAM SEARS, MD, and MARTHA SEARS, RN,**
co-authors of *The Baby Book*

"With just the right balance of humor and reliable advice, *Babytalk* does a terrific job of giving busy new parents the information they want and need."
—**Sesame Workshop™**

"*Babytalk* magazine is a trusted source for no-nonsense, solid advice for new parents."
—**ALAN FIELDS and DENISE FIELDS,**
authors of the bestselling *Baby Bargains*

"New moms have an endless stream of questions, and *Babytalk* has concise, entertaining answers—the magazine is a must-have baby accessory."
—**SAMANTHA ETTUS, editor of**
The Experts' Guide to the Baby Years

"*Babytalk* magazine is an excellent resource, providing parents the information that they need from late pregnancy throughout the first year of life."
—**JODI A. MINDELL, PhD, author of**
Sleeping Through the Night

more . . .

... AND FROM NEW MOMS

"I love *Babytalk* magazine. I love that there is real advice from real moms. The advice is always something I can actually use and not some old wives' tale. There are great articles, and the magazine is fun to read."
—Danielle, Indianapolis, IN

"I love *Babytalk* magazine because even a 'seasoned' parent (we have four children, ages six and younger) can learn a thing or two with each issue! The columns are great, the features are cutting-edge, and the covers are just so cute!"
—Shanna, Elk Grove, CA

"I love *Babytalk* because of all the input from real moms. Sometimes I wonder if authors of parenting books and magazines actually have children, because their suggestions sound noble, but are utterly absurd when put into practice. I know that *Babytalk* has ideas suggested by real moms."
—Susie, Boise, ID

"Why do I love *Babytalk* magazine? Because it's a mommy-girlfriend who tells it like it is and it's always there for you! The articles and advice on babies and mommies are so helpful to me, and they make me feel like I'm not alone. I usually get two or three copies, one for my office at home (I'm a work-at-home mommy,) one for my bathroom, and another one just in case a mommy-friend needs it!"
—Andrea, San Jose, CA

"I love *Babytalk* magazine because it makes me feel connected with other moms and their babies. I find it comforting to know that there are other moms out there who experience the perils and joys of motherhood like I do."
—Elizabeth, Centreville, VA

THE **babytalk** INSIDER'S GUIDE TO

Your Baby's First Year

BY STEPHANIE WOOD AND KITTY O'CALLAGHAN, CONTRIBUTING EDITORS, **babytalk** MAGAZINE

WELLNESS CENTRAL

NEW YORK   BOSTON

This book is not intended as a substitute for the medical advice of physicians. The reader should regularly consult a physician in all matters relating to health, and particularly in respect of any symptoms that may require diagnosis or medical attention.

Text copyright © 2008 by The Parenting Group, Inc.
Illustrations copyright © 2008 by Hachette Book Group USA, Inc.
BABYTALK is a registered trademark of The Parenting Group, Inc.
All rights reserved. Except as permitted under the U.S. Copyright Act of 1976, no part of this publication may be reproduced, distributed, or transmitted in any form or by any means, or stored in a database or retrieval system, without the prior written permission of the publisher.

Wellness Central
Hachette Book Group USA
237 Park Avenue
New York, NY 10017

Visit our Web site at www.HachetteBookGroupUSA.com.

Wellness Central is an imprint of Grand Central Publishing.
The Wellness Central name and logo is a trademark of Hachette Book Group USA, Inc.

Printed in the United States of America

First Edition: February 2008
10 9 8 7 6 5 4 3 2

Book design and illustrations by Giorgetta Bell McRee
Text composition by L&G McRee

Library of Congress Cataloging-in-Publication Data

Editors of Babytalk Magazine.
	The Babytalk insider's guide to your baby's first year / the editors of Babytalk Magazine.
		p. cm.
Summary: "From Babytalk magazine, a comprehensive guide to your baby's first year, complete with expert advice and the secrets that nobody tells you about"—Provided by the publisher.
	ISBN-13: 978-0-446-69804-7
	ISBN-10: 0-446-69804-0
		1. Pediatrics—Popular works. 2. Infants—Care—Popular works. I. Title.
	RJ61 . B133 2008
	618.92 22
						2007021122

Contents

So it's the end of life as you know it . . . You're about to embark on a real-world roller-coaster ride, but the highs will soon outnumber the lows, and the view from the top will be glorious. When you truly respect your and your baby's unique personality and needs, you're going to do a stellar job as a parent—your kid and you both win.

Consider this section the baby owner's manual they forgot to give you at the hospital, with the lowdown on: sponge baths and tub baths; circumcision care; umbilical cord care; diapering and rashes; nail know-how; spotting jaundice and what to do about it; layette lingo; coping with visitors; dealing with the house; bonding, and why you don't need to worry about it just yet; and a few words about your postpartum recovery and whirlwind emotions.

A guilt-free guide to everything you need to know about the feeding choice you make, be it breastfeeding, bottlefeeding, or doing the combo—and why it's important that your method suits your *own* style (your baby will get the nutrition she needs regardless).

CHAPTER 3: *Everthing You Always Wanted to Know about Babies and Sleep—But Were Too Tired to Ask*   93

No, you won't get much, but you will spend the rest of your days (and nights) for some time to come dreaming about it. Here are some realistic thoughts about how to help make sleep happen—for your baby and you—and how to cope when it doesn't.

CHAPTER 4: *How to Keep Your Baby (and Yourself) Calm(ish), Cool(ish), and Not (Too) Crazy*   122

Next to feeding and sleeping, your other priority will be soothing your little one—and your own nerves! We'll begin with understanding crying and dealing with colic, then segue into attachment, security, routine, and personality issues.

CHAPTER 5: *The Growing Year—A Real-Life Look at Your Baby's Development*   160

Insight into the nothing-short-of-miraculous way your baby grows and develops—despite the "mistakes" you may make along the way! Beyond the physical skills, we'll include cognitive, social, and language skills, and look at how play and stimulation feed into all this. Plus: a milestone reality-check chart—when moms think babies should reach milestones (the commonly believed ages) versus the average window when they actually do it.

CHAPTER 6: *In Good Health—Must-Know News on Vaccines, Baby Bugs, and Keeping Your Kiddo Well*   199

There's nothing scarier to a new parent than the thought of her baby getting sick. But when it comes to healthcare, there's a lot more to learn about than fevers and runny noses. We give you the lowdown on everything you expect—well-care checkups, immunizations, and garden-variety illness like colds, rashes, fevers, ear infections—as well as a healthy dose of reassurance.

CHAPTER 7: *Feeding, Part II—Time to Chow Down on the Solid Stuff*   237

Just when you get the liquid diet down, it's time to think about those first bites of baby mush, then on to the eventual total table-food diet (good-bye, ounce markers and measurable little jars; hello, stress). In this chapter, we help you gauge what's really going in and how much it matters—or not.

CHAPTER 8: *Babyproofing and Beyond—The No-Panic Guide to Safety and (Eeks!) First Aid* 270

Busy, mobile little babies are as dangerous as they are adorable. Here's all you need to know to protect your precious bambino from injury, plus how to keep calm and handle every type of emergency, from boo-boos to the really scary situations.

CHAPTER 9: *The Stuff of Motherhood—Great Gear Guaranteed to Make Your Life Easier* 326

There's a whole new world of shopping at hand, and just as with your own home and wardrobe, you definitely don't need it all (not that you won't want it). Before you head to the local baby retail outlet or worldwide baby Web, check out our insider's guide to gear you need and gear you don't for everyday life and travels with your baby.

CHAPTER 10: *What's Up with You?—Time to Think about Mom (for a Change)* 347

Finally, it's time to turn our thoughts to numero uno: You, you, you! We'll hold your hand through everything from adjusting to this weird new body you now inhabit; to your evolving relationship with your partner in parenthood (Dad, not the baby!), and how to reconnect if you're having trouble finding together time; to what working or staying home has to do with it; to how to keep your act together and learn to love your new life (easier than you think!).

CHAPTER 11: *Special Families, Special Needs—Real-Life Advice for Parents of Premature Babies and Infants with Medical Issues* 381

New parenthood is hard enough when you're blessed with a healthy full-term baby. An unexpected health issue or surprisingly early arrival requires a whole additional level of support, both physical and emotional, for your baby, yourself, your partner, and any other siblings on the scene. In this chapter, we point you in the right direction to find the very best care for your baby and everyone else in the family.

Adoptions, both within the United States and internationally, are on the rise. So are twins and multiple births, in part due to huge leaps and successes in infertility treatment. However you happen to come by your baby (or babies), you have special concerns that the average parent of a singleton (now, there's an affectionate-sounding description if we ever heard one!) simply doesn't. Here's some customized advice on coping, bonding, and caring for these extra-special-in-their-own-way babies.

Our favorite resources on whatever parenting issue—health, development, sleeping, traveling, you name it—you might find challenging during the year ahead.

Acknowledgments

One bitter January day in 1997, seven months pregnant with my second child and sitting at my desk daydreaming about the magical but mythical maternity leave that all moms-to-be manage to convince themselves is ahead, I received a phone call that steered my career in an unanticipated direction. Having spent much of my professional life employed by, and then freelancing for, a competing publication, I was surprised to hear the voice of Janet Chan, the new editor-in-chief of *Parenting*, and editorial director of the Parenting Group, which includes *Babytalk*. That conversation evolved into a decade-long relationship with Janet and her talented staff, as well as with Susan Kane who took the reigns at *Babytalk* two years later. I owe the better part of my career since to all those involved in that chain of events, as well as many terrific and fun editors on both the *Parenting* (Lisa Bain, Linda Rodgers, Josh Lerman, to name but a few) and *Babytalk* staffs (lots more on them to come).

Still, I owe my biggest debt of gratitude to Susan Kane for giving me the opportunity to nurture and mold this very important offspring in her own impressive career. That she trusted me with such a precious and humongous baby of a project still surprises me when I think about it, not to mention the sheer fact that we actually managed to get it done relatively on schedule. Susan's endless cheerleading and pep talks along the way, even when I knew well that she was at least as stressed as I was, were a significant factor in my ability to maintain both my momentum and my sanity the past year and a half. I'm continuously amazed at how she manages to maintain her level of passion and perfection in all she does every day. Susan's vision of, and endless aspiration for, *Babytalk* is the singular secret to its success.

My co-author, Kitty O'Callaghan, was also a pure pleasure to work with. I envy her ability to take the most mundane moments in motherhood and twist them into side-splitting tales that reassure, entertain, and remind us that life with kids is really quite the same for all of us, no matter how different and special our families are. I couldn't have asked for a better partner, and I hope her talents for both writing and parenting have rubbed off on me at least a little.

Of course there were many other players within the *Babytalk* family who gave me endless assistance, advice, and support. They include our research editor, Jennifer Geddes, who is as sharp a woman and mother as she is a reporter and fact-checker, which is to say extraordinary. It is because she has backed me up on this book that I sleep at night. I also want to thank Executive Editor Lisa Singer Moran, Managing Editor Maureen Shelly, and Senior Editors Patty Onderko and Christina Vercelleto, all of whom were quick to lend a hand, an eye, a tip, or a less-used adjective when necessary. I'm also grateful that they each, at times, overlooked the fact that I was often late with other deadlines because of the book (and that I never hesitated to whine about it).

I am also indebted to Assistant Editors Margaret Williams and Caitlin Stine, who were on top of my every e-mail practically before I hit the send button, gathering research, rounding up the many, many mom quotes that are the true voice of *Babytalk*, posting polls on our Web site, and generally helping me make every brilliant middle-of-the-night brainstorm actually happen. Margaret Williams, in particular, must be thanked for completing the tremendous but thankless task of pulling together our gargantuan resource list as the final manuscript deadline was looming and I could no longer tell my *p*'s from *q*'s or diaper rash from cradle cap.

Finally, I must thank our intrepid editor at Grand Central Publishing, Natalie Kaire, whose sharp, insightful guidance, and keen eye for detail helped keep us on track and cutting edge. Her endless patience, composure, and understanding every time we freaked out about the next looming deadline are the traits of a true professional.

Of course none of this would have been possible without the support of my husband, best friend, and partner in the excellent adventure of marriage and family life, Patrick Mullen. He has had endless patience with me and my stubborn attempts to be both career woman and mother, probably leaving him in the dust a little too often. I must also thank my three beautiful children—Matilda, Anthony, and Charlie—for their unconditional love, admiration, and pride in what I do professionally, even when it interferes with their desire to be picked up, dropped off, or entertained at times. I just hope they don't hold it against me when the objects of future crushes discover they can Google their toilet training travails and behavior faux pas online someday. I would also be remiss if I didn't thank my mother- and father-in-law, Mary and Patrick Mullen, and my numerous brothers- and sisters-in-law for their many parenting anecdotes and free babysitting during the course of this (and many other) projects.

Finally, words can never express my gratitude to my very own mother and father, Jane and Roger Wood, who taught me the most important aspects of being a good parent, which cannot be found in any book—only in your memories and your heart.

—*Stephanie Wood*

I owe a huge debt of gratitude to everyone who had a hand in this project, but the biggest payout is reserved for my co-author, Stephanie, for her prolific efforts and vast reserves of patience. Her knowledge on everything confronting new parents is beyond compare, as is her ability to write it all down (on time!) in an informative, organized, and entertaining manner. Without her Herculean strength and fortitude, this book would never have happened.

In addition, I would like to thank the wonderful editors at *Babytalk* for their guidance and input. In particular, Editor-in-chief Susan Kane deserves my deepest gratitude for her insightful comments and questions, which not only were a great service to the reader, but also made me look good.

I would also like to thank my husband for his endless calm assurance that, yes, I would get everything finished. And, finally, a big thank you goes out to my mom and dad for teaching me everything I know about parenting, and to my children for showing me everything I don't.

—*Kitty O'Callaghan*

Yes, You Can Raise That Baby!
(And It Doesn't Have to Be Aunt Edna's or Anyone Else's Way)

There are several inalienable rights of new motherhood:

> You have the right to be tired.
> You have the right to be stressed.
> You have the right to cry for no apparent reason.

But most importantly:

> You have the right to enjoy this time, and . . .
> You have the right to bring up your baby, your way.

Now, there's a novel idea (or two). To believe that these rights exist, however, we have to believe that most mothers come equipped with the brains, the instincts, and the loving hearts to nurture their children in their own ways. Why would we do such a crazy thing? Probably because we're moms—imperfect, loving, and always learning. We are *Babytalk* editors because we have (and adore) babies, just like you do.

And because we're moms whose job it is to publish helpful advice, our mission at *Babytalk* is to tell it like it is about life with a baby, to help women navigate not just the practical realities of being a new mom, but the emotional roller coaster as well. We believe that too many parenting magazines and books sugarcoat the challenging experience of life with a new baby, downplaying just how difficult sleep deprivation and weeks or months of colic can be. By telling the truth instead—from the ecstasy of this experience to the agony—we help women feel less alone and build their confidence. Yes, the pages of this book will still give you all that you expect to keep your baby safe, secure, healthy, and loved. You'll learn in-the-trenches secrets of figuring out what your baby needs during those hazy, confusing, sleep-starved first days and nights home from the hospital; how to devise a feeding style that works for your lifestyle (and yes, that means you don't have to exclusively breastfeed, or even breastfeed at all, if it's too much of a challenge); the gear you really need to get around efficiently (and the stuff you can skip); how to handle that first fever, first tooth, and first spoonful of mush (not necessarily in that order); and even how to tell Grandma or that annoying know-it-all mom in your playgroup to kiss off (tactfully) when you're bombarded with outdated or unwanted advice. In sum, we will go beyond the expected to talk about the things no one else reveals; the reality of parenting versus the ideal. Because we reflect a mom's true experience, we think you'll find this book refreshing, gutsy, and compelling, as well as encouraging and warm.

Another important *Babytalk* difference: We're not going to tell you there's only one right way to care for your child, be it how she eats, sleeps, cries, soothes, or entertains herself (if only!). There are, of course, myriad experts, books, grandparents, friends, neighbors, co-workers, nannies, TV shows, TV shows *about* nannies, and, of course, complete strangers telling you *their* way, and making you feel like a total screwup in the process. But our feeling at *Babytalk* is that there's no point in dispensing my-way-or-the-highway advice when it just doesn't work and only kicks a mom's confidence to the curb.

Of course, there are obvious, ironclad safety issues where there is only one right way to do things—such as putting your baby to sleep on her back or always using a car seat. But when it comes to just about anything else, you have many more choices than you may realize. As all parents know, each baby is an individual with his or her own character and needs, and often you have to experiment with different tactics to find the best ways to meet those needs. And trust us when we say that the best ways will meet *your* needs as well.

Here are two quick examples of what you'll find in these pages that you won't find anywhere else. A truism floating around out there says that once your baby is a mere six to eight weeks old, you need to get in the habit of putting her to bed when drowsy but still awake, so she can learn to fall asleep on her own. This is a scenario that works for some babies with mothers luckier than Powerball winners. The rest of us often find that no one in the entire house gets any sleep when you try and try and still fail to employ this method. If you know that the only way your baby can go to sleep is by rocking her and then gently transferring her to her crib, we're not going to teach you how to get her to zone out some other way, and we'll help you make your method even more goof-proof. We're also here to tell you that a child who feels his mother is tuned into his heart's desires is a child who can happily fall asleep on his own when he's ready—even if it's later than the "ideal."

Let's look at another "rule" we mothers with babies will hear again and again: Wait at least four weeks, until breastfeeding is well established, before you allow your husband or Grandma to introduce a bottle and finally let you get a stretch of sleep longer than two hours. If you're someone who needs sleep to feel sane, you may find yourself—as many of us here at *Babytalk* did—a sobbing mess at the two-week mark of exclusive breastfeeding. Here's what we say: Go ahead and have Dad give your bambino a bottle *now*. Most babies can go back and forth between breast and bottle by this point with no problem. We'll tell you how to do the combo, and we won't tell you formula is poison because people who say that are lunatics. Deep inside, you know that. And it's that voice deep down inside that we will teach you to hear and to trust.

Pep talks aside, we promise not to whitewash the tough stuff. *The Babytalk Insider's Guide to Your Baby's First Year* will indeed tell it like it is, with all the humor, anxiety, sadness, joy, and intense love that having a baby brings. You'll get expertise born of experience and solutions rooted in sympathy. We know what your day-to-day life is like—we're living it right along with you.

While blanket policies and recommendations about issues like weaning and bedtime won't always apply to you, guidelines from august bodies such as the American Academy of Pediatrics (AAP) do exist. We respect them, and we're going to tell you about them. But we're also going to give you the variations, the windows of expectation, and the things that might happen if you don't follow the guidelines *exactly* (which are not always as bad as you might think). Your pediatrician might do the same: Many are moms and dads themselves and know just where you're coming from. If yours is more dogmatic than you'd prefer, you'll find reassurance throughout the book in our little boxes titled "Voice of Reason"—these are snippets of advice from pediatricians and child development experts who know that few parents or babies fit the perfect mold. You'll also see tips and quips from lots of real women like you in our "What Nobody Told Me About . . ." sections, as well as plenty of baby care choices in our popular lists of "Five Ways to . . ." do just about anything that pertains to your little one.

This book is a road map through the toughest times and wonderful moments of parenting for you and your little passenger. We'll travel the highways of tried-and-often-true advice, but also the back roads, winding paths, and shortcuts that will safely take you where you need to go. If along the way you find you'd like some company on your trip, we invite you to visit Parenting.com/babytalk, where plenty of other moms just like you will be both bragging and bitching, venting and dishing. And here's the very best part: Because you're in charge of your own journey, it's much less likely to be a guilt trip. Let's begin, Mama!

THE **babytalk** INSIDER'S GUIDE TO
Your Baby's First Year

CHAPTER 1

Baby Boot Camp

How to Keep Your Baby Alive and
Your Sanity Intact the First Six Weeks (or So)

Welcome to Club Mom. You are now a card-carrying member of the world's biggest, longest-enduring, least exclusive, yet most sought-after group in the world (and if you're a second- or third-time mom, you can add a gold star to your card). Your cronies include incredibly organized, creative, talented, athletic, and socially gifted women. They also include incredibly confused, stressed-out, tired, cranky, and nervous-about-keeping-the-baby-breathing women. Most often, any given mom has characteristics from both categories.

That said, when you meet another member of the club who seems to have it all together—or even just seems to be freshly showered—you might start to wonder if you are fit to wear the burp cloth. Rest assured, you are not alone in your doubts. We all feel them. So let us be the first to tell you that not only is that spit-encrusted shield of honor yours to keep, but your moment or day or week of feeling inadequate is temporary. It is just a stage, and it, too, shall pass along with:

- The stage wherein your baby screams like a banshee at the stroke of 12, 2, 4, and 6 AM, then sleeps until noon while you try to clean the house and do the laundry in a trance-like state.
- The stage wherein he regurgitates what appears to be twice the amount of liquid he just consumed.
- The stage in which he enjoys playing with the electrical outlets far more than the tony educational gadgets you have just invested in.

- The stage in which he unrolls all the toilet paper from all the bathrooms in the house on a daily basis.
- The stage in which he loves to say potty words, especially at the dinner table when company comes over. (The number of potty words he spews forth is in direct proportion to the age of the dinner guest, for prime shock value.)
- The stage during which he only eats food that is the color white or begins with the letter *p*.
- The stage when he insists on sleeping in full firefighter gear.
- The stage when he insists he doesn't need to do his homework because he will be playing major-league football for a living.
- The stage when he tries to con you into a Mohawk for his school pictures.
- The stage when he insists on believing in Santa Claus a little longer because he knows *you* would never actually spend $600 on PlayStation XIV, or whatever version we're up to at that point.
- The stage when the girls start to call (whatever happened to playing hard to get?).
- The stage wherein he stops asking you if he can borrow the car and wants to know instead when you will be buying him one.
- The stage wherein you cry all summer because he's about to go off to college.

Way, way, way before all these stages (every one of which will seem like the last one you can survive), you will emerge from Baby Boot Camp and realize that you are quite capable of keeping your squirming, whining, tiny infant alive. In fact, you might even be good at it. This chapter is a crash course that will help you get through the first phase, the postpartum period of about six to eight weeks when the learning curve is steepest, days and nights blur together, and your confidence ebbs and flows like the milk dripping from your breast: one minute, not so much, the next gushing everywhere. Here is a very loose description of what to expect: Your baby will need to eat approximately every two hours, and will sleep off and on around the clock in roughly the same time increments. Therefore, so will you. You will feel not just exhausted, but also physically uncomfortable as you heal, depending on the type of birth you experienced, for approximately one to three weeks. (We give you all the physical recovery details beginning on page 30.) You will no doubt also experience difficulty and discomfort for roughly two weeks as you learn to breastfeed, if that's the method you've chosen. (Again, all the insight, advice, and secrets you need on this topic can be found in chapter 2, beginning on page 39.) Somewhere toward the end of this postpartum phase, you'll probably be surprised and delighted to discover your baby will be sleeping for slightly longer stretches (like three hours instead of two), and thank heaven for small blessings. Feedings will be less stressful and may space out a bit as well, timing-wise. Your ob-gyn will probably pronounce you healed somewhere around six weeks, maybe eight weeks if you had a C-section or otherwise complicated delivery. Your partner will make the mistake of thinking that you actually want to have sex again just because your body is capable (not!). In between, you will call and run to the pediatrician often for checkups and emotional support (see chapter 6, page 199, for a complete breakdown of when your baby's checkups need to occur and what to expect during them). And someday you will look back on all this and remember the emotional peaks, forget the frustration, and actually feel like doing it all again!

Yes, having a baby truly is the end of life as you know it, and if we may invoke another cliché, your new life may feel like a roller-coaster ride, complete with exhilarating highs and nauseating lows. But let us assure you that taken as a whole, the entire experience will be as wonderful as it is wild. Seriously.

First things first: Before you and your baby can begin your new life together, you must actually *leave the hospital*, a rather scary scenario for any new mom. After all, for the last forty-eight hours or so, you have been in the protective custody of nurses and doctors who know exactly what they are doing. Now, for some bizarre reason, they seem to have the impression that you do, too.

While you may not feel confident in your maternal skills yet, you can still be prepared to make the trip home. You only need four essentials to go from point A to point B: an infant rear-facing car seat, a change of clothes for the baby, some diapers, and another pair of hands—whether they're attached to the baby's father, your mom, or a good friend. Going mano a mano with your newborn is possible, but not advisable, particularly for the first week or so when you're losing sleep and gaining more work. So repeat after us: Two pairs of hands to one baby. (Frankly, a third pair wouldn't hurt, either.)

The trip home will be thrilling and a bit frightening. Don't be surprised if you suddenly think that every car on the road is careering at breakneck speed or that your baby needs you to check that he's breathing every few minutes. Your apprehensions will finally melt away, however, when you arrive home. Stepping into totally familiar surroundings, you will experience a sense of relief. You don't exactly feel fabulous, but it's better then having a thirty-pound weight sitting on your pelvis while simultaneously choking your lungs and chest. And you can look forward to spending a night in your own bed. A night without being disturbed by squeaky hospital carts rolling up and down the corridors or nurses barging in to take your vitals at 1 AM (like you're going to die now, after all you've just been through).

Sure, your baby will wake up now and again, but for the first few hours or even days he may be so exhausted from his long, strange trip that he may shut down and sleep. Our advice: Go with it. Ignore the well-wishers on the phone and let the answering machine do its job. Ignore the mess your partner made while he was on his own in the house (you might as well start training yourself now). This is the time to rest and get your bearings if you can.

It's also the perfect time to psych yourself up for Murphy's First Law of Motherhood: Newborns invariably wake up from their stupor, and continue to do so day or night. We're sorry to tell you, but those two or so days in the hospital when it looked like you were going to have the world's most contented baby were but a tease. He was simply recuperating from delivery and checking out the world in small doses. Once your baby sees how exciting it is, he'll enter party mode. He may seem to stay awake forever, especially at night, and when he does sleep it will be at the least convenient time for you (like right before his doctor administers a shot, or when your breasts are ready to explode).

This is the type of newborn behavior that inspires descriptions like *haze, daze,* or *fog.* In your exhausted, uncertain, yet extremely vigilant state, you will be trying to make sense of those cues everyone told you your baby would send your way. You know, the ones that signal that she's tired or wet or curious or hungry. The funny thing is that no matter how hard you look or listen, you will definitely not be able to decode every gurgle, wince, whimper, or cry. Don't worry. Your baby barely knows what she wants and needs during these first weeks, let alone how to communicate it to you. So instead of driving yourself crazy trying to read her mind, relax and concentrate on the basics: feeding, burping, changing, and snuggling.

Think of it as autopilot baby care. It's not that you're ignoring your baby's needs, it's just that at this point they are so fundamental—and your sleep, so minimal—that worrying about what your baby is thinking is a waste of precious energy. Do what needs doing and slowly, slowly, slowly, some sense will emerge for both of you.

"WHAT NOBODY TOLD ME ABOUT HOW MUCH TIME BABYCARE TAKES"

"I felt like I was topless for a month straight! The baby needed to be fed so often and it took so long, there were days when I would look up and it was already 4 PM and I was still in my PJs. To cope I had to learn to manage my own expectations about what was an appropriate dress code around my own house. I grabbed a bathrobe and began answering the door in my pajamas with a smile like it was normal!"
—*Nicholle, St. Louis, Missouri*

"The hardest part was learning to do things for myself with a baby strapped in a front carrier. My son loved it, but it was very hard to eat without getting crumbs all over his little head, and brushing my teeth was really not an option. I learned how to squat so I could load and unload laundry."
—*Trisha, Armonk, New York*

"The first month entailed a trilogy of sanity challenges: the hormonal roller coaster, the physical changes, and the responsibility for this little creature."
—*Tina, Monroe, Wisconsin*

"The lack of a regular routine was hard. I'm someone who thrives on organization and I learned soon enough that a good deal of motherhood is flying by the seat of your pants! But I learned real patience for the first time in my life, and I've become more relaxed about the little things. My sweet baby girl is the greatest chaos in the world!"
—*Lizzie, Villa Park, Illinois*

The Bottom Line

We might as well start with the fine art of diapering, because next to feeding and trying to get your baby to sleep (both of which get their own chapters), this is what will hog most of your time and brain cells. You've probably read those horrifying statistics about how many diapers you are going to change in your baby's first few years, and how much they're going to cost you. Banish those thoughts, pronto. Disposable diapers today are nothing short of a godsend: They're so easy compared with what previous generations of moms went through that they're worth every penny. (Just imagine soaking, washing, and bleaching loads of cloth diapers every single day and having to put on rubber pants on top of them at every change. And of course you had to change cloth diapers a lot more, because they didn't absorb anything. Not to mention the nasty rashes that resulted from all that wetness.)

STUFF YOU NEED FOR NEWBORN CARE . . .

- ❏ Lots of wipes (get the ones for sensitive skin).
- ❏ Diaper bag.
- ❏ 8–10 burp cloths (cloth diapers are cheap and work great).
- ❏ A few packs of diapers with umbilical stump protection (but don't go overboard, because your baby will grow out of these unbelievably quickly).
- ❏ Rectal thermometer.
- ❏ About 6 "stretchies" (footed long johns—your baby will live in these 24/7).
- ❏ Swaddling blanket (one that's specifically made for this purpose will simplify your life a bit).
- ❏ Petroleum jelly (for the thermometer and circumcision care).
- ❏ Baby nail scissors.
- ❏ Pacifier (grab 3–4 extras when you find one she likes).

. . . AND STUFF YOU DON'T

- Rubbing alcohol and cotton swabs. These are no longer recommended for drying up umbilical stumps.
- Bassinet/cradle/moses basket. The crib is fine, even for the first night home from the hospital.
- Small "drool" bibs. The burp cloths can do double duty.
- Baby powder. There's just no reason for its existence.

If becoming a woman of the cloth appeals to you, we cannot tell a lie: They are a fair amount of work. But so is breastfeeding, and many of us manage to put that fact aside to provide that great nutrition for our babies. The upside, though, is that today's generation of cloth diapers are far from what your mom used. There are fitted styles with tabs that don't require pins, liners for times when you need extra absorbency (read: bedtime), and comfortable terry-cloth covers instead of those old plastic pants you may remember. Some brands even combine diaper and liner into one product (called all-in-ones). If you don't want to wash them yourself, diaper services can eliminate that hassle for a fee. (Bear in mind, however, that you may well end up spending as much as you would on disposables in the long run.)

If you want to save the cost and you have the time, washing cloth diapers isn't as bad as it sounds, once you get into the routine. Not only is bleach unnecessary, but it's not even recommended anymore because it destroys the fabric. With today's more efficient washing machines, you usually just need to do a presoak cycle, then a hot wash with regular detergent. Some moms like to do an extra rinse with about half a cup of baking soda or vinegar (not both) added every few loads, too, to keep the diapers looking fresh and smelling good. As for diaper pails, those smelly soaking things have been done away with, too. You can usually use a regular "dry" pail if you empty solid contents into the toilet first, and line the pail with a plastic bag. (It's generally recommended that cloth diapers be washed every two to three days, but frankly we think three days is pushing it a bit—you're going to dread opening the diaper pail at this point.) Check online (just do a search for "cloth diapers" and you'll find plenty of sites that weigh in on the topic) for lots more cloth diapering and cleaning tips. Moms who go this route tend to be passionate and willing to share their tricks.

Still a little uncertain? You can certainly supplement with disposables on the go and at night when leaking is more likely. You'll save some money and some hassle. There's also a flushable biodegradable diaper on the market now. Called gDiapers Flushables, they're a new concept brought over from Australia, where they've been used by families for more than a decade. The system consists of a washable, reusable outer pant and a super-absorbent flushable pad, which has been tested and accepted by the National Sanitation Foundation. They're a bit more expensive than regular disposables. For more information, check them out at gdiapers.com.

STUFF YOU NEED FOR CLOTH DIAPERS . . .

- ❏ 6–8 covers.
- ❏ 24–30 cloth diapers.
- ❏ 6–8 liners (also known as doublers or inserts). These are optional, but a handy way to increase absorbency for longer periods like nighttime or outings, to minimize leaks.
- ❏ 15–30 all-in-ones—a combination diaper and cover so you don't need to buy both if you go this route.

. . . AND STUFF YOU DON'T

- • Pins. Velcro tabs are found on most designs now.
- • Rubber pants. The new cloth wraps are waterproof, cute, and much more comfy.
- • Bleach. It ruins the fabric and may be harsh on your baby's bottom.

If like most moms you decide to go the disposable route, you'll need to plan on going through about a dozen diapers a day at first. Once you master the art of the diaper change (the basics of which will take but a few tries), you will actually find you enjoy it. Not only do you get to marvel over that incredible little body of work you've produced, but you will become obsessed with your baby's various forms of pee and poop, because that's pretty much the main barometer of whether he is eating enough or not. In fact, future cocktail party conversations with other novice parents (and some not so novice) will likely involve diaper contents a significant amount of the time.

Meanwhile, here are the real secrets successful diaperers need to know:

1. Place a few paper towels or some toilet paper under your baby's bottom to contain leaks or sprays (babies inevitably pee as soon as the cold air hits their privates). If you have a boy, cover his penis, too, which makes for a fine fountain.

2. Move a poopy diaper far enough away from your baby that he can't stick his toes in it.

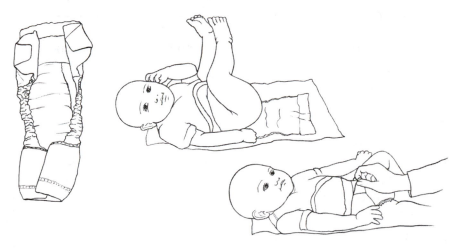

Figure 1.1 Today's disposables are almost foolproof. Just lay the diaper flat, position your baby on top of it with the fastening tabs behind him, wrap the front over his belly, and secure the tabs at his waist. The fit should be snug, but not uncomfortably tight.

3. If you have a girl, remember to wipe from front to back to keep germs away from her vagina.

4. If you have a boy, tuck his penis in the downward position before you fasten the new diaper to minimize leaks.

5. If your brand of diaper has elastic around the leg openings, check to be sure that the ruffled edge is folded out around the leg to create a leak-proof seal (you wouldn't believe how many people mess this one up).

VOICE OF REASON

"It's not uncommon to hear that wipes are not to be used during the newborn period. Like many parenting recommendations, we're not exactly sure why this one exists. Wipes are safe to use on newborn skin. In general, they are thought to be as mild as using a wet washcloth. The best advice we have to give you on the subject is that if they seem to be causing a problem, don't use them. Otherwise, wipe away!"

—*Laura A. Jana, MD, FAAP, and Jennifer Shu, MD, FAAP, authors of* Heading Home with Your Newborn: From Birth to Reality

---

Changing Table Checklist: What You Need within Reach

- ☐ Diapers.
- ☐ Rash ointment.
- ☐ Petroleum jelly.
- ☐ Cotton balls.
- ☐ Baby wipes, or a bowl of lukewarm water and a washcloth.
- ☐ A diaper pail or diaper disposal system (your nose will thank you for the latter).
- ☐ Tissues or paper towels.
- ☐ Cloth diapers for patting dry sensitive bums.

Tushie TLC

There's nothing that seems to suggest *bad mom* like a nasty case of diaper rash. Fortunately, most newborns don't get diaper rash—their parents are so uptight about keeping them clean and dry that nothing stays on that precious bottom for long. Plus, their diet is one-dimensional, which means there's not much that's irritating at this stage (but just wait until you get to baby food).

When your baby does eventually develop a rash, and most do, try not to let it guilt-trip you. Some babies are just more prone to diaper rash. Breastfed babies may also get it because they have more frequent stools. To avoid this rash behavior, change your baby's diaper often and ASAP after bowel movements. (Don't worry about changing pee-pee diapers in the middle of the night unless they're super wet, however. You'll just end up making the baby wider awake than ever.) A preventive application of a diaper rash ointment or petroleum jelly is key if your baby seems to be tending toward frequent outbreaks. Otherwise, you really don't need to bother using anything.

When her tushie is really sore, you may want to skip rubbing it clean with prepackaged wipes and rinse your baby's bottom instead with a squirt bottle of water followed by a gentle patting with a soft baby washcloth. Baby oil followed by cotton balls also cleans very gently. Then apply a coating of a mega-moisturizing diaper rash treatment, such as Triple Paste (triplepaste.com). Boudreaux's Butt Paste (buttpaste.com) is another effective brand. If the rash persists for more than three or four days, or you notice bright red little bumps, your baby may have developed a yeast infection. You'll need to see your pediatrician for a prescription remedy.

Everything You Wanted to Know about Baby Bodily Fluids (and Then Some)

What goes in must come out, and in the world of babies that fact takes on a whole new meaning. It will seem like your baby pees, poops, and spits up way more than he takes in, leaving you wondering if he's getting any nourishment at all. To reassure yourself that he is not going to wither and die from malnutrition anytime soon, you will find that you inspect diaper contents with a zeal once reserved for an elegant gourmet dinner, then discuss them ad nauseam with your partner, relatives, friends, and strangers in the grocery checkout line. Anyone who has ever been a parent will relish the conversation, fully sympathizing with where you're coming from. (Anyone who has never had this privilege will find you revolting, but who needs them right now anyway?) Meanwhile, there are really only a few things you need to get straight.

Pees and q's. First off, it's going to take a few days to jump start your baby's system. If you're breastfeeding, it may not be until your milk fully comes in (between two and five days) that she starts to wet the expected eight to ten diapers a day. The hospital staff will be keeping an eye on her

$$$ SAVER

If you accidentally tear the tab off the new diaper when fastening it, don't throw that unused diaper away! Simply slip a second diaper around the outside of the one with the torn tab, then fold the torn diaper around your baby, fastening the remaining tab as usual. Wrap the second diaper around the baby and fasten. At the next diaper change, you can just remove the inner torn diaper and reuse the outside clean one.

production while you're in there, but when you get home five or so wet diapers may be the norm for two or three days; then she'll up the ante. If your baby's urine output doesn't seem to increase, check with your pediatrician ASAP.

In this era of super-absorbent disposable diapers, it can be tricky to tell if they're actually wet. Our best advice is to familiarize yourself with the texture of the diaper layers when they're dry, then touch them to see if they feel a bit puffier at the next change. The gels inside inflate as they absorb the urine. This will also make the diaper feel heavier. Still uncertain? Go ahead and give the diaper a sniff at the front leg area and see if you get a whiff of that unmistakable urine smell. (You'll be doing a lot more gross stuff than this as time goes on.) Once you've started changing her, if you still can't be sure there's pee in it, put the diaper back on and wait another hour or so, then check again.

Poop parameters. You've no doubt heard that breastfed babies poop messy, runny, French's-mustard-colored stools at every feeding, but again, this becomes true only after about the first week. Immediately postpartum, babies produce a thick, black tar-like poop called meconium (this may happen in the hospital, so you may not see it). Then as breast milk and/or formula begin to make their way through the system, the stools become brown and pasty. Formula-fed babies will continue to poop this way (though it becomes more formed, and the color may vary), while breastfed babies will go on to the thinner, yellow, seedy variety of legend.

The next fun feature about baby poop you'll find yourself obsessing over is how often to expect it. Again, many breastfed babies have a bowel movement during or after almost every feeding. However, this truism does not apply to all. Formula-fed babies are definitely less frequent poopers, and may even go as little as every few days. This behavior usually sends grandparents into a total panic, and by default new parents as well. Because babies are also notoriously loud poopers—straining, grunting, and getting very red-faced—all of this can add up to major anxiety about the big C: constipation. Try to tune Grandma out on this one: Babies are seldom constipated. Like adults, infants are unique in their bowel habits, and your pediatrician is likely to dismiss your concerns. As long as the poop is soft when it eventually arrives, your baby will be diagnosed as quite normal.

Another related myth along these same lines pertains to the iron content in formula. As you yourself may have experienced very recently, iron supplements can be, well, binding in adults. Not so with babies, and don't be tempted by low-iron formulas (which most medical experts think should be pulled from the market). Full-iron formulas are essential for your baby's brain development and will not constipate him. Nor will the iron supplements your pediatrician prescribes for your baby if he's being breastfed. Don't let anyone tell you otherwise.

Spit happenings. The mouth, of course, is at the other end of the bodily fluid spectrum, and many babies spit up as often as ten or twelve times a day. Sometimes we're talking a major eruption; other times it just trickles out like overflow. Either way it's messy. One mom told us that whenever she was trying to get ready to go somewhere with her firstborn, she could never decide whether to dress herself first, then have her daughter spit up on her, or dress her daughter first and watch her spit up on herself. No matter how much experts describe spit-up as just a nuisance, it's these little issues that make moms go bonkers.

As for the science behind it, if you must know, the most common reason for spitting up is that a baby's digestive tract muscle between the stomach and the esophagus is immature (essentially, it's loose and will gradually tighten up by about six months of age). Most babies are not bothered by spitting up, and there's probably a lot less nutrition being lost than you think—typically about a tablespoon, but because the breast milk or formula mixes with other fluids, it can seem like more. Just keep plenty of bibs, towels, and clothes for quick cleanups on hand, especially when you go out. (Keeping an extra change of clothes for yourself in your trunk isn't a bad idea, either.) To minimize spitting up, try these tactics:

- Keep feedings smaller and more frequent.
- Don't pressure your baby to finish a feeding if he seems full.
- Hold or keep your baby sitting upright after feedings for a little while to let gravity help with digestion.
- Burp your baby regularly (see pages 14–15).
- If you're feeding your baby formula, talk to your pediatrician about a brand that might be easier for him to digest.

Occasionally, spitting up warrants medical attention. If your baby is very irritable and fussy and prone to spitting up, he may have a reflux problem that could be relieved with medication. If your baby experiences true vomiting—more forceful expelling of a greater amount of his stomach contents—diarrhea, bloating, and is not gaining weight adequately, he may have a milk allergy, so discuss it with your doctor. Both reflux and milk allergies are uncommon, but they do occur. Spitting up any blood is a sign of infection, and yellowish green bile indicates a blockage, so if you see either of these, call your doctor right away.

The Business of Burping

Some babies are born burpers, letting out Grandma-pleasing belches before you lay on that first pat. Others require major cajoling. But one thing's for sure: All that air they take in while sucking has just got to come out, or you'll have one cranky kid on your hands. You'll usually need to burp your baby halfway through each feeding, then again when the feeding is complete. If your baby gets fussy at any point during a feeding, stop and burp him—there's a good chance that's the problem. Here are four ways to help him let one rip. Keep in mind, too, that no baby burps every time, so if you've given it your best effort for a few minutes, go back to feeding or whatever is next on the agenda. Your baby will let out a belch when he's ready.

1. Put pressure on the baby's tummy by laying him facedown on your lap, then rubbing or patting his lower back. Ask your doctor to show you how forcefully you can pat him, if you're nervous. (See figure 1.2a.)

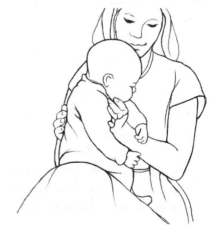

Figure 1.2a Laying your baby tummy down across your lap is one way to burp her.

Figure 1.2b Sitting your baby upright on your lap is another effective belch producer. (Be sure to support your baby's head and neck while she's young.)

2. Hold the baby sitting up in your lap, supporting him in front with your hand, and rubbing or patting his back. (See figure 1.2b.)

3. Hold the baby over your shoulder—again with pressure on his tummy—and rub or pat his back. (See figure 1.2c.)

Figure 1.2c Burping baby upright, with her head looking away from you is a time-honored method, but makes for plenty of spit-up stained shoulders if you don't keep a burp cloth handy.

4. Lay him on your lap faceup with his head at your knees and bicycle his legs.

The Care and Cleaning of Your Newborn

The first week or two at home will feature a number of challenges that try new moms' souls, but then they mercifully disappear. Aside from the basics of keeping her alive, your baby's body is going through a sort of healing process from the delivery that you also have to keep on top of, and work around, such as the umbilical cord stump, maybe a circumcision site, and a little thing called jaundice that can occasionally morph into a really big deal. Here's the lowdown.

Cord Concerns

Your baby's umbilical cord was probably the last thing you thought about when you were imagining what it would be like to take care of your baby, then—yikes!—there it was, staring up at you all icky-like at that first diaper change. The good news: Research shows we can relax the old standards on cord care. If this isn't your first baby, you may remember having to swab your other newborns' cord stump with alcohol at every diaper change. But in fact, it makes absolutely no difference if you clean that little leftover much at all. Not only is there less risk of infection if you just let the cord stump air-dry, but it's likely to fall off sooner, too—in about seven to ten days.

While you're waiting for that big event, simply keep the baby's diaper folded down below the stump, or use newborn diapers made with cord cutouts. When the stump does detach, gently clean the area with some baby soap and water. If you notice a little bleeding at that point, go ahead and swab the area with a little rubbing alcohol or apply an antibiotic ointment. And call your pediatrician right away if at any time you notice a ring of redness developing around the umbilical cord stump, pus, or odor, or if the area becomes warm to the touch. Though rare, it could signal a bacterial infection or irritation that would need treatment with intravenous antibiotics.

Circumcision Decisions

If you've had a little boy, now that you've gotten past the big question—to circumcise him or not—you need to know what's next. If you skipped this procedure, your only task is to keep clean the tip of your baby's penis and around the ridge of the foreskin. Don't try to pull the foreskin back; it will retract by itself by about three or four years of age.

If your son was circumcised, you've got a bit more work for the first week or so. At first, his penis will be a little red, and you will probably notice some yellow secretions. Don't panic: This is totally normal and a sign of healing. Keep the penis clean and dab a bit of petroleum jelly on it at each diaper change to keep it from sticking to the diaper. Your baby's circumcision site should heal completely in about a week; if you notice any sores, swelling, or bleeding from the tip of the penis, call your pediatrician.

Jaundice Watch

This is one of those mysterious and exotic illnesses that you never gave an iota of a thought to before you came home from the hospital, yet it can add an untold amount of anxiety to your first week at home. Then with any luck, you will forget jaundice exists—until you have your next baby.

So what's the deal, anyway? Remember the term *bilirubin* from middle school science class? (Okay, neither did we.) It happens to be a substance that occurs in the body when old red blood cells that are no longer of any use break down and then pass through the liver, the intestines, and out in the form of poop (that stuff again). Jaundice, a yellowing of the skin, occurs when too much bilirubin builds up in the baby's body. This is likely to occur in as many as half of all newborns, because their livers and intestines are not functioning at full capacity yet. Fortunately, most jaundice is not serious, though it always needs to be evaluated by a pediatrician, who may only recommend simple little treatments like allowing your baby to "sunbathe" in just a diaper by a window inside for about fifteen minutes a day (sunlight happens to help break down the bilirubin). Use your common sense about this: Of course you don't want to actually put your baby outside in direct sun where he could get burned, and if it's cold out, be sure to turn the heat up indoors so he doesn't get too chilly, either. Frequent feedings, hopefully followed by frequent poopings, will also help the excess bilirubin pass through your baby's system.

Jaundice levels usually peak between three and five days after birth. On your own, you can check for jaundice by gently pressing on your baby's skin then watching to see if there appears to be an underlying yellow tinge to the spot (a jaundiced baby will have the telltale yellowish color regardless of race). Jaundice usually begins at the top of the body and spreads down to the toes, so you can work your way down with this spot test to get an idea of how far it might have progressed. The whites of your baby's eyes may also become yellowed, and at the end of the illness they may flout the above pattern by being the last area to return to normal. Yellow skin sounds obvious, but it isn't always. One very fair-skinned mom told us she was delighted at her newborn's golden skin color, until a home nurse came for a postpartum follow-up and diagnosed jaundice the minute she laid eyes on the child. Many pediatricians now schedule an office visit for two days after you bring your baby home for this very reason; if yours doesn't mention it, request one yourself to be on the safe side.

Doctors usually diagnose jaundice levels with a heel stick—drawing blood by poking the heel with a needle then draining it into a tube for testing—so prepare yourself for some screaming. Depending on what the test reveals (how high the bilirubin level gets as well as how many days old your baby is), your pediatrician may have you come back and forth a few times to monitor it; if the bilirubin level gets very high and does not drop, there is a risk of damage to the nervous system. Often, careful monitoring is all that is necessary, but some babies with higher levels of bilirubin will need what's known as phototherapy—putting the baby under special lighting—several hours a day or perhaps overnight in the hospital. All of this back and forth can be physically and emotionally stressful (read: a real drag) on top of your own need to recover from childbirth, but rest assured that your baby will be fine. The jaundice, too, shall pass without any serious long-term effects.

When to Call the Doctor about the Baby

Of course you're going to feel like calling every other minute—that's why many pediatricians have regularly scheduled daily call-in hours. You will also have the opportunity to talk to your pediatrician face-to-face during checkups about four times during this postpartum period. Most docs schedule checkups within two to five days of bringing your baby home from the hospital (we say the sooner, the better), then again at the two-week mark, the four-week mark, and at your baby's two-month "birth-day." Meanwhile, it's fine to take advantage of this appointed chat time with any little questions that are worrying you, but call the doctor's office no matter what time it is about any of these real health issues:

- A fever of 100.4 degrees Fahrenheit or more up to two months of age (see chapter 6 for more specifics on fever as your baby grows).
- Bloody stools, or stools that seem more watery than they have been.
- Repeated or projectile (forceful) vomiting.
- Refusal to eat for more than two or three consecutive feedings.
- Bleeding or oozing from the umbilical cord or circumcision sites, which may signal infection.
- A yellow tinge to the skin or whites of the eyes, both symptoms of jaundice.
- White patches in the mouth or on the tongue, which may indicate a painless yeast infection called thrush, which requires treatment.

All That Skin Stuff

You expected the Gerber baby; you got a wrinkled, splotchy old man. "Don't worry," the nurses will all say, "in a week or so he'll be rosy and round and beautiful." That's true—for about another week. Then the rashes will set in. Most newborns are subject to a bevy of skin blemishes in the first two months that will make you recall the horrors of your teenage acne. Relax. These nasty blemishes are easily treatable and temporary—and you will eventually get that perfect-looking Gerber baby (probably by the time you actually feel like going out and showing him off). Meanwhile, here's a sampling of the mostly minor newborn rashes you might encounter. (Some rashes are more serious, of course, and we deal with those in chapter 6; check there if your baby's symptoms seem more significant than described here.)

What:	**Cradle cap (seborrheic dermatitis)**
Symptoms:	Brownish yellow crusty, flaky, or scaly patches on the scalp, forehead, eyebrows, and behind the ears
Treatment:	The traditional remedy is to apply a light coating of baby oil or olive oil to your child's scalp, then gently scrape off the softened scales with a baby comb or brush. That's what your mom will tell you to do, but most pediatricians now pooh-pooh this cosmetic fix, preferring a selenium-based dandruff shampoo instead (be careful not to get it into your baby's eyes!), which can actually cure the problem. You can gently loosen the scales while shampooing, but you may still have to scrape some off afterward as well. How your baby responds to this cradle cap treatment is as individual as she and her oil glands are: In some cases, it will disappear after two or three cycles of shampooing and scraping, while other babies battle it for months. (The good news: Eventually your baby will get enough hair that it's no longer visible and you can forget about it!)

What:	**Infant acne**
Symptoms:	Pin-head-size pimples (white or yellowish dots on a red base) usually on a baby's face, but occasionally on the back, chest, or belly as well. Infant acne typically appears between two and four weeks of age as your hormones work their way out of your baby's system.
Treatment:	None. Creams and ointments will just irritate your baby's skin more, and the acne will clear up on its own in a few weeks.

What:	**Milia**
Symptoms:	Little white bumps on your baby's nose, forehead, cheeks, and occasionally his trunk, limbs, or penis. Milia is caused by a buildup of sebum, a natural skin lubricant, or trapped skin fragments.
Treatment:	None. Just keep your baby's skin clean and dry, and it will disappear on its own at about two to four weeks (in a few cases it lasts a little longer), when your baby's oil glands and pores mature.

What:	**Miliaria**
Symptoms:	A raised rash of small, clear or white fluid-filled blisters that result from skin secretions or blocked pores.

Treatment: None. Just keep your baby's skin clean and dry, and avoid
              overheating; they will be gone within two weeks.

What: Erythema toxicum
Symptoms: A rash of red splotches with yellowish white bumps in the
              center, similar to a flea or insect bite, which appears in the
              first few days after birth.
Treatment: Although it sounds awful (who came up with that scary
              name!), there's nothing really toxic about these bumps, and
              no treatment is necessary. Just keep your baby's skin clean
              and dry and they will vanish within two weeks.

Nail Know-How

Your baby's fingernails grow so fast that they may actually be a danger to her.
She can accidentally scratch her sweet face while sleeping or during all that
twitching around that occurs as she learns to control her body. Still, taking
a pair of clippers to those tiny little fingers is nerve racking for new moms.
The secret to success: Use only baby nail scissors (they are rounded, not
sharp at the edges), which will be less likely to hurt her if your aim is off. The
best times to attempt a mini manicure are after baths when her nails are soft
and pliable, or when she's sleeping and more likely to lie still. With your
baby's palms facing up or down, press down on the pads of her fingers before
you clip so the skin isn't in the way. Do her fingernails about twice a week,
toenails about once a month. You can use an emery board to smooth rough
edges between trims (these also come in infant size).

Figure 1.3 Be sure to hold down the
pads of your baby's fingers when
trimming the nails so you don't snip
tender skin as well.

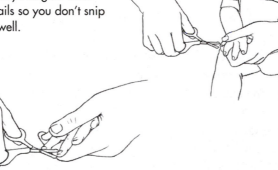

VOICE OF REASON

"My initial nail cutting attempt with my first child drew blood. Five more children and about two decades of being a pediatrician later, I'm no longer afraid of it, having learned a few tricks: First, try doing it backward, with the pad of the finger facing you (and be sure to use nail clippers designed for babies!). Use the thumb of the hand that isn't holding the clipper to pull the pad down slightly away from the nail, so you can see exactly where you are cutting. Second, distraction helps. Seat your baby on your lap facing a favorite video and she may not even notice that her nails are being clipped. Finally, nibbling is a viable alternative. All you nail biters out there can put your skills to good use—and no metal need come near your baby."

—*Claire McCarthy MD, contributor to* The Experts' Guide to the Baby Years *and* Parenting *magazine columnist*

How to Bathe Your Baby

For the first week or two until your baby's umbilical cord stump falls off, all she will be able to have is a sponge bath. (Whew—one less thing to worry about during these crazy, hazy days!) You'll need to put a waterproof pad or thick bath towel on the bed or carpeted floor and gather the following supplies: two bowls of warm water, two baby washcloths, and some baby soap or cleanser. Using the first bowl of water, gently wipe your baby down with the damp washcloth, using soap only in the areas that seem especially dirty, and not on her face. Clean her bottom last, so you don't spread any poopy germs from her bum elsewhere. Then use a clean washcloth and the other bowl of water to rinse her off. Work fast and dry each part of her right away so she doesn't get too chilly. It helps to cover her clean trunk with the towel while you're washing her nether parts.

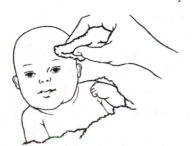

Figure 1.4a Use a fresh, moist cotton ball to wipe each eye. Clean your baby's face first.

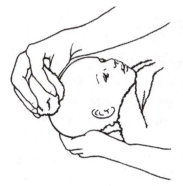

Figure 1.4b Gently wipe her scalp with a little baby soap or shampoo on a wash cloth.

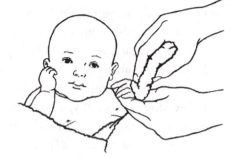

Figure 1.4c Cleanse her hands, belly, and legs next.

Figure 1.4d Turn your baby over on her tummy and wipe off her back.

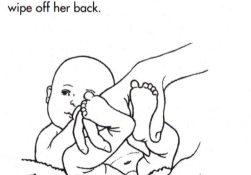

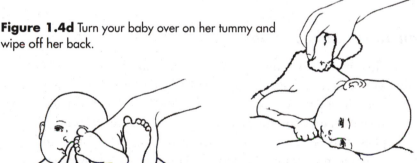

Figure 1.4e Cleanse the diaper area last.

When the time comes for that first real bath, enlist an extra pair of hands—Dad's, Grandma's—to help you hold on to your wet, squirmy little gal. The good thing is that babies don't really get very dirty, so you typically only need to undertake this task once or twice a week (though the occasional baby needs more; your pediatrician can advise you). Too much bathing, in fact, may dry out your baby's skin. When you do get down to business, follow these steps:

1. Assemble your supplies (see the box, page 25) and turn up the heat—or turn on a space heater in the room—so your baby doesn't get too cold. The room temperature while bathing should be about seventy-five degrees Fahrenheit (but remember to turn it back down for bedtime to between sixty-eight and seventy-two degrees Fahrenheit—you don't want her to get overheated while sleeping).

2. Line the bottom of the infant bathtub or sink with an extra washcloth or hand towel to keep your baby from slipping. Fill the tub with a few inches of warm (not hot) water and test it with the inside of your wrist. (See figure 1.5a.) Grandma may recommend the elbow, but the

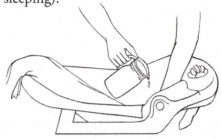

Figure 1.5a

skin there is tougher and less sensitive. Play it safe: Go cooler if you have doubts. If you're paranoid, you can always get a thermometer, but most of us do fine without one. Just for peace of mind, the ideal water temp for a baby's bath is between ninety-five and a hundred degrees. To achieve this, your home water heater should be set no higher than 120 degrees—the temperature at which you can put your hand in running hot water without getting burned. Then add some cold water to the bath to bring the temperature down a bit.

Figure 1.5b

3. Gently place your baby in the water, using one hand to support her head and neck. Use your other hand to pour some warm water over her body to keep her from getting cold. (See figure 1.5b.)

4. Wash her face first. Wipe her eyelids from the inside corner out, using a fresh cotton ball moistened with warm water on each eyelid. (See figure 1.5c.)

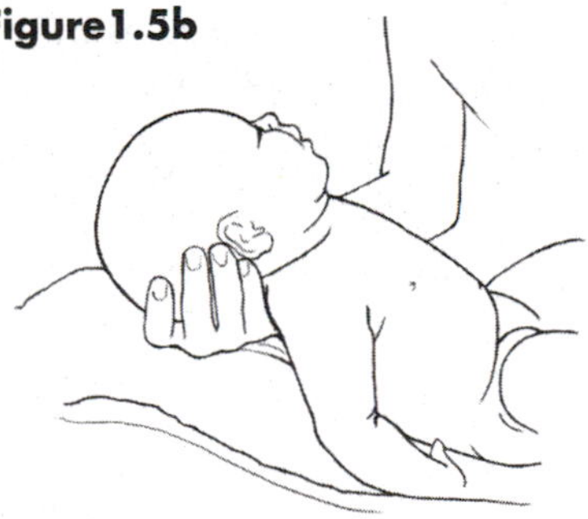

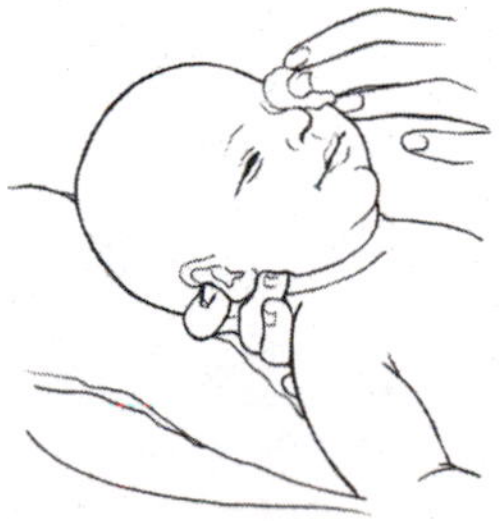

Figure 1.5c

5. Gradually work your way down her body to the diaper area (basically, from cleanest to dirtiest areas). Again, you may want to cover her torso with an extra towel as you go, to keep her warm. (See figure 1.5d.)

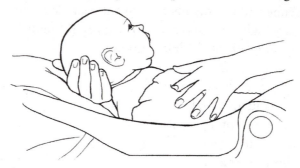

Figure 1.5d

6. Shampoo her head last (to keep her from getting too cold). Using a no-tears baby shampoo, gently lather and rinse her scalp. Don't worry—you can't hurt the soft spot this way! (See figure 1.5e.)

7. Wrap your baby in the hooded towel as soon as you remove her from the water. Keep as much of her body covered as you can while you dress her. (See figure 1.5f.)

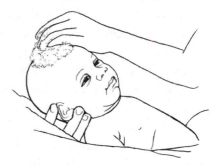

Figure 1.5e

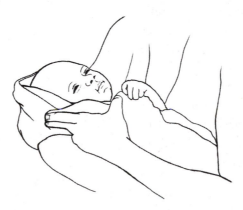

Figure 1.5f

STUFF YOU NEED TO BATHE YOUR BABY . . .

☐ Hooded baby bath towel and washcloth.
☐ Extra towel to keep her warm.
☐ Infant bathtub.
☐ Baby soap or cleanser.
☐ Cotton balls.
☐ Change of clothes, diaper.

. . . AND STUFF YOU DON'T

- Baby lotion (optional, if you like it).
- Baby powder. As we said before, not necessary, but if you like it, be sure it's talc-free.
- Baby shampoo. You can also use a liquid body cleanser that's tear-free.
- Diaper rash ointment. There's usually no need for it unless you are actually treating a rash.

What the Well-Dressed Newborn Is Wearing

Not much, frankly. If there were a best-dressed baby award, the winner would not be the one in the exclusive designer duds. No, what every seasoned mother (by that we mean one who has survived the first six weeks, because by then you will fully comprehend the logistics of dressing and undressing what is best described as a wet noodle) will tell you is that the stretchie and Onesie (also called a bodysuit) are where it's at, 24/7, depending on the season. What exactly is a bodysuit? It's an undershirt with snaps at the crotch. Depending on how you feel about the snapping, you can also use the traditional side-snapping undershirts you probably wore as an infant, and which your mom has fondly bought for your baby in bulk. The advantage of the bottom-snapping bodysuit is that it doesn't ride up under other clothing, so you can use them as undershirts in winter months, T-shirts with pants or shorts, and a complete albeit casual outfit in warm weather. But you will also do so many diaper and clothing changes throughout a typical day that after a while, crotch snaps will drive you nuts. You'll go from diligently snapping all those snaps to fastening only one, possibly giving Junior the wedgie of his life. Buy a few traditional undershirts, too, since they are easier to fasten and at least sometimes you'll prefer them.

For colder months, the other great baby outfit you will use the most is the stretchie, also called a romper or coverall—essentially a one-piece garment with long sleeves and legs that also cover your baby's feet. These outfits usually snap up one leg and the torso. Beware stretchies that snap up the back—they were originally invented as a form of torture, probably by some childless person in an office who had to pick up the slack while her colleagues were on maternity leave. One attempt at putting on this

---

The Real-Life Layette

- ☐ 6 snap-bottom undershirts, and 2 side-snap undershirts.
- ☐ 4–5 stretchies.
- ☐ 3–4 "dress-up" outfits.
- ☐ 6–8 pairs of socks if you find you like them. (You may rely on coveralls and never use these, but if you do, have plenty on hand because you will lose them constantly. Ditto for booties.)
- ☐ 4 "sleep sacks" or gowns for when bedtime becomes real. These function as blankets, so you don't need to put one in the crib. (Extra bedding is considered a risk factor for SIDS—sudden infant death syndrome—so the less you can get away with, the better.)
- ☐ A sweater and hat. (You may want more than one, hats especially, depending on the season in which your baby is born.)
- ☐ 1 snowsuit (for winter months).
- ☐ 2 large hooded bath towels.
- ☐ 2 plain baby towels.
- ☐ 4 baby washcloths.
- ☐ 4 or more receiving blankets (again, you may use more in the bouncy seat or stroller during winter months, or if your baby especially enjoys swaddling—see chapter 4, pages 135–36, for more on this).
- ☐ Lots of burp cloths (they can double as bibs until solid feeding begins).

awkward ensemble, which involves flipping your baby like a pancake from one side to the other, and you will toss it straight into the poopy diaper pail where it belongs.

Of course you will want a few cute outfits for showing off your baby to company or going out—but bear in mind that *a few* is just that. Resist the temptation to stock up on fabulous fashions; you won't be going out that much, and your baby will quickly outgrow them. You'd also be wise to return many of the outfits you receive as gifts. (Use the store credit to buy bigger clothes down the road when the gifts dry up.)

All that said, see page 26 for a quick rundown of what you probably want to have on hand, wardrobe-wise, for the first few months.

Figure 1.6 What the smartly dressed baby is wearing (*clockwise from top left*): sleep sack, side-snap undershirt, snap-crotch undershirt, one-piece play suit (also called a romper or stretchie), elastic-bottom nightgown.

Size Matters

The prevailing words of wisdom about baby clothes tell you, "Buy big," and if you have a large baby to begin with, you can pretty much count on him not fitting into the first and smallest category for long, if at all. Baby clothes are typically sized by age—newborns, three months, six months, nine months, etcetera—and it doesn't take a rocket scientist to figure out that not all babies are the same size at the same age. Look carefully at the weight and height ranges listed on the tags instead—that's the real barometer of what will actually fit your child. Keep in mind, too, that some babies do wear "their age" clothes perfectly fine. Certain brands also tend to

---

Five Ways to Dress a Baby

1. Avoid bending those delicate little fingers the wrong way by first sticking your own hand all the way through the sleeve, then taking hold of your little guy's hand and guiding it back through.

2. The guiding principle of stretchies and footie pajamas: Tuck that chubby little limb in the side with the shorter opening first, and tackle the longer opening last. Otherwise, you can end up twisting your baby like a pretzel.

3. *Button* is a bad word when it comes to baby clothes. Opt for easier zippers and snaps, accompanied by a rendition of the "Itsy Bitsy Spider" or "Wheels on the Bus" while you work.

4. Again, it's okay to cheat a little on the snapping. We doubt even Martha Stewart fastened all three snaps on her child's bodysuit every blessed time. Our hat's off to you if you snap even two of them more than half the time.

5. Steer clear of baby shoes unless you absolutely need them (for inclement weather, perhaps, but otherwise not until your baby starts to walk). They are a royal pain to get on (think of the way the Wicked Witch's feet curled up under Dorothy's house when it landed on her); then they fall right off anyway. Instead, try those cute Robeez—soft, flexible leather shoes with elastic around the ankle that prevents them from slipping off—at robeez.com.

run bigger, so you may find that your baby wears a smaller size from these stores. It may seem more complicated than algebra at first, but by about six months you will get a better sense of where your baby will fall in this sizing spectrum, and a pattern will emerge that may remain predictable well into preschool.

And Baby Makes . . . Chaos!

One of the great catch-22s of bringing your baby home from the hospital is the company issue. On the one hand, you're exhausted, uncomfortable, confused, and could really stand to hibernate for a few weeks. On the other, you love showing off your baby, opening all those adorable gifts, and recounting your delivery room war stories (payback to all those know-it-alls you've been listening to during these long, pregnant months). Frankly, we're not sure there is any great answer for handling it all, short of not always picking up the phone or answering the door. Anyone with any sense will call first and ask if they can stop by, so if you constantly screen your calls, they may get the hint after a few encounters with the answering machine that you're just not ready for visitors yet. If you do pick up, be noncommittal: "I'd love to see you but I'm not sure when we have to go back to the pediatrician. I'll call you back about a time."

If you're lucky enough to have some help at home—be it your partner, Grandma, a sister, or even someone you hired—let them entertain your visitors: "I've just got to lie down before the next nursing session. Mom's going to keep an eye on the baby for an hour if you feel like sticking around." (The hope here is that they'll get the hint and hit the road fairly soon.)

Should you have a pack of relatives or close friends clamoring for a look-see, you may want to tackle it all at once with, say, a brief open house on a weekend afternoon. Make sure you've got some help to put on a pot of coffee or tea, and a plate of store-bought cookies, then stop right there. No one expects a big spread, and it will only encourage your guests to stick around longer—which you really don't want.

When you are entertaining visitors, feel free to set some rules and stick to them. You can always blame them on your pediatrician: "The doctor said not to let anyone hold the baby for the first month, if at all possible." Of course you're probably going to have to cut a few people some slack

(Grandma, your sister-in-law), but that doesn't mean your cousin with her snotty-nosed kids sneezing and coughing all over the place. And when you have had enough of the company, you can always repair to the bedroom for a feeding: "Little Johnny doesn't eat well if he's distracted, so I have to go somewhere quiet. It was nice of you to stop by." Remember: When you're a new mom, there's almost no such thing as bad manners; it's everyone else who is being rude by not considering your and your baby's needs.

As for going out with your baby, most doctors recommend avoiding taking even healthy newborns to public places (malls, grocery stores, restaurants) for the first three or four weeks, perhaps longer if your baby was a preemie or has a medical condition. The season in which your baby was born is another factor to consider. During winter months, germs and illnesses are circulating everywhere, and both you and your baby are vulnerable to them in these early weeks. If the weather's warm, however, a short stroll in the park for some fresh air is likely to do both you and your newborn good. Be sure to dress him properly (one more layer of clothing than you would wear, plus a hat), and remember to keep him shielded from the sun (dressed in lightweight clothing that covers as much of his skin as possible, plus a hat, and under a stroller canopy). While one of us actually has a friend who took her month-old preemie son on a vacation to Ireland to visit relatives—and he came back unscathed—we recommend avoiding any such major travel early on. In addition to your baby's vulnerable state, you yourself will likely be overwhelmed with life at home, let alone having to pack it all up and take it with you. Plus, just imagine how nervous you would be if your baby needed a doctor and you were unfamiliar with the quality of medical care in the area. (For more on traveling with your baby, see chapter 9, page 342.)

Oh Yeah, *You*

Why is it that we get volumes of information on the pain and potential complications of labor and delivery, but no one ever seems to mention what recovery is going to be like until they're wheeling you out of the hospital? You're bleeding, cramping, sweating—and that's just from a run-of-the-mill vaginal delivery. Throw in an episiotomy or tearing and you've got stitches in the most tender part of your body, or a C-section that may result in serious postpartum pain for quite some time. Nobody ever seems

GRANDMA GUIDELINES

We love them, they drive us nuts. There's nothing like an overzealous grandma to complicate a maternity leave. Our advice: Use them when you need them, and send them packing when you don't. Here are some pearls of wisdom from the trenches.

Set some ground rules. Even grandmas need visiting hours. Tell them you'll be happy to see them at certain points—say, between 10 AM and noon, or maybe 5 PM and 7 PM—whatever suits *your* schedule right now. During other times, you and your baby will be resting until further notice. This way, you'll also be able to get yourself dressed (well, maybe) and psyched for the company.

Think carefully about whether you want her to move in or not. Temporary live-in grandmas work great for some new moms and are a disaster for others. Consider how in sync you two normally are; things won't improve just because you've now got this child in common. Also, consider your partner—if he and your mom don't always see eye-to-eye, you may end up running interference, and you really don't need that hassle right now.

You deal with the baby, let her do other stuff. Grandmas are great for cooking, housework, and tending to other siblings, so make it clear she'll handle these tasks and you'll take care of the baby (unless you specifically ask her to do something).

Remind yourself that she has "mommy amnesia," and believe it or not someday you will, too! Yes, your mother or mother-in-law will say "You never did that," or "That never happened with my kids," so just try to ignore it. She probably did go through all the same things, but as with the rest of life, you really do forget the bad and remember the good.

to mention that if you have a forceps delivery, you can remain bruised down there for weeks. And how about those burning, swollen, engorged breasts, gnawed-on nipples, the pins and needles of let-down, haywire hormones, and bowel movements that are as painful as pushing the baby out? (Sorry to be so crass, but after giving birth there's just not much left that's shocking anymore.) It's no wonder everyone keeps postpartum recovery such a secret: The human race would probably die out if women realized what else they were in for *after* they give birth. Oh, and did we mention you're not allowed to sleep, either?

On the upside, many of these symptoms abate in about a week. You will continue to be exhausted for quite some time, of course, and it's going to be another two to three weeks before breastfeeding becomes routine, but the serious aches and pains will pass fairly quickly. Meanwhile, take advantage of every offer of assistance.

Bleeding. The flow you're going to experience now is going to seem like those nine or ten periods you got to skip have come back to haunt you—and in a way, they have. All that uterine lining will come pouring out for a few days, especially when you nurse, which causes contractions and gushing. Be prepared. (Even if you had a cesarean birth, you will still experience the same amount of vaginal bleeding.) Expelling small blood clots is also normal. The fact that you can't wear tampons will make it seem even more prolific. The color will begin as bright red for about the first five days, change to a lighter pink then brownish for up to another ten days, then become yellowish white, then watery and colorless. It will all be over somewhere between four and six weeks. Most new-mom books call this postpartum flow by its medical name, *lochia,* but that's about the only place you'll hear the term—we've never even heard our ob-gyns use it.

The main thing you need to remember here is that if your bleeding increases suddenly (when it seemed to have been lighter for a few or more days), that could be a sign that you're exerting yourself too much physically (no mall prowling for you yet) and you need to get off your feet. Tell your husband this happened and he'll be in such a panic that he'll insist you go to bed for the next twenty-four hours (not that we're suggesting you lie, of course, but a little exaggeration on this topic may buy you some much-needed rest!). One more caveat: Though it's rare, continued heavy bleeding and large clots could be a sign that some of your placenta was retained in the uterus and may need to be removed, so call your ob-gyn ASAP if you experience this. Your body will bleed like crazy trying to expel that placenta, and you can be in danger of a serious hemorrhage.

Cramping. For the first few days postpartum, you can expect to experience some cramping that will rival contractions, especially when you are nursing. When your baby sucks, it triggers the release of the hormone oxytocin, which in turn stimulates contractions. This is your uterus squeezing out the leftover lining and shrinking back to its original size—a good thing despite the discomfort. Just like your basic period cramps, these may or may not bother you a lot. They tend to get worse with subsequent births. (Which is weird, because everything else about the process—from labor and delivery to healing—usually gets easier. But there you have it.) Ask your doctor about pain relievers while you're recovering; they will certainly make this brief phase more tolerable.

Incisions. Swelling peaks about seventy-two hours after delivery for both episiotomies and cesarean sections, so this is the day or two when you are in the most pain. Some soreness will likely continue for several weeks; still, when it comes to episiotomies, the worst discomfort is usually over in about a week. Pain, redness, gaps in the incision (your partner can help you inspect an episiotomy if you're concerned), or more than a few drops of oozing or bleeding could signal an infection, so call your healthcare provider. And even if you managed to avoid an episiotomy or tearing, your perineum—the area between the vagina and rectum—is going to be sore from all that stretching and pushing. Meanwhile, here's how to baby your bottom:

- Take frequent sitz baths for the first few days you are home. The hospital usually provides the special pan you will need, which you fill with warm water; then rest it on the toilet bowl and lower your bare buns and genitals into it for a few minutes. Afterward, if the hospital gave you some anesthetic spray to take home such as Dermoplast, give your perineum a spritz to numb the area a bit and help keep it clean. You can pat at your stitches with chilled witch hazel pads like Tucks, or wear them right on top of your sanitary napkin for the same numbing effect.
- While you urinate, squirt your perineum with a spray bottle (which they will give you to bring home from the hospital) of warm water to prevent stinging. Then repeat the squirting when you're done to clean any excess urine off your incision.
- Use a doughnut cushion (available at medical supply stores) or Boppy (the nursing cushion that has the center cut out of it) to sit on. This takes the weight off your perineum.

Bladder and bowels. Because they have the bad luck to be neighbors to your uterus, these two organs get traumatized in the birth process. The bowel in particular may just decide to take a holiday to recoup, leaving you constipated and full of as much gas as your baby has. Sore stitches and possibly hemorrhoids—painful, swollen, itchy varicose veins in the rectal area, which some women develop during the pushing stage—further complicate the ability, physically and psychologically, to, well, poop. In the old days, the first bowel movement was a sign that you were ready to be released from the hospital; now we are sent home in time for this blessed event, along with advice to eat lots of fiber and drink plenty of fluids to jump-start sluggish intestines. We say: Try not to get too worked up about it, and definitely take a stool softener (ask your doctor what you can use). Once you get through the first movement, your system may go back to normal. If you've got hemorrhoids, don't strain during bowel movements, which can make them worse, and alleviate the discomfort by wiping with Tucks pads rather than toilet paper, then using medicated numbing sprays or witch hazel compresses.

As for your bladder, your postpartum problems can range from one extreme to the other: urinary incontinence, when you can't stop the flow of urine, or feeling the urge to go and then being unable to produce a drop. In most cases, these problems are very short-lived. If you can't seem to pass urine like you used to, there is probably some temporary swelling of the muscles that control its flow. Drink plenty of fluids, and spray warm water over your perineum as you try to pee. Like running water in the bathroom sink, this can be a psychological prompt helping you to go, and it soothes soreness, too. This condition should subside in a few days.

Incontinence should also be a temporary problem, because the tone of your pelvic muscles improves in a few weeks' time (talk to your doctor if it doesn't). If it's driving you batty, you can do Kegel exercises to help it along. To perform Kegels, squeeze the muscles you use to stop the flow of urine, hold them there for ten seconds, then release. Do this exercise ten to twenty times in a row, about three times a day, for maximum results. Frankly, most of us don't bother with these (*another* thing you've got to do now?) and wind up just fine.

Cesarean specifics. If you've had a cesarean, you have a special set of needs. There's no question your incision will be painful longer than an episiotomy cut or tear (usually about three weeks). You can protect it by tucking an extra sanitary napkin into the front of your underpants; many women

"Instead of a birth plan, moms-to-be should make a postpartum chore plan. Husbands may want to be helpful, but they don't have a clue that we need the small things taken care of without us telling them what to do. So explain that he's completely in charge of, say, the garbage and the grocery shopping, while you'll do the laundry. Alternate days when you or he does the meals. Write down your plan to keep the house running smoothly, and then you can both concentrate on taking care of the baby."   —*Meredith, New York, New York*

"Visitors who come and sit and stare at the baby and don't lift a finger to help you when you've just forced a *human being* out of your body can be very stressful. Furthermore, I think they should be banned from being near new mothers for at least six months."
—*Laura, Williamstown, New Jersey*

also say it helps to hold a pillow against it when you laugh, cough, or sneeze. Of course you will have to be careful lifting. Keep it to just the baby—no laundry baskets or grocery bags (show this section to your husband!)—and limit doing anything even slightly strenuous, like going up and down stairs. You may be extra tired (whatever that is, considering no mom with a newborn gets to sleep regardless of the type of delivery she had), so take it easy as much as possible. The other big recovery symptom women who have C-sections experience is gas pains (yes, that again). The intestines pretty much shut down after a cesarean, and it can take up to a week to get them going again. The usual recommendation is to walk a lot to get the gas moving through your system, but really, who can do that after major surgery? Walk as much as you feel able to manage, and follow all the other constipation guidelines.

When to Call the Doctor about Yourself

Sure, you will feel sore and uncomfortable, but if you feel this bad, call your ob-gyn pronto:

- You have to change a "super" sanitary napkin every hour for several hours.
- You release what seems like several unusually large blood clots at any time or gushes of bright red bleeding a week or more after delivery.
- You develop a fever, chills, or painful, frequent urination. You may have a urinary tract infection.
- Your episiotomy site or incision site becomes red, warm, swollen, more painful, or starts to ooze. You may have an infection.
- You have a red or swollen area in a breast, especially with a fever. You may have mastitis.
- You run a temperature above 100.4 degrees Fahrenheit for more than a day.

The Baby Blues (and We're Not Talking about Decorating the Nursery)

Half of all new moms go through a difficult time known as the postpartum blues. They're impatient, anxious, irritable, and sad, without even understanding why. After all, they've got his beautiful baby, right? Yet they may cry suddenly and unexpectedly, and resent people who are trying to help—especially Dad when he gets to sail out the door to work. The thought of being left alone with the baby can seem terrifying.

It's normal to have mood swings and feel overwhelmed as you struggle with the relentlessness and fatigue of newborn care. For most new moms, these feelings begin three to five days after childbirth and can go on for several weeks, and the reasons are obvious when you think about it: If this is your first baby, you're in virgin territory. If you have other children, they need you, too. Then there are those wildly fluctuating hormone levels that can make PMS seem like a picnic. The best remedy is accepting any and all offers of help, and getting as much rest as you realistically can. In fact, women with less support are more likely to experience the baby blues. Another good idea: Continue to take your prenatal vitamins. While most doctors recommend this if you're breastfeeding anyway because it helps ensure you get adequate nutrition, research shows that the added folate (a key ingredient in prenatal vitamins) helps stave off symptoms of depression because it boosts brain function. Other good sources of folate include whole wheat breads, cereals, rice, and pasta. For most new mothers, this stage passes in a few weeks as your body mends and returns to normal, and you get a handle on your baby's demands.

A smaller group of new moms, however, may need more help. The more serious postpartum depression (PPD) affects somewhere between 10 and 20 percent of postpartum women. Do not feel even one iota of shame if this includes you. PPD is an illness some of us are just prone to get. Fortunately, celebrity mothers such as Brooke Shields and Marie Osmond have spoken publicly and written about their battles with PPD, eliminating some of the stigma of this all-too-common experience. Reading about their similar challenges may help you get through yours. Look for *Down Came the Rain: My Journey through Postpartum Depression* (Hyperion, 2005) by Brooke Shields and *Behind the Smile: My Journey Out of Postpartum Depression* (Warner Books, 2001) by Marie Osmond.

What triggers the more serious PPD? It's believed to be a combination of factors—biological, psychological, and social. You're at increased risk if you've had a previous diagnosis of depression, a difficult relationship with your spouse, a history of abuse, an unwanted or unplanned pregnancy, or a miscarriage or stillbirth in the past. PPD typically begins to peak two to four weeks after birth, and can continue a year or more if left untreated. The most effective remedy for PPD is a treatment plan that includes therapy and antidepressant medication (many of these are safe to use while breastfeeding, so you needn't worry about that).

If you experience even just a few of the following symptoms of PPD, don't keep them to yourself. Talk to your partner and your doctor so you can get on the road to getting well, and enjoying your new baby and new role:

- Feeling restless or irritable.
- Feeling sad, hopeless, and overwhelmed.
- Crying a lot.
- Having no energy or motivation.
- Having no interest in the baby.
- Eating too little or too much.
- Finding that you either can't drag yourself out of bed, or can't go to sleep when you finally get in it.
- Having trouble focusing, remembering, or making decisions.
- Feeling worthless and guilty.
- Losing interest in activities you used to enjoy.
- Withdrawing from friends and family.
- Having headaches, chest pains, heart palpitations (the heart beating fast and feeling as if it's skipping beats), or hyperventilation (fast and shallow breathing). See your doctor to rule out any physical causes.

- Being afraid that you might hurt your baby or yourself. This symptom can be a sign of the extremely rare—and dangerous—condition called postpartum psychosis, so don't waste a second getting help. Let your loved ones know you are in the midst of a crisis and need someone with you at all times until your doctor says otherwise.

And Finally, a Few Words about Bonding

When you were pregnant, you probably read a lot about bonding and looked forward to it. A typical new-mom fantasy goes something like this: You'd be sitting in a rocking chair in a white cotton nightgown. Your gorgeous newborn—also dressed in white—would be suckling contentedly at your breast as you gazed peacefully at the sunlight sparkling on the grass outside your bedroom window. You would at last know the true meaning of the word *bliss*.

Brrrrring! Time to wake up now. Like pretty much every other idyllic moment, this one is pure fiction. You hear the word *bond* and the dashing 007 probably comes to mind—not your baby. You're on automatic pilot at this stage of the parenting game—and life beyond the next diaper change is foggy at best. Sure, there are meaningful, memorable moments with your newborn, but it's not very likely that your relationship has evolved to the point that you could call it a bond. A bond is when you know exactly what someone needs and how to fulfill it, right? You may love your baby at first, but there's a good chance that you don't always like him . . . or know what the heck to do for, with, or about him.

Frankly, that's okay. And it's all totally familiar to the many women who have come before you. Caring for your baby and getting to know him and his unique personality is what will help you bond. Meanwhile, we can all aspire to the perfect relationship, the perfect instincts, the perfect nursery and layette, as long as we remember that these things reside mostly in fantasyland. Day by fuzzy day, somewhere along the way we start to get a little bit of it right, maybe a lot on a really good day, and that vision will keep us going. Hang in there . . . it's going to get way better. Bliss—or at least something close to it—really is around the corner.

CHAPTER 2

Feeding, Part I
The Liquid Diet

Yes! We are here to tell you that you can believe the hype: Feeding your baby can be one of the most fulfilling experiences of your life. Unfortunately, we also have to tell you that this glorious gift can only be received after you understand that feeding your baby can also be one of the most demanding and emotionally draining experiences of your life. As with most things worth having, feeding is one of those parenting jobs in which taking the good with the bad rewards you with the best results. Sounds a lot like childbirth, doesn't it? And just like that most natural of all functions, feeding your baby is a fairly basic task that is rarely simple to perform.

That's probably not what you expected. Indeed, feeding your baby may well have seemed one of the easiest things about motherhood—back when you were pregnant, that is. What could be more loving and natural? Today 70 percent of new moms leave the hospital attempting to breastfeed—up from 55 percent in 1993, just a little more than a decade ago—because that's what's emphasized by healthcare professionals, not to mention the very vocal legions of women who promote nursing from a personal standpoint as well ("breastfeeding activists" or "lactivists" is the politically correct way to refer to them, though you may have heard other, less positive descriptions!). All the information out there about breastfeeding screams its superiority: It's healthier, cheaper (both true), and more convenient (debatable). Then there's that fabulous bond that will develop between you and your child (if the nursing goes well). To really top it all off, there was until recently a controversial public health campaign that went so far as to claim in advertisements that choosing to not breastfeed puts babies at risk, and is as careless as smoking or drinking during pregnancy (utter nonsense!). With all that propaganda, even those who are—and let's be frank—a little squeamish about the concept of nursing can usually talk themselves into giving it the old college try.

Enter: baby. Exit: confidence. "What *was* I thinking?" many a gnawed-up new mom moans in the wee hours as she stumbles to the crib, bracing herself for the pain that latching on may bring to novice nipples (yes, even if you're doing it right) in the first week or two. It doesn't take long to realize how demanding breastfeeding actually is. Even if you and your baby are both pretty quick studies and your milk flows smoothly, it's an incredible physical drain on an already beat-up body. Once you recuperate, there's still the time-suck factor (pun intended). Your other life—you know, the one where you take a shower and get dressed each morning, go to the grocery store, meet a friend for coffee—is basically on hold. Your new schedule revolves around your baby and around the clock: Specifically, your day and your night are divvied up into one- or two-hour chunks of "free time" between feedings. But throw in burping, changing the baby (who will probably have a nice messy little poop after virtually every feeding), possibly caring for your sore breasts, and that time shrinks down to, oh, say, about forty-five minutes and you're back at it all over again. Just going out for a quick trip to the mall or dinner with your husband involves a demanding regime of pumping, storing, trying to stay comfortable and avoid leaking all over yourself while your baby is in someone else's blessed hands for a few hours. All these challenges contribute to a huge drop-off in breastfeeding by six months, when only a little more than a third of moms are still nursing—36 percent at last count. And at one year of age, only 17 percent of moms can claim they breastfed their babies the whole first year, which is what the American Academy of Pediatrics considers the ideal scenario.

Okay, we know we're coming off sounding negative. We really do agree that breast milk is the gold standard in infant nutrition. In fact, we caused quite an uproar in August 2006 when we published a groundbreaking *Babytalk* cover depicting an infant nursing: At last count, we received eighty-five hundred letters about it, the vast majority in support of our choice. Still, some women felt the cover photo was "disgusting," "immoral," or "a sexual thing" they believed they needed to hide from older children. That cover was chosen to illustrate our feature article, "Why Don't Women Nurse Longer?" and we were thrilled with the literally worldwide coverage we received for the image as its appropriateness was debated across the airwaves, over the Internet, and in other newspapers and magazines. We did just what we'd set out to accomplish: raise the consciousness about the challenges of breastfeeding so that the powers that be in our society would make it easier on moms, from providing places to nurse and pump in public or at work to physically, emotionally, and verbally supporting them in this oh-so-important endeavor.

Yet these very challenges are also why, if you're among the other 30 percent—the new moms who felt from the get-go that bottlefeeding was more your speed—you're not going to get any flak from us. We also know how much you've given over of your life to have this baby in the first place, how indescribably demanding newborn care is, and that something like 60 percent of you are going back to work, not to mention the fact that you may have other children who aren't too thrilled to be sharing you. At *Baby-talk,* we recognize there's no one way to feed a baby, and we believe that using formula can be just fine. Sadly, there are other moms who will gasp at the sight of a bottle and a newborn together. The fact is, breast versus bottle has become about as polarizing as Republican versus Democrat or working versus staying home. A few years ago, *Babytalk* surveyed more than thirty-six thousand women and discovered that both methods garnered their share of criticism. We were shocked to discover that almost three-quarters of breastfeeders felt that formula feeders were selfish and deliberately depriving their children! Meanwhile, 83 percent of breastfeeders said they had been criticized for their choice by formula feeders, usually in the form of subtle but deprecating comments like "You're still doing *that?*"

It sure shouldn't be this way. Whichever feeding camp you fall into, feeding your baby is an act of love. Most children end up perfectly healthy regardless of the choice you make. We're here to tell you: Listen to your heart, not the statistics. We all know plenty of bottlefed babies who never seem to get sick and breastfed ones who practically live on antibiotics (despite the fact that breastfeeding is supposed to confer the gift of a strong immune system). Look around and you'll see that breastfed babies also get fat (formula is allegedly the early obesity culprit) and formula-fed babies aren't that much more likely to be colicky (another claim). Your baby will thrive if you love him, and feed him in whatever way works for both of you. Sometimes that means an exclusive choice, a combination of both methods, or breastfeeding for a few months, then switching over to the bottle. So here's the lowdown, no-holds-barred, nothing-but-the-truth take on how to feed your baby. Prepare to be liberated.

What's in This for Me?

It sounds practically sacrilegious to look at the feeding options from your perspective (rather than your baby's), but let's be blunt here: You're the one doing all the work. We all know that breast milk is the optimum form of nutrition. No one's going to argue that. But we also know that for many women, it's darn hard to pull off exclusively for the recommended year. We admire you if you love it and can do it, but we also respect you if you can't. And you can only make the right decision if you're armed with all the information. You wouldn't buy a car or house based on a one-sided review, so start by truly considering your options here.

Choice: **Breastfeeding**
The Benefits: Breast milk is indeed best. Research shows that it can protect your baby from illness and infection, possibly enhance brain development, and also lower the risk of developing chronic illnesses such as asthma and diabetes. There is also mounting evidence that breastfed babies are at less risk for developing weight problems later in childhood, an important concern as childhood obesity rates have escalated to epidemic proportions in our country. You may benefit, too: Research shows that breastfeeding for more than a few months may reduce your risk of ovarian and breast cancer, as well as adult-onset (Type 2) diabetes, rheumatoid arthritis, and possibly osteoporosis. In theory, nursing your baby should help to melt away postpartum pounds to the tune of about five hundred calories a day, though many women find that they don't lose the weight that quickly because they also need to consume more calories to make the darn stuff. Nursing can be convenient (no bottles to wash or formula to mix), and certainly it's inexpensive (you only need a few nursing bras, breast pads, and, usually, a breast pump, though some moms don't even bother with them). If you pump your breast milk, someone else can feed it to your baby by bottle if you go back to work (though keeping up nursing under these conditions is a project, to say the least) or when you need a break (and you always need a break). Last but far

from least is the tremendous pleasure you will get from being able to provide your baby with this incredible gift, and the marvelous, magical bond that will develop between the two of you when breastfeeding is going well. Really.

The Drawbacks: Since a newborn can feed every two or three hours around the clock, and you still need to pump even if your partner gives the baby a bottle of expressed breast milk, nursing gives new meaning to the expression *24/7*. The fact is, you just can't underestimate the fatigue that comes from nursing. Starting out, breastfeeding can be a bigger physical drain than pregnancy was. (We know it's blasphemy to say that, but virtually all of us at *Babytalk* nursed our children, so we know whereof we speak!) The learning curve may have more twists and turns than a fun-house ride, and sore nipples, plugged milk ducts, and engorgement are some of the low points you may have to ride out. Once you reenter the world at large, nursing in public may make you feel self-conscious, and scheduling can be a challenge, especially for working moms. Some jobs may not allow for multiple pumping breaks (and even if they do, pumping carves a good chunk out of your workday); bosses and co-workers can be intolerant.

Choice: **Bottlefeeding**

The Benefits: Although you don't hear them promoted much, there really are some nice perks about feeding your baby from a bottle. It's comforting to see just how much food your baby is consuming, after all. Bottlefeeding is still an act of nurturing, and can provide an emotional closeness just like breastfeeding (maybe more so if you personally feel more comfortable or secure doing it). There's a far shorter learning curve as well. Sure, some babies prefer certain types of nipples or bottle shapes, or are intolerant of certain brands of formula, but the majority of infants are off and running—er, sucking—pretty easily. And you certainly can't underestimate the relief of not being the sole nutritional provider: You can share the feedings with Dad or a sitter, which frees you up to rest, work, care for other kids, or—and here's a wacky idea—maybe even do something for yourself.

The Drawbacks: Formula is costly, though it varies by brand and preparation. The most expensive and convenient is ready-to-serve liquid. Condensed liquid that you mix with water costs less, and powdered formula, which also has to be mixed with water, is cheapest. You can buy in bulk for greater savings, or splurge on pre-packaged individual servings when convenience is at a premium, such as while traveling. Bottles and nipples also need to be purchased, initially sterilized, and washed pretty much daily. Feedings have to be prepared and then packed for most outings with your baby. As for the babies, constipation can be a side effect, which you don't see as often in breastfed infants (of course they have very runny stools, which aren't fun, either). And sometimes you may need to try several formulas (in consultation with your pediatrician, of course) to find the one that your baby digests best. Finally, overfeeding and excessive weight gain are possibilities, especially if you get hung up on wanting your baby to finish every bottle.

Choice: **Combining the two methods**

The Benefits: Breastfeeding some of the time and bottlefeeding the rest can be an ideal choice for many moms. You're still providing your baby the health benefits of breast milk while giving yourself a break. If you're a working mom, adding formula bottles to your baby's feeding routine will save or at least limit how often you need to pump at work and schlep equipment back and forth. Supplementing is also a relief for moms who aren't making a lot of milk or are having trouble developing a good latch-on technique. Exhausted or frustrated by nursing? This route's for you. Giving your baby expressed breast milk is even better for her. If pumping works well for you, your supply can be maintained while you're at work if conditions allow it, and nursing can continue at home.

The Drawbacks: With formula, you may be giving up some of the health benefits that are maximized when a baby is exclusively breastfed. And while most babies can easily switch between breast and bottle, some find it difficult at first. Some babies may prefer the faster flow of a bottle and decide to nurse less frequently (since it is more work on the baby's part), which means your milk production will decrease. Others steadfastly refuse the bottle (the longer you wait to introduce it, the harder it might be). Pumping also does not always yield the same amount of milk as nursing does. Because a breast pump doesn't "work out" your breast as efficiently as a baby sucking on it, this may—but not always—contribute to some decrease in production as well.

For all these reasons, the usual advice is to wait three to four weeks to introduce a bottle so you can build up your milk supply, but many experts and moms (us included) say you can do it at more like two weeks if breastfeeding seems to be going smoothly. To avoid clogged ducts as you add bottles, wait four to seven days before dropping a nursing session (if you won't be pumping the milk then, that is). Your breasts ingeniously follow the principle of supply and demand: The more you breastfeed, the more milk you produce, and vice versa. If done carefully, you can nurse as few or as many times a day as you like and your milk supply will adjust to the timetable you set.

The Breastfeeding Choice

So you want to breastfeed. Good for you. But there's no getting around it: Very few women can simply put baby to breast for the first time and expect instant maternal nirvana. As with any other skill, proper technique is the secret to successful breastfeeding. Getting it right makes all the difference in your comfort level and your baby's nourishment. Plenty of mothers find breastfeeding to be easy after the initial learning period; if you can stick it out for about six weeks, everything tends to fall into a more predictable flow, and your confidence increases.

A good latch is the most important step. If your baby doesn't lock lips correctly with your nipple, he won't get enough to eat and he'll ravage your breast in the process (nope, we're not exaggerating). Yes, he's born with a rooting reflex that makes him turn toward the breast and open his mouth (when he feels like it), and a sucking reflex that's activated when the nipple touches the roof of his mouth. But even though your nipples have ballooned to the size of a dartboard and are as dark as a bull's-eye in the center, some babies still can't manage to hit the mark.

To steer him right, hold your newborn close to your body, with his head directly facing the breast. (You want to line up your nipple with your baby's nose and chin, his lower lip touching your breast.) Tickle the area between your baby's nose and upper lip with your nipple, which will stimulate his rooting reflex and cause him to open his mouth very wide. Then quickly but gently RAM—short for "rapid arm movement"—your baby onto the breast so that he folds his mouth over the nipple. Don't try to bring the nipple to him: He won't take enough in and you'll be uncomfortably hunched over, with an aching back to add to your postpartum complaints. The goal is to get his gums to land at least one inch past the base of your nipple with his lips protruding out. Think "fish lips," says *Babytalk* contributing editor and pediatrician William Sears, MD, coauthor with his wife, Martha Sears, RN, of *The Baby Book*.

To help your baby grab the breast and areola (the area around the nipple) more effectively, you can also try an "asymmetrical" latch, suggests another of our contributors, the pediatrician Marianne Neifert, MD, author of *Dr. Mom's Guide to Breastfeeding,* who has nursed her five children and sure knows what she's talking about. (Dr. Neifert is also the co-founder of The Lactation Program sponsored by the Colorado Health Foundation in Denver.) Dr. Neifert recommends that instead of centering the nipple in the middle of your baby's mouth, you should aim for his upper lip. This allows his more powerful lower jaw muscles to cover more of the breast.

You may feel some discomfort (okay, a good pinch!) for the first minute or two, but it should ease up after your baby begins a deep, rhythmic sucking-and-pausing pattern. When your baby is latched on correctly, he's not only sucking on your nipple, but also putting significant pressure on all those tiny little dots that circle your areola. The milk doesn't flow just from the tip like on a bottle, but out of all those little holes, too—more like a showerhead. You should feel your baby's jaw sucking and compressing almost this whole areola area. Also, his nose should be resting against the upper part of your breast, and his chin pressed against the underside

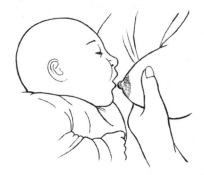

Figure 2.1a Gently tickle your baby's lip with your nipple.

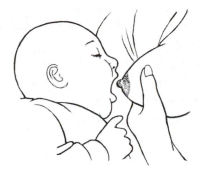

Figure 2.1b When he opens his mouth wide, quickly pull him onto your breast.

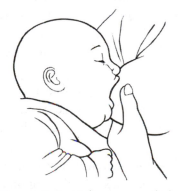

Figure 2.1c Make sure your baby's mouth covers a large part of the areola and his lips are turned outward.

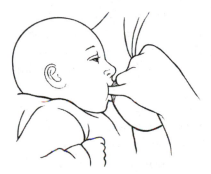

Figure 2.1d To unlatch your baby, slide your little finger into the corner of his mouth to break the suction before removing him.

below the nipple. Don't freak: Your baby can still breathe, because his nostrils will be flared. We all get neurotic about this, but you really don't have to worry.

If your baby has a bad latch, remove him by inserting your pinkie into his mouth to break the suction, then try again. We cannot overemphasize how important it is to get your baby latched on your breast correctly. If you have to repeat the attempt twenty times, do it. How do you know that your latch isn't working? A few good indications:

- Your baby is grasping just the nipple and none of the areola.
- Her lips are tucked or curled inward.
- You hear clicking noises.

- The sucking sounds are rapid and light, rather than deep and regular.
- You don't hear much swallowing.

The best signal, however, is pain. Make that toe-curling pain. Nursing is a natural function, so it shouldn't hurt, the theory goes. Of course, childbirth is natural, too, and we all know what a breeze that is, right? Here's the deal: A certain amount of nipple pain at latch-on can be expected in the first week or two, as this tender body part adjusts to the trauma of being suctioned with the kind of power Hoover only dreams about every other hour around the clock. If, however, the pain does not subside fairly quickly after your baby latches on, she's just not on right. If your pain lasts throughout each feeding, and is so severe that you dread nursing, you need to get help from a lactation consultant immediately. Breastfeeding is a need-based system, and the amount of milk you make is directly related to how frequently and successfully your baby nurses. You don't have to tough it out. Breastfeeding shouldn't be like a test on *Survivor*. The only way to win immunity from a bad latch is to keep asking for help until you and your baby can manage on your own. (To find a lactation consultant, ask your ob-gyn, your baby's pediatrician, or go online at http://gotwww.net/ilca. Lalecheleague.org can also hook you up with a free breastfeeding support group.)

If you're pretty sure your baby is latching on correctly and your nipples just need time to adjust, soothe them between feedings by lathering on a medical-grade lanolin cream (such as Lansinoh)—it will keep your skin supple and doesn't need to be washed off before nursing. Some women also find that coating the nipples with a little breast milk after each feeding then letting them air-dry helps.

There are a few other discomforts that accompany the early stages of learning to breastfeed, but they're all usually manageable. Most women can expect the initial uterine contractions that breastfeeding triggers in the first week or so. (This prevents hemorrhaging and shrinks your womb back to normal size—both worth a bit of suffering for.) You can head off the uterine pain with over-the-counter analgesics such as acetaminophen (Tylenol) or ibuprofen (Advil or Motrin), which are safe for nursing moms. It's best to avoid the over-the-counter pain reliever naproxen (Aleve) when nursing because it can build up in your baby's system, though infrequent use is usually acceptable. If you happen to be taking a prescription pain reliever for an incision or tearing, that will certainly do the job. Just try to get off these (especially if it makes your baby sleepy at the breast) as soon as you're comfortable.

You may also experience a pins-and needles sensation when your milk is released from your breasts. Some women find this more uncomfortable than others, but it lasts only a minute or two, and the sensation tends to lessen as breastfeeding becomes more established.

Then there's engorgement, when your breasts look like zeppelins (and we're fond of saying *lead* zeppelins, because they'll also be rock-hard!). Engorgement is an all-too-common side effect the first few days, when your milk comes in abundantly. When your breasts become engorged, you'll certainly know it. The clinical definition is that your breasts will look and feel swollen and firm, and be very tender to the touch. They'll also probably drip like a leaky faucet, since there's nowhere else for the milk to go but out at this point. The real definition: You'll be horribly sore and uncomfortable and desperate to literally get this stuff off your chest. The best remedy for engorgement is to nurse and nurse some more, so your body learns to regulate milk production. As the expression goes, however, that's easier said than done, because engorgement can also cause your nipples to flatten out a bit, making it more difficult for your baby to latch on—think of trying to suck on a basketball. To help him, express some milk either with a pump or by hand first. To hand-express your milk, wash your hands first, then gently massage your breast, working from the outer areas in toward the nipple to get the milk flowing. Warm compresses can also help your milk let down. Then place your thumb above and about an inch back from the base of the nipple. Your next two fingers should be in the same position below the nipple. Lean forward, holding a clean container to collect the milk in front of your nipple with your free hand. With the hand cupping the nipple, push back against the chest wall, then gently roll your fingers toward the tip of the nipple. You might only get a few drops at first, but if you're putting pressure on the ducts around the areola, the flow should pick up in a few minutes. Express just enough so that your baby can latch on.

If your baby still has problems, try using a thin silicone nipple shield that fits over your own nipple to help it protrude more so your baby can grab on (these shields can also be great for inverted nipples). Also, double-check your baby's latch. A poor latch can mean poor drainage, leaving milk behind to cause blocked ducts. If the latch is the problem, unlatch ASAP. Then try again, as often as necessary, making sure that most of the areola goes into your baby's mouth. Don't get discouraged if this part proves challenging: Your baby has to learn his part of the dance—a duet—just like you.

Between feedings, apply cool compresses to reduce swelling and the hot feeling radiating from your leaden blimps. It sounds a bit bizarre, but placing plastic Baggies of frozen peas or crumpled cold cabbage leaves inside your bra may also soothe engorged breasts. Practitioners of alternative medicine have long believed cabbage and its juices have medicinal value; though there's no scientific proof, many women attest to relief from this method. Taking acetaminophen or ibuprofen also helps, and you may need them for other postpartum discomforts anyway.

Finally, wear a bra 24/7 while you're engorged—but no underwires, please, which can put pressure on your ducts. This may sound uncomfortable, but the extra support will actually be a relief. Lactating breasts are firmer and heavier than usual, and many women, especially those who are large-breasted to begin with, find wearing a bra to bed worth doing the entire time they're nursing. Of course your bedtime bra doesn't have to be an old-style Jayne Mansfield boulder-holder; a nice stretchy spandex sports bra will suffice (as long as it's not too snug—binding your breasts tightly can inhibit milk production) or a comfy cotton one.

A common side effect of engorgement is a clogged duct—a localized backup or blockage of milk that will feel like a tender, hard knot. If you develop one, place a warm compress on the area and gently massage it just prior to nursing your baby to get the milk flowing. Begin the next few feeding sessions on the affected breast—your baby will be hungrier and drain it better. If he doesn't drain it well (your breast will feel much softer and slacker if he has), pump the breast afterward. Varying your nursing positions (see pages 52–54 for how) can also help ensure that all the lobes are emptied. A clogged duct is usually painful enough that you can't ignore it, but it's still worth saying that if you don't take immediate steps to relieve it, a clogged duct can quickly develop into a breast infection, commonly known as mastitis. Mastitis is an unmistakably miserable flu-like feeling, including fever, chills, and headache. Your breasts will develop red or pink splotches that are actually warm to the touch and tender. This sore area may also feel firmer than the rest of your breast (due to clogged milk below it). Contact your healthcare provider right away; you will need to be treated with antibiotics, and it will be two or three days before you feel better. You can, however, continue to nurse your baby while you have mastitis. In fact, you need to, to get that clogged milk out of there!

All that said, there is one fairly easy way to prevent engorgement and the spiraling side effects we just talked about: Learn to anticipate your baby's hunger. Watch your baby for subtle feeding cues, such as putting his fists in his mouth or making sucking or smacking motions with his lips. Keep an eye on the clock, too: If it's creeping up on two hours since you began the last feeding, those lips are going to be getting lively. What you don't want to do is deal with a crying, ravenous baby: You'll get stressed and he'll have a harder time latching on because he's screaming, creating a difficult situation for both of you.

The usual advice is to allow your baby to nurse for about ten minutes on the first breast, then switch to the other side and let him continue until he's done—you'll probably notice the sucking slowing down or ceasing altogether. Sometimes your baby will just drop off the breast himself. Other times you may have to break the suction or "unlatch" him—*never* just pull him away without doing this, unless you want to discover the true meaning of pain! To unlatch, slide your little finger into the corner of his mouth, then remove him from the nipple. The next time you feed your baby, start with the opposite breast, since the breast you used first was more drained. If you have trouble remembering which goes next, attach a safety pin to your bra or switch a ring from one hand to the other.

"WHAT NOBODY TOLD ME ABOUT BREASTFEEDING"

"I had read all the books and gotten plenty of advice from my friends before I gave birth, but when it came time to actually do it, I was a wreck. My beautiful little girl wouldn't latch on and only wanted the bottle! I pumped day and night in hopes that she would nurse. I often found myself crying in desperation. I was about to give up when my doctor recommended a silicone nipple shield that fits over your breast while nursing. Wow! What a difference! It was inexpensive and my daughter latched on right away. After a week, I was able to nurse her without the shield. This wonderful invention allowed me to continue breastfeeding her when I thought all was lost."

—*Elizabeth, Fairfax, Virginia*

"The breast pain was the worst. No one can prepare a new mom for that. It was a great experience all in all afterward, but painful at first."

—*Tracy, Middletown, Delaware*

(continued on next page)

"I wanted to nurse my baby, but my son did not want to nurse. He preferred to drink from a bottle! I was stressed because I felt that I was doing something wrong—not holding him properly, not producing enough milk, et cetera. Pumping every three hours so that I did not dry up made me tired, and my own goal of providing breast milk for at least six months was overwhelming me. I soon realized that if he had a tired and unhappy mom, he would be unhappy also. I calmed myself down, and then he learned to nurse from my breasts on his own!"

—*Sujatha, Edison, New Jersey*

"The physicality of it . . . my breasts were not my own . . . they cracked and hurt, they leaked, I had to wear a bra 24/7, I had to pull them out every two hours, wear a pin to remind me which side to start on next time, hope I could express enough for daycare . . . the list is endless. But I loved seeing how my son was thriving because of *me*!"

—*Nancy, Fort Edward, New York*

There's yet another caveat to this line of advice: Babies have different nursing styles. Some are vigorous suckers who can consume their entire meals in seven to ten minutes before you've even switched breasts. You'll know when your baby has just about emptied your breast because it will feel much softer and slacker. Other babies tend toward slow, endless feeds, content to keep sucking you like a pacifier long after their bellies are full. With newborns, experts often recommend letting them hang on to that second breast for a little while longer, because this comfort sucking (also known as non-nutritive sucking) helps your baby bond with you and feel secure. This assumes your nipples aren't gnawed to death, of course, because if they are, extensive sucking is going to make them worse. We say a pacifier sure comes in handy for these situations, especially if nursing is otherwise going well and your baby is gaining weight nicely, so don't overlook that possibility if you've got a nurser who treats you like the proverbial all-day buffet.

Comfort Counts, Too

The right position or hold can go a long way toward helping you establish a good latch. After all, you're going to be sitting this way for a good twenty to thirty minutes, and the last thing you need is more aches and pains. There are four common breastfeeding holds that will ensure you and your baby are both cozy. Most women begin with the cradle hold—unless they've had a cesarean birth, in which case the football hold usually works best because it puts less pressure on your incision. Feel free to experiment, and definitely use a nursing pillow like the Boppy for support. These are perfectly created to position the baby where you want him, whereas standard bed pillows will require more maneuvering on your part (and you don't need any extra complications at this point!).

Cradle hold. While sitting upright, cradle the baby's head in the crook of your arm on the side you want to nurse from. His body should be lying across your lap (on the nursing pillow) and facing toward your chest. Cup your breast with your free hand by placing your thumb just above the areola (the darker area around the nipple) and the other four fingers below it—this is called a C-hold. Then use the arm your baby's resting on to pull the little sucker toward you.

Figure 2.2a The cradle hold.

Figure 2.2b The football hold.

Football hold. In this position, your baby lays alongside you, rather than on your lap. Tuck his legs underneath your arm so that they're behind you with him looking up at your nipple. Hold your breast in the C-hold with the hand opposite the side you're nursing on. Place the nursing-side hand behind your baby's head, and pull him onto the breast when his mouth opens wide. The football hold is good for a number of reasons: If you've had a cesarean birth, it avoids putting pressure on your abdomen. It also gives you good control over your baby's head during latch-on, and can help relieve clogged ducts.

Cross-cradle hold. The arms are switched in this variation on the cradle hold. The baby is supported by the arm and hand of the side opposite from the breast being nursed, with her head resting on your hand (rather than the crook of your arm) for more control. (See figure 2.2c.) Her feet are instead in the crook of your opposite arm, and you're using the hand on the side of the breast she's nursing from to "C-cup" the breast while your other hand supports her head. This position is ideal for small babies, and can also be helpful for those who have trouble latching on, because you're able to use your hand to bring her head and mouth to the areola.

Figure 2.2c The cross-cradle hold.

Lying down. Many breastfeeders grow to love this position because it takes the pressure off their backs. Lying on your side with your head on a pillow, position your baby parallel to you with her head in the crook of your arm, tummy-to-tummy, and her mouth pointed toward your nipple (the nipple of the breast supported by the bed). Beginners should cup the breast in the C-hold with the opposite arm (seasoned nursers can eventually forgo the C-hold in this and other positions). Then, pull your baby onto the breast.

Figure 2.2d Lying down.

Five Ways to Learn to Breastfeed

1. Do your homework: Take a breastfeeding class at your hospital before your baby is born and read this chapter a couple of times. Have the nurses in the hospital coach you, and get phone numbers of good lactation consultants from them or from friends.

2. Enlist your sister or closest friend who's an experienced breast-feeder to come by often in the first few days and watch you RAM that baby on until you get it right.

3. For the first week or two, hire a baby nurse who can help you with your technique and do some of the grunt work between feedings so you can get as much rest as possible. (Get word-of-mouth references from friends, relatives, your childbirth educator, or physician's office, if possible, or do an online search for "baby nurses" and you'll probably find local agency listings.)

4. Acquire every possible piece of equipment to assist you in your success: a good breast pump; comfy, easy-to-use nursing bras (see pages 67–68 for suggestions); shields, shells, pads, and cold packs; nipple cream; and a nursing pillow. (See page 57.)

5. Cross your fingers and say your prayers—some moms and babies are naturals at breastfeeding, and we hope you fall into that category—but keep the number of a lactation consultant posted on the fridge *just in case.*

"Is My Baby Getting Enough?"

One of the scariest aspects of breastfeeding is not being able to measure how much milk your baby is consuming. You can tell she's eating enough if she meets the following criteria:

- She's nursing every two to three hours around the clock.
- She latches on well and sucks vigorously, leaving your breasts obviously softer and slack (drained) after feedings. (The breast you began on may be more drained than the second breast, so start on the fuller breast the next time.)

- She wets six to eight diapers a day.
- She has several yellow, loose, seedy bowel movements a day.
- She's gaining weight at a consistent rate. Newborns lose as much as 10 percent of their body weight in the first days after birth, but should gain it back by two weeks. So if your baby weighs more than her birth weight at her two-week checkup, she's doing great.

Worried? Don't be afraid to call the doctor immediately if you have any doubts or concerns about how much your baby is consuming. Most pediatric practices are happy to let you come in for a weigh-in as often as you want, to ensure that your baby is gaining and not losing pounds. And if they're not, too bad for them. Go in anyway if it helps you stay sane and ensures your baby's well-being. If you're having trouble with nursing, your baby's doctor may be able to help you improve your technique and can refer you to a lactation consultant, if necessary. You can also rent a scale just like the one your pediatrician uses for a little less than $100 a month. They're made by Medela, a manufacturer of breast pumps and other nursing products. Call 800-835-5968 and ask about the Medela BabyWeigh Scale, which will give you a precise electronic reading before and after each feeding so you can see exactly how much your child ate.

We don't want to make you unnecessarily paranoid, but it's important not to wait until problems are extreme. If your baby isn't eating enough, she can become dehydrated, which is a dangerous condition. Signs of dehydration include decreased urination, sunken eyes, and excessive drowsiness. A sunken soft spot on your baby's head is a sign of severe dehydration; if you see this, get yourselves to the emergency room immediately.

Your Breastfeeding Rights

1. If you have a right to be somewhere with your baby, you have a right to breastfeed there. While there are a few places, such as courtrooms, where babies aren't permitted, women can legally breastfeed in most public places—stores, restaurants, parks, and malls. In fact, most states now have laws that protect a woman's right to breastfeed (visit lalecheleague. org/LawBills.html to see if yours does), and no state outlaws it. Still worried about obnoxious comments? Download *Babytalk*'s breastfeeding rights card at Parenting.com/babytalk and stick it in the face of anyone who gives you, er, lip.

STUFF YOU NEED FOR BREASTFEEDING . . .

- ❏ Nursing pillow (eases neck and back strain).
- ❏ Burp cloths (lots of them).
- ❏ Can of formula, just in case (like when our suburban editor was stuck in New York City during the 2003 blackout and her stored breast milk ran out).
- ❏ Breast pump (see pages 74–77 for guidance on which type of pump is right for you).
- ❏ 3–4 nursing bras. Make sure you can open the cup with one hand, since you'll be holding your baby with the other.
- ❏ Nursing pads to absorb leaking milk. Experiment with different kinds—some are useless and slide around inside your bra like falsies.
- ❏ Phone number of a lactation consultant (yes, you will need to call at least once!). There will likely be one affiliated with the hospital where you delivered, or you can check with your pediatrician's office or other mom friends for a recommendation.
- ❏ Freezer storage containers.
- ❏ Nipple cream. Look for one that doesn't need to be removed for feedings, such as Lansinoh, because washing it off will just irritate your nipples more.
- ❏ 6–8 bottles (for feedings by Dad or a babysitter).
- ❏ Breast shells. These wide shields are designed to be worn in your bra between nursing sessions to prevent friction and chafing; you may need them if your nipples are sore.
- ❏ Nipple shields (silicone shields to be worn while nursing to help draw your nipple out; you may need them if you're engorged or have inverted nipples).
- ❏ Warm/cool relief packs (a lifesaver if you're engorged or have blocked ducts).

(continued on next page)

. . . AND STUFF YOU DON'T

- Nursing shawls. Just use a receiving blanket.
- Lots of specialized nursing clothes. Shirts with hidden openings can be more hassle than they're worth because the darn holes can be too small and never seem to line up with your bra opening when you need them to. Instead, try the ones that pull down or across from the top—check out the selection on Babystyle.com. Or just wear button-front shirts or a top you can lift up from the bottom. Many moms find this works just fine.

2. You have a right to pump comfortably at work. Technically, American employers aren't required to provide moms with a specific place to pump. Yet ironically, some states do mandate that employers "enable" women to breastfeed. How you can be enabled without a place to do it is beyond us. What you can insist on is break time to pump, and a spot other than a bathroom stall to do it in. Ask for a room with a lockable door, a place to sit, and an electrical outlet for the pump. Still no go? You can pump in your car (you won't be the first mom to do this!). You probably need a pump that can run on a battery or a manual pump. (See pages 74–77 for more buying info.)

3. You have a right to breastfeed for as long as you'd like. The American Academy of Pediatrics (AAP) recommends all moms nurse until their baby's first birthday, but they also don't think you need to stop there. The AAP policy also states that extended nursing is fine "for as long as mutually desired." The jury is out on whether nursing past the first year provides any health benefits to your child, but there is evidence that women who nurse for lengthy time frames have reduced risks of breast and ovarian cancer, as well as osteoporosis and adult-onset diabetes (Type 2). And extended nursing certainly contributes to a strong bond between mother and child, so don't let anyone tell you it's time to quit if you don't really want to. Even if you want to stop at the year mark, weaning is not something you can typically accomplish overnight. Take the time your baby *and* you need to make this physical and emotional shift.

The Emotional Side of Breastfeeding

When you see a title like this, you are no doubt expecting some lilting flowery words about bonding and attachment, and how utterly fulfilling nursing your child is. Since you know all that already (or are at least working to get to that point), we're not going to waste your time. What we want to tell you about here is the emotionally challenging stuff—the feelings every nursing mom encounters at some point and dares not admit. Here's the thing: You're entitled to those feelings of frustration, as well as to resentment and annoyance at your partner. They don't make you any less of a mother; they simply make you human. Many of these mixed emotions will pass when the postpartum fog lifts and you and your baby have aced Breastfeeding 101 (but you can still expect to get ticked off at times). Between now and then, don't be surprised if you have a few crying jags along the road to that rewarding, exhausting, magical maternal experience.

The sleep factor. Sure, babies sleep fifteen hours a day; they're just not consecutive (or necessarily the same hours when *you* expect to sleep). Instead, your newborn may snooze a couple of hours here and twenty minutes there, with no regard for day or night. Needless to say, trying to take care of yourself so that your body can keep breastfeeding is not an easy task. Even if you were able to get a full night's sleep, chances are you'd still be wiped out. In fact, some experts say it takes more energy to feed a baby

VOICE OF REASON

"Learning how to breastfeed is like learning how to drive a car with manual transmission. If you survive the technique test, you get to move on to the engorgement phase when the milk actually comes in. Your breasts may be more impressive than your neighbor's boob job. Your husband will want to take pictures. This too will pass. If you make it to the two-week mark, you are on cruise control. That should be your goal. You may need a great deal of moral support to get to two weeks, however."

—*Ari Brown, MD, pediatrician, mom, and co-author of* Baby 411:
Clear Answers & Smart Advice for Your Baby's First Year

than to make one, which explains why you're possibly thirstier and hungrier than you've ever been, even during pregnancy. Respect your body's need for these additional calories (you should be taking in a minimum of twenty-two hundred calories a day, and preferably closer to twenty-seven hundred) and provide them in a healthy fashion, along with a death-by-chocolate-type dessert now and then. We are talking about your emotional well-being, after all.

The classic "sleep when the baby sleeps" pearl of wisdom can't be underestimated. But unless you adjust your priorities during your awake time, you'll never sneak in the shut-eye you need. To give your REM real restorative power, plan to shift your daily responsibilities. Remember, your main agenda the first few weeks and months is to feed and care for your baby and yourself. Clear your calendar, limiting visitors and your regular duties. Ask your husband to be a bouncer, nudging visitors out the door when they cut into your naptime. He can also pick up burping and diapering tasks, which will give you anywhere from ten to twenty extra minutes of sack time after a feeding. Learn to delegate daily tasks, such as folding laundry or emptying the dishwasher, to your partner, mother, or a good friend, and cooking to your local pizza guy or a neighbor who knows her way around a casserole. In short, accept any and all offers of assistance.

Other lifesaving tips: Put as many of your regular bills on automatic payment as you can, and consider hiring a weekly housecleaner for a while. Once breastfeeding is going well—the baby has no trouble latching on, you have a good milk supply, and your pediatrician agrees that he's gaining the right amount of weight—you might also consider stockpiling pumped milk, so that you can hand off one feeding a night to your partner. (See page 70 for guidelines on storing and serving expressed breast milk.)

As corny as it sounds, positive thinking can also go a long way toward powering you through, especially during those first weeks. Try to think of those middle-of-the-night feedings as a gift to your baby. They help him get the best nutritional start possible while ensuring that your milk supply stays high. You can also cling to this little piece of good news: When you're breastfeeding, you'll benefit from high levels of prolactin, a hormone that helps your body foster deep, restorative sleep—whenever you can get it.

"Is there another mommy in the house?" Wouldn't it be ideal if, when those 2 AM wails penetrate your dreams, you could shout this and a wet nurse would answer the call for help? Alas, your engorged breasts begin to spring leaks, and you curse in the dark under the covers. What would your girlfriends think? How could you feel this way about your baby, for God's sake? You end up consumed by guilt as your baby consumes his meal.

Been there, done that, as the saying goes. Who the heck wouldn't be resentful of everyone who doesn't have to endure this torture, not to mention the little terror in the crib? You're not Attila the Mom for feeling this way. You're just plain old, everyday, normal Mom (now isn't that an attractive description). The challenge really isn't how you can eliminate guilt. You might as well stop breathing. If you didn't feel guilt now and then, you'd be a robot and wouldn't be able to breastfeed, not to mention love, your baby in the first place. Guilt is part of the job description; the other talent you need is knowing how to prevent it from paralyzing you.

Think of the three R's (no math involved): recognize, reiterate, and relax. First off, recognize that guilt is a normal human emotion. There are no warning labels issued for breasts, but if there were, they might say: "Warning: Breastfeeding may cause drowsiness and be downright hazardous to your sanity at times. Be sure to take regular naps and drink plenty of water, and consume chocolate or an occasional glass of good wine as needed." The truth is that breastfeeding—while a wonderful means of nourishing and bonding with your baby—doesn't automatically make you feel warm and fuzzy each time you lift your shirt. It's more like sex (remember sex?): Sometimes you're really into it, and sometimes you just have to go through the motions for the sake of your, er, partner.

An important antidote for these seesawing emotions is good old talk therapy: Confide in a trusted friend, relative, or pretty much anyone with enough experience at it to be able to reassure you that it does get easier, that feedings get shorter, and that the baby will sleep longer between meals. Try keeping a journal—your progress may be more obvious in its pages—or seek out other breastfeeding moms to chat up online. Finally, relax. Just because a negative thought comes to your mind, it isn't transmitted via breast milk to your baby's brain. He still adores you, and you still adore him. Enough said.

What's Dad got to do with it? Plenty, though it may not seem like it. He didn't carry the baby, suffer through labor, or deliver her. Now he can't even help feed her. Which leaves you cursing under your (bad) breath every time he sails out the door to work. His very existence can be enough to annoy you. There's no argument here: Breastfeeding takes away some— okay, lots—of your freedom. (Then again, so does having a baby.) In the beginning of your baby's first year, you're constantly on the clock, with your newborn whistling *time's up* every two hours. Not so with your hubby. So even when he's running out to pick up a pint of your favorite ice cream, you may resent him for it.

When you're ready to burst with anger because he doesn't understand what you're going through, remember this: He doesn't understand what you're going through! And, as you've probably already guessed from other situations in your relationship, he's no mind reader. To get the me time that you need—whether it's to take a nap, take a walk, or take a spoon to that ice cream he just fetched—you will have to be vocal about your needs. (Don't consider yourself the whiny type? Get over it. It may be the only way to get any attention from him or the kids for the next few decades. They will surely all outdo you at this game if you decide to be a martyr.) Then start shifting some additional baby duties his way. Many new dads are dying to get their hands on the baby, if we moms will only let them. The bigger the asset your man can become, the less resentment will simmer in your soul. And the baby really won't feel any pain when she's wearing her diaper backward. Later, after you've settled into a daily rhythm with your baby, you may be surprised to find that your feelings of resentment turn to pity as you think about how your partner can never know the beauty of breastfeeding.

Banishing the busybodies. You may have thought of breastfeeding as a personal choice, but you will soon find out that it's a very public issue. Everyone from the security guard at the mall to your aunt Evelyn wants to have a say in when, where, and how long you breastfeed. In a recent *Babytalk* survey, about a quarter of breastfeeding moms said they were made to feel uncomfortable about nursing their babies at some point. That's no surprise, because other research from the American Dietetic Association indicates that 57 percent of Americans disapprove of women breastfeeding in public.

What this means, of course, is that you're bound to be put in a position of needing to defend yourself eventually, and it's tough to think straight—not to mention be tactful—when you're tired, hormonal, and feeling a wee bit grumpy that anyone other than your husband and baby is paying attention to your breasts. Whether the comments ("How long are you planning to nurse?" "Isn't he on solids already?") are occasional or frequent, they will be annoying, like a mosquito buzzing in your ear. Wouldn't it be nice if you could just zap them away with bug spray? Since no one makes pesticides for intrusive friends, family, or even strangers, you need your wits and a few pieces of valuable medical information to shoo away the offenders. A simple response like "The latest studies show that this is the best thing for babies" or "Our baby's doctor highly recommended that we do it this way" may send the message that the busybody is out of bounds. It's hard to argue with medical experts and scientific research, after all. You can also bring up how the American Academy of Pediatrics recommends that women breastfeed for at least a year, and how breast milk is the best food for boosting your baby's immune system.

It's helpful to remember, too, that most people aren't knowingly trying to sabotage your efforts. If your aunt's kids are all grown up now, there's a very good chance that she's not aware of the latest information. If it's your husband who's resisting your efforts (yes, this happens when he feels like the odd man out in the love triangle or when nursing makes lovemaking awkward), you may want to have your pediatrician tell him about the health benefits of breastfeeding at a checkup. You can also soothe his hurt feelings by emphasizing that you understand why he's feeling neglected and that the situation is most definitely temporary. In other cases, friends who made different choices for their children may have trouble imagining what it's like to walk a mile in your nursing bra. If you don't receive any positive feedback from your immediate circle of family and friends, then it's time to cast a wider net. Look for nursing support groups in your area or, again, chat with other like-minded moms online.

"WHY BREASTFEEDING WORKED FOR ME"

"It was so easy and natural—and always ready when my little one was hungry. I can't imagine having to wake up in the middle of the night to prepare a bottle. Nighttime was always such a sweet time for me to be awake, just me and my baby. I work from home by telecommuting, so there was never any need to worry about leaving for work, which made it easy for me. Another thing that helped is living in a place where most women nurse and for a long time, at least a year if not longer. In fact, I have to say that nursing was the best part of being a new mother!"
                                                    —*Mary, Athens, Georgia*

(continued on next page)

"At six months I started to stop nursing, but it was so much easier than making formula, I kept reverting. I continued for another three months till my daughter was more interested in solid food and sippy cups. I'm now pregnant with number two and will probably do the same."

—*Mina, Montclair, New Jersey*

"I always had it on me; it didn't require refrigeration, heat, or stirring. I already washed it on a regular basis. And it was *free*."

—*Angel, Wilson Borough, Pennsylvania*

"I thought it was a lot easier and more convenient. I didn't have to worry about warming bottles, and as long as I could find a somewhat private area, it worked well in public, too. I even was able to work and still nurse at least once during the day since she was at a daycare at the same place where I work."   —*Amy, Alpharetta, Georgia*

"Breastfeeding was great in the end, but tough in the beginning. I pushed through the first two weeks and it was stressful, but then things mellowed out and got easier every day. Nothing to carry around, heat up, buy, or clean. The true secret of breastfeeding is that the longer you do it, the easier it is. Once the baby is eating solids, you nurse so much less. It helps to put them to sleep, calm them down. In many ways it's the lazy mothers' choice. The funny thing is you get so much credit for doing it at all and then if you do it for over a year people think you are this selfless person. Meanwhile I always found it to be convenient, ready to go, inexpensive, and it made me skinny again. Kind of a win—win for everyone."

—*Meredith, Ridgefield, Connecticut*

Nursing-Mom Diet Myths: What You Really Can and Can't Have

For nine months, you've given your body over to your baby so she would enter the world healthy, happy, and with every advantage. It's about time you get to indulge in a little treat for yourself—but wait! You still can't have that double espresso, down a glass of Chardonnay, or pop a pain reliever for that aching episiotomy, because you're nursing! Or can you? It's true that a lot of things travel from you to your baby through breast milk, but not every substance you ingest will enter your baby's bloodstream as it did when it passed through the placenta. And what does wind up in your breast milk is usually not as concentrated as it was when the baby was in your womb. Here's what you really need to know about treating your-self—and treating your baby to your breast milk.

Caffeine. Now that you really need it, you can have it, although slugging down a potful of black coffee isn't exactly recommended. Two caffeine-containing beverages a day is usually fine. For the record, coffee contains the most caffeine; tea and soft drinks have less, depending on the brand. That said, some babies do become cranky or have trouble sleeping if their mothers consume caffeine, so watch for signs that it might be affecting yours and cut back if necessary.

Herbal teas and supplements. This is a bit of a gray area, so you should discuss it with your healthcare provider and your baby's pediatrician if you want to indulge. Herbs in any form are not regulated by the Food and Drug administration (FDA), so it's not always possible to know the amount and strength in a preparation. Teas or supplements that contain the herb fenugreek, for instance, can have potent effects on heart rate and blood pressure; so you should avoid them. Ironically, fenugreek has been touted as increasing milk production, but to do so it would need to be taken in such large amounts that you and your baby could well experience the negative side effects as well. Other herbal no-nos, whether they're in the form of teas or supplements, include comfrey, ginseng, ginkgo, kava, valerian, and St.-John's-wort.

As a rule, brand-name teas that you can readily find in a grocery store with clear ingredient labeling, such as Celestial Seasonings or Bigelow, may be fine in the following flavors: chamomile, orange spice, pepper-mint, raspberry, red blush, and rose hip. (But it's still a smart idea to check with your doctor.) Be wary of any teas that appear homemade or are not clearly labeled with an ingredient list.

Alcohol. Don't believe the myth that a glass of beer will increase your milk supply—it won't. And regular alcohol consumption can harm your baby. But you can indulge in an occasional drink, because alcohol passes through breast milk about an hour and a half to two hours after you drink it. So if you nurse first, then have your cocktail, then wait at least two hours until your baby is ready to nurse again, there's little chance he'll be sharing your Chardonnay. If you want to be extra cautious, you can always "pump and dump" the next feeding of breast milk, then give your baby some of your backup supply from the freezer, or formula if you've been supplementing.

Medications. While both over-the-counter medications and prescriptions can pass into breast milk, in most cases it's only a small amount that won't affect your baby adversely. For instance, acetaminophen and ibuprofen are fine to take for occasional or short-term discomforts, and some prescription painkillers may also be, but most doctors would caution against their regular use. Let your ob-gyn know that you are breastfeeding so she will be sure to prescribe an acceptable postpartum pain reliever. Many antibiotics, antihistamines, antiseizure medications, and blood pressure medications are also okay. If you've got a chronic condition such as epilepsy, diabetes, or asthma, it's important to keep treating it, and you can usually do so while breastfeeding. You and your doctor can work out the how-tos. On the other hand, illicit drugs like cocaine, marijuana, or heroin are most definitely not okay while breastfeeding. The effects of antianxiety medications such as Valium, and antipsychotics such as Thorazine, are unknown and may be of concern, so be sure to tell your doctor if you are nursing. And there has been much in the news lately about taking antidepressants during pregnancy and while breastfeeding, so you should talk with your doctor about them before making your decision. New studies seem to come out every few months, but as of this writing, Zoloft (sertraline) is believed to be the safest antidepressant for breastfeeding mothers: It shows up in breast milk in only very low levels. The same goes for Paxil (paroxetine). On the other hand, Prozac (fluoxetine) is less desirable because it appears in breast milk in larger quantities and takes longer to clear out of the milk. Side effects such as colic, insomnia, sedation, and jitteriness have been observed in babies exposed to Prozac. Finally, there is some evidence that Wellbutrin (bupropion) may contribute to reduced milk supply.

Cigarettes. Sorry, but there's still nothing good to be said about smoking—for you or your baby. Some studies have demonstrated that smokers produce less breast milk than nonsmokers, and while there is no hard-and-fast research, it is possible that chemicals from cigarettes and the pesticides used in growing tobacco may be passed on to your baby through your breast milk. The biggest dangers, however, are the side effects of secondhand smoke: Smoking in the presence of your baby increases her risk of infections, asthma, and SIDS (sudden infant death syndrome). In fact, studies show that exposure to cigarette smoke at least doubles your baby's risk of SIDS. If you smoke, it's still a good choice to nurse your baby to help negate some of these side effects, but never do it in the same room of the house as your baby or while in the car with her. Best of all is to go outside to smoke, and keep your home and car totally smoke-free environments.

Spicy stuff. Much is made over offending foods in a mother's diet, but the reality is that many babies happily tolerate whatever it is that's flavoring their milk, from the spicy (garlic, onions), to the gassy (broccoli, cabbage), to the allergenic (peanut butter, eggs, citrus). Those moms with a family history of food allergies are more likely to notice reactions to their diets in their infants, so you should discuss this with your baby's pediatrician; there may be an increased likelihood that your baby will develop the same allergies if exposed to these ingredients prematurely. Typical symptoms of an allergic reaction in a breastfed baby include skin rashes, red cheeks, congestion, diarrhea, vomiting, and fussy or colicky behavior. If your baby seems to be reacting to your breast milk, discuss it with your pediatrician, who will likely suggest eliminating the one or two most likely culprits for five to seven days and seeing if the symptoms improve. There's usually no need to drastically cut back your diet, and doing so may adversely affect your milk production.

Nursing Accessories We Love

It's the little things—like having a bra you can unfasten with one hand—that mean the most to the nursing mom. Many manufacturers claim this feature, but you've really got to road-test a bra, or at least try it on in a fitting room, to be sure. (If you're shopping at a store without a fitting room, when you get the bra home, remove it carefully from the packaging and don't take off any tags until you try it on and are sure you like it.) Not all models are created equal. Here are a few accessories we found can really make your life easier:

> **The Easy-Zip Nursing Bra** has cups that can be quickly unzipped with one hand; it's is made of a stretchy, soft microfiber fabric that

always fits expanding breasts (a tank top is available, too). $40; available at amazon.com.

Easy Expression Hands-Free Pumping Bra or **Bustier.** The breast shields attach right to the bra (available in traditional or bustier styles), so you can pump hands-free. Ingenious! $34; easyexpression products.com.

Second Nature Wide Neck Nurser baby bottle and **All Stages Nipple**. Virtually all bottles and nipples claim to mimic Mom, but this system is the closest we've seen. The nipple has twenty-five microholes so the milk flows just like in a breast, at a baby-directed speed. When your baby stops sucking, the holes close—dripping is minimized. Ideal for combo moms and babies reluctant to try a bottle. Available in most baby retail outlets. A set of bottles, nipples, and caps ranges $12–20 depending on size and retailer.

Glow-in-the-dark digital clock. Keep it in the room where you breastfeed at night so you can keep track of how long you've been nursing on each breast without having to disrupt your baby by turning lights on full blast. Nursing in the dark will also hopefully lull him back to sleep a little sooner!

Working without Weaning

For many moms who plan to remain employed, just when they find their breastfeeding groove it's time to return to work and rethink their routine all over again. The challenges ahead include pumping and stockpiling breast milk, introducing a bottle, negotiating a time and place to pump at work, and dealing with co-workers who may not understand your decision. On top of all that, you've still got to do your job. Despite these obstacles, some women do manage to continue to provide breast milk exclusively for their babies. If you're lucky enough to work for one of the 17 percent or so of large companies with on-site or very close-by childcare, that task is a whole lot easier. If you're not, take a cue from the Boy Scouts: Be prepared.

1. Get pumped. The first step is to rent or buy a good-quality electric breast pump (see pages 74–77 for pointers) that empties both breasts at once. They're more expensive than other types, but the time savings will be well worth it. You may also want to keep a lower-cost but efficient manual pump at home so you don't have to haul the machine around (though many of us keep the heavy motor part of the electric pump at work Monday through Friday, and tote only the bottles back and forth).

Now a few words about learning to pump: This, too, can seem overwhelming when coupled with everything else you're going through. Paradoxically, the more relaxed you can be about pumping, the easier it will be to get the milk flowing. So the last thing you want to do is attempt to master it just a few days before you're due to return to work and under pressure. Instead, give yourself about two weeks before you go back to practice and begin storing your breast milk. Consider tapping into your husband's inner mechanic, that guy gene that enables him to interpret how-to manuals in his sleep. (He'll probably jump at the chance to assist you in any way possible with your breasts, desperate as he is for attention at this point.) Or, if your partner's the type that breaks more things than he fixes, ask a girlfriend who knows her way around a breast pump to come over and give you a demo. These contraptions seem like they require a course in advanced physics at first, but unlike actually breastfeeding, you can usually get the hang of them quickly and painlessly.

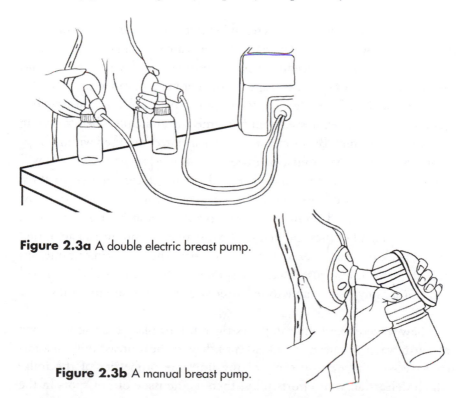

Figure 2.3a A double electric breast pump.

Figure 2.3b A manual breast pump.

2. Stock up. Once you know how to hook up, you're ready to start your freezer stash of pumped breast milk that a caregiver can use to feed your baby while you're at work. Start pumping after each morning feeding, when your supply is at its peak. Expect to pump between fifteen to twenty-five minutes with a double electric pump that allows you to empty both breasts at once. How much milk you will be able to pump depends on the age of your baby, the time of day, and how well you're able to maintain your milk supply. During your first at-home morning pumping sessions, it may be an effort to get as little as two ounces of milk from both breasts, since your baby has drained them already. But once you are away from your baby, you may find that you can produce from five to eight ounces at a time, assuming you are able to pump about three times during the work-day. (Again, this amount is an average from the total of both breasts, but be aware that output can vary widely from mom to mom.) Seasoned pumpers report that the first pumping session of the day is often the most productive, with less milk being produced the second and third times they flip the switch. As your baby gets older and solids are added to his diet, you may find that the amount you can pump decreases, since your baby is relying less on breast milk.

You can store breast milk in resealable plastic bags with ounce markings in single-serving portions. These handy items are generally available wherever you can buy infant feeding supplies (bottles, nipples, breast pads, and the like). Be sure to label the bag with the date you pumped the milk. It's also okay to "layer" milk from different pumping sessions in the same bag as long as you have expressed it on the same day and chill it before adding it to the frozen milk. Breast milk can be refrigerated and used within forty-eight to seventy-two hours, or frozen for much longer periods. It will keep in a freezer compartment inside the refrigerator for two to three weeks, in a separate freezer unit of a refrigerator for three to six months, or in a stand-alone deep freezer for six to twelve months. Keep in mind, however, that all of these guidelines are just that. If you find a bag buried in the back of your freezer that's a week past the ideal time frame, it's probably still fine to use. Like any spoiled milk, breast milk will smell bad if it is, so you'll be able to tell after you thaw the serving if it's okay or not.

Thaw frozen breast milk in the refrigerator, or place the bag in a bowl of warm water. It's never a good idea to thaw or heat breast milk in a microwave—it will destroy some of the immune properties of the milk, which defeats all your efforts. Plus, there is the issue of hot spots in the baby bottle (due to microwaves' tendency to heat unevenly) that can burn your baby's mouth. For more on the controversy surrounding microwaving baby bottles, see page 91.

3. Introduce a bottle. At least two weeks before your maternity leave ends, have someone else—such as Dad, the new caregiver, or Grandma—give the baby a bottle. Practice this new feeding technique, once a day to start, so that your baby gets used to it before you actually have to be separated for a long period of time. (See pages 72–74 for tips on how to introduce a bottle.) When you return to work, you may want your partner to give a bottle during the night so that you can have at least one solid block of sleep.

4. Start politicking. Logistics are one thing; human nature, quite another. You may well need to negotiate a time and place to pump and deal with strange, even hostile, looks from co-workers. It's best to try to tackle these issues before you return. Find out what arrangements your employer already has in place. If something is lacking, such as a private space to pump, see if other employees also want a change. Try to be clear and firm about what you need without being antagonistic. Nursing moms are no longer an aberration in the workplace, so don't be shy.

If diplomatic efforts don't pan out, try giving your boss a note from your pediatrician explaining the health benefits of breastfeeding—a healthier baby can mean fewer days that a parent has to miss work. If that fails, know your legal rights. (The National Conference of State Legislatures Web site, ncsl.org/programs/health/breast50.htm, has a state-by-state list.)

One unexpected pocket of resistance may come from your colleagues. Moms shouldn't have to justify their breastfeeding to others, of course, but you will likely have a better experience if you have understanding co-workers. Toward that end, you may want to try to open a dialogue about what you're doing, in terms of both breastfeeding and your work, making it clear that you don't intend to use your pumping breaks as an excuse to slack off.

5. Get to work. Expressed breast milk should be kept chilled, so if you're pumping at work, you'll need a refrigerator or cooler to store it in until you go home. You'll also need an insulated bag and cold pack to transport it during your commute. Try to dress in easily accessible clothing: blouses that unbutton in the front, or sweaters that pull up easily. You may find that favorite one-piece dresses, for instance, aren't worth the bother of having to disrobe entirely to pump. It's also a good idea to keep an extra neutral-colored blouse or sweater for those days when you can't get to your pump fast enough and you start to leak. It goes without saying that you should wear a good set of breast pads at all times, and keep some spares in your desk or locker.

The Nipple Confusion Myth

If you attempted in any way to prepare for breastfeeding—took a class, read a few books, did some online research, chatted up some girlfriends—you have probably heard the following hazards about introducing a bottle:

- Your milk supply will be permanently crippled and quickly dwindle down to nothing (hmm . . . sounds suspiciously like the theory that all epidurals lead to C-sections).
- The dreaded "nipple confusion" will occur, leading your baby to permanently (there's that word again) reject your breast.

Bunk. Nothing more, nothing less. Sure, the theory makes sense: Nursing is more work for the baby because she has to suck harder (bottles have gravity on their side, which keeps the milk flowing at steady pace), so why shouldn't the poor kid prefer the easy way? Don't introduce a bottle too soon, breastfeeding advocates warn, or your novice nosher will turn up her nose when you serve up her dinner. But moms in the trenches (on our Parenting.com/babytalk Web site) beg to differ. An incredible 82 percent said their breastfeeding babies could switch-hit with a bottle, no problem. We also personally know not only moms who introduced a bottle as soon as they got home from the hospital, but even moms who had the postpartum nurses in the hospital give middle-of-the-night bottles so they could get some sleep and recuperate from delivery. All of these women were able to successfully breastfeed, no nipple confusion, no lack of milk.

While the common wisdom advises introducing a bottle at four to six weeks, we say most babies can handle it at two to three. If you can wait four weeks, fine. But if you can't, there's probably no harm in introducing a bottle sooner. We're not exactly implying that some overzealous breastfeeding advocates made up nipple confusion to keep moms nursing exclusively (though some would agree to that theory), but it's definitely been blown out of proportion. In fact, if you want to bottlefeed at some point, you may want to introduce a bottle by around six weeks, before your baby gets too entrenched in his nursing habit. We've all heard of older babies who refuse to ever take a bottle, which can lead to serious feelings of entrapment for some moms.

The fact is, there's no way to prove a concept like nipple confusion. A baby can't explain himself, and he may be having trouble nursing for a variety of reasons, so it's obvious why a bottle may become an easier food source to him. That's why our contributor Dr. Marianne Neifert says *nipple preference* is a more accurate description. In fact, the authors of one of the more comprehensive papers on the topic, published in 2001 in *Newborn and Infant Nursing Reviews,* advised healthcare providers to take "a more moderate position" on bottlefeeding a breastfed infant, which we interpret as "Of course you can!" In our experience, if the baby can smell you, he prefers you, even if you've been offering bottles.

Using a pacifier in conjunction with breastfeeding has also gotten a bad rap, largely for the same reasons. Yet another recent study found pacifiers didn't cause breastfeeding problems, either. What the study did find: Early bottles and pacifiers may shorten the overall length of time that a woman ends up breastfeeding, though it's not exactly clear why. Perhaps women who are using bottles and pacifiers are having trouble nursing already or are less motivated to continue. But the benefits can't be ruled out, either: The added flexibility of pumping and bottlefeeding can allow working moms to continue breastfeeding (even if it's just on a part-time basis) longer than they would have otherwise.

All that said, every baby will react differently when introduced to a bottle. Some will love it from the get-go, others may be harder to convince, but most can soon learn to switch between breast and bottle effortlessly. If you're aching to sleep more than three hours at a stretch, or to finally use that spa gift certificate your BFF gave you postpartum, say no more. Here's how to make the concept palatable to your budding gourmet:

- Let someone else serve up the first few bottles, so your baby continues to associate you (and your smell) with breastfeeding. After a while, he'll accept a bottle from you, too.
- Give expressed breast milk in the first bottle, if possible, since your baby is familiar with its scent and taste.
- Choose the right time. Don't wait until your baby is starving before offering her a bottle for the first time—the surprise may make her

more hysterical, and less likely to accept it. Instead, aim for an hour or two after her last feeding.

- Babies love skin-to-skin contact, so if Dad is doing the feeding, for instance, your baby may take to it better if she can nuzzle his bare chest at the same time.
- Stay calm. Your baby can pick up on parental anxiety, so try to stay positive.
- Don't force-feed. If she only wants to take a few sips the first time, that's fine.
- Get help if you hit a stumbling point. If you find that your baby begins to prefer the bottle to the breast, seek help immediately from an understanding lactation consultant. (That is, be sure she's someone who's fine with bottlefeeding and won't be a big pain in the rear.) Perhaps your baby isn't getting what she needs from breastfeeding. Improving your technique can make it more satisfying for her to nurse. Just be sure to keep pumping to maintain your milk supply while you work things out.
- Don't give up if your preemie requires a bottle. If a premature baby isn't able to nurse—his sucking mechanism might not be fully developed— he may end up being fed from a tube or bottle first. But this doesn't mean he'll never breastfeed. Once preemies reach their due date, they're often able to learn to latch on and nurse. And if you've been pumping all along, you should quickly be able to build up your milk supply.

Pump-Choosing Pointers

Breast pumps can be a busy mom's best friend. They allow you to continue to provide your baby with the best nourishment while resuming your lifestyle (well, somewhat anyway). Fortunately, breast pump design has improved with increased demand. If you're tempted to borrow a friend's decade-old model, do a little window-shopping first. Quieter motors, cushioned breast shields, and personalized suction strength can all be yours these days, making for a much more comfortable and efficient experience. Here's what else you need to know.

Type:	**Hospital-grade rental**
Best Used For:	A preemie or a baby who's having trouble learning to breastfeed. The super-powerful suction will help build up

and maintain your milk supply until your baby gets the hang of doing it on his own. This type of pump is also a good idea if you're unsure about wanting to breastfeed and therefore aren't ready to invest in your own pump. Rent one for use at home while your baby is a newborn; you can buy a good-quality double electric (see the next category) down the road when you're about to return to work and feel more certain about being able to keep up with the demands of nursing.

Pros: Fastest, most efficient pumps available. Inexpensive to rent for short periods of time.

Cons: Heavy and unwieldy; not practical to carry to work.

What to Check Out: Many hospitals can put you in touch with a lactation consultant or company that offers rentals. Prices range $1–3 per day, plus $60 for your own personal accessory kit (required for hygienic reasons).

Type: **Double electric**

Best Used For: Long-term daily pumping, or working full-time outside the house.

Pros: Powerful and efficient, allowing you to pump both breasts at the same time. Portable.

Cons: Expensive. They're also a bit cumbersome to transport on a daily basis. Then again, as we noted earlier, if you're pumping pretty much only at work, you can get away with leaving the motor (the heavy part) at your job. Then you just need to carry the bottles and cold pack to and from home during the workweek.

What to Check Out: Working moms now have a choice of several really good pumps (whew! one thing to make your life easier, at least). We like the Medela Pump In Style Advanced with both a let-down mode (which simulates your baby's faster initial sucking) and an expression mode (which simulates the slower, deeper sucking your baby settles into), built into either a shoulder bag or backpack case. The rechargeable battery pack allows you to pump without an electrical outlet, if necessary ($350; medela.com for more info). The Playtex Embrace earns points for its unique baby-mimicking suction. This pump has five speeds and five suction levels, and the super-soft cups are very comfortable against the breast. All the parts fit neatly into labeled pouches within a black tote bag ($249; playtexbaby.com for more info). The Ameda Purely Yours is a very light (only one pound) and quiet pump that features eight suction and four cycle speeds so you can customize it to your needs ($200 and up, depending on bag style; 800-323-4060). Finally, the makers of the world's best lanolin nipple cream have recently introduced the Lansinoh Double Electric Pump with a very reasonable price tag. Moms like the instructional DVD that comes with it, and the fact that it has fewer parts and is easier to clean but just as efficient as high-end electric models ($150; available at target.com and walmart.com).

Type:	**Single electric**
Best Used For:	Somewhat frequent use, though probably not efficient enough for the mom who's going to work full-time.
Pros:	Portable, lightweight, affordable.
Cons:	Obviously, pumping only one breast at a time is going to take you a bit longer.
What to Check Out:	The Avent ISIS iQ UNO is the luxury-model single pump, with a state-of-the-art memory feature that responds to your personal pumping style and massage cushions to help stimulate let-down ($150; 800-542-8368). It's a no-frills model, but the Medela Single Deluxe Electric pump has been a best seller for years because it gets the job done fairly efficiently (about fifteen minutes per breast) and runs on batteries or electricity ($65; medela.com).

Type:	**Manual**
Best Used For:	Occasional use (a missed feeding here, engorgement there). This type is also great if you need to pump where electrical outlets are not available and without the noise of an electric- or battery-powered motor.
Pros:	Lightweight, simple, inexpensive, and quiet.
Cons:	Requires a little effort, and you can only pump one breast at a time (unless you buy two).

What to Check Out: Many moms rave about the Avent ISIS for ease of use. Once let-down is achieved, some women find that they don't need to squeeze the handle as often as with other manual pumps to keep the milk flowing. Best of all, the whole thing goes in the dishwasher ($45; 800-542-8368).

THE PUMPING-ONLY OPTION: WHO'S DOING IT AND WHY?

Some women want to feed their children breast milk, but don't get comfortable with the actual nursing experience for one reason or another. Perhaps they feel too self-conscious in public, can't seem to develop a good latch, or don't get over the early nipple soreness that most new moms experience in the first week or two. Moms of multiples may find it too difficult—or too crazy—to nurse two babies at a time. Health issues can get in the way of breastfeeding, too: Moms of preemies frequently have to pump and deliver their milk to their babies in the hospital, then these same babies may find it hard to latch on once they do get home. In still other cases, babies may refuse to nurse because of a mom's unusually shaped or inverted nipples. Whatever the reason, these moms have the option of pumping their breast milk regularly and feeding it in a bottle. Admittedly, it takes work, but your baby will still get the health benefits of breast milk. And some moms swear by it. Here's what a few have to say:

"I wanted to breastfeed very badly for all the benefits to me and my son, but he just wouldn't take to the breast at all no matter what we did. So I ended up pumping my breast milk into bottles and feeding him like that. I never knew what to say when people asked if I was breast- or bottlefeeding because I was bottlefeeding breast milk. It actually worked out better and more conveniently for us that way. My son still got the full benefits of breast milk, it allowed me to see how much he was taking in, and his father was able to feed him. We both got to have just as much bonding with him; my son and I are extremely close."

—*Heather, Worcester, Massachusetts*

(continued on next page)

"I pumped for twenty-three months exclusively for my twin sons. They both had really weak latches that even a lactation consultant couldn't seem to help with. And I found it difficult to hold them both to directly breastfeed. All that pumping was a pain, but I didn't want to feed them formula."   —*Catherine, Columbus, Ohio*

"I pumped and bottlefed for nine months. I did it because I was concerned about how much my daughter was eating since she was only five pounds when we came home from the hospital. It was definitely more time consuming, but I wanted her to receive the benefits of breast milk."   —*Holly, Winsted, Connecticut*

"I pumped breast milk and fed it to all my babies in bottles. I found it so much easier with other children to take care of. It was less stressful and took less time to pump than to sit and nurse for thirty minutes or more. Of course it was more time consuming than preparing a bottle of formula, but the benefits of breast milk made it very much worth it. If you go this route, I would invest in a very good electric pump!"   —*Jamie, Tabor, Iowa*

When "Exclusive" Breastfeeding Is No Longer Possible

The number of American women choosing to breastfeed when they are in the hospital postdelivery is at an all-time high (again, 70 percent)—and that's a great thing for babies. However, the number that reaches the AAP's "ideal" recommendation of breastfeeding for the entire first year of life is substantially lower: 17 percent, or fewer than one in five moms. In fact, by six months the number of moms breastfeeding is almost half the number that started, down to 36 percent. What makes women throw in the burp cloth? There are myriad reasons.

Discomfort. The physical aches and annoyances of breastfeeding can be frequent at first; most novice breastfeeders experience sore nipples and engorgement to some degree in the early days and even weeks as their body adjusts to the process. Others get hit with mastitis and clogged ducts, which can occur at almost any point in the breastfeeding process due to overproduction, underconsumption, poor milk flow in general, or the need to drop feedings when supplementing or weaning. That's why, in a nationwide *Babytalk* survey, 45 percent of moms switched to the bottle of formula eventually. It's fine if you do, too, but first you may want to try out our remedies on pages 48–50.

Exhaustion. An all-or-nothing mentality among zealous proponents leaves many women with the feeling that they can't introduce a bottle of pumped milk or formula when, ironically, those two options may give them the break they need to keep going. Almost half—47 percent—of the moms in our survey felt supplementing with formula was "cheating." Do your best to tune out that nagging little voice.

Lack of support. When you don't know where to get help, and your own mother is pining to feed the baby every bottle (not to mention murmuring, "Why are you putting yourself through this?"), who wouldn't feel like caving in and just taking a nap? These are great times to call up or get together with a pro breastfeeding friend. Even an online support group can help restore your confidence fast.

Work. Even if you have a private space and understanding employers and colleagues, keeping up with the demands of pumping first three times a day (then two when your baby starts eating solids), storing, and transporting breast milk is tough. It's practically impossible under less desirable circumstances. In a 2005 report from the Centers for Disease Control and Prevention, 90 percent of full-time working moms had quit breastfeeding by six months. See our ways to make it all work if you've got your heart set on working without weaning on pages 68–72. If it's still just too tough, you can cut back to only morning and evening at-home nursing sessions—or none at all. And congratulate yourself on the nursing you've accomplished.

The world at large. Whether they're nervous about nursing at the mall or in the Little League bleachers, or the disapproving glances get to them, it's tough for some women to go public with breastfeeding. Turn to "Your Breastfeeding Rights" on pages 56–58 for those moments when you need a quick comeback or pep talk.

Doing the Combo

Talk to a hundred women who added formula to their baby's diet or switched from breast to bottle altogether and you will get a hundred reasons why. The reality is, even if breastfeeding comes easily to you and your baby, and you enjoy doing it, the incessant demands can still wear you down. And guess what? There's absolutely nothing wrong with that. You can still be a good mother, and raise a healthy baby, by supplementing with formula, or switching to all formula eventually. Whatever amount of time you've breastfed, your baby will benefit from it.

Once you've made the decision to forgo nursing exclusively, you'll need to devise a game plan for weaning away some or all of your baby's breast-feeding sessions. Just as your body didn't learn to make milk overnight, it can't stop suddenly, either. Quitting breastfeeding cold turkey would be a painful experience—think how hard and sore and ready to explode your breasts start to feel when your baby nurses just an hour later than his usual feeding time simply because he took a longer nap than usual. In addition to the excessive engorgement that would occur, you would be in danger of developing clogged ducts—milk would become backed up, which can be excruciatingly painful. And the clogged ducts can then become infected and result in mastitis.

That's why the general wisdom is to gradually drop breastfeeding sessions, at the rate of about one a week, so that your body has time to adjust. You'll still feel a bit swollen and sore for the first two or three days at the time you skip the feeding, and will possibly leak more than usual, but it should be more than bearable. Some women find that as little as four or five days is enough for their breasts to get the signal that they've turned off the tap at that point in the day. If you get engorged, express just enough breast milk to relieve the pressure (pumping too much will simply make your breast produce more milk again). The feedings you choose to drop will likely depend on the age of your baby. It may be the middle-of-the-night nursing session when your partner feeds a bottle, and then you take on the early-morning feeding while your hubby takes his turn getting some shut-eye. Or it can be the midday feedings if you're going back to a nine-to-five job. For whatever reason you're weaning, it's usually best to save the bedtime feeding for last, since that's often the most soothing for your baby, and the easiest for you to pull off. In fact, many working mothers continue just the morning and night nursing sessions to maintain a close bond with their babies. As long as you wind down your feeding schedule slowly enough that your body is comfortable, your miraculous breasts can keep up this truly personalized and pleasant routine for as long as you desire.

"WHY THE COMBO WORKED FOR ME"

"I started off breastfeeding. However, after I went back to work, it was hard to pump enough to keep up with the demand. I started supplementing with formula only at daycare. At home, I nursed my son morning and night, and on weekends. This continued for ten months until I weaned him from breastfeeding. Even though I was unable to fully provide breast milk, I still felt good knowing he was getting some."
—*Beth, St. Louis, Missouri*

"We did both breast and bottle. And each home bottle, we made half-and-half from the formula and pumped milk. It gave me the satisfaction that my baby was still getting breast milk."
—*Sara, Roswell, Georgia*

"I had low breast milk production and after a few frustrating weeks I resigned myself to supplementing with formula in bottles. It took a load off. I am still nursing him at two and have decided to let my son wean himself. I work full-time and even though I pumped at work I never worried about the lack of milk because I knew he could have formula if we ran out of breast milk. And he never got nipple confusion. He preferred me when I was around and took the bottle when I wasn't, which saved me from worry."
—*Melissa, Long Beach, California*

"In the beginning I breastfed solely. Once it was time for me to go back to work, I began to pump, and my daughter was fed my breast milk in bottles at daycare. At about seven or eight months, I began to send formula to daycare instead, but still nursed when we were both at home. When I was ready to wean, I found that this had helped me out a lot. I was able to easily and gradually wean her off, without having painful, overfilled breasts. My daughter was happy, too. I didn't even have a problem weaning her off of the bottle."
—*LaToya, Summerville, South Carolina*

(continued on next page)

"I used a combination of breast and bottle for both of my daughters. I loved the closeness of nursing my girls, but found that using a bottle allowed me to be more flexible (this was especially helpful when my second daughter was born). Using the bottle also gave my husband a special chance to bond with our babies as well as gave me some downtime between nursings."   —*Elizabeth, Fairfax, Virginia*

The Bottlefeeding Choice

Some women choose to bottlefeed their babies from the get-go—in fact, up to 30 percent, according to the latest statistics—and despite all the pro-breastfeeding info out there, we certainly support your choice. People who say formula is wrong or bad or unhealthy are just plain mean as far as we're concerned. While many women find breastfeeding to be magical, others would describe their own experience as closer to frustrating or even miserable. It's hard to feel something special when you're more sore than serene, more exhausted than elated. (One caveat: Breastfeeding might be much easier with your next baby, so if your feelings are mixed, it won't hurt to give nursing a shot the second time around. You know more than you did before, and this new baby may simply be a better nurser than your first child.) That said, if you're one of the many moms who prefer bottlefeeding or turn to it after a period of breastfeeding, you have every right to do so.

If you don't nurse at all, you may have some discomfort during your first few postpartum days as your body begins to make milk anyway, but an over-the-counter pain medication should relieve it. While your postpartum body starts out with the intention of making human milk, if no one demands it, the supply side simply shuts down. A few decades ago, the norm was to give new moms a drug to dry up their milk supply, but that's no longer deemed necessary. If you're taking prescription painkillers for other postpartum discomforts, they will certainly do the trick. Wearing a bra with good support 24/7, and making it as snug as you can stand, will also help. A few other tips: apply an ice pack or bag of frozen peas to your breasts (at brief intervals, of course!) to minimize swelling, and when you shower, avoid letting hot water land directly on your breasts.

Because your baby doesn't suck on your breasts and stimulate the milk production, you won't produce as much milk as a mom who is trying to nurse, so any engorgement should be minimal, and your milk will naturally dry up on its own in about a week, maybe even less. Meanwhile, if you have moments of self-doubt, or if anyone gives you any grief about your choice, give yourself a pep talk by reading your rights, below.

Your Bottlefeeding Rights

1. You have a right to bottlefeed without feeling guilt-ridden. Whatever your reason for not breastfeeding, you shouldn't have to explain yourself to anyone. Go ahead and fall back on a "health" reason, like needing to take a medication that could be problematic for your baby, if it helps—we won't tell! If you feel good about yourself and your choices, those positive feelings will contribute to a positive relationship with your baby.

2. You have a right to supplement nursing sessions with formula or breast milk fed from a bottle. Don't feel you have to choose one method or the other. Many women prefer a combination of breast and bottle.

3. You have a right to bottlefeed from the start. Sometimes a mom knows in her heart she would prefer to bottlefeed, but is persuaded by others to breastfeed and just isn't happy or relaxed until she weans. Many women describe a feeling of tremendous relief when they switch to the bottle, can see how much milk the baby is taking in, and can feel liberated from something they found hard to do. And let's face it: There's not a lot of encouraging literature out there about bottlefeeding. What's most important to your baby's development are love, affection, and a close emotional bond, which you can provide with either feeding method.

Bottlefeeding 411

While moms who bottlefeed ultimately have more day-to-day inconveniences, including buying and preparing formula, and washing bottles and nipples, the learning curve in the early postpartum period is much less steep. Bottlefed newborns typically eat every three hours at first, with smaller babies sometimes wanting to eat every two hours and larger babies sometimes going four. So you may be feeding your baby slightly less often than a breastfeeding mom, but not a lot less. And your baby will need to be fed around the clock and on demand, so that hard-and-fast four-hour feeding schedule Grandma keeps suggesting will probably have to wait a few months, unless your baby happens to settle into it on his own. You do have the terrific advantage of backup, however: Anyone can give your baby a bottle at any time, so you can get more rest initially than a nursing mom who's going it alone.

STUFF YOU NEED FOR BOTTLEFEEDING . . .

- ❑ 6–8 small bottles (and soon 6–8 large ones).
- ❑ Formula (stock up only after you're sure the brand agrees with your baby).
- ❑ Bottle-drying rack for handy storage.
- ❑ Dishwasher basket (great for nipples, rings, and the small spoons and sippy-cup parts you'll later use).
- ❑ Bottle brush (with nipple brush attached).
- ❑ Burp cloths (lots of them).

. . . AND STUFF YOU DON'T

- Sterilizer. Just boil new bottles, nipples, and rings before the first use.
- Bibs. Again, you can use a burp cloth until your baby starts solids.
- Bottle warmer. Save your money; you can run hot tap water into a bowl and stick the bottle of formula in it until it warms up, or even just feed your baby a cold bottle—there's no law that says it has to be warm, and most babies don't mind it this way if they're used to it.

How much your baby will eat is another variable. A newborn can consume anywhere from half an ounce to two ounces a feeding. Since you shouldn't reuse leftover formula in a bottle (bacteria can accumulate once it's been warmed and served), it's best to start out with a small amount and add more to the bottle if your baby seems to be still hungry. As with breastfed babies, weight gain is the best barometer of whether or not your baby is eating enough. While it's tempting to look at those ounce markers and try to coax him to finish three instead of four, or chugalug those last few sips, your baby knows what he needs to fill his little tummy; you should respect his decision when he decides enough is enough. (And if you force it in, he's probably just going to spit it up on you anyway.)

Figure 2.4 Hold your baby's bottle at a slight angle (or use one with an angled design) so that the nipple stays full of formula or breast milk to prevent him from swallowing too much air.

The trickier part can be deciding exactly which formula to feed your baby, which is why we highly recommend just following your pediatrician's advice to start with. One look at the formula aisle in your local grocery store and your head can start spinning. Before you get too excited, however, consider this: Virtually every product labeled "formula" is safe and nutritious for your baby. That's because all formula manufacturers in the United States must adhere to a government-approved recipe carefully calculated to ensure adequate infant growth. For the most part, price has nothing to do with quality. Your baby will receive the same nutritional value whether you buy a store-brand formula or one made by a popular manufacturer. There's also no reason to splurge on a more expensive organic formula unless you personally prefer it for your own lifestyle reasons.

What *is* important on the ingredient front is that the formula you choose contains enough iron, so make sure the label says "with iron," "iron-fortified," or something similar. (Serving your baby a "low-iron" formula could put him at risk for an iron deficiency that may impair his development; only use a low-iron formula if your pediatrician recommends it.)

Other ingredients you are probably hearing a lot about are the polyunsaturated fatty acids DHA (docosahexaenoic acid) and ARA (arachidonic acid). Abundant in breast milk, they aid in the development of a baby's brain, eyes, and nervous system. Most formulas—even the specialized varieties such as lactose-free and hypoallergenic—now come in DHA- and

ARA-enhanced varieties. A flurry of new research is showing that the positive effects of supplemental DHA are valid for both preemies and full-term infants. Not only are DHA and ARA formulas increasingly being recommended, but pregnant moms are now being encouraged to take DHA supplements. When they first came out, some brands of this type of formula were as much as 20 percent more expensive and were not available in large economy sizes. That's all changing as they become more widely used. This is one ingredient we *Babytalk* moms feel is worth splurging on.

The next thing you need to know is that infant formula comes in three variations: ready-to-feed liquid that requires no preparation; concentrated liquid, which must be mixed with equal parts water; and powder, which also must be mixed with water. Not surprisingly, the more convenient, the more expensive the type. A good way to balance the work-versus-expense issue is to use powder at home most of the time, then treat yourself to the ready-to-feed variety when you're traveling or on a daylong outing. Some formula manufacturers offer ready-to-feed four- or six-ounce bottles that you just open and pop a nipple on, so you don't even need to worry about keeping them cold (or warming them, since they're room temperature). Powder is also better for occasionally supplementing a breastfed baby: You only need to mix as much as you want to serve, and a once-opened can of powder keeps for thirty days, whereas an opened can of liquid must be used in forty-eight hours. (Frankly, all of us at *Babytalk* are huge fans of powder formula. It's so much easier to travel with—you just tote your supply of water and powder at room temperature, then mix and serve. No need for cold packs or warming bottles because everything's just right! Plus, it's cheap!)

Beyond that, there are lots of different factors to consider: taste (your baby's preference, not yours), price, special additives and whether you're willing to pay a little extra for them, digestibility, and convenience. Your baby's pediatrician probably has a specific brand of cow's-milk-based formula she recommends to start with. If you find that a particular formula seems to be causing your baby distress, call the doctor's office to discuss some other options. Here are the pros and cons of what's available and what might suit your particular child.

Type: **Cow's-milk formula**
What It Is: A cow's milk-based formula is usually the first choice of pediatricians because it most closely resembles breast milk, is the best source of protein, and has the most efficiently ab-

sorbed calcium. According to the AAP, 80 percent of bottle-fed infants drink a cow's-milk-based formula.

Pros: Because they're so widely used, there are a lot of different options in size, price, and convenience, from ready-to-serve portable bottles for travel to large economy-size cans of powder. They're also often available in discount warehouses.

Cons: Some babies with colic, allergies, or other digestive difficulties may not tolerate this type of formula.

Type: **Soy-based formula**

What It Is: Soy formula uses soy protein in place of cow's-milk protein. While the AAP still considers soy formula an acceptable alternative for full-term infants, it has come under fire recently for the phytoestrogens it contains and their possible links to early puberty, thyroid disorders, and attention deficit disorder. Be sure to talk to your doctor first if you are considering it. If you decide to feed your full-term baby soy formula, your pediatrician might recommend additional vitamin and mineral supplements for you to give her.

Pros: Soy formula is acceptable to families who prefer their child not consume animal-based products for religious or ethical reasons.

Cons: Soy formula tends to be more expensive; it may not be available in large economy sizes, and its brownish color is also more likely to stain clothes. Also, consider the concerns mentioned above.

Type: **Lactose-free formula**

What It Is: A cow's-milk formula for babies who are sensitive to lactose—a condition that can cause fussiness, gas, and/or diarrhea. Lactose intolerance is actually rare in infants and usually develops in older children or adults. Sometimes, though, babies have trouble digesting lactose after a stomach virus, and may need this special formula for a few weeks—with your doctor's approval.

Pros: Very helpful for lactose-intolerant infants.

Cons: May be more expensive and unavailable in large economy sizes.

Type: **Hypoallergenic formula**

What It Is: A cow's-milk-based formula made with special predigested (broken down into their most basic elements) proteins, for infants with a milk allergy or gastroesophageal reflux disease (GER or GERD for short). While rare (it's found in just one or two out of every hundred babies), a milk allergy can cause colic, vomiting and/or diarrhea, hives, blood in the stool, and failure to thrive (a term used when a baby is not gaining enough weight). Hypoallergenic formulas may also be recommended for babies at high risk for developing allergies due to a strong family history of them.

Pros: A godsend for babies with more severe allergies and digestive difficulties.

Cons: These formulas are quite a bit more expensive than others. Some of them also don't taste like regular formulas, but a hungry baby will happily drink them if they are what makes him feel good.

Type: **Organic formula**

What It Is: Organic brands contain all the nutritional value of regular formula but are produced without antibiotics, hormones, or pesticides.

Pros: These formulas may provide peace of mind for parents who want to keep their baby's diet as pure as possible, but there's no scientific evidence that they are in fact better for your baby.

Cons: More expensive, and may be harder to find (although you can order them online; try babyorganic.com).

Type: **Generic (versus brand name)**

What It Is: While there may be a few slight differences in makeup, both generic and brand-name formulas provide the same nutrition and must be approved by the Food and Drug Administration. If your baby needs a special formula (or simply enjoys the taste of one over another), brand name may be the way to go.

Pros: Cost savings.

Cons: Generic formulas may not come in as many variations (with DHA and ARA, lactose-free, and so on).

WHEY TO GO?

Cow's-milk formulas actually contain two types of proteins: casein and whey. Most formulas are made from predominantly casein proteins with a little whey. One brand, however—Nestlé Good Start Supreme—is made with 100 percent whey protein, which the manufacturer has dubbed "comfort proteins." These whey proteins are also a little more broken down than in traditional formulas (though not as much as in the hypoallergenic varieties). If you've got a baby who is gassy or extra fussy, and there's no medical explanation for his discomfort such as allergies or GERD, this formula is worth considering (but always ask your baby's doctor before switching formulas). Pediatricians are often quick to dismiss the idea that a particular type or brand of formula can relieve the crankies, but there's a lot of playground buzz among moms supporting this theory. So what have you got to lose?

Bottlefeeding Bunk: Myth versus Reality

Breastfeeding advocates are quick to point out that bottlefeeding requires more "work," but many moms who do it disagree (breastfeeding certainly has its share of demands, too). One thing's for sure: Formula feeding isn't as labor-intensive as it was in Grandma's day. Here are some shortcuts you'll love to know.

Myth: **You need to sterilize your baby's bottles.**

Reality: It's a good idea to sterilize bottles, nipples, and rings before you use them for the first time, but repeat sterilization is not necessary unless you have well water or concerns about your local water supply. Washing bottles in a dishwasher or hot soapy water does the job just as well.

Myth: **You always need to boil the water you use to mix formula.**

Reality: Some pediatricians recommend doing so for the first three months or so to be safe, but others don't feel it's necessary at all, unless, again, you have well water or concerns about your local water supply. Either way, it should only be necessary for a little while, if at all. Talk to your doctor about what she recommends. To sterilize your tap water, bring it to a gentle boil for about one minute. Then let it cool before mixing it with your baby's formula. To save time, you can boil enough to feed your baby for twenty-four to forty-eight hours. Store the water in a cleaned plastic milk jug and let it come to room temperature, then just mix it with powdered or concentrated formula as needed.

Myth: **You need to use bottled water when preparing your baby's formula.**

Reality: Tap water may be better in many cases, as long as it's safe, because it most likely has the added benefit of containing fluoride, which is a real plus for your baby's teeth (most municipal water supplies have fluoride added to them; check with your local water company if you don't know). If you use bottled water, you need to be sure it's a brand that has fluoride added— for which you'll pay a higher cost, naturally. Finally, bottled water is not sterile, so if you're using it to make formula for a newborn, you may want to boil it anyway. That means it's not necessarily more convenient, either.

Myth: **You must keep your baby's formula cold when you take it on an outing.**

Reality: Not always. You can get away with skipping the cold pack if you know you'll be feeding it within one hour of taking it out of the fridge for a newborn, or two hours for an older baby. Another option is to bring a container of powder, a measuring spoon, and a bottle of water and mix it immediately before serving. Some manufacturers also offer single-serve packets of powder that you just empty into a bottle of premeasured water and shake (also handy for middle-of-the-night feedings), as well as ready-to-feed single-serving bottles you just open and pop a nipple on.

Water Supply Wisdom

Unsure of your water quality? You can always call your local water company and ask to have the water from your faucets tested; also if you live in an old house or building, have your pipes tested for lead. Your water company is required to provide you with an annual report on the quality of your municipality's water by July 1; it should be automatically provided to you either with your water bill or as a separate mailing. You can also go online to epa.gov/safewater and see if your local water report is posted online (many are). In general, most large municipal water systems are very safe, and public service announcements will be widespread in the rare event that a water supply becomes contaminated in an emergency situation (such as a natural disaster like flooding). Still not convinced? Consider buying a water filter for your kitchen faucet.

To Microwave or Not? A Quick Look at the Controversy

You've no doubt heard that you should never use a microwave to warm your baby's bottle because of the risk of the formula becoming overheated and burning your baby's mouth. The warning label is even right on the can of many brands. Yet you probably also know a mom who does it. We asked *Babytalk* readers in an online poll, and 61 percent confessed to nuking their babies' bottles. What gives? Well, warming the ba-ba in your microwave is a lot more convenient than letting it sit in a pan of hot water for a few minutes until it reaches room temperature. We all know how long that seems to take at 2 or 3 AM when the baby is screaming. Look, we can't in good conscience tell you to do it: There's the possibility of hot spots that would burn your baby's mouth. But if you do decide to microwave, always be sure to:

> **Only use microwave-safe plastic bottles** while heating. And always take the nipple and cap off before microwaving.
> **Warm the bottle for only about three to five seconds per ounce**. That's somewhere between eighteen and thirty seconds for a six-ounce bottle, depending on how powerful your microwave is.
> **Shake the warmed bottle vigorously** to distribute the heat.
> **Test the temperature** of the formula by squirting some on your wrist before serving it to the baby—every time.
> **Never nuke breast milk**. In addition to the previous safety issues, you will also destroy some of the immune properties of the breast milk, which negates some of your efforts to provide your baby with the very best nutrition.

"WHY BOTTLEFEEDING WORKED FOR ME"

"Bottle was what worked best for us. I don't know if it had anything to do with our lifestyle . . . it just made everything easier. We started out with breastfeeding but our daughter didn't really take to it. The moment we went to the bottle she was so much happier. And so was I! Breastfeeding isn't for everyone." —*Jamie, Schenectady, New York*

"I was thirty-five when I had my daughter, Jordan, and I don't know what changed from when my son was born (I was twenty-one), but I could not breastfeed this time. I couldn't get her to latch on properly, no matter what I tried. She was so frustrated and I was so frustrated, and I had postpartum depression pretty bad, so I switched to the bottle. I decided it was best for her since I wasn't feeling good or comfortable, and what was best was for me to get myself out of the hole I felt like I was in. All in all, I think it was the best decision I could have made!"   —*Christy, Mission Hills, California*

"I always planned on breastfeeding. I took classes, bought dozens of books, special expensive 'breastfeeding' clothes, and for only a mere three weeks did I get to use any of those. Unfortunately, I came down with a horrible case of mastitis, during which breastfeeding was nearly impossible for me, so I switched to a bottle and we never looked back. Thank goodness my baby didn't seem to mind! It was a good decision for both of us. Sometimes you just have to go with the flow, no pun intended!"
—*Jessica, Portland, Tennessee*

"With my oldest, I tried breastfeeding for about a month. The pain involved was emotional and physical. I dreaded feeding her. Then mastitis set in. That was it for me. I switched to the bottle full-time. She was happy. I was elated. Finally, I couldn't wait for her feeding times. She has been an extremely healthy child (no prescription meds ever and she is almost six years old) and very bright academically. With my son (born almost three years later), I decided to once again try breastfeeding. This time it was a complete success from the very beginning and I did it exclusively for one year. I loved not having to wash bottles. My son is also very healthy and bright. I have told anyone who will listen: Do what is best for the mother and don't let anyone make you feel guilty about any way you choose to feed your baby."   —*Jill, Ozark, Missouri*

CHAPTER 3

Everything You Always Wanted to Know about Babies and Sleep

But Were Too Tired to Ask

It's a sacred truth that parenthood requires love and sacrifice. It's a *secret* truth that what parents sacrifice is *almost all of their sleep.* For a long, long time. Sure, you probably heard that you'd be sleep-deprived. But the degree to which you will suffer has certainly been whitewashed. While some moms enjoy a chunk of four or five hours by the second month, others can only scrape together two or three at a time far into their new-parent gig. No matter which category you fall into, though—and you will fall, because you're so friggin' tired you can't stand—sleep will be as elusive as your sex drive.

Unlike sex, however, you will actually miss your sleep. In fact, after months and months of interrupted REM cycles, you may find yourself tendering Faustian bargains in your head, just in case a higher power might be listening. (*I swear I'll never eat another bite of chocolate, if I could just . . . have . . . a . . . full . . . night's . . . sleep!*) Unfortunately, this type of desperation often begets resentment. And no one is immune from it. Not your husband, not your mother, and not even your baby.

Yeah, you heard us. Your baby. Don't worry. Your infant is still your reason for living. It's just that while she's getting all the rest she needs—what with napping all day—you've long ago used up your energy reserves and are running on empty. After any given night, therefore, you shouldn't be surprised if you find yourself regarding your angel's contented face like a parched Bedouin squinting at his smug camel (*#&**$ lucky hump!*). It's not that you don't love your baby. It's just that you need your rest and, like every other mom from the beginning of time, you sometimes feel a tad out of sorts that this helpless creature holds your sanity in her tiny, vise-like fist.

Why You're So Damn Tired

Experts are fond of saying that newborns spend most of their time sleeping. But we wonder what would happen if an expert actually repeated this reassuring fact to a new mom's face. What might *she* be fond of saying? Nothing that can be printed here, that's for certain. And who could blame her? After weeks of logging no more than two consecutive hours each night, with no end in sight, a mom might equate the frequently mentioned factoid that a baby clocks as many as eighteen hours of sleep each day with her newborn's diaper: They're both full of crap. Because while the number of stated hours is correct, there is a whopping difference between sleeping for eight hours straight and sleeping for one hour, eight times. (Not to mention that the number eighteen is an average; you could get stuck with the one who only sleeps ten hours.)

Why does your baby insist on waking up around the clock? First, there's food. The combination of a tiny tummy and a liquid diet means that she eats little, digests quickly, and in two hours is coming back for more. The second, less intuitive, reason has to do with the circadian rhythms, or what we call an internal clock. While our tickers keep our bodies in sync with sunrise and sunset, newborns, having been cloistered in a pouch of amniotic fluid, never learned day from night. So it's up to you, Sensei, to teach your baby that concept. Meanwhile, your tiny pupil may keep hours more reminiscent of a college kid who naps during the day and parties all night.

Another reason why your baby can sleep as much as a house cat while you're quickly running through all nine lives is rooted in her sleep cycles. Unlike grown-ups, newborns spend 50 percent of their shut-eye in active sleep complete with random body movements and facial grimaces, irregular breathing patterns and rapid eye movements beneath their closed eyelids. In adults, this phase is called REM sleep (for "rapid eye movement"), and we spend a paltry 20 percent of our sleep time in this semi-agitated state during which we experience dreaming. The extra dream time that occurs during your baby's lengthy active sleep stage is vital to stimulating his developing brain (that's what sleep researchers like to think, anyway). Unfortunately, it's also stimulating your already fatigued brain—particularly if your baby is lodging in your room at night or if you have a baby monitor cranked up on your nightstand. You might even think that any given whimper or snort means that your baby is waking up—wrong-o! It's no wonder that you're not sleeping well, even if your baby is. While you're just starting to float in the soothing waters of your deep sleep state, guess what? A tiny, hungry lifeguard yells *Everyone out of the pool!* It's time for another feeding. Because you barely dip into any stage of sleep—be it light, deep, or dreaming—these spurts of shut-eye are seriously unfulfilling. In short, no matter how you count the number of hours, your sleep is shortchanged.

How long can you go on like this? The first month is the worst. By the second month, your baby may give you three hours here, four hours there. Finally one day, probably after one particularly bad all-nighter, she may even grace you with five or six hours in a row (which pediatricians define as sleeping through the night and new moms define as nirvana). There's just no telling when any baby will get the hang of sleeping all night. (Even more maddening, some babies start out as champion snoozers and for who knows what bizarre reason decide to reverse course after a few months.) The good news is that they all do eventually get the hang of it. *Babytalk* readers tell us that 55 percent of their infants were sleeping through the night at three months of age; another 16 percent were between four and six months old when they hit this marvelous milestone. Whenever it happens, you will finally be able to lay your obsession with getting a good night's sleep to rest, as it will be replaced with a new obsession: getting that much sleep every night.

What's Weight Got to Do with It?

Nada, frankly. You may have heard the common wisdom that by the time a baby weighs more than twelve pounds or so, she should be capable of sleeping through the night. You can toss that proverbial baby fable out with the bathwater. While it's logical to believe that the bigger the baby, the fewer nighttime feedings she'll need, wouldn't you know it, baby sleep often defies logic. The fact is, there's no proven poundage that guarantees better or longer sleep, no matter what your mom, your mother-in-law, and every old-school pediatrician may say.

Breastfeeding may also contribute to your baby's wakefulness at night. Because breast milk is digested faster than formula, babies who are nursed tend to wake up more often looking for food. The upside, of course, is that breast milk is the best possible food. And this alone goes a long way toward mitigating feelings of fatigue—this and the fact that you can brag about it to your mother-in-law.

Still, you'll meet breastfed babies who defy that logic, too, sleeping through the night within weeks of coming home, and formula-fed babies who get up every two hours for months. You're also going to meet moms who try every sort of sleep "remedy," from those who still spike bottles with cereal to fill nighttime tummies (even though pediatricians rightly warn against it as a choking and chub hazard) to breastfeeding moms who give a bedtime bottle of formula to "hold their babies over longer." When you're desperate for sleep, we know you'll be tempted to try anything within reason. Talk to your pediatrician if you feel really confused. While the introduction of solids around six months sometimes does coincide with sleeping through the night, there's no guarantee that this will do the trick, either.

Looking Forward to Lala Land

It sounds simple enough: Bathe, feed, cuddle, place in crib. Maybe you will even get one of those really good-natured guys or gals who fall effortlessly into a predictable eating, sleeping, and napping routine. Maybe you'll also win the lottery and never have to worry about the cost of college. But if you're like most of us, figuring out how to get your baby to fall asleep at the right time and in the right place will take you a good part of the first year of her life—sometimes longer, but we won't go there just yet.

The first thing you need to know is that there is no right way to get your baby to sleep. Oh, you'll hear lots about the ideal situation: Each night at the same appointed hour, you should lay your baby in her crib when she's drowsy, but not sleeping. That way, she will learn to "self-soothe" (fall asleep on her own). A lovely concept. One that does work with a small percentage of easy, adaptable babies. But for many a drowsy baby, there is no Self aside from Mom who can soothe her.

The second thing you need to know is that there is no sleeping arrangement that is best for every family. Some parents insist that co-sleeping (having the baby sleep in your bed or in a bedside sleeper—a bassinet designed to attach to your mattress) leads to longer blocks of sleep for everyone. Others swear that putting a baby to bed in his own crib in his own room is the only way that you will ever get any sleep. Still others go the middle route: They want the baby in the crib, but the crib in their room adjacent to their bed. What is right for you? Only you can say. If you are a very light sleeper, for example, co-sleeping may not be the way to go. If, on the other hand, you sleep better knowing that your baby is next to you, then co-sleeping might work for you, though you have to know about its risks (see pages 102–5).

If you choose to actually use that nursery that you so painstakingly decorated, don't underestimate the possibility that it, too, can contribute to how much—or how little—your baby sleeps. When you were very pregnant and very excited about all that adorable decor in the baby super centers, it probably didn't cross your mind that some styles would be more restful than others. Then again, it probably didn't cross your mind that you'd actually be getting less sleep than when you were pregnant and couldn't even roll over without waking up or needing to pee. And if it did, you still couldn't fathom how desperate you would be to get your baby to nod off. But we digress. Back in the baby bedroom department, no matter how trendy or cute a particular wallpaper, carpet, or crib bedding set may be, bear in mind the possibility that if it is bold, bright, or a busy pattern, it could be too intense, or even too much fun, for your baby. While there is no research suggesting that pink or blue rooms are more conducive to sleep than, say, teal or orange, we can imagine that whoever christened those two pastel hues the official baby shades had some idea of how relaxing they can be. And while you may use your bed to surf the Internet, watch *Survivor,* or pluck a few chords on the guitar, try to reserve your baby's crib solely for sleeping, not entertainment. It's not only safer this way (see chapter 8, pages 279–80, for much more on crib safety), but will help cue your baby into what's coming. Some little guys and gals might enjoy an overhead mobile to gaze at before they nod off, but others will be too stimulated by such crib toys. (If yours is the latter type, you can always clip the mobile on the rail of the play yard instead, so it doesn't go to waste.) There are also some gadgets out there that clip on the crib and produce white noise or even vibrations to help babies sleep, but again, some find this soothing, others distracting, so you'll have to experiment. Still, rest assured that most safety and sleep experts advocate the less-is-more approach when it comes to where your baby bunks.

So while there is no shortage of experts and books and Web sites and girlfriends to offer theories on how best to get your baby to sleep, there is a serious shortage of absolute truths. We at *Babytalk* have been saying for a while now that there is no one right way to put your baby to bed (you're probably already getting weary of hearing it), but now we've got some bona fide research to crow about. Noted Philadelphia psychologist and sleep researcher Jodi Mindell, PhD, author of the book *Sleeping through the Night*, headed a task force organized by the American Academy of Sleep Medicine to assess the effectiveness of the various approaches to teaching infants and toddlers to go to sleep and stay asleep. What they found was no surprise to us: The task force reviewed fifty-two studies of behavioral methods and found that forty-nine of them had positive results. In fact, 82 percent of the children who participated showed a significant improvement in their sleep habits. Despite the differences in the various methods, which ranged from minimal crying to allowing babies to wail for extended periods, and a variety of soothing-to-sleep approaches in between, there was one common denominator that contributed to their success: The parents were consistent about employing the method they chose.

"WHAT NOBODY TOLD ME ABOUT SLEEP DEPRIVATION"

"It is the worst form of torture anywhere. You get groggy, goofy, grumpy, crazy, delirious, and your body and mind can't function. I have a seven-month-old who still breastfeeds three times a night and a three-year-old who still wakes up five nights out of the week. My husband and I have permanent dark circles under our eyes. It's the one and only thing that's deterring us from having a third baby."
—*Tina, Upland, California*

"Why can't the baby just be awake and not need me to hold him? I don't mind if he stays up all night—just don't expect me to hold him all night. And what's with deciding to sleep all day and, as soon as *my* bedtime rolls around, all of a sudden you think my breasts become an all-night buffet?"
—*Caryann, Salt Lake City, Utah*

"No one told me how irritated I would become with my husband. I get up to nurse and hear him snoring away, so peaceful over there in lala land! Then morning comes and he actually has the nerve to tell people he hardly got any sleep because the baby was up all night!"

—*Heather, Phoenix, Arizona*

"I have come to the simple conclusion that I will catch up on my sleep when I am dead!" —*Tiffany, Garland, Texas*

"Huh? Did you say something? My head is in a fog. My brain works like molasses with no sleep. And my days of perfect fingernails and my hair down instead of in a ponytail are long gone."

—*Andrea, Byfield, Massachusetts*

"I found that when I did follow the advice to sleep when the baby slept, I felt *much* better. It was so hard to put aside all those other things I wanted to get done, but it was well worth it. Even if I only did it a few times a week, it made a huge difference in my behavior and ability to cope overall." —*Shelly, Chandler, Arizona*

"Once my mom found me asleep on my breast pump. And I know there were many more times that it happened because I'd wake up when I felt the milk trickling down my side because the suction cup had fallen away from my breast!"

—*Renee, Spartanburg, South Carolina*

"No one warned me that I would be the one to need remedial toilet training. I was so exhausted with my first child that in the middle of the night I got out of bed, walked into the bathroom, sat down on the commode, began to pee, and suddenly realized it had all been a dream. All, that is, except the peeing part. I was wetting the bed! I couldn't believe it!" —*Janey, Lexington, South Carolina*

And that brings us back full circle to what we've been trying to say all along: What matters most is that you feel good about how you're handling your baby's nighttime routine. A strong sense of security is going to be a far better predictor of how your baby sleeps at night than how much he weighs, how much he eats, where he sleeps, and how many months he's logged here on Planet Earth—or whatever else you heard at your last mommy group. Some moms would rather keep waking up and warming bottles than let their baby cry themselves to sleep. Other moms suffer a few nights of wailing for the payoff of four or five hours of uninterrupted sleep. Still others like the closeness of "the family bed" and nighttime nursing. Any expert will tell you that a predictable routine is best, but hey, you're the one who gets to create that routine.

That said, here are five baby bedtime strategies worth a try. It's up to you and your baby to figure out what it will ultimately take to ensure that everyone in your family is getting as much sleep as possible.

1. The Drowsy Tuck-In

Almost regardless of where you turn for sleep advice, you will discover the golden rule of baby bedtime: Tuck your baby in sleepy but not yet konked out, so he learns to self-soothe and nod off on his own. The benefits to this approach are many: For starters, your bedtime routine will be shorter and less stressful. For another, your baby will go back to sleep more easily after his nighttime feedings. Finally, after he reaches the blessed point that he no longer wakes for nighttime feedings, he will still wake intermittently (as we all do), but he'll be able to roll over and go back to sleep on his own. In short, you won't be his sleep crutch, which means more rest for both of you.

How to get to that heavenly place? The general wisdom is to begin to establish a routine—including a bath or massage, for example—that lets your baby know nighttime is near. Of course you can do some preliminary soothing—you'll want to feed him, and maybe rock or sing or read—but then lovingly deposit him into bed groggy but still awake and lying on his back to minimize the risk of SIDS (sudden infant death syndrome), which we explain in more detail on pages 113–15. Then whisper your good nights and good-byes and hightail it outta there. Like all new habits, this one may take a few attempts before your baby gets it. Try not to snatch her back out of bed at the first whimper. Some babies need to make "settling" sounds to calm themselves; others may yelp at first but quickly stop. A helpful tip in the early weeks is to follow the two-hour rule during the day (see page 108). If you can get in the habit of laying your baby down when she's starting to feel drowsy for naps in this way, she may accidentally begin to nod off on her own and realize it's not so bad at bedtime, either.

If the drowsy tuck-in works for you, you've probably got what's called an "easy" baby. Chances are your gold-star girl or guy was also a natural at latching on, burping, and passing gas. With these wee ones, bedtime may be effortless compared with what other moms go through (although we're sure everyone is very happy for you). The typical pattern for these very regular, predictable babies is that by six or eight weeks of age, you will probably see a longer sleep period emerge at night—about four hours. By three months, many of these babies will go to sleep as early as 6 or 7 PM and rise for the day (so to speak) around 6 or 7 AM. Some may be sleeping through the night, but others will continue to wake every three or four hours for feedings. During the day, you'll probably first notice a consistent morning nap at about 9 AM and your baby may be ready to nap again about every two hours. As awake periods gradually stretch out to about three hours at a time, a consistent afternoon nap will emerge as well. Most babies then stick with the two naps—morning and afternoon—for quite a long time; some even squeeze in a third short nap between the afternoon and bedtime (in which case they'll also go to bed a bit later).

2. Soothing Your Baby to Sleep

This is more a natural instinct than a method. Of course your early attempts at inducing sleep are going to include feeding, rocking, singing, and swaddling. And all babies do need a wind-down routine. The catch is that not all babies tolerate the drowsy tuck-in that's supposed to follow. Some resist loudly when unceremoniously plopped into the crib, and some moms feel like crap walking away from those wails. Or you may have a "high-need" or "challenging" baby (politically correct terms for colicky, fussy, difficult, or whatever else you really feel like calling her by now). This type of baby might want to be held constantly, fuss or cry often, and demand her dinner loudly.

If you yourself are a very patient sort and for whatever reason you just don't have one of those infants who eats, sleeps, and poops on schedule, you may be content with taking this more laid-back approach to bedtime. The continued sleep deprivation is tough, but you may feel that letting your baby cry is worse still. Plenty of us feel that way, or have drama-queen babies who are just too sensitive to soothe themselves and end up inconsolable without an elaborate routine. These are the babies who refuse to be sleep-trained—left on their own to drift off to dreamland—at least at this stage of the game.

It's fine to rock a baby like this to sleep if that's what your instincts tell you to do. If she loves sucking, lay in a stash of pacifiers—especially if you're nursing, so you don't become a human pacifier (for more on how to get a reluctant baby to take a pacifier, see chapter 4, pages 142–43). And don't let the aforementioned breastfeeding evangelists tell you a paci will put an end to breastfeeding—we already addressed the myth of nipple confusion back in chapter 2, remember? Then once your baby is out cold, hold your breath, rise from your rocker ever so gently, tiptoe across the room, and lower her slowly, slowly, slowly into the crib. One of the biggest challenges of this approach is that babies often wake up the minute your arms are no longer around them—and you'd jump out the window yourself if there wasn't a window guard on it! Here's a good tip if you find yourself in this situation a little too often: Since a cold sheet can be a rude awakening for these sensitive babies, keep a blanket over the sheet until just before tuck-in, and the sheet will feel warm and cozy on her little body. You can also try the soft and cozy crib sheets made by fleecebaby.com, for a warmer landing and safer rest. The deep-fitted sheet pockets hug the mattress tightly so it won't come loose and pose a SIDS risk.

Let's be frank: Not many sleep experts will endorse such a laissez-faire approach to bedtime. Yet many parents follow it because it's the only thing that works for them. The upside is plenty of snuggle time; the downside is you may become your baby's own personal snooze inducer, and she will then require snuggling-to-sleep (and maybe nursing or a bottle) every time she wakes up in the wee hours. We say, "So what?" If you're a patient enough sort to pull it off for the time being, then no harm, no foul. Parents who've taken this path add that the period of desperate dependence is brief, and that giving your baby the security she needs when she needs it during her first year will actually help her become more independent later. One more caveat if you are breastfeeding: Do yourself a major favor and introduce that bottle so Dad can do some of those middle-of-the-night feeding-and-soothing sessions. Otherwise you will absolutely lose your marbles.

3. Co-Sleeping

If you like following the concept of attachment parenting, the style of childrearing that involves lots of close physical bonding (breastfeeding, babywearing, et cetera), you may love the close connection of sleeping in the same bed with your baby, too. (You can read more about attachment

A SLEEP CRUTCH YOU DON'T HAVE TO FEEL GUILTY ABOUT

As a new mom, you're constantly being told what you *shouldn't* do to get your baby to sleep—don't rock your baby to sleep, don't nurse your baby to sleep—but some kids just don't seem to get it when it comes to self-soothing. If your baby missed out on that gene, here's a sleep crutch that can be a dream come true for both of you: white noise, such as the quiet hum of a fan, the low buzz of radio static, or a CD of waves crashing against a beach. Everyday household noises can be very distracting to a baby who is trying to learn to fall asleep on his own, so flipping on some white noise can be a soothing way to drown them out. Strangely enough, it actually calms your baby's nerves by inundating the ear with a multitude of tones to the point that the brain stops trying to distinguish the sounds and surrenders to them—in a way, it shuts down. Once your baby perfects his falling-asleep skills, he may no longer need white noise to calm him, but there's no harm in continuing to use it. And while you can buy a white-noise machine for your nursery, it doesn't have to cost anything. Just put a radio dial between stations, or make a tape of the sound of a running vacuum, shower, hair dryer, or treadmill.

parenting in chapter 4, on page 125.) Some moms like the idea of this approach even before their baby is born. They may have been raised this way themselves or are attracted to the emotional connection that lots of physical contact brings. Moms who are exclusively breastfeeding may find that sleeping alongside their baby makes the constant nighttime feedings of the early weeks and months easier to manage. Still others have a high-need baby and fall into the so-called family bed because it's pretty much the only way anyone in the family can seem to get any sleep. A baby who is fussy and demanding, or shy and introverted, may really thrive on this intimacy and immediate meeting of his needs. Bear in mind, however, that there are some infants who are easily overstimulated and may not do so well in the bed with Mom, and you may have to accept that even if it's not what you had in mind (it's just one of the first clues you will get that your baby makes plenty of the decisions!).

If you go the family-bed route, you also need to realize that babies who sleep with their parents are at a higher risk for sudden infant death syndrome. In 2005, the American Academy of Pediatrics came out with a strongly worded policy stating that infants under six months should not sleep in the same bed with their parents because research shows it ups the risk of SIDS. In fact, nearly 50 percent of babies who die of SIDS are in a bed-sharing situation, according to the AAP. One in about two thousand babies dies of SIDS each year—not a huge number, but huge to the devastated parents who lose their children this way. For more on SIDS, see pages 113–15.

As the AAP's new guidelines indicate, a co-sleeper, crib, or bassinet next to your bed is safest, but if you choose to go to sleep with the baby in your bed (or it's the only way to get your little guy to nod off), make sure you are vigilant about these ground rules:

- Keep your baby safer by putting him down on his back.
- Keep him away from any blankets or pillows.
- Don't sleep with your baby on a water bed, on a sofa, or in an armchair. These are even more dangerous than a traditional adult bed.
- Maintain a smoke-free environment.
- Never use alcohol, drugs, or any medication that might make you unaware of your baby's presence.
- Remember that your baby's bedtime should be before yours, so avoid keeping him up until you turn in. Lie down with your baby to get him to sleep somewhere between 6 and 8 PM, and then move him into a co-sleeper by your bed so he's safe until you return. Move him next to you when you go to bed if that's what you choose to do.
- *Babytalk* contributing editor William Sears, MD, co-author of *The Baby Sleep Book,* recommends that babies sleep next to their mothers, rather than between both parents, because he feels a mother will be more aware of the baby's presence and less likely to roll over on him. That probably sounds like a horrifying thought to you—and it's uncommon but has happened (hence the previous warning about drugs and alcohol). Some experts feel that the presence of a man in the bed can be a bigger threat in this way because he's likely to be physically larger and sleep more soundly—he's not the one being called upon to feed the baby constantly. While we hate to tell you to boot your first love out to the living room sofa, some couples find it's really not such a bad idea in the early months. After all, that's when your baby is tiny, most vulnerable, and waking frequently for feedings. Both you and

your partner are so exhausted, you're not feeling terribly amorous anyway, and if Dad can get a good stretch of sleep he can then spell you for a while and perhaps give your baby a bottle of breast milk or formula the second half of the night. If you do all three stay in the same bed, consider this arrangement: a mesh guardrail on one side of the bed, then baby next to the guardrail, Mom next to the baby, and Dad next to you. In fact, once your baby can roll over, it's safest to have guardrails on both sides no matter who's in the bed with the baby.

How long should your baby stay in your bed? That's a decision that's up to you and Dad. He may well tire of the arrangement before you, but if you're still breastfeeding during the night, you can't underestimate your own need for sleep, either. Weigh that with the fact that you've also got a marriage to maintain. Remember, too, that sex doesn't have to happen in a bed, and a little creativity can go along way toward keeping the spark in your relationship and your baby still in your bed, if that's what you prefer.

For some parents, the addition of a second baby means it's time to move the firstborn to a crib. You'll need to do this gently, however. Consider helping your older child transition to a crib or toddler bed well before the new arrival so it doesn't send the signal that he's being "replaced." Proponents of the family bed say many children will naturally leave it at around the second or third year, anyway. If you get anxious for it to happen sooner, you can help the process along by letting your child move to a crib in your room first, and eventually to his own space for good.

4. The Gentle Good Night

If you began your sleep routine with lots of soothing in the early months and now find yourself wearying of all the work, yet you don't have the nerves for crying, or a baby adaptable enough to segue smoothly into a drowsy tuck-in routine, there is still another in-between solution for older (at least five months old) babies: You can attempt to gradually wean your child off an extended bedtime routine with what experts refer to as deconditioning or modified sleep training. You can try it on any baby, but it may work best on one with a fairly easygoing disposition; babies who are clingy and sensitive or high-energy and intense may put up more resistance. The big benefit here is that you get to take back your night eventually, with fewer baby tears and less maternal angst than traditional cry-it-out methods entail. The downside: You have to be very patient and very consistent for several weeks. Here's how it works: Adopt a very consistent bedtime wind-down routine (always nurse or give a bottle in the same spot, then read a book or sing a song); then tuck your baby into her crib while she's still awake, only instead of hoofing it out of there, pull up a chair next to her crib. If she fusses—and she probably will at first—talk to her and touch her intermittently (patting her tummy, back, or head) to soothe her. Try not to pick her up—but you can do so briefly if she's really hysterical. Stay as long as it takes for her to fall asleep, then leave the room; repeat the method if she wakes during the night. Perform this routine consistently for the next three days at nap- and bedtime. On day four, move your chair about halfway across the room, between the crib and the door, and reassure your baby verbally from there until she falls asleep and you can leave. Again, stick with this routine for three days. On days seven and eight, move the chair all the way to the doorway and if necessary again give your reassurances verbally from there. By about day nine, with any luck you should be able to tuck your baby in and promptly leave without wails.

If your baby seems especially distressed when you begin this program, you can give her more time to adapt by keeping the chair a little closer—for instance, only move it a quarter of the way across the room instead of halfway. You'll end up adding from three to six days to the ritual before you're successful, but if you've got the patience and you think your baby will be better able to tolerate the eventual separation, so be it—you'll accomplish the same goal in the end.

5. Ferberizing

Okay, you're in the same place as the last mom: Your're fed up with the complicated routine and night wakings, but you want faster results and think you can handle some crying. And deep down, you know you'll be a better, more loving parent when you get your life in order again, too. If your baby is no longer a newborn, you can try Ferberizing—a method popularized by Richard Ferber, MD, in the classic book he recently revised, *Solve Your Child's Sleep Problems*. Over the years (the book was first published in the 1980s), critics have dubbed Ferberizing the "cry-it-out" sleep method, and possibly because he himself wearied of the callous reputation he'd developed, the new edition offers some caveats. Ferber now emphasizes that his method doesn't always work, especially on really sensitive infants, so consider your baby's personality before you attempt it.

Ferberizing is best used after four months (you should always respond quickly to newborns) and before eight months, when babies haven't fallen into hard-to-break habits. It's also ideal for an initially easy baby who may be getting more active and thus more resistant to going to bed because his world has suddenly become much more engaging.

You yourself will need nerves of steel. If you're the type who feels like crying whenever your baby does, don't even bother to read on. But if you're exhausted and just can't take it anymore, here's how it works. Begin with your usual bedtime routine, but (and by now you know what's next . . .) tuck your baby in when he's sleepy but still awake. If he cries—and he will if he's not used to being deposited in his crib awake, no matter how lovingly—respond by consoling him with a soft, reassuring voice and by rubbing his tummy, but explain that it is bedtime and you are going. Your soothing tone should help even when he can't understand the words. Leave the room for a brief period—about five minutes at first—then return to console him if he is still upset, but don't take him out of the crib. Repeat this pattern until your baby falls asleep on his own, and do so again if he wakes in the middle of the night. Each consecutive night, lengthen the time you let him fuss by a few more minutes, then go in to comfort him, until it is no longer necessary.

Depending on the temperament of your baby, this process can last a few days or a few weeks. Some babies may fuss a little as they settle in, then drift easily off to sleep. Others will wail. A baby who's typically a good sleeper but has had his routine disrupted—because of a vacation, an illness that required extra nighttime soothing, or even a new developmental leap like learning to crawl or pull himself up, for instance—may get with the program within a night or two. If your baby is crying for hours, or throwing up because he's so upset, you may need to reconsider and try another method.

Listening to your beloved infant scream with fury is brutal even if it only lasts a short time. But this method works like a dream, when it works. You'll know you're going in the right direction if the length of crying drops off dramatically the second night—say, from half an hour to just fifteen minutes. These are the babies who get with the program fairly quickly. (If after a few nights, your baby shows no progress, you may want to consider method 3—the Gentle Good Night—because as we noted earlier, some babies do refuse to be Ferberized.) If you succeed with Ferberizing, don't get too cocky: Even sleep-trained babies tend to slip back into their old habits when something upsets their routine, so you can count on needing to offer refresher courses from time to time. Many moms feel Ferberizing is the best thing they've ever done for their child and themselves. Others give up after a night or two, and continue to sob long after their babies have stopped.

THE TWO-HOUR RULE

The two-hour rule will apply to many things in your new life as a mother. Your baby will need to nurse every two hours. You will probably change his diaper about every two hours. You will rarely get more than two hours of sleep at a time. But there's one more two-hour tip that eludes many new moms: *A newborn usually can't stay awake for more than two hours at a time.* Seriously. Of course your baby doesn't want to let you in on this little secret, so instead of rubbing his eyes and yawning, he may do something to confuse you, like get wide-eyed or cranky. To avoid this, watch the clock. When he's been up about an hour and a half, feed him again and put him in his bouncy seat or crib, turn on some lullabies or a musical mobile, step back out of sight, and see what happens. If he nods off, you're on your way to starting a routine.

When Most Babies Sleep

Yes, Virginia, there is a pattern, though it's not always visible in the fog of sleep deprivation. If you can see your way clear to maintaining whatever sort of routine works for the two of you, by six weeks you may notice a longer sleep period (about four hours) emerging at night. Should the pattern continue on track, by about three months many babies will wake in the morning around six or seven o'clock, and then take a consistent morning nap at about nine that lasts an hour or two. Typically, by four or five months most babies will be napping for a predictable stretch in the afternoon as well (this nap may be the longest—up to three hours for some babies), and be ready to turn in for the night at about seven. Your baby may still be continuing to wake for a nighttime feeding at this point, but hopefully he will go right back to bed. (See "Teaching the Bambino Day from Night" on pages 110–11.)

According to the AAP, by four months most healthy babies *should* be able to sleep for a five- to six-hour stretch without being fed, but we moms quickly learn that there's a difference between *needing* to be fed and *wanting* to be fed. Some infants get attached to their middle-of-the-night snack more for comfort than survival, and that's okay if you can muster the energy and enthusiasm to keep at it. If not, consult with your pediatrician about whether your baby really needs the feeding or not, and if the answer is no, you can try shortening his wee-hour snack at the breast, or providing a bottle of water instead of formula, so that your baby comes to the realization that it's not worth waking up after all. By age one, and often earlier, that nighttime feeding habit will cease, if your luck holds out.

How Much Sleep Your Baby Needs

This is the sort of information that makes most moms laugh, or cry, depending on how well you're holding up. While it does little to explain your unique baby's sleep style, it may help you see some semblance of predictability in your wacky new life.

Age: **One week**
Average Hours: Anywhere from ten to eighteen.
Time of Day: Anytime.

Age: **One month**
Average Hours: Fourteen and a half.
Time of Day: Anytime.

Age: **Three to four months**
Average Hours: Fourteen and a half.
Time of Day: Increasingly more at night; about three daytime naps.

Age: **Six months**
Average Hours: Fourteen and a half.
Time of Day: Eleven at night, three and a half during the day (two to three naps).

Age: **Nine months**
Average Hours: Fourteen.

Time of Day: Ten and a half at night, three and a half during the day
(two naps).

Age: **Twelve months**
Average Hours: Thirteen and three-quarters.
Time of Day: Ten and a half at night, three and a quarter during the day
(two naps).

Age: **Eighteen months**
Average Hours: Thirteen.
Time of Day: Ten and a half at night, two and a half during the day
(one to two naps).

Teaching the Bambino Day from Night

One of the first parenting skills many of us have to acquire is teaching our
newborns that nighttime is not party time (she can save that concept for
college). There seems to be no scientific explanation why newborns' internal clocks often seem to be reversed at first, but it must have something to
do with pregnancy. Remember how your doctor explained that your baby
sleeps in your womb during the day when you are active and literally rocking her to sleep as you move around, then—when you lie down for the
night—the kick fest in your belly begins? Perhaps it has to do with that
nine-month cycle of events. But unless you were accustomed to working a
midnight shift job prior to parenthood, this is not likely to be a welcome
scenario. To reroute this sleep routine, you are going to have to do two
things that go totally against your instincts: wake your baby if she sleeps
too long during the day, and not tiptoe around her when she is napping.
You're going to be so desperate for some downtime yourself that your inclination is going to be to unplug the phone, turn off the TV, and whisper
when your newborn does nod off for a nap, but that's not what's best for
you in the long run (sorry!). She needs to learn that your home has a certain hustle and bustle during daylight hours, and that it's totally quiet
when it's dark at night *because everyone else is asleep, too* (hopefully). Here's
what else you need to do to reset that internal clock:

Let the light in at the right time. Keep shades up and lights on during daylight hours (though some babies may need their room darkened at naptime). At night, do the opposite: Darken her bedroom as much as possible

and feed and change her with only a night light and perhaps a glow-in-the-dark clock on.

Keep quiet at night. Avoid stimulating your baby in the middle of the night, so she has a better chance of going right back to sleep after a feeding. Resist the urge to talk to her, sing to her, or play peekaboo. Be quiet and matter-of-fact while changing her diaper, then kiss her and put her back to bed. *Boring* is the operative word in the wee hours.

Ditch the nighttime diaper change. Of course your instinct is to keep your child as clean and dry as possible, but you'll just rouse your baby even more if you attempt a 2 AM diaper change. Don't do it unless it's full of number two, or so soggy with pee-pee that you think it will fall off.

Fill that belly during the day. Newborns need to eat every two to three hours, tops, but some do have trouble waking up from naps for feedings. While Grandma probably loves the old adage *Never wake a sleeping baby,* save it for later. In the early weeks and months, you need to make sure she gets those daytime feedings in. And if you spend a little time playing with her after those daytime dinners, she will get another lesson in the difference between daytime and nighttime: *In the daytime, we play; at night we don't.*

Five Ways to Wind Down Your Baby

1. Give those meaty little limbs a slow and gentle massage (see chapter 4, pages 136–39, for how-to instructions).
2. Add a little lavender-scented baby wash (several major brands now make it) to your little guy's bedtime bath if that's part of your routine (you don't have to bathe your baby every night).
3. Dim the nursery lights, put on some soft music, and slow-dance your way to your partner's crib.
4. Zen out with some white noise while you nurse or bottlefeed: the hum of a fan or air conditioner, or a tape of waves crashing or womb sounds.
5. Wear your baby down in a front carrier or sling for about half an hour before bedtime; the beat of your heart against her chest will calm her.

The Sleep Aid That (Unfortunately) Isn't

Go ahead and admit it: You've been so exhausted at times you've considered giving your baby a dose of Benadryl to help her sleep. Maybe you've even done it. This over-the-counter allergy medicine is known throughout the mommy rumor mill for safely inducing sleepiness. Indeed, almost half of all pediatricians in one study a few years ago reported that they have recommended a dose of Benadryl to parents of children under age two at least once in the past six months to help them sleep. Well, we're sorry to tell you that the jury has reached a verdict on this popular practice and it doesn't really work—at least not in terms of improving sleep habits in the long haul. According to a study published in the *Archives of Pediatrics & Adolescent Medicine,* when forty-four babies between the ages of six and fifteen months were given a small dose of diphenhydramine (the generic antihistamine found in Benadryl) thirty minutes before bedtime, or a placebo, the drug appeared to reduce nighttime awakenings in only one infant. In fact, the six-week study was halted early due to diphenhydramine's lack of effectiveness. Researchers used a very low dose of the OTC medication—1 milligram per kilogram of body weight—and it's possible that a slightly higher dose of 1.5 milligrams per kilogram of body weight (which is still within the medically accepted range) would have a more sedating effect. However, the study authors noted that the use of any sort of medication to induce sleep isn't going to get at the root of the problem—the baby's inability to soothe himself to sleep without your help. (Okay, we knew that, but you can't blame us for wanting to try.) It may well knock your baby out for a few hours, but it's not going to keep him asleep all night or train him to stay that way on a regular basis. Plus, diphenhydramine may cause unpleasant side effects, ranging from dry mouth and grogginess the next day to hyperactivity in some children. (It's also worth noting that Benadryl's manufacturer, Pfizer, does not promote it as a sleep aid for babies, even though diphenhydramine is approved as one for adults and children over twelve.) Still, there is one thing, besides allergies, that an occasional low dose of Benadryl can be good for in short-term use: a quick fix for tough-to-nap times, such as when you're traveling on an airplane and a sleeping baby would make the flight easier for your child, yourself, and everyone else in the surrounding area! (But always check with your baby's doctor before giving it.)

SIDS: Keeping It in Perspective

It's cavalier, and in fact idiotic, to suggest you don't need to worry about something as serious as sudden infant death syndrome (SIDS), the unexplained death during sleep of an otherwise healthy baby. This horrific tragedy typically has no predictable signs, symptoms, or obvious causes. How can you *not* worry? You simply will—but you can lessen your anxiety to the extent that you're not glued to the side of the crib watching your baby sleep. First, arm yourself with knowledge: SIDS is more likely to occur within a very specific time frame. Ninety percent of SIDS victims are younger than six months, and the peak time is between two and four months. Other risk factors for SIDS include premature birth and babies whose parents, especially the mother, smoke. Boys are slightly more likely to die of SIDS than girls, as are African American and Native American babies.

All that said, the rate of SIDS deaths has dropped dramatically in the last decade, certainly due in part to a widespread public health campaign promoting safe sleeping habits, which we're going to give you in detail here. In addition, there's been an exciting medical breakthrough in trying to determine if there is in fact a biological basis for SIDS—it's looking more and more like that is indeed the case. Researchers at Children's Hospital Boston, examined brain autopsy specimens of thirty-one infants who'd died of SIDS and ten who'd died from other causes. The researchers were able to document abnormalities in the SIDS victims' brain stem serotonin system, which regulates breathing, blood pressure, body heat, sensitivity to carbon dioxide, and arousal. Serotonin is a chemical in the brain that transmits messages from one nerve cell to the other, almost like an alarm system, suggests study author and neuropathologist Hannah Kinney, MD. Dr. Kinney and her colleagues previously studied two other populations of SIDS victims and found brain stem abnormalities in them as well. The difference: The earlier research involved just one aspect of the serotonin system—the receptors. The newer study also looked at the cells that produce the serotonin and the transporters that help "recycle" the serotonin so that nerve cells can reuse it. Thus, the new research pinpoints multiple defects within the serotonin system.

Of course that's an incredibly complicated description for your own compromised (for other obvious reasons) brain stem to absorb. Essentially, here's what the researchers say is—or rather isn't—likely happening to

SIDS babies. When any baby sleeps facedown or gets his face near soft bedding, he is in danger of rebreathing his own exhaled carbon dioxide, cutting off his oxygen intake. Normally, when carbon dioxide levels rise, the serotonin system stimulates the baby to arouse himself enough to turn his head and start breathing faster, but for the SIDS babies, it appears that this alarm isn't going off. These new findings, then, support the theory that SIDS is no freak accident—it's a disease with a biological basis. That makes the message about following all the rules for reducing your baby's risk—which we already knew were helping because of the steep drop in SIDS deaths since they've been put into practice—even stronger. Here are the precautions you should continue to take; implement them and your whole family can rest easier.

- Put your baby to sleep on her back for as long as you can possibly get away with it. That usually means four or five months, when most babies begin to roll over. Back sleeping lowers your baby's risk of SIDS, possibly because in this position her face is away from the mattress and she can't rebreathe the dangerous oxygen-depleted air that she just exhaled. Before 1992, when the American Academy of Pediatrics and other health organizations recommended that doctors promote back sleeping, 70 percent of U.S. infants were stomach sleepers. But now that parents have been warned to put their babies to sleep on their backs, the number of SIDS deaths has been cut by more than half. Another interesting finding from the serotonin study was that 65 percent of the SIDS victims were found sleeping on their stomachs, supporting the theory that stomach sleeping does further compromise the impaired alert system in the brain. The one side effect of back sleeping is that some babies do experience a flattening of the head (known as positional plagiocephaly), but doctors say that providing adequate "tummy time" while your baby's awake and supervised can help prevent this. (See chapter 5, pages 171–72, for more information on avoiding positional plagiocephaly.)
- Stop smoking! If you need another reason to make tobacco taboo, this is it. Exposing your baby to cigarette smoke significantly increases his chances of SIDS; don't let other people smoke around your baby, either. Dr. Kinney and her research team suspect that one possible cause of the serotonin system defect is "prenatal insults" such as maternal smoking and alcohol use.
- Consider giving your baby a pacifier at bedtime. The latest research shows

that pacifier use when sleeping may protect a baby from SIDS because it may improve the baby's level of arousal or help his airway stay open.

- Don't overheat your baby with too many clothes or make his room too warm; the recommended temperature is between sixty-eight and seventy-two degrees Fahrenheit. Dress your baby for bed as you would dress yourself.
- Make sure your baby's crib meets safety standards, and don't put soft bedding, comforters, pillows, sheepskins, or stuffed animals in it. Use a one-piece sleep sack, rather than a blanket, to keep your baby warm in bed.
- If you are practicing the family bed, follow all the safety guidelines we set forth earlier in this chapter (on pages 104–5) and seriously consider using a bedside sleeper rather than bringing your baby into bed with you.
- If you can, breastfeed your baby. There's no guarantee that providing your baby breast milk will reduce her risk of SIDS, of course. But breastfeeding may boost her immunity, which may, in turn, help her resist upper respiratory infections, and some researchers believe the latter may contribute to SIDS—it's just one more complication in a baby who already has an impaired serotonin system to begin with. That sounds like a lot of caveats, but breastfeeding has many other benefits; it's worth attempting for as long as you can manage it.
- Make sure that your baby's other caregivers—relatives, daycare workers, babysitters—are aware of and follow these safety rules. As many as 20 percent of SIDS deaths occur when a caregiver other than a parent is watching the baby. No exceptions—not even for Grandma.

Super Swaddling

Wrapping up your baby in a blanket to keep him feeling snug and secure is an old soothing trick that's gained new respect in recent years thanks to scientific research proving its value. A study of six- to sixteen-week-old infants conducted in Brussels, Belgium, showed that swaddling them snugly in a blanket before tucking them in actually did help the young babies sleep better and longer. Why is this safe when we just told you to keep your baby away from any blankets when he sleeps? For starters, when properly swaddled, the blanket is wrapped so snugly around the baby that it won't come loose. The infants in the study who slept better while swaddled were also more easily aroused from their sleep, and because they're lying on their backs, they're less likely to get their faces buried. Both of these factors could be helpful in the fight to prevent SIDS. No one knows exactly why the babies were more easily aroused when swaddled, but some experts have suggested that the touch of the blanket on the skin may be soothing, providing a constant but hypnotic stimulation. The new research also supports the belief that when done properly with a lightweight blanket, swaddling does not elevate a baby's body temperature—more good news, because overheating is another risk factor for SIDS. Still, if it's summertime or you happen to live in a hot climate, you may want to swaddle your baby in only a diaper; skip the PJs.

No matter where you are, swaddling isn't much good if you don't know how to do it. Fortunately for those of us who can't fold our own clothes, much less perform blanket origami, there are a number of special swaddling blankets on the market now that make the practice foolproof even for moms with brain drain (which is most of us at the swaddling stage). You can find these blankets at baby retail outlets or online. For the record, the general wisdom is that babies enjoy swaddling from their first newborn days to about three months, then get annoyed at being tied up, but some mellow guys may be into it a little longer. For more on how to swaddle your baby, see chapter 4, pages 135–36.

 BABIES WHO DON'T NAP AND THE MOMS
WHO STILL LOVE THEM

"When our daughter was an infant she would nap in thirty-minute intervals! I couldn't believe it—breastfeeding every hour and a half and now this! She'd nap three times a day and you could set the clock by her thirty minutes. It seemed like thirty seconds. And the worst part was, she needed more sleep! Over time, she began to sleep a little longer and now sleeps an average of two hours in the afternoon. She has the most trouble napping if she gets overstimulated. She actually sleeps better if she has a routine and kind of boring morning around the house! The worst is if she has an out-of-the-house activity in the morning and nods off in the car on the way home. Even a five-minute catnap will prevent her two-hour nap in the afternoon."

—*Leigh, Los Gatos, California*

"It has been very difficult to get my son onto a nap schedule since my mother-in-law has him four days a week for a few hours, my husband has him a few hours the rest of those days, and my mother has him the other weekdays. No one will stick to one routine. When I end up with him on the weekend I tend to put him down around the same times, twice a day. On the days he doesn't nap I just try to get him to bed earlier."   *—Danielle, Indianapolis, Indiana*

"Isabel was never a good napper; I used to go to such great lengths to get her to nap that I would spend an hour trying to get her down for what amounted to a forty-five-minute nap. At two years old, she still hates to nap in her crib, so I take her for a drive and let her sleep in the car, but with the price of gas these days, it's an expensive alternative! A stroll in her carriage sometime works, too."   *—Liz, Morris Plains, New Jersey*

"When I had my first child everyone warned me to get him on some type of schedule, and he slept well from practically the day he came home. He always took naps at the same time during the day and I thought being a parent was a breeze. I cannot say the same about my second child. I have tried to put him on the same schedule as I did my first son. He just will not sleep. I try not to get upset and still keep a positive approach to parenting. I still try to put him on the same nap schedule every day. Some days he will sleep, other days he waits until it is his bedtime. Those are the days I just smile and try not to rip my hair out of my head!"   *—Cindy, Fort Lee, New Jersey*

"Regular nap routine? Ha! My son never read Dr. Ferber's book, let alone the one written by Dr. Sears. I do whatever works. Often that means taking him for a ride in the car. Don't try to force your baby into napping on a schedule because if someone told you when to lie down and go to sleep, you wouldn't like it, either."   *—Laura, Williamstown, New Jersey*

"My daughter is an absolutely horrible sleeper. Yes, we've tried everything. On the occasional good day, Ella Rose will take a twenty-minute

(continued on next page)

nap and go to bed at 10 PM. When I do get one of those days, I cherish it—and think back on it often. However, when one of the not-so-good days is upon me, I just say to myself, with a spoonful of ice cream in hand, that she will sleep someday. Those are the days that I do the dishes with my iPod on, or actually lock the door to the bathroom when I'm in there. I know they seem like simple things, but taking just little time-outs for myself when no one can interfere helps me cope. Bad sleepers do eventually come around. It just helps to be very flexible and patient, and to abandon the desire to watch a foreign film. It's quite hard to read subtitles as you're chasing your little one around at eleven at night." —*Kate, Rochester, New York*

Naptime Know-How

It's funny, but as much as you love your baby, you might begin each day looking forward to when he goes to sleep again. Don't feel bad about this. It's not like you're going to be doing your nails or anything remotely connected to a leisure activity. Naps are simply crucial to your routine so you can wash spit-up off all those to-die-for little outfits, schedule checkups, load the dishwasher, e-mail baby pics to your child's nationwide fan club, and chat online with other moms about what you're doing wrong (or right, if you're in the mood to brag or feel confident enough to dispense advice).

So how do you get to these baby-free pockets of time? With a combination of patience, perseverance, and, yes, pure luck. Moms of successful nappers usually attribute it to the fact that they stick to a very predictable routine every day. No one's going to argue that point, but there are some babies who simply refuse to be controlled this way, no matter how consistent you are. There are also moms who don't want to be so rigid about their day-to-day existence. If you're a spontaneous, carpe-diem type of gal, you're not going to say no to a sprint around the lake with the running stroller on a gorgeous spring day if the opportunity presents itself at naptime, or miss out on a Starbucks rendezvous with a college friend passing through town just because your little guy might be feeling a tad cranky at that time of day. Regular naps are important, of course, but if your baby refuses to cooperate and will only nod off in his stroller or car seat, we say do what you have to do to get through your day. A less-than-predictable routine won't damage his sense of security. On the contrary, you may be building his adaptability skills—another handy thing to have in life.

If you happen to like the idea of a routine, your best bet at getting a nap routine going is following the two-hour rule we discussed back on page 108. That's going to be your basic barometer for your nap routine for the first four to six months. Then, like the amount of time between feedings, the wakeful period will gradually stretch out to more like three hours. As we said before, infants will usually become overstimulated, tired, and cranky if they are kept awake longer than their little bodies can handle. Paradoxically, when you exceed the awake limit, it will probably become even harder for your baby to wind down and go to sleep because she's overtired and emotionally keyed up. If you want to get a regular nap routine going, try following that two-hour rule and setting the stage by doing a mini version of whatever your bedtime routine is. Of course you won't be going as far as putting her in PJs, but you may be nursing, rocking, or helping her wind down by reading a story. Then tuck your baby into her crib (asleep or not, depending on what's working for you at night).

If you've got a relatively easy baby and create such opportunities, the typical routine of about three naps a day will begin to be obvious; after about six months, your baby will consolidate that into two longer naps—maybe an hour and a half in the morning, than two- or two-and-a-half-hour nap in the early to midafternoon. Sticklers for routine will want to stay home around this time, so their baby spends his naptime in his usual crib, which may ensure he sleeps longer and maximizes your "free" time.

Of course, none of the above may apply to your baby. Just as with bedtime, no two infants have the same sleep style during the day. Yours may outright refuse to nap, preferring instead to take in all the sights and sounds around him. Or he may catnap for twenty minutes here, half an hour there, and derive enough energy from these short siestas to get him through the day. You, on the other hand, are left out of gas and possibly out of your mind as well. Sometimes you can improve on this situation a bit. If your baby has been up awhile and should by all rights be ready for a nap, don't head off to the grocery store—he'll undoubtedly fall asleep on the ride and be quickly rejuvenated. Make sure he's got a full tummy (to help him sleep longer), then try putting him in a quiet spot at home instead—say, the crib with a musical mobile turned on to entertain him, or on his back on a blanket or in a play yard with a gym-type toy suspended over his head. Then go quietly about your business and hope he nods off—there's no rule saying he can't nap on the floor, after all! A few days of this routine (done at the same time each day), and you may have yourself a regular nap, even if it is a short one. And while the usual party line among experts is that babies are best off napping in the crib, if yours prefers his bouncy seat or stroller, so be it. Any nap is generally better than no nap, moms in the trenches will quickly tell you.

 SECRETS OF SUCCESSFUL NAPPERS

"Ashlyn sleeps 12 hours at night and takes two 2-hour naps. She's typically 'up for two, down for two.' We started out loosely following the order of eat, awake, sleep. When Ashlyn would wake up from her nap, I'd feed her. Then she'd play for a while, then go down for a nap. Whether it had to do with our attempts or she's just a great sleeper, she fell into this pattern and still continues it now. She's so active when she's awake that she must need the sleep to recuperate. And lucky for me, because I need lots of sleep, too!"

—*Abby, Belmont, Michigan*

"Our now two-year-old has been a regular napper since she was two months old. I think the reason this was easy is because her caregivers and I have always worked together for continuity. We create a calming atmosphere by keeping the lights low and making sure she has a full tummy. Even if she doesn't sleep, we insist she has quiet time in her crib."

—*Amanda, Bronx, New York*

"My baby is a good napper, but I certainly can't take all of the credit. I work outside the home and my child goes to an in-home daycare. Our daycare provider has a set nap schedule, and we keep her on the same schedule on weekends, weekdays that I'm home from work, and vacation days."

—*Lizzie, Villa Park, Illinois*

"My eleven-month-old daughter is a great napper. She takes about a three-hour nap every day as long as we're home. We just got into a routine of always rocking her and having quiet time. Unfortunately she only naps in her crib. If she falls asleep in the car and we try to get her out, sometimes she will stay asleep, but other times she wakes up and then is crabby for the rest of the day!"

—*Leah, Sterling Heights, Michigan*

Tricks of the Tired

You're sitting in the oh-so-comfy new glider, feet propped up on the ottoman, baby at your breast, a glowing moon outside your window, and nothing but the sound of breathing, gurgling, tiny swallows. The next thing you know, your head hangs closer and closer to your chest, you close your eyes for just a minute or two—then suddenly you do that jerking thing, your head bolting back up-right. *My God! What if I'd dropped the baby*, you scold yourself, staring into those big startled eyes as your baby tries to refocus on her rudely interrupted repast. We could tell you to get more sleep, but let's tell you something you don't already know: ways to get through the day when sleep just isn't possible.

Soak up some sun. If it's warm enough, go outside on your deck or porch for the baby's first morning feeding. If it's not, sit by a window instead. The rays will reset your body's internal clock to daytime and minimize the urge to snooze.

Wash away weariness. Use an invigorating shower gel with a scent like peppermint, jasmine, or grapefruit.

Eat smart. Pace your protein for maximum energy: Eat a protein-and-carb-combo breakfast (say, a hard-boiled egg and whole wheat toast) to get you going, snack on protein (cheese, yogurt, a fruit and yogurt smoothie) during the day for a boost, then eat a few extra carbs at dinner to wind you down. Easy, one-handed foods: Wrap up veggies and hummus, or grilled chicken and salad greens, in a whole wheat pita. Still too much to pull off? Grab protein bars or a healthy, balanced frozen dinner, if that's the best you can manage.

Drink up. Dehydration can make you feel sluggish, so try to drink eight to twelve glasses of fluids a day—and (hooray!) caffeinated drinks count!

Take a power nap. A twenty-minute nap may not make up for the hours of sleep you're missing at night, but clocking short bouts of shut-eye can help you rest your eyes and recharge your brain. Better yet, enlist visitors to watch the baby while you take a more involved nap. They'll delight in the babysitting opportunity.

Get moving. Once you're past the postpartum recovery stage (about six to eight weeks after your baby's birth), try gentle workouts, like walking or yoga. While aerobic exercise, which ups your heart rate, is best for fighting fatigue, any activity can help.

Schedule a sleepover. Enlist Grandma, Aunt Mary, or your best friend who's still childless to come spend the night and get up with the baby. Even if you're breastfeeding, you need to introduce a bottle eventually, so why not pump some milk and get going now?

CHAPTER 4

How to Keep Your Baby (and Yourself) Calm(ish), Cool(ish), and Not (Too) Crazy

They say that every mother possesses the innate ability to differentiate her baby's cry from all others. This makes sense, of course, as she listens to her special someone's whimpers, screeches, and howls at some point every day. What is *not* innate, however, is every mother's ability to soothe any cry, anytime. Even if you've got a so-called easy baby who rarely cries full-throttle, there will be a day or a night that you will be confronted with a wail that just won't go away. And at some point, you will join in. But don't feel bad. Sympathy crying doesn't make you an emotional wimp or wreck. It just means that you love your child. After all, nothing is more deeply upsetting or maddening for a mom than the inability to make her baby happy. But while you can't expect to stop every tear from flowing, there are ways to prevent a few and manage the rest.

We're going to address lots of those soothing strategies in this chapter, along with two other important issues that contribute to your ability to keep your baby feeling contented and secure. The first is a phenomenon commonly called bonding—or attachment in more scientific terms. As the feelings between you and your child deepen, you'll both feel more confident: you in your ability to care for her, and she in the knowledge that you will be there to help her out no matter what it is she needs. The strengthening of this bond will mean that your baby just generally has less to cry about (she'll learn to let you know what she needs in other ways), and when she does decide to vent, you'll find it easier to figure out what she's complaining about and fix it. The second important ingredient in this mother-child duet is your baby's inborn personality. Just as you've learned to work around the penchants and quirks of your in-laws, your work colleagues, or your busybody neighbors, you'll also cultivate strategies to deal with your baby's personality. Recognizing whether she's a laid-back little mama, a go-getter filled with curiosity and chutzpah, or a slow-and-steady-wins-the race type will also go a long way toward helping both of you keep your cool. Naturally, none of this happens overnight, which adds to that steep learning curve of those first months.

Why You Just Can't Hurry Love

All those months when you were planning and living your pregnancy, you scarcely imagined anything less than feeling head-over-heels in love with your baby. That's why it probably came as quite a surprise when you felt that first twinge of resentment. Maybe it was in the throes of pain in the delivery room; or a few days later, when your nipples were gnawed beyond recognition; or weeks later, when you still couldn't stem the tide of tears from him or you. Or perhaps what you were feeling was more like ambivalence: It's not that you don't care for your baby; it's that you're pining for your old life and aren't sure that the trade-off is going to be worth it. The fact is, love at first sight is a bit of a maternal myth for many of us. Previous generations of parents may well have realized this, but some researchers back in the 1970s led us all temporarily astray. They put forth a theory implying that moms and newborns needed to spend the first twenty-four hours or so in close physical contact to emotionally bond. The initial repercussions of this theory were actually quite positive: They resulted in less delivery room anesthesia (many moms slept through or were too wigged out to participate much in the birth process prior to this new bonding concept); dads were suddenly welcomed into the delivery room; hospitals began to offer rooming-in; and there was newfound interest in the ancient art of breastfeeding. All this was terrific unless you were the unlucky mom who had her baby whisked away due to medical issues or an out-of-touch hospital staff, and were left to feel that your moment of bonding was forever stolen, meaning you'd never have the chance to be the mother you could have been. The idea that a lifelong relationship could hinge on what happens in the first twenty-four hours of life sounds laughable now, but back then plenty of new moms were left crying instead. Think what else was going on: The feminist movement was turning life upside down and inside out for women who were being told they could be and do anything they wanted—yet the doors weren't always open, or the keys couldn't be found, when they finally figured out where they wanted to go. This was one more missed opportunity to contend with. A generation and much misplaced guilt later, the delivery room bonding theory has taken its rightful place on the garbage heap of maternal lore. We all know it's nothing but a bunch of rubbish, yet many new moms continue to feel like lowlifes when a less-than-loving thought about their baby passes ever so fleetingly through their heads.

We're here to tell you: Get used to it. It's totally normal to have mixed feelings, not just in these overly romanticized newborn weeks and months, but throughout childhood as your baby evolves from middle-of-the-night nursing creature to defiant toddler to potty-mouthed preschooler to spitball-slinging seven-year-old . . . you get the idea. And guess what? Your newborn isn't exactly sure what to make of you, either. He's got a lot of mental processing to do before he actually connects the voice, the smell, and the taste of you to the fact that his tummy feels better after you've been around. Bonding is a two-way street, and then there's Dad trying to hitch a ride from the side of the road. It'll be a little while before you all find your way.

Meanwhile, cut yourself some slack. You've got all those postpartum discomforts weighing on you, haywire hormones, a wreck of a house, too much company and not enough help, and a child who doesn't know who he is, where he is, or what he wants most of the time. Try to put yourself on automatic pilot and learn the basics of babycare one step at a time. It's actually those simple (okay, not as simple as they seem) acts of diapering and feeding and holding and singing to your baby that promote the mother-child bond. As you respond to your baby's needs, she learns about you and the fact that you are her universe. Her sense of security grows as she develops the expectation and understanding that whenever she feels hungry or tired or out of sorts, you'll know just what to do to make her feel better. Of course you may not always feel like you know just what to do, but you are in fact learning right along with her. Think back on your first dates with your partner: You were nervous about what to order in the restaurant (*Is the scampi going to give me such bad breath that he'll be too disgusted to kiss me?*); what to say during the football game (*Did he ditch his last girl-friend because she thought fourth and ten was a trendy new store?*); what to wear for a jog in the park (*Am I going to look worse with no makeup or if I put it on and then the sweat makes it drip down the side of my face?*). Yet here you are still together after all these years. You and your baby will be also, and he won't care what you look like first thing in the morning, either, as long as he, too, has got easy access to your boobs.

Now, all that said, we need to discuss another concept you've no doubt heard about: attachment parenting. In traditional childcare lingo (as defined by experts with an "MD or "PhD" after their name), *attachment* is generally used as a synonym for *bonding*. When a baby becomes "attached," he feels secure in his relationship with you, knowing you will always be there to love and protect and meet his needs. It's basically a somewhat clinical-sounding way to describe a close emotional bond between mother and child. Attachment can (and should) also occur between a father and child, and another caregiver and child, such as a grandparent or babysitter who takes care of your bambino while you work. For obvious reasons, however, the bond or attachment between a mother and her baby is usually the primary relationship.

Here is where things can get a bit confusing: The term *attachment parenting* also happens to refer to a specific style of childrearing. When we think of how we want to raise our children, we don't usually choose a "method." There aren't typically "styles" of parenting as there are in, say, decorating: traditional, contemporary, or eclectic, for instance (though you could probably describe some parents in these ways, if you want to get creative, but we digress). Most of us simply go with our gut instincts, relating to and interacting with our children in the ways that feel most comfortable to us. It may involve adopting some of the very same attitudes and habits our own parents had, or doing an about-face if we have less-than-ideal family or childhood memories. Shrinks would have a field day discussing this topic, but in a nutshell most of us probably tend to take a Chinese menu approach ("one from Column A, one from Column B") when it comes to our kids. We do what feels right, and what seems to be working for them and us at any given moment. In fact, that sort of flexibility is exactly what we consider the ideal at *Babytalk*. (How many times have we already said, *There's no right way to raise your baby* so far in this book?)

There is, however, a movement or group of parents out there that subscribes to some very specific tenets of childrearing, and they describe themselves as attachment parents or AP parents. This is not to say that they're inflexible, of course, but that they do have a philosophy that can be defined, and it's a wonderful approach for many families. For others, not so much. Some moms-to-be read about attachment parenting (we'll refer to it from here on out as AP, for short) before their babies are born and know immediately that they would like to raise their children in this way. Others may fall into it as they search for ways to keep a high-maintenance baby content. In keeping with our motto *Raise your baby your way,* we'll fill you in a bit about the AP method, and you can decide what you think.

The main thrust of AP during infancy is lots of close physical contact like breastfeeding (always a great thing if you can pull it off), bed sharing (a very personal choice), and lots of babywearing (carrying your baby on your chest in a sling or front carrier—which, again, some parents get into and some don't). AP parents are probably more likely to continue to nurse beyond the first year of life, and co-sleep with their babies. Routines and schedules may mean less to AP families, because they prefer to follow their infant's lead in day-to-day life (a good idea in the early months, but many parents and their babies prefer the predictability of a schedule as time goes on). Of course an AP mom could have a very predictable, regular baby who eats and naps like clockwork, but the difference is that she's not likely to force the issue if her baby isn't into it. Moms and dads who really get into attachment parenting are also more likely to resist outside influences in their family life. For instance, they may prefer an at-home childbirth with a midwife; choose to stay home rather than go back to work because they want to avoid prolonged separation from their babies; and may eventually choose to homeschool their children because they want to convey a very specific set of values within their families and keep peer distractions to a minimum. *Babytalk* contributing editor and pediatrician Dr. Bill Sears is the expert most associated with the concept of attachment parenting. He and his wife raised their eight children this way; two of them grew up to be pediatricians themselves, working with their father and advocating the same childrearing philosophy. You can read much more about the concept on his Web site, AskDrSears.com.

Just like choosing a neighborhood to live in or a church to go to, attachment parenting is a lifestyle choice you need to consciously make. Because it involves in many ways putting your own needs on hold for probably a longer time than more mainstream parenting styles, some moms and dads will find it too restrictive. Indeed, many critics say that AP in its purest form puts undue stress on the mothers, especially, because they are expected to be so totally available to their children. And rest assured, your baby will become attached if you choose instead to have him spend his nights in his own bedroom, or switch to bottlefeeding when you return to work, or give up on the baby carrier after the second month because your back is going to give up on you if you don't. There are many ways to bond with your child, and as with that old delivery room theory, no one should be made to feel guilty about their choices or circumstances.

Building the Dad-and-Baby Bond

Once upon a time, fathers paced back and forth in hospital waiting rooms in anxious expectation of the doctor bursting through the doors to announce the arrival of a healthy baby boy or girl. We even know a few grandpas who claim they dropped their wives off at the hospital entrance and went back to the office (okay, maybe that was for baby four or five . . .). The prevailing wisdom in those days—and it really wasn't all that long ago—was that the early months and years belonged to Mom. Dads bonded when it came time to have a catch or teach their offspring how to ride a bike.

Fatherhood has changed in many ways since then, not the least of which is that dads want and are expected to have a bigger role from the get-go. Yet they still face some of the same challenges their own fathers and grandfathers did. Sure, men today make more time to be around for prenatal exams and tests, shop for nursery furniture, and coach their partners in labor. But for the most part, they still head back to the office within days of their babies' births. Even though the Family Medical Leave Act has been around for more than a decade, we all know that the concept of men taking paternity leave is still taboo in plenty of workplaces. Dads today certainly change more soggy bottoms than previous generations, with the exception of Donald Trump, who proudly boasts he doesn't "do" diapers (what's up with that?). Still, if someone bothered to keep score, we all know who'd win. And with the renewed emphasis on breastfeeding, men are probably less likely than ever to participate in feeding their infants, at least in the early months. (Promoting Dad's role is one of the reasons we at *Babytalk* believe in introducing a supplemental bottle sooner than some other experts, at two to three weeks postpartum.)

Not surprisingly, it's easy for Dad to feel as left out as ever. In an effort to help you read your man's mind, we polled nearly fifteen thousand new parents—men and women both—in an exclusive national survey. What we learned: While two-thirds of men said that the person they feel most emotionally connected to is still their wife, the same percentage of moms now give that numero uno designation to their bambino. And this re-alignment of your attention and affection is not lost on Dad: Over 60 percent of men said that their partners don't give them as much attention now that they're parents. While 42 percent of those men generously ac-knowledged that they understood and expected this change, another 44 percent were far from happy about it. Rather, they felt jealous, angry, sad, and resentful. One dad noted that while he understood his wife's new job was very demanding and tiring, "She needs to realize that I have feelings, too, and I feel neglected."

You're hardly alone if your first response to that is "Pass me the baby wipes and get over it"—but know, too, that 80 percent of the men also admitted moms should put their babies ahead of their spouses, at least in the early days of parenthood, which makes them feel just as guilty as you over their conflicting emotions. One chivalrous dad who responded to our survey actually said he was a bit depressed over the sudden lack of atten-tion from his beloved, but that he tries to keep it to himself because "I don't need her worrying about my needs as well." Note to him: Have you entered our Father of the Year contest yet?

And though he hasn't lost as much freedom or sleep as you, your part-ner probably misses his sex life way more. In fact, 71 percent of the men said they were "never" too tired for sex, but only 27 percent of the moms could relate to that level of libido (and if we had to put money on it, we'd bet that their young'uns are a bit older). We'll talk more about how babies fit into the marriage and sex equation, and when you will actually begin to care about all that again (yes, you really will), later on in chapter 10 (see page 347).

Meanwhile, in these early months, one of the most important things you can focus your mental energy on is helping Dad get involved in his baby's life. This will benefit you on several fronts: Most obviously, you'll have more help, more often. If you need to rationalize this for him, simply explain that less babycare stress for you adds up to more time you can devote to him once again. Next, the stronger the bond between Dad and his child, the easier it will be for him to deduce and fulfill the baby's wants and needs; 61 percent of our survey respondents felt their babies responded better to Mom, so they know there's room for improvement, too. And if you're really lucky, maybe he won't whine quite so much about his diminished sex life because he knows deep down that you still do really care, even if you won't be putting his deepest desires ahead of the baby's for the near future (anticipation can be a beautiful thing). Here are a few ways to help make all that happen.

Don't hesitate to ask. Yeah, we know it's frustrating, but most men aren't clairvoyant, no matter how well they do in their fantasy baseball leagues. Just like your partner probably didn't remember to put out the garbage on his own before you had your baby, he's probably going to forget you told him to pick up some extra nursing pads if you don't put them on the shopping list with a detailed map to the babycare aisle. We know it's kind of like having another child, but try to think of it as practice for when you have to nag your kids to help around the house.

Remind him how important he is to the family. Did you have an equal partnership during pregnancy, labor, and delivery, or was your husband your "helper"? Most likely, you did most of the nesting, sweating, and panting, and all of the pushing, crying, and lactating, while your husband took on very important secondary jobs—like driving you to the hospital or letting you curse his loins during a contraction. The simple fact is, you are the sun in this solar system, and he is but a peon of a planet. After seeing the miracle of birth, your partner might feel a bit like Pluto: downright declassified in significance. To keep him from feeling akin to a distant ball of gas, see below.

Let him help. It may sound like an oxymoron when you are in fact desperate for assistance, but no matter how inadequate we new moms feel at times, we are usually pretty sure we're better at childcare than our partners. There's a good reason for this: Because most dads have a different day job while you're on maternity leave or have become an at-home mom, they just aren't going to be as in sync as you are with your baby's ever-changing schedule of eating, pooping, and sleeping. So point out the baby tasks (diapering, burping, rocking) as necessary, then resist swooping in and fixing things when he screws up (which he will). After all, a backward diaper is still better than a dirty diaper. And your baby is probably going to enjoy hearing a raucous football game recap from *Sports Illustrated* just as much as you reading *Goodnight Moon* in motherese. If your hubby's learning curve seems steep, it's okay to dumb things down a bit (trust us: He won't mind). Teach him how to strap on the front carrier, for instance, and let him get comfortable toting the bambino around without having to worry about supporting her head. Then show him that it's possible to actually use his hands—perhaps raking leaves or folding laundry—while wearing his baby. Rocking is another foolproof task; short of dropping the baby, there's not much he can do to screw that up. And your little guy or gal is getting to know about Dad's manly scent, and hairy chest, in the process, which will prove to be good substitutes when you take on the next step.

Leave—often. Yeah, you read that right. We mean every few days or so, for as many hours as you can manage without your breasts rivaling Mount St. Helen's last eruption if you're breastfeeding. If you don't, your baby will begin to identify your loving arms (and any of your other available appendages, for that matter) as the center of his universe, and your husband will be lost in space. To beam him back, it takes sheer Dad-and-baby time, which can best be accomplished when Mom is out of viewing and smelling range. If it's hard to tear yourself away, just give your baby to his father and bolt. Quickly. Any wailing and gnashing of teeth (yes, we mean from Dad) won't last long, and they'll both be forced to develop the coping tools they need to get along with each other and without you.

Your Baby's First Language: Crying

Your baby came into this world with a shriek, and at the time, that was a good thing, a thrilling sign those little lungs were hard at work. Soon enough, however, your baby's cries will cease to be exciting. The average newborn cries two to three hours a day, peaking at a month or so, before dropping off dramatically by the third month. This is normal. You may have heard the theory that these first twelve weeks are actually the "fourth trimester." The thinking goes that unlike some animal babies, which remain in utero for twelve months and are born literally able to not just walk but also run, human babies have to come out three months earlier than is really comfortable for them (thank you, large craniums). The result, then, is that our babies are still fetal-like and not fully ready to adapt to life outside the womb. Hence, all of the crying, colic, digestive upset, and stimulus sensitivities. Whether or not this theory holds water, the indisputable fact remains that babies cry more during the first three months and that it's up to you to help them stop.

Most babies pass through this fussy stage fairly quickly, and some barely whimper at all. Then there are the real screamers who seem to defy all attempts at soothing. Excessive crying, commonly described as colic, afflicts about one in five infants (not to mention their parents), or close to a million babies a year in the U.S. We'll get more into colic later in this chapter on pages 143–48, but parents of the other 80 percent of infants are going to find themselves in frequent need of soothing strategies, too. The basic baby-soothing rule of thumb is to first eliminate the usual suspects. What those wails might typically mean:

- "It's been ninety minutes. Feed me, woman!"
- "Get this soggy diaper off me!"
- "Where the heck is my binky?"
- "I've been stuck in this seat too long. Pick me up now!"
- "Tone down the lights, will ya?"
- "A little volume control, puh-lease!"
- "This outfit's itchy."
- "Why don't all these people get out of my face?"
- "This scene is getting old. Can we go someplace more interesting?"
- "I'm tired and I'm not going to take it anymore!"

For the generally good-natured baby, simply remedying one or more of these issues is likely to work. Other infants require certain types of sensory stimulation, and nothing but experimentation will give you the answer. Here again, experts are fond of saying that babies tend to grow out of the crying phase, but we can't help but take some of the credit. Who can argue that as our abilities as mothers increase, and as we get to know our babies better, we are going to recognize what works and respond more efficiently, too? In this case, familiarity breeds comfort rather than contempt (save that for your hubby, whose soothing instinct is to hand the baby over to you).

A Cry-Baby Breakthrough?

If all this seems rather primitive in our scientifically sophisticated world, well, it is. The challenges of trying to communicate with a preverbal being are obvious and have stumped experts and not-so-experts for centuries. More recently, however, one mom decided she wasn't going to just sit back and cry herself. When Priscilla Dunstan, an Australian musician with a great ear for sound, gave birth to an extremely colicky son, she turned her finally tuned hearing skills to finding a pattern in his newborn wails. Sure enough, she was able to decipher five specific sounds he made when he was hungry, tired, needed to burp, had gas, or was otherwise uncomfortable. From there, Dunstan studied more than a thousand other infants and was able to document the very same sounds, finally giving support to the widely held but never defined theory that there is a language behind an infant's cries. While this science is in its infancy—pun intended—it's welcome news to many parents.

So just what are these five, uh, "words" your baby may well be uttering (or rather, screaming)? Dunstan says they're natural reflexes (kind of like a hiccup or sneeze) the baby body makes accompanied by sound; that's why they're the same in every baby. Not surprisingly, each expresses a physical need. When you first see them written, you'll probably think they all look alike, which begs the question: *Don't they sound alike, too?* To the untrained and overly stressed ear, yes, but Dunstan aims to change all that. Here's what you're listening for:

- *Neh* means "I'm hungry" and is the sound of the baby's tongue pushing against the roof of his mouth (the sucking reflex).
- *Owh* means "I'm tired." It's basically a yawn with sound.
- *Eh* means "burp me." It's made when a baby's chest tightens up because there's an air bubble in it.
- *Eairh* means "I have gas" and is the sound of the stomach muscles trying to push that air bubble out of the other end. (Listen for the *r*-sound to distinguish it from *eh*.)
- *Heh* means "I'm uncomfortable" and comes from a sweaty feeling (listen for the initial *h*-sound).

To truly recognize these baby words, however, you need to hear them repeatedly with your own ears. You can practice with the *Dunstan Baby Language* DVD, available at dunstanbaby.com (the two-DVD set is $59.99 plus shipping). The tutorial also includes lots of soothing solutions and tips on tuning your own ears. One caveat: The Dunstan approach has been found most effective between birth and three months of age. After that, you've still another nine months of cranky moments to contend with, so you'll need to have some other soothing strategies up your sleeve.

Ways to Soothe Your Cranky Cupcake

While no soothing strategy will work all of the time, these tried-and-true calm inducers work for many babies, much of the time. Experiment and see what's most likely to push your little one's relaxation reflex.

Method: **Get in touch**

What It Does: Touch stimulates pressure receptors in the brain that calm your baby and make her feel secure.

How to Do it: Massage her, swaddle her in a blanket, or "wear" your baby in a front carrier or sling. Other takes: Gently stroke your baby's cheek or scratch her back. The touch of warm water from a bath can work, too.

Method: **Rock and roll**

What It Does: Any sort of rhythmic swaying—up and down, side to side, back and forth, or a combination of the two—mimics the experience of being in the womb. It's called vestibular motion because it works on the motion sensors in your baby's ears, producing a hypnotic, calming effect. Different babies respond to different types of movement, so try them all. Fortunately, mechanical swings now usually have both side-to-side-and back-and-forth capability. One baby we know needed Dad to pick him up and set him down while in his car seat over and over (exhausting!).

How to Do It: Rocking her in a chair, using a mechanical infant swing, dancing, taking a stroller ride, or going for a car ride can all work. Variations include bouncing gently on a fitness ball while holding your baby, or putting him in a carrier and climbing on a treadmill or stair machine. (We should add the caveat *Don't try this if you're too tired,* but of course you're probably always too tired. Have your partner do it if your knees are buckling.)

Method: **Pucker up**

What It Does: It makes sense that the innate survival instinct to suck also switches on a calming reflex in your baby's brain—he can relax when his physical need for fuel is answered.

Sucking physically lessens babies' stress levels, lowering heart rate and blood pressure while stimulating natural pain-relieving chemicals in the brain.

How to Do It: Take advantage of this reaction by providing opportunities for sucking other than just at mealtime. Offer your baby a pacifier at bedtime to help him learn to self-soothe, or when he's out of sorts or overstimulated at, say, a noisy family gathering. Sucking on your finger or your breast—even when it's not feeding time—can also do the trick, but be forewarned: Too much comfort nursing can make mincemeat out of your nipples. You will often see the advice to provide a pacifier or the old boob when your baby is getting a vaccine, but we have to wonder if the latter isn't a bit risky—couldn't the baby come to associate your breast with pain after an experience like that? And God forbid if your tot's got a tooth.

Method: **Noisy does it**

What It Does: Believe it or not, more of the right kind of sound can help your baby shut out other surrounding stimuli that are annoying her. One of the reasons this works is that when your baby was in the womb, the sound of your heart beating and your blood whooshing through your veins was loud, clear, and consistent. The operative phrase here, however, is *the right kind of sound.* That means noise that is similarly dull and predictably repetitive, which is typically known as white noise—the sort of sound that comes from mixing many different frequencies together. Imagine trying to pick out someone's voice in a crowded room with everyone talking at the same time, the same speed, and the same decibel level. You'd just give up. That's how white noise masks distracting household sounds: It basically tricks the brain into relaxing by overwhelming it with too many frequencies. You almost *feel* white noise rather than hear it. Before you tune out that complicated explanation, realize that white noise is readily available—your only responsibility is to turn it on.

How to Do It: Turn on a fan, hair dryer, vacuum, dishwasher, or other similar appliance, or play a soothing-sounds CD (such as waves splashing), or a musical instrument like a guitar, piano, or flute. Some say making shushing sounds in your baby's ear works (especially combined with movement), as does running water in a sink or shower. You can also make a tape or CD of a vacuum cleaner running (but your house won't be nearly as clean).

Method: **Indulge in eye candy**

What It Does: A pleasant sight gives your baby something specific to focus on when the world at large is overwhelming him.

How to Do It: Lay your baby down in a spot where he can look at an overhead mobile; let him stare at a brightly colored pattern on a sofa, a comforter, or a colorful painting; or give him a change of scenery by moving to a different room or going outside. Keep in mind that too much visual stimulation can also freak out a baby, so consider your nursery decor if your baby has frequent trouble settling—maybe those tartan plaid sheets or the busy patterned quilts hanging on the wall are driving him berserk.

Swaddling

Also known as the Baby Burrito, swaddling is an ancient soothing method found around the globe. Why such staying power? Because it usually works. Newborns are used to the snug feeling of the womb, having lived there for nine months. By mimicking that secure enclosure with a blanket, a baby may feel right at home. Not only is swaddling calming, but new research suggests that young infants who are swaddled sleep longer, and may sleep safer: The babies in the study were more easily aroused, and experts surmise that this may be because the constant tactile stimulation could make them more likely to wake up if they are having any breathing difficulties. In addition, a baby who is swaddled is on his back—the safest sleep position. And from a practical standpoint, swaddling can help keep your baby warm in cold-weather months. All that said, here's how to pull off a perfect wrap (see figures 4.1a–c):

1. Get a large square blanket and lay it flat in a diamond shape with a point at the top. A standard receiving blanket will do, but the oversize, specially designed swaddling blankets may be easier (or preferable if you're trying to turn a big guy into a little taco).

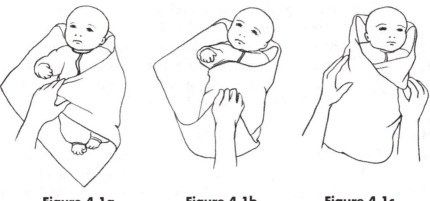

Figure 4.1a   **Figure 4.1b**   **Figure 4.1c**

2. Fold the top point (corner) down to the center of the blanket. You should have a horizontal line at the top of the diamond.
3. Position your baby on her back on the blanket with her neck centered at the top edge of the horizontal line (and her head slightly above it).
4. Hold your baby's left arm down at her side. If she fusses or tries to keep flailing it, continue to hold it down a few more seconds with gentle pressure; she will relax and straighten it out (honestly).
5. While you hold her left arm down, fold the same side of the blanket down and across her body, and tuck the end tightly under her right lower back and buttock (see figure 4.1a). It should be snug, so that she can't move her left arm (no, you won't hurt her).
6. Straighten her right arm (the one on your left) at her side. Bring the bottom blanket corner up (see figure 4.1b). A large swadling blanket may be long enough to go over her right shoulder; in this case tuck the tip under her right arm in the back.
7. Fold the right side over your baby and wrap it snugly around her (see figure 4.1c). A large-size swadling blanket may be long enough to tuck the tip into the fold in back, at her neck, or even to wrap all the way around her and tuck into a V fold at the center of her chest.
8. Most babies stop wanting to be swaddled by eight to twelve weeks—and for safety's sake and leg development, you should stop swaddling then anyway, when the bambino can kick the blanket off!

Massage

The benefits of touch have been well documented. Research shows that preemies who are consistently massaged gain more weight and leave the hospital sooner. And its calming effects on all babies are obvious. We all love a good massage (hey, Dad: How about giving one to a weary mom?), and though we're going to give you a pretty thorough step-by-step here, it doesn't have to be nearly this complicated. If you don't have the time or energy for the whole enchilada, simply rub a little baby oil into your palms and give your little guy a few long, slow strokes on his legs, arms, and back—and you're done.

What's the best time to give your baby a massage? Frankly, there's not really an easy answer. Usually it's not a good idea to begin a massage if your baby is in the midst of full-throttle crying; it could upset him even more. However, if he appears to be suffering from gas pains, massaging his tummy may provide relief. Otherwise, you should probably try to first calm your crying baby, then proceed to a massage. And while before bed seems like a logical time, some experts advise not doing it just before or after a bath, especially with a young infant, because the combination of the two activities can be overstimulating. In short, you're pretty much going to need to experiment to find out how your unique baby reacts (what else is new?). You can learn more tips and tricks from the Infant Massage Information Service, found at infantmassage-imis.com, or the International Association of Infant Massage at infantmassageusa.org.

When you've got the time, try this skin-to-skin, step-by-step guide to giving your baby a massage. Perform each stroke slowly, for about a minute, and use the pads of your fingers, not the entire palm of your hand. (Check with your doctor first if your baby is a preemie or has any medical conditions.)

1. Gather what you'll need: a flat comfortable surface such as a bed or thick rug, a small amount of oil (baby or olive), a blanket and a soft towel, and your naked or diaper-clad baby. Turn up the heat in the room before you start if the weather is chilly. Low lights and soft music are great, too.

2. Put the towel on the bed or rug, then lay your baby on his stomach with his head turned to one side. Keep the part of your baby's body you are not massaging covered with the blanket to make sure he's warm enough. Moisten your hands with the oil, then stroke from his forehead across the top of his head and down to the nape of his neck. (See figures 4.2a–c.)

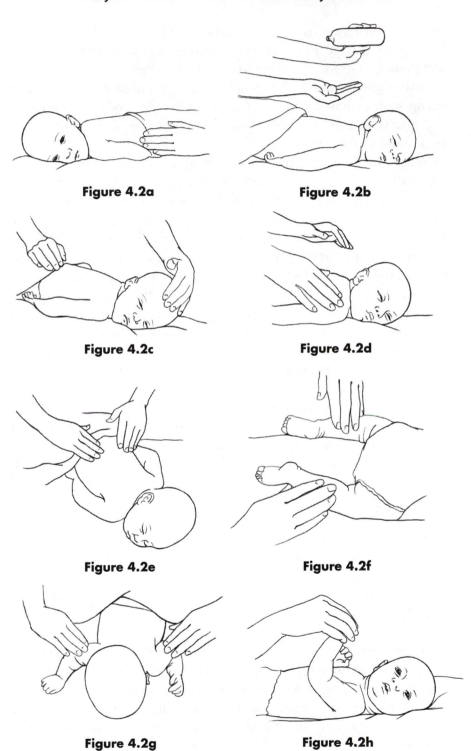

Figure 4.2a

Figure 4.2b

Figure 4.2c

Figure 4.2d

Figure 4.2e

Figure 4.2f

Figure 4.2g

Figure 4.2h

3. Stroke across each shoulder from the center of the neck out to the arm, one side at a time, with the pads of your fingers. (See figure 4.2d.)

4. Stroke from the top of your baby's back down to his hips with both hands, one on each side, being careful to avoid the spine. (See figure 4.2e.)

5. Run the pads of your fingers down the back of your baby's legs at the same time, then go back up again. (See figure 4.2f.)

6. Repeat the same down-and-up stroking on the backs of your baby's arms. (See figure 4.2g.)

7. Turn your baby over to his back, and repeat the same down-and-up strokes on his chest and the front of his arms and legs. (See figure 4.2h.)

A Pacifier

To plug or not to plug, that is the question. And depending on whom you ask and what the latest scientific study reports, the answer is either "absolutely" or "never." Well, right now we're happy to report that the pendulum seems to have swung back to the pro-pacifier side. We're happy about this because the editors at *Babytalk* have pretty much always endorsed binky use. Why? Because we're moms ourselves and totally aware of how much the right silicone soothie can mean to both your baby and you. If you're a nursing mom, for example, a synthetic pacifier can save you from becoming a human one. And despite all those ultrasound photos of fetuses sucking their thumbs in utero, it is often a few months (if ever) before babies find the favored digit once out in the real world—they simply can't move their arms well enough to get their thumbs to land in their mouths. So why endure the wail-a-thons when the perfect substitute is cheap and readily available? (Of course, pacifier preference depends on your little guy's taste, as with everything else. Some babies resist taking them. See pages 142–43 for what to do about that scenario.)

But don't just take our word for it: The AAP now endorses pacifiers especially during the first six months at nap- and bedtime because numerous studies have shown that pacifiers appear to reduce the risk of SIDS. No one's exactly sure why, though it may be that the use of a pacifier during sleep improves the level of arousal or helps the airway stay open. And despite popular opinion, pacifiers have not been shown to interfere with breastfeeding.

Want to know more pacifier facts? You will if you have an in-law who insists that they should be banned, so here they are:

- Pacifier use probably won't lead to staggering orthodontia bills—unless your child continues to suck on one after age six.
- Pacifiers won't prevent your baby from learning to talk—unless he's got it in his mouth all day. If he gets to the verbal stage and still relies on it, limit its use (only in the crib, for example).
- Pacifiers don't cause nipple confusion—we pretty much hammered the whole concept of nipple confusion even existing back in chapter 2. However you will need to be sure your baby is eating regularly if he's enjoying his paci often—sometimes smaller infants have less-than-voracious appetites and can almost forget they're hungry because they're so satisfied by their synthetic nipple.
- It doesn't have to be difficult to wean a baby from a pacifier. If you do it at around six months, when the AAP recommends, you can simply stop offering it and your baby will probably forget about it in a day or so. (You, on the other hand, may still be sorely tempted to whip it out again.) After one year, putting the pacifier away gets a little more challenging, but there are loads of parent-tested tricks, such as wrapping them up and having your toddler give them to someone's new baby as a present. And plenty of children simply grow tired of them and lose interest on their own, so it may not even become an issue.

If you do opt for a pacifier, keep these health and safety guidelines in mind:

- Choose a one-piece dishwasher-safe model and keep it clean. Resist rinsing it off by putting it in your own mouth.
- Avoid pacifier clips. The safety recommendation for these gadgets is that the strings and straps should be short—never long enough to wrap around your baby's neck—and it goes without saying that they should never be used in the crib. We think, however, that the potential risks are not worth the supposed convenience. Just buy plenty of extras of your baby's preferred pacifier model and keep them in a Baggie in your diaper bag. If one drops to the ground and you don't have access to a faucet for rinsing it off, replace it with a fresh one and clean the other when you get home.
- Let your baby be the judge of his preferred style. Orthodontic pacifiers are designed to promote proper oral development, but whether they're necessary is debatable. And again, research shows that a child

would have to suck any type of pacifier intensely for years to develop dental problems.

- Choose pacifiers with vented shields (the part that surrounds the lips and mouth area), which provide rash protection. Without the vents, saliva can collect underneath and irritate the skin.

- Replace pacifiers when they show signs of decay—typically a nipple that's become, sticky, bumpy, or cracked, or a once firm shape that has gone soft and squishy.

- Once you hit on a pacifier style/model/brand that pleases your baby, immediately run to the store where you found it and buy every one in stock. Murphy's Rule of Pacifiers is that particular style/model/brand will be instantly discontinued and you'll lose the last one in existence and be up all night trying to soothe your hysterical child who will hold this act of abandonment against you until she grows up, has her own baby, and makes the same foolish mistake herself.

- Don't stress too much about the ear infection connection. We will admit that, as much as we like pacifiers, there is some evidence of a link between their use and the frequency of ear infections. Still, like a lot of medical research, the findings need to be taken with a couple good shakes of salt. First off, the initial study of 845 children under the age of three in a daycare center in Finland found that pacifier use increased the frequency of ear infections by as much as 50 percent. However, it's impossible to say if there's something happening in the ear related to the sucking mechanism that contributes to the development of an ear infection, or if toddlers in daycare centers are sharing more germs along with their pacifiers. After all, it's long been known that children in daycare develop more infections in general. Another study by the same group of researchers followed 484 children visiting well-baby clinics; it was found that babies who stopped using pacifiers after six months of age had a third fewer ear infections than those who continued sucking their pacifiers. The AAP's position on all this is that since ear infections are pretty uncommon before six months, and up until six months pacifiers can have a protective effect against SIDS, pacifiers are worth recommending to this age. After six months, it's your call. Certainly if you have a baby older than six months who is plagued with ear infections, stopping the pacifier may be worth considering—and definitely easier than prophylactic antibiotics or surgically inserting drainage tubes in your child's ears.

VOICE OF REASON

"Used correctly, pacifiers can be wonderful. When babies suck on pacifiers (or thumbs), they are able to create their own mini vacations reminiscent of some of their favorite moments—feeding in mother's arms or the quiet stillness before they were even born. What a nice gift to allow them to make this magic for themselves!"

—*Alan Greene, MD, drgreene.com*

Some wary babies fight the pacifier despite our best efforts, popping out the offending plastic as soon as we let go. But you can con your reluctant user into sucking one anyway. Pediatrician Harvey Karp, author of a very good baby-calming bible, *The Happiest Baby on the Block,* has a strategy we find practically foolproof. Here's his advice:

1. Experiment with different styles. The orthodontic model your neighbor insists is the best may turn off your particular tot. Some babies prefer a long, narrow nipple; others like the short, stubby ones. Then there's the silicon-versus-rubber issue, and the round base versus the style shaped sort of like butterfly wings. No matter what the consensus of your mommy group is, your baby's preference will be the deciding factor!

2. Offer it when she's not hysterical. An already screaming baby is only going to get more pissed off at a pacifier she doesn't want. Calm her down, then proceed to the next step.

3. A soon as your baby starts to suck, attempt to lightly tug the pacifier just a little bit out of her mouth. That's right, we said *out.* Prevailing wisdom has always been to do the opposite—hold the pacifier in place, jammed onto your baby's face, which will probably feel a bit cruel when you try it. Fortunately, for some wacky reason, pretending to tug the pacifier out actually works better. Maybe it's some previously undiscovered innate reflex, or maybe it's just your first lesson in an important principle of parenting: reverse psychology. Either way, the vast majority of the time, your baby's inclination is going to be to hold on to what you want to take away, and suck even harder. Dr. Karp suggests repeating this little tug ten to twenty times in your

early attempts at getting your newborn to accept and like a pacifier. We've tried it and can attest that it works. And it's a strategy you'll be able to use for years to come in infinite ways, like when you tell your teenager she has to watch her younger sibling and can't do her homework until later, and she develops an immediate need to spend an hour and a half on calculus.

How to Survive the Dreaded Colic

It starts as a whimper. Just an uncomfortable sigh from your newborn. Soon, though, these little sounds modulate into sharp squeals, which in turn balloon into full-throated wails. Alarmed, you bounce her, shush her, and try to feed her, but she won't have any of it. After a few hours of staring at a red face and quivering tongue, you reach for the phone and call your pediatrician. The provisional diagnosis: It's probably colic. The next day, you're at the doctor's office to get the official diagnosis: It is colic. "Don't worry," the doctor says. "Colic usually disappears in about three months."

Say what? Colic is best defined as extreme crying that may worsen as the day goes on. Some experts identify colicky babies by using the well-known rule of threes: They cry for more than three hours a day, at least three days a week, for a period of at least three weeks. This may work scientifically as a diagnosis, but it is a ridiculous description to the parents of these babies who would simply describe the crying as "endless." No one at home is clocking it, believe us. You know if your baby has it.

Fast-forward two weeks: Your baby is still screaming and you're as wild-eyed and desperate as she is. Parenting books litter your bedroom, all of which say the same thing: Run the vacuum, go for a ride in the car, avoid eating garlic if you nurse. Even if one of these techniques seems to do the trick, none of the books has told you it will only work for fifteen minutes. Then the howling begins again. "Hang in there," say all the advice givers. "Three months is over before you know it."

Not three months of colic. Three months of colic is sheer hell, a sanity-testing eternity, and anyone who tries to trivialize it should be sued for libel. If you're living this nightmare, you need way more than a list of tips and a hearty clap on the back. You need validation that what you're going through is truly awful, and advice for helping *you*—not just your baby—survive it as best you can.

The Newest Thinking on Colic Causes . . . and Cures

While there's a prevailing myth that colic is more common among formula-fed babies, it's not. Plenty of breastfed infants have it, too. Premature infants may be more susceptible to colic. Some new research also shows that women who smoke during pregnancy or around their babies are more likely to have colicky infants. The most commonly accepted theory for the cause of colic has pretty much always been an immature digestive system. As food moves through the baby, it causes discomfort that makes him not only cry, but typically extend or pull up his legs and pass gas. But more and more, the medical community is recognizing that sometimes a specific health-related condition may be behind a baby's colic. Though more often than not doctors have no explanation for a particular baby's colic, here are some possibilities:

- GER, gastroesophageal reflux. This disorder causes stomach acid to back up into the esophagus and create a burning sensation in the chest and throat. These infants may spit up more often than a normal baby, struggle through feedings, and be especially irritable after eating. Babies with GER are also more likely to be fussy all day long, not just at night. GER is common in preemies, so if your colicky baby is one, talk to your doctor. Prescription antacids can help control this condition. So can special formula with rice cereal added to it (but don't try this without first talking with your doctor).
- A cow's-milk-protein allergy, which causes digestive distress. According to the AAP, a very few actually develop a milk allergy. It's more likely to occur in a baby with a family history of food allergies. If you have such a history, you may want to make a special effort to breastfeed, because feeding your baby a cow's-milk formula from birth also increases the chances he'll develop a milk allergy. On the other hand, it's not that likely that a baby will develop a milk allergy from his mother consuming milk and passing it on her in breast milk (though some nursing moms find that their babies are happier when they eliminate dairy from their own diets). If you're feeding formula and your baby seems to have a cow's-milk allergy, talk to your pediatrician about switching to a hypoallergenic formula, which can improve the situation.
- A sleep disorder. Many colicky infants are simply not getting enough sleep and are so exhausted and overstimulated that they cry constantly. A children's sleep expert can help you get your baby on a healthier

sleep schedule, which will likely improve his overall mood and eating habits as well. To find one, contact a nearby children's hospital, many of which have sleep disorder centers. Your pediatrician should also be able to refer you to a behavioral pediatrics expert who deals with issues such as colic and sleep difficulties.

- A sensory processing disorder. Some infants dislike noise and novelty so much that they essentially flip out when exposed to too much. Things like bright lights, itchy clothing, and even too much holding can also set these babies off. While many babies outgrow this sensitivity in a few months as their neurological systems mature, others have a true lifelong neurological condition in which the brain has trouble processing sensory experiences, making them feel overloaded. For now, minimize environmental annoyances (wet diapers, cold or scratchy clothing or blankets, high-pitched or loud sounds, crowded places, strange faces, to name a few) as much as possible. You'll have an idea where your baby falls in this spectrum as she exits the colicky first three or four months. If she mellows out, her sensitivity issues are also probably abating. If not, talk to your pediatrician, who can give you advice about the need to seek treatment. Typically, these children may need to work with an occupational therapist to learn to manage their reactions to stimuli and improve their fine- and gross-motor skills, which can be compromised by the disorder. Most are perfectly intelligent, however, so don't let it scare you. They simply learn differently from other children. For more information on this condition, you can check out the classic book on the topic—*The Out-of-Sync Child* by Carol Stock Kranowitz (Perigee, 2005), recently revised and updated—or the Web site of the Sensory Processing Disorder Network: kidfoundation.org.
- Even without any diagnosis, some babies' sensitive tummies require that you adjust your diet while breastfeeding or switch to the very gentlest hypoallergenic formulas (talk to your pediatrician about this possibility).

Finally, we never hesitate to recommend the advice of our contributing editor, pediatrician William Sears, MD: Camp out on your doctor's doorstep until he comes up with some way to help your baby. Dr. Sears doesn't buy the idea that colic is something you and your child simply have to endure until it passes. A truly colicky baby is a "hurting baby," he believes, and with effort, a medical solution can be found to relieve her discomfort. Of course, some babies are simply "high-need," meaning they cry often because it's their temperament to communicate this way. But if there's a medical reason for your baby's colic she's probably not thriving in other ways either—she may have poor weight gain, sleep fitfully due to the physical pain, and seem to be getting worse, not better, after the peak age of six to eight weeks. For more details and insight, check out his Web site, askdrsears.com.

Gripe Water: Miracle Cure or Myth?

If you've got a colicky or just fuss-prone baby, chances are you've heard of a miraculous-seeming substance called gripe water. Testaments to this herbal concoction's ability to soothe cranky infants, practically in an instant, abound online, and many foreign nannies and caregivers also endorse it. That's because the recipe for gripe water came from Europe and has been more widely used in other cultures. Original forms of gripe water may well have worked like a charm because they contained alcohol, which probably knocked those poor little souls right out soon after they ingested it. Gripe water formulations that contain alcohol are now banned in the United States (too bad—some of us moms could probably use a swig), but more acceptable variations are for sale. Modern-day versions of gripe water usually contain a combination of herbs that may include fennel, ginger, chamomile, or peppermint, and may produce at least a temporary calming effect, if for no other reason than it will be a surprising new taste to your baby. There are, alas, no clinical studies proving that gripe water is at all effective at soothing babies. And it's worth noting that if there were such an easy treatment for colic, it wouldn't be a medical mystery. Still, if you're at your wit's end with a screaming child, there's probably no harm in trying it. Just be sure to stay away from homemade remedies or anything for sale on the Internet that may contain alcohol, and run the ingredients by your pediatrician.

"WHAT NOBODY TOLD ME ABOUT COLIC"

"My son had colic for three and a half months. It was awful. Thank God for the baby swing; it was the only thing that soothed him at all. Some of my friends' kids had colic-like symptoms that turned out to be acid reflux. I wish I had known more about both colic and reflux so that I could understand what he really had. I never pushed my pediatrician to check him. I'm still kicking myself."

—*Erin, Springfield, Illinois*

"I don't care what anyone says, colic is intestinal distress. Something is causing the baby to be in pain. My first had really bad colic that started at three months, which is unusual, as it's usually over by then. I was breastfeeding, and I did an elimination diet and found out he was sensitive to wheat, dairy, and tomatoes. When I eliminated those things from my diet, his colic disappeared literally overnight. It's not easy to do, but you can get all your nutrients and eat a healthy diet as a mom. It's just not that big of a sacrifice. I also had to change my medication for high blood pressure (I developed postpartum high blood pressure after having preeclampsia). An allergy medicine I also take bothered him. I am a strong advocate of breastfeeding, so I didn't want to quit. Soothers: gas drops, Tylenol, riding around in the car. And know that it doesn't last forever." —*Denise, Hugo, Colorado*

"Our daughter was colicky pretty much from birth until almost four months. The earliest problems were due to milk allergy and caffeine sensitivity, which went away when I gave up all dairy and caffeine products. Apparently the stomach sensitivity continued, because the one thing I wish we'd known to try (and didn't learn about until week ten!) was Mylicon drops. She would still be very cranky in the evenings but most of the out-and-out full-lung screaming stopped after someone recommended the gas drops. On an unusual note, on her worst colicky evenings, she seemed to be soothed by music with very low tones—something about the vibrations, perhaps? She liked classical cello (Yo Yo Ma) and also my husband's deepest humming.

"Looking back on it, I think most of the crankiness not explained by a sensitive stomach was probably overtiredness. I tried to get her on a sleep schedule but she wouldn't take a pacifier and didn't find her thumb to help her self-soothe until after three months. However, I would recommend to all moms to get their babies on a sleep schedule as soon as they can. Once we got the stomach sensitivity under control and also

(continued on next page)

got her caught up on her sleep, we magically had a happy, content baby and we have ever since." —*Julie, Coppell, Texas*

"Unfortunately, I didn't cope very well with colic. From eight to eleven or even midnight, every night, for three months, we tried everything—swaddling the baby tight, doing the football hold, walking the baby up and down stairs, laying him across our thighs, saying *shhh* nice and loud and steady near his ear, breastfeeding more—you name it, we tried it. We finally just ended up letting him cry (scream) himself to sleep on our chests every night (mainly my husband's chest) while we patted his back. It didn't really make any difference what we did; it happened every night and we all just exhausted ourselves. But after the three months were up, it was over, thank God! My advice is to sleep during the day, whenever the baby is sleeping, because you know you won't get any sleep later on. Also, hand the baby off to someone else when you get impatient or need a break." —*Dawn, Alexandria, Virginia*

"Our first child hardly ever cried . . . we thought we were the *best* parents! All the other babies cried, but not ours. Must be something the other parents were doing wrong! Then we had our second child, who cried from the moment he exited the womb until he was three months old. Nothing would make him happy. We went to the pediatrician thinking something had to be wrong with him or our parenting skills. She said, 'Babies cry.' Well, duh, we'd figured that one out! He would be peacefully sleeping, then it was like someone flipped a switch . . . boom . . . screaming for hours on end. I would sit on the stairs and cry.

"Looking back, I should have been more realistic. We were just really lucky with the first. Several times people offered to take him for a while so I could escape the noise, but I always declined. I thought he would be more upset if I left him. For my sanity and his, I wish I had taken them up on it. It really is true: Babies cry. And sometimes there's just no reasonable explanation for it. Sometimes the best thing to do is make sure the baby is in a safe place (crib, playpen, et cetera) and leave the room. Crying doesn't hurt them, they won't end up in therapy because they felt abandoned, and you will be able to regain some strength to get back in the trenches."

—*Jennifer, Raleigh, North Carolina*

What's Personality Got to Do with It?

Plenty, actually. How your baby is hardwired to handle life's ups and downs will, at least in part, help dictate whether she laughs or cries in the face of change, whether she soldiers on when frustrated or gives up and crawls away, and maybe even how soon she attempts feats like cruising and walking or is willing to try broccoli. The other half of the equation is how you respond to and cultivate her unique habits and propensities. A shy baby who is given time to warm up, for instance, may be blowing raspberries and drooling all over Aunt Rita and Uncle Phil by the time the visit wraps up. Try thrusting her immediately into their arms, however, and she may not get near them again before kindergarten.

Infant temperament researchers believe that all children start life with an inherited set of nine personality traits. The specific combo of traits your baby comes bundled with then puts him into one of three categories: easy (adaptable, pleasant, sociable, falls into a regular schedule); slow to warm up (cautious, less physically active, tends to whimper rather than scream, and is not always in a good mood); and challenging (highly intense reactions, defies routine, very cautious in new situations, and more inclined toward bad moods than other babies). This doesn't mean you should have a cow if you ended up with a challenging baby, however! These last, super-sensitive kids have their positive traits, too—that intensity may well be accompanied by a long attention span that helps them focus on and perfect their areas of interest, and they often grow up to be extremely creative types.

In other words, your baby's personality will evolve to a certain extent as he learns to cope with the world, as well as focus on what makes him happy and avoid what upsets him. You'll see this occur somewhat in the first year, for instance, as your baby first learns to express himself in ways other than crying; a sensitive baby who seemed to cry a lot at first will learn to simply push away a rattle or crawl away from a TV that's too loud or a sibling who's getting on his nerves. An alert and playful baby who may have seemed easy at first can become quite a challenge when he becomes mobile and begins climbing on top of furniture to try to get to what excites him. These are primitive expressions of personality, so to speak, but they'll continue to evolve in more sophisticated ways throughout childhood. Your shy baby may always be that way to a certain extent (some children do outgrow this trait), but find lots of pleasure if you steer him to friends and activities that suit his demeanor: maybe the highly focused sport of karate instead of aggressive team sports, or chess club over drama club. You can't change your baby's inborn personality any more than you can change your spouse's annoying habits (though we will all try to a certain extent), but you can help her find happiness and realize her full potential by providing her with the opportunity to experience and discover what best suits her.

How soon will you know your baby's personality? Some traits are obvious almost from birth; others will become apparent by three or four months. And while your baby's personality will be with her for life, some inborn traits may evolve in intensity. For instance, her low frustration level may improve as she gains confidence in her abilities, or her no-holds-barred desire for activity may subside a bit as her attention span grows and she discovers that coloring or painting is kind of fun, too. Even the most challenging traits can become less problematic as she learns to cope with life's ups and downs, and figures out what makes her happy—all in conjunction with your support and guidance, of course. Here are the clues you need to recognize the kid your baby will soon become.

Trait 1: Activity level. Does your baby often seem content watching the world from her swing or bouncy seat? Or does she wriggle from one end of her crib to another, create a flood at bathtime, and turn diaper changes into wrestling matches? The former baby has a low activity level, so you may not want to overwhelm her with too much physical play. Instead, give her plenty of options—a hanging gym, an activity bar on her stroller—to keep her motivated. The highly active, baby, however, enjoys frequent stimulation. The positive side of this is that she may reach gross-motor milestones such as crawling, cruising, and walking sooner than other babies. The downside: You need to be especially vigilant about safety, because she's more likely than mellower babies to get herself into trouble. Remove all crib accessories the minute she learns to roll over, always use the safety belt on the changing pad, and never leave her unattended in a bouncy seat or other device she might be able to flip over. Of course you may also be able to count on her being a good sleeper, since all this activity is bound to wear her out!

Trait 2: Regularity. Do you have a baby who seems to sleep, eat, and even poop like clockwork? Or does he defy every attempt at routine—catnapping throughout the day and grazing at the breast or bottle as the urge strikes? The first type of baby is regular. Structure your day around his habits as much as possible for now—his sense of security depends on it— and he'll make your life easy. When he gets a little bigger, he'll be more able to tolerate missing an occasional nap, because he knows you're there for him even when his reality gets rocked a little. If your baby is irregular, try not to be too rigid or you'll only make yourself crazy. Don't obsess about routine, but do try to add elements of predictability to it. For instance, nurse him in the same chair, and stick to his favorite soothing methods. And definitely be persistent about bedtime—these babies still need their rest and will become super cranky without it.

Trait 3: Sociability. Will your baby smile and coo at just about anyone who scoops her up, no matter how abruptly? Or does she seem to have been born with stranger anxiety, resisting even her doting grandma's advances? If you've got the first type, a highly sociable baby, provide her with lots of opportunities to interact with others—join a playgroup, go to the park, and bring her along when you run errands. The clingier baby is what psychologists call withdrawal-oriented, a complicated name for what pretty much amounts to shyness. Don't force this type of baby into unfamiliar situations. Keep her close until she signals that she's ready to interact or explore by making cooing noises at her company or, if she's older, perhaps trying to wriggle off your lap and crawl around. (Note: Most babies go through a clingy stage somewhere around eight or nine months, known as stranger anxiety, which will pass on its own if it's not your baby's usual nature. You'll learn more about this in chapter 5.) As a general rule, it's seldom a good idea to force a reserved child to be more outgoing; a person's inborn level of sociability stays surprisingly constant throughout life. Try not to fret about it too much. Your child will still make friends—just at her own pace.

Trait 4: Adaptability. Does your baby typically "go with the flow," napping if he needs to in the middle of a boisterous party, or quickly becoming comfortable with a new Saturday-night sitter? Or does he refuse to sleep anywhere but in his own crib, cry if you cut your hair, and spit new foods right back at you? The first type of baby is highly adaptable. His flexible nature usually means he easily tolerates changes to his routine and new people in his life. Traveling is usually no sweat with this personality type, either: He can go to sleep in a hotel room or at Grandma's as easily as in his nursery. Enjoy his flexibility, but don't take advantage of it. Even though he warms up to a new babysitter, for instance, make sure they are playing together before you take off. If your baby isn't very adaptable, go slow when introducing changes in his life. Little-seeming things like you getting new glasses or Dad shaving off his beard can be downright scary for him. If you are on the go, pack familiar objects, such as favorite blankets, books, and toys, so he has some reminders of home.

Trait 5: Intensity. If your baby makes her feelings known—and loudly—with earthshaking cries or contagious laughter, you probably don't need to be told she has an intense personality. While you're going to want to soothe her every cry, don't feel guilty when you can't. This is how these babies show their feelings. If you can't take it anymore, put her in the crib and take a time-out yourself. And take heart: One day that same intensity may make her an excellent student or accomplished musician or artist, because she'll put all her energy into those interests, too.

If your baby isn't very intense, barely reacting at all or whimpering instead of shrieking, life may seem easier, but you have to work harder to understand what she's thinking and feeling. Pay careful attention (watch for scowls or signs of boredom like looking away) and talk your baby through her feelings—"Oh, you don't like that noise!" "Isn't this rattle fun?"— so she knows you're there and involved.

Trait 6: Disposition. A baby with a positive disposition wakes up with a smile and keeps it all day long. This is the baby you can bond with just by having fun: singing songs, blowing raspberries at each other, and playing silly games. If, on the other hand, your baby tends to scowl and whimper and whine, don't beat yourself up—it doesn't mean he doesn't love you. Do your best to make sure he isn't unhappy because he's uncomfortable or ill, and provide him with plenty of smiles and affection to help him view the world more optimistically. As he gets bigger and learns to express himself better, his crying and unhappiness should diminish. The secret to keeping these children happy is to let them be just who they are, and not force them to be someone else. Challenge him to go out and provide the opportunity to make some friends, for instance, but don't try to turn him into the proverbial life of the party. One or two close friends who tend to view the world the same way he does may be just perfect for him, and you will get a chance to see that there are other kids like him who are functioning beautifully in their own way.

Trait 7: Distractibility. Is your baby quickly soothed by a change in scenery or a new toy? Or is she the type that won't calm down when upset until she gets exactly what she wants? The first kind of baby is highly distractible, which will go a long way toward keeping her out of trouble or averting temper tantrums. Simply steer her away from the light socket and she'll forget about it. But keep in mind that things may also distract her in a negative way—for example, a lot of commotion in the room may disrupt her feedings—so keep such stimulation to a minimum. If your baby is less distractible, she may not notice, say, lawn mowers or fire truck sirens when she's trying to settle down for a nap, but be prepared to act fast—with toys, food, and extra pacifiers—when distress strikes.

Trait 8: Persistence. Do you have a baby who doesn't give up easily, whether he's trying to bat a toy above him or resist a diaper change? Or is he quickly frustrated by toys he can't master, or simply the kind who flits from activity to activity? The highly persistent first type needs you to work with him. Let him take a rattle to the changing table or change his diaper wherever he's playing, for instance. Keep him engaged by increasing the complexity of his toys, introducing the shape sorter when the stacking ring is no longer a challenge. If your baby isn't very persistent, do just the opposite: Don't rush into toys geared to ages above him, and have lots of activities on hand to occupy him whenever you need to accomplish some grown-up thing.

Trait 9: Sensitivity. Some babies fuss at the slightest provocation: too much noise, too many people, a soggy diaper, or cold crib sheets. These babies are highly sensitive and tend to have strong reactions to stimulation. Keep her environment soothing whenever possible: low lights, soft music, and not too much company at once. Talk to her in a low voice; avoid too much activity before bedtime, or she may have extra trouble settling herself. If your baby isn't very sensitive, changes in environment or routine will seldom set her off. Do check her regularly to make sure her diaper's clean and she's comfortable. Babies with a low sensitivity level may not even react much to pain, so they may become subdued or lethargic when sick, rather than cranky or irritable.

Regardless of your baby's early inclinations, try not to get too caught up in labels in the first few months. Many parents are caught off guard by those initial personality traits, then calm down or become more accepting when they take a second look. That stubborn streak your partner has coupled with your tendency to speak your mind may explain why your baby protests loudly whenever you whisk her away from her playthings for a diaper change. Or your propensity for adventurous activities like skiing or mountain climbing could translate into a baby who scales milestones early, leaving her peers in the dust. Petrified of public speaking? Maybe your baby will bury her head when a friendly admirer approaches. But clingy doesn't have to mean cranky, and almost all temperamental traits can be positives when you learn to work with your child's particular constellation. That's what's known as goodness of fit: the ability to accept your child and help her adapt. Your perceptions and reactions to her behaviors and tendencies go a long way toward shaping her into a happy, well-adjusted child, not to mention improving your satisfaction level. The flip side: When parents and babies have personality clashes, the end result can be frustration and guilt.

When the baby you get is not the one you expected, avoid an upsetting scenario by looking at the strengths your baby's temperament offers. A persistent baby won't back away from life's challenges, a shy baby may grow into a keen observer, and a cautious baby is less likely to get hurt than his very active peers. Try to look at personality traits in the long term, too. An easy baby now may turn into a more challenging toddler because that same carefree, independent personality may lead him to wander off exploring when you're engaged in a conversation at the park, for instance, while the clingy baby stays by your side and out of mischief. By decoding your infant's personality in this way, you both stand to have a much happier life together.

If you can pick your baby out of this lineup of characters, and have hit upon a few soothing tactics you can rely on, you're getting to know this amazing little person and figuring out what makes him tick. He's probably got you under his thumb now, too, and soon will be trying out his own little arsenal of tactics to get you to do things his way. The part of the mother–child bond that makes you want to feed and protect him is in place even before birth, but the real strong love evolves as you get to know and read each other and become secure in your abilities. For some moms and babies, that's a two-month process; for others it takes more like four. But rest assured, you're getting there.

From Siblings to Playdates:
How Your Baby Interacts with Other Kids

When it comes to new-baby-and-bigger-sibling relationships, there's one thing we can practically guarantee you: Your latest-born will adore her older brother(s) or sister(s), regardless of how close or far apart they are in age. Babies are absolutely enchanted with other children, and those who live under the same roof get top billing. When it comes to the bigger sibling, however, there are fewer predictables. Some welcome their new home-mates—sometimes roommates—with open arms; others feel more like belting them (and yes, they sometimes do). Even if your older child is initially excited, it may not take long for the blissful growing-family bubble to burst. Once your firstborn realizes the baby is getting more attention and presents (which she ironically has no clue about), the bigger sib will likely resort to sticking Play-Doh up her nose and using the furniture as a trampoline every time you attempt to feed, change, or otherwise turn your attention to your newest addition. The reality of living with a baby brother or sister—not to mention multiples!—is to little kids what sleep deprivation is to moms: You can't fathom how tough it is until you actually experience it. And unfortunately, most firstborn children are still too young to have the language skills to express their feelings (which brings us back to the hitting issue again). Sometimes what's perceived as a negative response to the baby is in fact a response to Mom's stress and exhaustion (read: no time left for me). Here's what each of your children—little and big—just might be thinking.

Your Baby's Viewpoint

Why do babies love babies? One theory about this phenomenon is that humans have an innate sense of what's attractive, and that usually includes features that are soft and round and not too big or small or oddly shaped—just what most babies look like. Then there's the possibility that we're all programmed to love babies so we want to care for them, ensuring the survival of the species. Thus babies exit the womb with an innate tendency to find their peers attractive. And you can't argue with the fact that a baby's features are much more appealing than many of us adults with pointy noses, hairy chins, big brown moles, huge-seeming glasses, or overly bright collagen-enhanced red lips (we're not talking about you, of course).

The typical baby's fascination with faces in general also most certainly plays a role. Those first few weeks home from the hospital, your baby can only focus on what's close up, and most often that's the faces of you, Dad, and his bigger siblings. Coupled with the sounds of your voices and your scents, your baby learns to recognize his family and begins to respond to their attempts to entertain him, resulting in that first social smile somewhere around six weeks. From here on out, he won't be able to get enough human interaction (except when he's overly tired or ravenous, at which time he'll let you know just how he feels).

While your baby also enjoys the faces of strangers—you'll notice him staring enraptured at other babies on TV or in videos—those of his family members will generate the most excitement as his familiarity and security grow. It also helps that little siblings are more often at your baby's eye level, and more likely to do wacky things like play peekaboo, sing songs, or do the hokey-pokey for the baby (they're hankering for attention, too, after all).

As your baby enters the second half of his first year, the condition of stranger anxiety typically sets in, making him fearful of strange faces. Siblings, however, continue to provide that familiar comfort, and curiously enough most older babies are not fearful of other babies or toddlers. They somehow seem to recognize their peers as being safe.

Still, if you bring two babies or young toddlers together—siblings, relatives, or playdates—keep a close eye on them. Hair pulling and eyeball poking may well ensue, not so much out of meanness but for curiosity's sake. Discipline them with distraction or separation, rather than reprimands. And bear in mind that playdates at this stage of the game are more for Mom's sake; while kids are interested in each other to a certain extent, they really don't play with each other in a reciprocal fashion until they're past their second birthdays. The ability to share—and feel good about it—comes later still, typically between the ages of three and four.

Your Older Child's Viewpoint

As your expanding belly literally starts to come between you and your firstborn, your guilt is likely to grow as well: How can this one not feel a loss when you have to divide your time between two (or three or more?). Well, we're not going to lie and say there won't be a period of adjustment for both of you, but in the long run your capacity to love him will actually grow, rather than shrink. Think of it as how you began to view and love your husband differently when he became a father the first time around. Now you'll see your older child evolve into "the big one" (no matter how little he was just yesterday), and he'll probably take on that role with relish eventually, making you burst with pride as he helps his little sibling learn who-knows-what (it will become such a daily occurrence you'll barely notice, and if you're lucky you'll only have to teach shoe tying once).

Begin this process by helping your oldest feel involved in the preparations for the new baby: Choosing the nursery color from a few preapproved selections, shopping for baby items, and picking out a special gift to give the new baby when he comes home from the hospital (and a big-sister gift for her, too). Talk about all the ways your firstborn will be able to help you with her new little brother or sister, and let her practice tasks like diapering her dolls, then be your assistant when you're doing the job for real. You can also show your child his own baby pictures and tell him how he acted when he was small. You can prepare him for the day-to-day with a newborn by saying that he cried a lot because he couldn't talk, and Mommy and Daddy had to pay a lot of attention to him. Emphasize that though the baby will take up a lot of your time, she'll eventually be a big kid just like her brother.

When you bring the baby home, have someone else carry her into the house and keep your arms available for a big hug. Or arrange for your older child to be away when you first get there so when he comes in, you're settled and ready to focus just on him. Either way, your firstborn is going to be more interested in attention from you than gushing over the baby, and the newest addition isn't going to know the difference yet.

Once the baby arrives, of course, you'll have to be judicious about your time and your responses, and expect there to be some negative reactions when, for instance, the visiting relatives rush past the big sister to gush over the new baby brother. (You'll find this as painful as she does.) Here's some advice for those maddening moments when your family multiplies a bit faster than you can handle.

"What do you mean I can't hit the baby?" Since many of us are crazy enough to bring a second child into the world when our firstborn is a high-maintenance toddler, we're likely to be stretched so thin that whenever our eldest is being good, we take advantage of this to tend to the new baby's needs, not his. So what does the firstborn do? He gives the baby a good pinch or a whack. Sometimes the aggression can seem accidental—your oldest is on the other side of the room when the baby suddenly gets whacked up the side of his head by a wayward building block. This is the stage when you just can't leave your firstborn alone with the baby. Put your infant in her car seat by the shower if you must.

Naturally, most of us are horrified by our eldest's darker side, but remember that negative feelings are normal. The result: Little, not-so-verbal kids lash out—they pinch, throw things, or hit to express their anger. And even if the older child isn't feeling negative, she may get dangerous ideas into her head. One mom we know woke in the middle of the night and discovered her toddler daughter had made her way out of her new big-girl bed and was lovingly wheeling the three-week-old baby's bassinet up and down the hall like a stroller, which would have been a disaster if she'd accidentally tipped it over or headed for the not-yet-gated staircase. (The lesson of this story: It's a good idea to put a safety gate in your toddler's bedroom doorway if she can get out of her bed on her own and you're so sleep-deprived you won't hear her, which pretty much applies to all of us.)

Of course, you also need to set limits on such behavior, but try not to overreact. Keep your cool and take advantage of the opportunity to acknowledge your child's feelings: "I know you want to do the puzzle, but I can't help you now because the baby's crying. It's okay to feel angry, but you can't hit your sister." Then you might suggest that your older child get out the puzzle and set it up so the two of you can get started once the baby quiets down. The sooner you let your older child know you understand, the sooner he'll calm down.

You can also try to head off the aggression. If you see your son heading toward his little sister, for instance, jump in and say, "You want to touch Sarah? She really likes to be hugged this way because it doesn't hurt her." Chances are, your child really does like the baby; he's just acting out his confused feelings.

You can also try appointing the big sibling the baby's protector (this works best with a child who's at least three and probably four years old). Explain that it's his job to make sure that people are very gentle with the baby's fingers and toes. He'll feel important and get the basics of newborn safety.

"Why does she get to stay up later than I do?" Second babies also have a bad habit of arriving on the scene just when your firstborn has begun to use the potty regularly or has adjusted to preschool. Then, in a flash, all the routines are out the window and you've got two kids with no schedule. Staggering bedtimes can be a convenient solution to the evening chaos. If you can get the baby down first (even just for a little while), then you can spend an hour or so with your oldest and have him asleep before the baby wakes up to party the night away (where you fit into this sleep picture, we're not so sure). Or try taping yourself reading bedtime stories, and when your oldest begs for one more, you can turn it on and let him nod off to the sound of your voice while you nurse the baby in the next room.

"I don't want to give up my stuff." Second-time parents-to-be are often advised not to take away their eldest's crib when the baby comes home. Make the transition well in advance, the advice usually goes, or get another one if your firstborn isn't ready for a bed. We get that, but some siblings are reluctant to pass down other gear as well, even if they can't possibly remember using it. What to do? Some moms just let their toddlers climb into the baby tub and pretend they're newborns again—a game they usually tire of soon enough. Chances are there's also a new improved model of whatever you had the first time around, so if you've got the bucks, you can always consider springing for a new whatever for the baby.

When it comes to bedrooms, if your kids must share one, it's a good idea to let the eldest help set it up. She might pick out the baby's bedding, for example, or something decorative for the baby's wall. And even if space is tight, try to designate an area of the room that's all hers—a corner or a bookcase, for instance. The baby won't be able to invade it for a while, and by then she'll likely be over her hurt feelings.

"But you promised we could go to the playground!" Big kids may need their own space, but they also need time to do all the things they used to do with you. Only now there's one of you and two of them, so that's not always feasible. A solution to this time bind can be to hire a sitter now and then— but just for the new baby, while you do something fun with your firstborn. If you have relatives on hand, great. Or Dad can take the older child under his wing when you're nursing or bathing the baby. But don't forget to give your firstborn some mommy time, such as doing a craft project or playing a game while the baby naps. That need for individual attention is the root of sibling rivalry. Simply telling your eldest that there's enough love for everyone is too abstract. He needs something more concrete. For those moments when you must tend to the baby, invite him to have a snack while he sits next to you, or let him hold a book up for you to read to him while you nurse. Store a small stash of treats and books in a spot he can reach in the nursery or wherever you do most of your babycare.

Too exhausted to consider an outing or the mess of finger paints? Do whatever you can to work in some cuddle time. If the baby's napping, you can tell your older child, "I'm too tired to play in the yard. But why don't we put on a video and watch it together in bed?" Everyone wins: You get some rest, and he gets some one-on-one attention and affection. Playing doctor is another great idea: You can lie on the sofa and be examined, and your child gets some interaction (sort of). And speaking of physical contact, sometimes it can be the antidote even to serious misbehavior. If your older child starts to act out and you know you've been guilty of neglect, fight your urge to reprimand him. Instead, put the baby down, go over, and say, "You look like you need a really big bear hug." Later, you can talk to him about his behavior if you really feel it's necessary. But if you work in these sorts of responses, there's a good chance the need for repercussions will diminish fairly quickly.

CHAPTER 5

The Growing Year
A Real-Life Look at Your Baby's Development

WARNING: THE SURGEON GENERAL HAS DETERMINED THAT COMPARING YOUR BABY WITH OTHER CHILDREN HER AGE CAN BE HAZARDOUS TO YOUR MENTAL HEALTH.

O f course you're going to do it anyway; we do it, too. How the heck else can we know if our babies are normal or not, right? The problem with this bit of reasoning is that the very definition of *normal* can be as slippery as a newborn in a bathtub. Since most parents don't realize that the developmental time line provided by most parenting books (including ours) is actually a *guide*line, each milestone is cause for joy or angst. Either your baby pulls off a feat early and you fantasize about her future induction into a hall of fame or onto a dean's list, or she's a bit behind and you scour the textbooks for clues to the problem (and it's usually the worst possible prognosis). Meanwhile, neither scenario is likely to be true. There's a huge, and we mean huge, window of expectation when it come to normal progression of most developmental skills.

You can and should coax and encourage your baby to reach for her toys or try rolling over, but her development is going to come at its own unique pace. It will be motivated by an array of factors, from personality (perhaps he's more cautious than curious) to gender (girls tend to be talkers, boys walkers) to true potential (maybe he really did get your athletic gene).

While we aren't dumb enough to say that you should never compare and contrast your baby with her peers—that's like saying you shouldn't breathe— we will say that you should try to keep this natural tendency in check or

160

you'll start hyperventilating. In fact, it can be quite helpful to measure your baby against other children her age. Getting a sense of where your baby sits, or crawls, or walks on the developmental time line tells you what she does well and what might benefit from more mommy input. It can even help you pinpoint any real areas of concern that you can broach with your pediatrician. If, however, comparing your baby with others starts you obsessing about how fast or slow your baby is plotting her course, then each approaching milestone will turn into a millstone around your neck, dragging you down with worry. (Hmmm . . . how do we know this?)

To prevent a monthly freak-out, it helps to understand what development is. Or, more accurately, what it is not. Development is *not* the same as growth. *Growth* refers to physical changes, and involves a series of measurements neatly put into a graph to illustrate how small or large your baby is compared with other kids her age. Generally speaking, if your child is consistent in her growth, whether she is petite or zaftig, all is well. By contrast, *development* encompasses a wide range of changes including physical, emotional, and cognitive skills, many of which overlap and inform one another. To help you get a handle on what developmental learning involves, and why normal parameters aren't carved in stone, check out how many categories figure into this equation:

Cognitive (aka intellectual) development. How your baby's brain figures out the world around him.

Social-emotional development. How he adapts to and interacts with others.

Language development. His ability to communicate, which in the first year includes receptive language, the ability to understand what's being said to him even if he can't say it back—as well as expressive language, which refers to actually saying words.

Fine-motor development. The ability to use small-muscle groups, especially the fingers, to perform tasks (holding a spoon, grabbing your hair).

Gross-motor development. Using large muscles to roll over, sit up, crawl, walk. (FYI: Whoever wrote the ditty *Head, shoulders, knees, and toes* knew something about development, because that's exactly the order in which infants achieve gross-motor skills. First they gain head control, then use their shoulders to roll over and sit up; next comes knee control, which allows them to pull up and cruise. Finally, they walk with the support of their feet and toes!)

Now that you know how many variables are involved in computing *normal,* we're going to go ahead and give a month-by-month developmental time line anyway. We are experts in our own right, after all, and we have a responsibility to provide you with the accepted rate of progression for developmental milestones. But as you walk the line, keep reminding yourself that even if your baby may fall slightly behind or ahead of the pack, chances are he is still just an average kid. (And if you think that description sounds bad now, wait until he gets to school and his teachers refer to him as "an average student"—then you'll really cringe!)

The First Month

Newborns live by the credo *Stick with what you know.* And what they know is how to sleep, eat, and cry. (Pooping is an acquired talent.) This limited skill set, however, belies some behind-the-scenes talents blossoming in their brains, including how they see and hear the world. As the month progresses, you'll notice some very alert moments after each feeding. Your baby's eyes will open wide and her face will take on a sparkle as she studies her surroundings. There are a lot of misunderstandings out there about what babies can see and when, and frankly the explanation of how the eye works at birth will cause your already heavy lids to sag even farther. Suffice it to say that not all the parts are functioning at full capacity

HOW DOES YOUR PREEMIE GROW?

Calculating the development of any baby can be nerve-racking, but if you're the mom of one of the half a million babies born prematurely each year in the United States, you're in the advanced math class. Preemies are typically described as having two ages: a chronological age, dated from the day they were born, like other children, and an adjusted age (also referred to as corrected or gestational age). The adjusted age is based on the baby's due date—when she would have been born if she had been full-term. Because a preemie doesn't get a chance to fully mature in the womb, you can't expect her to be at the same point developmentally as other full-term babies born at the same time as she was. The adjusted age takes into account that she is actually developmentally younger than her peers. For instance, if your baby was born two months early, three months after her birth date she will be expected to be more like a one-month-old than the three-month-old the calendar indicates. When she is six months old, her doctor will be looking for behaviors and milestones of a four-month-old. How much your preemie adheres to this adjusted development schedule depends on many factors, including how early and how small she was when she was born. For example, a three-pound baby born at twenty-eight weeks may take more time to catch up than a four-pound baby born at thirty-four weeks. It's also not uncommon for preemies to achieve some milestones close to their chronological age, and others closer to the corrected age. One mom of a preemie born almost two months early told us: "It seemed like one day my son could barely sit up, and the next he was crawling. Meanwhile, two other preemie girls I know were all caught up by about six months." Because preemies have such different catch-up rates, the important thing for you to focus on is that your baby is moving forward. It's also helpful to keep in mind that there's a wide range of normal for milestone development even among full-term babies. Typically by age two or two and a half, most preemies are fully caught up and there is no longer a need to view them in terms of an adjusted age.

If you have a preemie, your doctor will likely keep an especially vigilant eye on her development, but don't hesitate to raise any concerns yourself. Preemies are at greater risk of developmental delays and other health problems, so you want to be sure your baby gets every kind of care available to her. For more on the special needs of raising a premature baby, see chapter 11, page 381.

for the first few months, so your baby can't see as well as you. Thus, the closer things are to her face (think eight to twelve inches), the more she will enjoy them. It's also somewhat of a myth that babies can only see in black and white. They can see colors, but similar shades (such as red and orange) blur together, while contrasting patterns are clearer, hence all those black and white and red toys. A graphically patterned rattle or mobile will interest your baby, but take care not to overwhelm her with a lot of this type of visual stimulation. In fact, what your baby most wants to look at right now is your face.

Because their vision is limited, young infants are what experts call auditory learners, which means they learn more about their world from hearing than seeing at this stage. Your baby learns to recognize you, and bonds with you, when you get close and converse with her in "motherese"—that high-pitched, lilting, singsong way of talking to a baby that seems to reflexively appear in all of us practically minutes after the cord is cut. Infants benefit from motherese (also known as just plain "baby talk") in a number of ways. For one, when you exaggerate the sound of the words, it helps your baby hear and recognize them. We tend to use shorter sentences, so they become easier for your baby to understand. Our emotions are also exaggerated when we use baby talk, which helps your child recognize happiness, sadness, pain, and sympathy for her when she's upset. And that special tone tells your baby you are only talking to her and no one else. Motherese is not just for mothers—dads do it, and so do older siblings. Language researchers have actually studied one-month-olds' reactions to conversation and found that they prefer motherese to adult-sounding speech. So go with your gut and babble often to your baby.

Along with sights and sounds, your baby is beginning to understand her body. Namely that she has one. Talk about a neurological hurdle: Your little being isn't even aware that she has toes at the other end of her body, or that you and she are separate people. So you can forgive her if her movements are jerky and twitchy. These are the result of inborn reflexes (see "Baby Self-Defense," page 167) rather than intent, and will smooth out over time. As for physical changes, look for increasing strength of your baby's neck muscles, and greater head control. You still have to support her neck, and will for weeks to come, but you'll soon notice her trying to lift her head when she's lying on a flat surface. This is a sure sign that both her curiosity and her capability are growing.

    NEWBORN SENSIBILITIES

Sense: **Sight**
Baby's Ability: Your baby sees clearly at birth but is nearsighted—
                   objects farther away than eight to ten inches are
                   blurry until focus improves in the second month.

How to Encourage It: Two words: *face time*. As we noted earlier, the most appealing sight to a newborn is a face—especially her mother's, father's, or sibling's. Look into your baby's eyes as you diaper, hold, and feed her. Put an unbreakable mirror by your changing table or in her play yard to encourage her to practice turning her head side-to-side.

Sense: **Hearing**

Baby's Ability: Your little guy should hear clearly from the moment of birth, although not quite as well as an adult. He jumps at sudden noises, is soothed by the sound of your heartbeat, which he lived with during pregnancy, and is interested in hearing human voices, especially yours.

How to Encourage It: Talk to your baby often—he's listening even if he seems to be staring off into space. Use the lilting sound of motherese, raising your pitch, slowing down your speech, and repeating key words. Pause often so your baby can respond with his own vocalizations.

Sense: **Smell**

Baby's Ability: For having such teeny nostrils, newborns have a large capacity for distinguishing smells, particularly the ones emanating from you. As amazing as it seems, your baby can recognize your body fragrance within forty-eight hours of arriving in the world and can distinguish the scent of your breast milk from another mother's milk. So don't worry about skipping a shower. Think of it as a learning tool for your baby's olfactory nerves.

How to Encourage It: Don't wash your nightgown too often (though we know you can only live with so much spit-up on your shoulders!). Your body odor can actually be very soothing to your baby, if not your partner, particularly if she's prone to colicky nights or unable to settle

(continued on next page)

herself back to sleep after a wee-hour feeding. Some older babies even take comfort by cuddling with a piece of your nightgown or a shirt while you're away and a sitter is in charge.

Sense: **Taste**
Baby's Ability: Babies are born with several thousand taste buds, some of which die off and aren't replaced as we age. That may be one of the reasons it's tough to get kids to eat foods adults like; they taste everything more intensely, so if you find foods like spinach challenging now, imagine how your child feels about it! In these early months, however, everything your baby encounters is pretty yummy, be it the simple flavor of formula or the evolving experience of breast milk, which is colored by what you last ate. Still, as you might expect, sweet tastes are every baby's favorite, and bitter is the least enjoyed.
How to Encourage It: If you're breastfeeding, don't shy away from adventurous foods (unless your baby is clearly upset by them, of course). Experts believe that tastes such as garlic, onion, spices, and other strong cultural preferences in breast milk will help your baby accept different foods when he graduates to the table.

Sense: **Touch**
Baby's Ability: Perhaps to make up for weak peepers, your baby has an extremely sensitive sense of touch. He begins to know the world through his skin and quickly learns to distinguish someone familiar by touch alone. Your baby is also comforted, and more active, alert, and responsive when he is massaged.
How to Encourage It: Just before bedtime, gently stroke your baby's face, arms, legs, back, and torso with the pads of your fingertips. About ten minutes makes for a good mini massage, but watch your baby for clues that he's had enough—not all infants enjoy prolonged touch.

The Second Month

Four weeks gone already? It seems like just yesterday you were bringing your newborn home and wondering whom he would take after. This month offers up the first clues, as he begins to develop his own personality. You'll probably witness his first true social smile (rather than a gas bubble grimace, or the little grin you may glimpse when your tot is feeling content) at around six weeks, and he may even begin to coo at your delightful face, or a stuffed animal, or a shiny spoon. Initially, cooing is an automatic behavior, but as your baby realizes that he can make the sound himself, he'll begin to do it more often. The more you respond to his coos with a smile or encouraging words, the longer he'll continue it, because he's enjoying the attention.

Both of these behaviors are early signs of emotional growth: Your baby's gotten the idea that when he smiles at you, you'll smile back, and it makes him feel happy. When you make a funny face, he may try to mimic you to maintain the interaction. He also feels sad or scared at times, and will begin to cry in response to those feelings now, too.

Your baby is also busy trying to make sense of his world. He'll begin to hold up his head for a few seconds at a time as he checks things out, turning to look in the direction of new sounds. And he'll seem to spend countless minutes lying there studying his own hands and their movements, which he can't yet control. He's also picking up on familiar routines: When he sees your breast or a bottle coming, he'll suck excitedly.

Baby Self-Defense

Because a newborn has limited control over his body, Mother Nature equipped him with many innate survival skills. These reflexes, while necessary, can make him seem like a bundle of nerves—twitching, jerking, and kicking at odd times—but they're actually signs that everything is working just fine. Many of these primitive responses will disappear in a few months as your baby's body becomes more organized and he no longer needs them. Meanwhile, you can keep tabs on his development by performing these fun and fascinating little checkups.

What It Is: **Rooting reflex**

Check It Out: Stroke the side of your baby's cheek with your fingers or breast and he'll turn his head toward it, open wide, and begin to make sucking movements with his mouth. This most basic of survival instincts can be a big help to nursing moms trying to teach their babies to latch on.

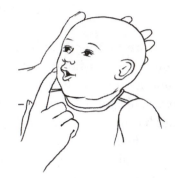

Figure 5.1a The rooting reflex.

When It Disappears: About four months.

What It Is: **Moro (or startle) reflex**

Check It Out: Sit your baby upright for a few seconds with your hands lightly gripping her underarms, and your fingers supporting her neck then suddenly but gently lower her back a bit. She'll throw out her arms and legs and extend her neck, as if to say, *Pick me up!* Loud, unexpected noises may elicit this reflex, and she may even cry when especially startled.

Figure 5.1b The moro reflex.

When It Disappears: Around two months.

What It Is: **Walking (or stepping) reflex**

Check It Out: Hold your baby under his armpits with his legs dangling, then lower him so his toes touch the floor. He should immediately place one foot in front of the other and start to "walk" in place.

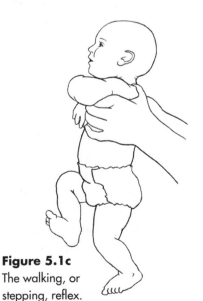

Figure 5.1c The walking, or stepping, reflex.

When It Disappears: Around two months. (Perhaps it's nature's way of telling him he's not *really* ready?)

What It Is:	**Grasp reflex**
Check It Out:	Stroke your baby's palm with

Figure 5.1d
The gripping reflex.

Stroke your baby's palm with your finger. She'll immediately grab your finger and hold on so tight you might have to pry her little fingers off. It's her way of holding you and trying to get as much skin-to-skin contact as she can. If you stroke the sole of her foot, she'll curl up her toes in the same way, too.

When It Disappears: Gradually, beginning in about the third month.

What It Is:	**Tonic neck (or fencing) reflex**
Check It Out:	When your baby is lying on his back, gently turn his head to the right. His right arm will shoot out in front of him and he'll raise his other arm above his head. He'll do the same thing on the opposite side if you turn his head to the left. Doctors have no idea what this reflex is for, but it does help your baby focus on the hand that's out in front of him.

When It Disappears: Between four and five months

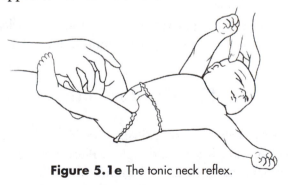

Figure 5.1e The tonic neck reflex.

What It Is:	**Righting reflex**
Check It Out:	Gently drop a blanket over your baby's face. She'll automatically shake her head from side to side and flail her arms until it falls off—it's your baby's way of protecting

herself. As she gets bigger, this reflex will evolve as necessary. For instance, when she's learning to sit up, she'll automatically stick her hand out to catch herself if she begins to topple over.

When It Disappears: Toward the end of the first year, as muscle tone and control improve.

What It Is: **Tongue-thrust reflex**

Check It Out: Touch a baby spoon to the tip of her tongue and watch her push it back out. This reflex prevents her from choking on foreign objects.

When It Disappears: Between four and six months, which is one reason why it doesn't usually make sense to attempt solid feeding any earlier—except in the rare instance of gastroesophageal reflux disease (GERD), when doctors may recommend slightly thickening infant formula with rice cereal in a bottle (see page 144).

What It Is: **Withdrawal reflex**

Check It Out: When your baby is sitting contentedly in his bouncy seat, suddenly bring your face close to his. He'll quickly turn his head away in another attempt at self-protection. He'll do the same if it's an object headed his way (you may have noticed it in the blanket test just above), to avoid a collision.

When It Disappears: Fortunately, it lasts a lifetime! Or at least until that cute chick from algebra zooms in for a kiss.

The Third Month

Finally, the Gerber baby has arrived! All those icky skin rashes have subsided and her skin now has a healthy glow. Plus, those scrawny plucked-chicken limbs have plumped up and rounded out, thanks to the endless hours of feedings you've been providing. Her legs and arms will have unfolded and her fingers have broken out from her once clenched fists, all making her appear much longer. Your baby will put her newfound limbs to work, flailing excitedly when she is interested in something. Her neck has also gotten strong enough to hold her head up at least at a forty-five-degree angle, and possibly a ninety-degree angle, for a minute or two when she is lying on her tummy.

Most babies are crying a lot less by this point (knock wood) because they've figured out other ways to express themselves. Your baby is also feeling more secure about you and her world. She's coming to realize that you will always feed her when she's hungry, and comfort her when she's upset, so she has less reason to get worked up. All this contentment may be making her confident and sociable now, too, so bring on the company. Many babies this age will smile and babble at all who hold them.

Your baby's vision has improved to the point that she can differentiate similar-looking colors, and the muscles have strengthened so she will follow a slowly moving object with her eyes. This skill, combined with her developing hand–eye coordination, will make it easier for her to play. She'll be able to bat at toys as they hang above her, or try to grasp a rattle as you shake it for her.

Doing (Tummy) Time

You've no doubt learned that there have been loads of improvements in babycare since your mom raised you (don't put it that way to her, of course!), but one that has a little bit of a downside is that today's infants spend a lot less time on their tummies than previous generations who slept that way. Less tummy time can translate into a lag in achieving certain skills, such as rolling over, sitting up, and crawling, because babies may not build up neck strength as quickly as they used to. There's also an increased risk of positional plagiocephaly, or flat-head syndrome, due to infants spending excessive amounts of time on their back. Fortunately, all these concerns can be easily remedied by giving your baby a daily tummy workout. Tummy time gives him a break from lying on his back, of course, but it will also strengthen his neck muscles so that he is able to move his head on his own. Here's how to make tummy time fun:

- When your baby is a newborn and can't support her head on her own, turn her head to the side so she can lie tummy-down across your chest to cuddle, or across your lap for burping. This is a good way to help her get used to being on her tummy while also avoiding burying that delicate little face and nose in your lap or chest.
- During the second month, begin to hold tummy-time sessions for about ten minutes, twice a day (carefully monitor her at all times

during these sessions). You might lay your baby on a colorful play mat to look down at, or in her crib with an interesting toy or crib mirror directly in front of her. Another good idea: Lay her upper torso on a nursing pillow with her arms over it. Slightly elevating her this way may be more comfortable for her and also gives her a new view.

- At about eight weeks, you can begin to play airplane: Lie on your back with your baby on your belly so that she's vertical, face-to-face with you, her toes on your lower abdomen. Then hold her arms up so she lifts her head; make faces or silly noises to keep her engaged and holding her head up.

MILESTONE MADNESS

Admit it: You get a tad nervous when your baby isn't the first kid on the block to accomplish something. You wouldn't be normal if you didn't. But as we've said before, there's a wide range of normal, and just to prove how wide that chasm can be, we've put together this handy chart you can consult when your baby is asleep while you're still awake (stressing out about how normal he is, no doubt). Typically you might see a "When to Worry" caveat added to this kind of time line, but we've got our own take on that: It's called "Worry Whenever." And we mean it. Talk to your pediatrician anytime, about anything. It's your prerogative as a mom. Even if you know in your heart you're being overly obsessive and just want some reassurance, you've got a right to ask. And any developmental expert will insist it's better to pursue a concern than wait and see—in the world of developmental delays, early intervention is always the best intervention. (Which also means that if your pediatrician strikes you as a bit too laid-back about something that's nagging at you, get another opinion, pronto.) That said, we did put together a list of possible warning signs to help you recognize some issues that you'll want to bring up with your pediatrician. (See "The Lowdown on Late Bloomers," page 194). Again, try not to let them freak you out—they don't always mean something terrible is amiss, just that there is a *possible* developmental delay and it's worth talking to your pediatrician about.

Milestone: **First smile**
Window: One to three months.
Average Age: Two months.

Milestone: **Head control (the ability to hold his head up without support)**
Window: Two to four months.
Average Age: Three months.

Milestone: **Rolling over (from front to back)**
Window: Two to six months.
Average Age: Four months.

Milestone: **Sitting up independently**
Window: Five to nine months.
Average Age: Six to seven months.

Milestone: **Pulling up to a standing position**
Window: Eight to twelve months.
Average Age: Nine months.

Milestone: **Crawling**
Window: Six to ten months (but some babies never crawl).
Average Age: Eight months.

Milestone: **Cruising (walking while holding on to furniture)**
Window: Eight to twelve months.
Average Age: Nine to ten months.

Milestone: **First tooth**
Window: Three months to eighteen months.
Average Age: Six months.

Milestone: **Walking**
Window: Nine to eighteen months.
Average Age: Thirteen months.

Milestone: **First words**
Window: Nine to fourteen months.
Average Age: Twelve months.

The Fourth Month

Your baby's development is rolling along, and he is, too. This may be the month that he discovers how to turn from his stomach to his back. Turning from back to stomach is harder (try it and you'll see what we mean), so that skill comes slightly later. Your baby's probably becoming much more wiggly in many ways, in fact, so you need to be extra vigilant about his safety, and never leave him unattended, even for a moment. If you've been placing his infant seat on a table to keep him at eye level, now's the time to break that habit, before he gets strong enough to flip it—and himself—over. On the bright side, by the end of this month he'll be heading out of the peak SIDS risk period (most SIDS deaths occur between two and four months of age), so you can relax a bit when he begins to roll around in his sleep despite your best efforts to keep him on his back.

Other physical accomplishments may include raising his body up on his arms; trying to "airplane," or balancing on his tummy; and grasping and

VOICE OF REASON

"I wish all parents could put away the time lines. When parents focus on achievements only, they lose the chance to enjoy—to revel in—their baby's process of development. It's like taking a train trip through a glorious countryside but only looking out the window when you're about to pass a station. This doesn't mean, of course, that parents shouldn't provide stimulating, enriching activities—we just needn't be so goal-oriented about it. Listen to music because it brings joy, because you can dance together, not because it might predict later math ability. Play with blocks because your baby likes them and don't worry about the outcome; if the pieces don't fit and the building crashes, he's still learning. We need to let our children make their way through the process of learning—with all its stops, starts, and detours—on their own terms."

—*Anita Sethi, PhD, clinical psychologist, research scientist at the Child and Family Policy Center at New York University, and* **Babytalk** *contributing editor* shaking a rattle if you first stroke his palm with it. He probably has achieved full head control now, and his back is getting stronger, too, so prop him up with some pillows behind him for a new perspective on his world. He can see colors well, and distant objects come into focus, so there's much more to look at, and he'll squeal with delight when he sees something he likes. In fact, babies this age often squeal just to entertain themselves, so expect things to get a bit noisier around your home (but squealing will sure be a lot more pleasant than all that crying in the early months!).

The Fifth Month

For a contented little guy, your baby may start acting like a fish out of water, flipping from back to front and rolling whenever there is room to move. His movements are more controlled by this stage, however, and your baby can actually direct his body to do as he says, which is often *Grab those earrings!* or *Swipe those eyeglasses!* He may also be able to transfer objects from one hand to the other when he gets hold of them. He's developing a self-concept, turning when you call his name or giggling when he sees the two of you together in a mirror. Don't be surprised if he performs little attention-getting tricks, either: He may cough or make other funny sounds like "raspberries" to get you to notice him, or wiggle around excitedly in his infant seat when you enter the room as if to say, *Hey, I'm over here!* Blowing raspberries has yet another benefit: They help your baby master moving his mouth, tongue, and lips together, which is a precursor to being able to form words.

As your baby hurtles toward the six-month-mark (remember when you were so sleep-deprived you were afraid you'd keel over before the next nursing session?), you will also notice that she is awake for increasing amounts of time during the day, typically taking a morning and afternoon nap that amount to about three to four hours in total. The majority of babies are doing what pediatricians define as sleeping through the night now, but that often means more like midnight to 5 or 6 AM, not exactly the solid eight hours you once enjoyed. Others may still be waking for a nighttime feeding, especially if you've managed to exclusively breastfeed this long, so don't think you're doing something wrong. Overall, your baby should be getting fourteen to fifteen hours of sleep a day, so if she doesn't get in eight to twelve hours at night, she may nap even more. All this activity really wears out a little body!

FIVE EASY WAYS TO GAUGE YOUR BABY'S GROWTH

Sure, the doctor is already charting your baby's growth, but you only get to see his version every two or three months. If you'd prefer an update more like, oh, every week, here are some do-it-yourself ideas:

1. Keep a journal of your baby's accomplishments and your feelings as you both navigate this action-packed year. Down the road you can look back at it and laugh at your new-mom anxiety or pat yourself on the back for your prescient observations.

2. Use a growth percentile chart to monitor your baby's height, weight, and head circumference. You can download them (and instructions on how to use them) from cdc.gov/growthcharts. Then when she doesn't hit a milestone right when you're expecting it, you can comfort yourself by reviewing the fact that she seems to be A-okay physically, which means she'll get to it in her own good time.

3. Point, click, scrapbook—online, that is. Kodakgallery.com, shutterfly.com, and snapfish.com all offer easy scrapbooks; you just upload your photos and drag faves into a premade book. Then— voilà—you'll have a beautiful keepsake of your baby's growth. You'll be the envy of the mommy-group members who can't see their way past the spit-up.

4. Go ahead and compare notes—within reason—with your friends, neighbors, and relatives (though you may further compromise your already limited ability to get a good night's sleep). You'll almost inevitably discover that all kids are different and mature early in some ways while lagging a bit in others.

5. Since you'll bring up any concerns to your pediatrician as necessary, try to just relax and enjoy your beautiful bambino.

The Sixth Month

Welcome to the honeymoon phase. By the end of this month your little one will be halfway through his first year, and he has you to thank for it.

And he will express his gratitude in many different ways, including adopting a happier demeanor (his tummy has finally gotten used to itself and ceased its constant barrage of gas rockets and spit-up) and granting everyone more than a few hours' sleep at night. You'll enjoy the regularity in the daily routine, because it finally gives you a sense of control over your life once again, and so will your baby, because it helps him feel secure and loved. Most babies will be in the early stages of solid foods—the AAP recommends introducing them between four and six months—which makes for lots of mealtime mayhem, as well as photo ops for that scrapbook! (See chapter 7 for advice on baby food and beyond.)

Your baby will probably be showing signs of attachment to certain toys and people, especially you and Dad. In general, babies this age are quite sociable, preferring interactions with people to objects. However, when left alone to amuse himself with a toy for a few minutes, he may do so happily, often using his mouth to aid in this exploration, now that he can get things to it.

Physical coordination is moving right along, too. Most babies this age can hold their head straight when pulled up by their arms into a sitting position. By the end of this month, he'll probably also be able to tripod—sit up for a few seconds with his arms extended on either side of him for balance—or even sit upright without support for a few minutes. Still, this is a skill that requires practice, so make sure he's always on a soft surface, and expect plenty of toppling over in the early weeks of learning to sit upright. Once he's mastered it, however, there's no turning back!

The Truth about Teething

Every parent looks forward to the clink of that first tooth on the silver spoon, but when and where it will appear is a bit of a mystery even to the experts. On average, the first tooth rears its pearly head between six and seven months of age, but it can show up as early as three months or as late as the first birthday. Complicating the situation is lots of conflicting evidence about whether the behaviors traditionally considered signs of teething—drooling, chewing on fingers or toys, crankiness, night awakenings—have any connection to teething at all. Most pediatricians tend to pooh-pooh them, and most seasoned mothers insist they're true. Which leaves the decision about whether to take them seriously or not pretty much up to you. Consider that babies drool because they often just don't know what to do with the spit rolling around in their mouths, for instance, and that just about anything can make a baby cranky. Diarrhea, fever, and coughing are also symptoms that Grandma might attribute to a pending eruption, whereas your doctor would probably insist a baby who's feeling or acting this way is just plain sick. While there doesn't seem to be any reliable medical link, bear in mind that they don't call it cutting a tooth for nothing. What you can count on: Teething patterns tend to be hereditary, so knowing when you and your partner began to sprout yours can be a reliable clue. Ditto for siblings: Older brothers and sisters who were late teethers may well set the family trend.

Once baby teeth begin to make their appearance, they usually arrive in predictable fashion. The two lower central incisors are most likely to appear first, followed by the four upper central and lateral incisors, the two lower lateral incisors, the first four ("one-year") molars, the four pointed canines, and finally the second four ("two-year") molars. Still, there can be variations to this pattern, and that's absolutely no big deal. What matters is that by his second birthday, your baby should be sporting about sixteen pearly whites—and that's practically a guarantee.

As usual, all babies react differently to the arrival of their chompers. Some babies are irritable and uncomfortable with every pending breakthrough, while others take no notice and go about their daily life quite happily. Most typically, discomfort is the worst with the first tooth or teeth because the sensation is new to your baby; the rest aren't as big a deal until the molars arrive (their very size may make them more of a production). If your baby seems to be bothered by teething (waking more at night, gnawing on his fingers, generally crankier than usual), try these comforts:

- Rub his gums with your (clean) finger.
- Give him a chilled teething ring to chew on.
- Offer a bottle or sippy cup of chilled water to help numb sore gums, or a frozen ice pop (for an older baby).
- Consider a topical teething gel, which can provide temporary pain relief, or a dose of infant acetaminophen or ibuprofen (the latter is only for babies over six months) if your baby can't seem to sleep at night because of teething pain.
- Two traditional teething remedies to be wary of: rubbing an alcoholic beverage on your baby's gums, which is downright dangerous, and the giving of hard frozen foods like waffles or bagels, which may break apart and create a choking hazard.

As for dental care, most experts recommend cleaning an infant's gum with gauze after feedings to prevent plaque buildup, and beginning brushing (with a fluoride-free toothpaste or none at all) as soon as the first tooth has arrived. Reality check: You're going to be way too busy to do the gauze thing when your baby is eating every few hours! Do it when you can get to it and skip the guilt trip. You can get more serious when there are some real teeth there to brush. At that point, you'll just need a soft-bristle, baby-size toothbrush. Toothpaste is not recommended until after age two, because fluoride should never be swallowed (ingesting too much is actually dangerous), and children younger than two don't usually understand how to spit it out. There are some fluoride-free "toddler" toothpastes available, but we can't see bothering at this early stage since it's not actually necessary—your life is complicated enough!

The Seventh Month

With the ability to sit up comes the desire to move (darn that free will!). It won't be long before your baby figures out the best way to get from point A to point B, whether it's rocking, rolling, or scooting on her bottom. So don't be surprised if you put her down on a play mat and turn around a few minutes later only to find she's halfway across the room. Some babies may even be crawling by the end of this month. If you haven't begun to childproof your house, let this gentle reminder get you started—before you know it, your baby will suddenly have access to all kinds of dangers such as electrical outlets, cleaning products, and choking hazards. Turn to chapter 8, "Babyproofing and Beyond," for a thorough, room-by-room guide to making your home as safe as possible.

This is a key month for the development of fine-motor skills as well. In contrast with younger babies, who can only hold objects with their palms (known as the palmar grasp), your baby will begin to start holding objects with her fingers. She may touch them before she picks them up, and will show an increasing interest in stroking and patting. If your baby drinks from a bottle, she may be able to hold it by herself now—though that doesn't necessarily mean she'll want to! She may love being held and yes, "babied" by you.

In keeping with that, you may also notice that your previously sociable guy or gal is becoming a bit wary—or maybe even downright panicked—at the sight of other people, from the grandma he knows so well to the unfamiliar faces cooing at him in his stroller. This stranger anxiety is actually a bit of a backward compliment: Your baby has become so attached that he prefers you to everyone else and is exercising his capacity to differentiate you from others. Some babies put up a big fuss; others are less bothered by it (but don't worry—they're still just as attached!). Either way, you can expect your baby's stranger anxiety to persist for three to five months. While he's in the throes of it, you can reassure him by giving him time to warm up to others. If someone comes to visit, for example, don't thrust your baby into the visitor's arms. Hold him snugly on your lap while you chat and demonstrate that you are comfortable with the "stranger" first. Then wait for him to make the first overture. You can nudge him along by, say, responding happily when your vistor offers him a toy. Expect your baby to have an easier time meeting someone in his own home, because he feels more secure when things are familiar. And your behavior also comes into play: If you act surprised or nervous or taken aback, he'll pick on those feelings and echo your discomfort.

Be Wary of Walkers

For years, safety experts and pediatricians have been calling for a ban on baby walkers, entertaining contraptions that consist of a seat on a wheeled base that allow not-yet-mobile infants to scoot around the house, and often down staircases or up to hot stoves, resulting in way too many injuries. In response to a potential ban—and no doubt a bad reputation—walker manufacturers voluntarily developed new safety standards, literally putting brakes on these mini vehicles and widening the base to keep them from fitting through doorways. (This means you should definitely not buy an older model from a garage sale or use a hand-me-down from a friend or relative unless you know for sure it was made in the last few years.) Now a new study has demonstrated that walker injuries have in fact been greatly reduced—67 percent fewer since the early 1990s—but the pediatric safety researchers who conducted the study still adamantly believe parents should avoid walkers. Some important caveats to consider about walkers:

- The new design may not be the only factor contributing to the injury decline: A greater awareness of injury may have resulted in less use as well.
- Infants in the redesigned walkers can still reach hot stoves or other dangerous objects, or pull something over on themselves.

- Research shows that the average age of walker use is between eight and nine months, which is a bad time for your baby to be bearing so much weight on his legs. After all, if his legs were strong enough to support his body, he'd be walking instead.
- Babies lean forward in an abnormal position in the walker, and tend to tiptoe, both of which can also hamper physical development.

All that said, there are two similar types of gear that your baby can safely enjoy. The first is the stationary exerciser. This item looks like a walker but has no wheels; instead, a saucer-like base wobbles and rocks, and the seat spins and bounces, so that your baby can have active fun without actually being mobile. The second is often also termed a walker, but it has no seat to contain the child. These push toys with wheels are for babies with the leg strength to cruise or who are just starting to walk on their own, typically about nine months and up. By standing behind and pushing the toy, a baby can have fun while acquiring his "sea legs," so to speak. A baby at this stage is already pretty mobile and going to get around with or without the toy, so constant supervision is the name of the game.

The Eighth Month

This could be the month your little one really takes off—many babies discover they can get around on all fours about now. The act of crawling is actually a challenging maneuver to pull off. Your baby has to first dig his knees into the floor surface and use them to push off, while at the same time pulling himself forward by alternately rotating his arms—just think of the coordination involved, not to mention how hard his muscles are working! It's no wonder many babies start to slim down—and sleep better—at this stage (if only we could, too!). Because a baby's arm muscles are now generally better developed than his leg muscles, it's not unusual to see a child crawl backward first, then learn to go forward. You'll know your baby is getting close to crawling if you see him rocking on all fours—it's like he's contemplating going full steam ahead, but can't figure out which body part to move first. This activity can go on for a few weeks, in fact, before your baby actually puts it all together. Meanwhile, you can encourage him by placing a favorite toy just beyond his reach for motivation. One of our babies was so intrigued with a singing, crawling, wing-flapping butterfly that she'd haul her whole body forward, mustering all the arm strength she could to get to it. The end result: She crawled to reach the object of her desire.

Another strategy: When you see your little guy rocking on all fours as if he's trying to get going, hide behind a chair or table slightly ahead of him, then pop out and say "Peekaboo!" Repeat this game a few times; chances are he'll be so delighted, he'll suddenly shoot over to find you without thinking first. Once your baby begins to crawl, you can help him become more proficient and have fun at it by creating little obstacle courses with throw pillows, sofa cushions, boxes, and other objects to crawl around or over—just be sure to keep a constant eye on him so he doesn't get trapped or scared. Really proficient crawlers will go from crawling to sitting to crawling again, almost effortlessly. They also move their arms and legs in an alternating style—when the left arm is forward, so is the right leg, and vice versa, which helps them gain speed. (If your baby isn't yet crawling at the end of this month, there's no need to panic. See "Not Crawling? No Problem" on page 185.)

Crawling is just one of the many physical feats ahead: In the next few weeks, your baby may well figure out how to pull himself up to a sitting position from lying down, and from there pull to a standing position while holding on to a piece of furniture. This can become quite a challenge at bedtime for a few days as he excitedly practices his new skill: As soon as you tuck him in, he'll grab the crib rails and pop back up to his feet like a jack-in-the-box. It's adorable at first, but there is a catch—isn't there always? Once he's up, he might not figure out how to get back down, and thus he can't go to sleep. After a dozen or so times of laying your baby down and watching him pop back up, you won't know whether to laugh or cry. But rest assured, this stage will pass quickly, like all the rest.

As your baby begins to explore in a big way, you may find that he's less content when confined: Gear such as stationary exercisers or play yards or even just sitting in the high chair gets annoying for a guy who knows he could get across the room to those pretty objets d'art on the coffee table . . . if only he were free! Consider ways to make larger areas safe enough for him to explore—using safety gates to block off certain rooms, for instance, and clearing breakables from his path.

In addition to her multiplying motor skills, your baby has also made an impressive cognitive leap by now: She's come to understand object permanence—that is, something still exists when it's out of her sight. This skill ushers in new ways to have fun—playing endless games of peekaboo, for instance, or delighting in a jack-in-the-box.

Your little one's verbal skills are increasing, too. Her coos turn to babbles as she begins to combine vowels and consonants, making sounds like *ga-ga-ga* and *ba-ba-ba*. She'll also have endless fun making raspberries, a wet razzing sound with her lips, just as you will when you repeat them back to her. Good times.

Hands-On Advice

With all the physical acrobatics hogging the stage right now, you may not notice a significant improvement in your baby's fine-motor skills—the ability to use her hands and fingers with greater dexterity. At six months of age, most babies can grip a small toy, rattle, or sippy cup with what's known as a mitten grasp (fingers as one, thumb at the side). But around the eighth or ninth month, they progress to a tweezer-like pincer grip that allows them to pick up much tinier objects with their index fingers and thumbs. Here are some fun ways to help your baby get a grip:

> **Read in 3-D.** Purchase an activity book with textures and shapes your baby can finger.
>
> **Be a builder.** Creating towers of any shape and size exercises big and little motor skills, and they're always a blast to knock down.
>
> **Play ball.** Gather a big (unbreakable) bowl and a collection of smaller balls (tennis balls will work), and help your baby practice dropping the balls into the bowl—it'll boost his hand-eye coordination and maybe pique his interest in the NBA.
>
> **Bring on the finger foods.** The high chair tray is the perfect surface for learning to scoop, and dining on finger foods means your little gripper gets a treat when she succeeds. (Of course, you will also be finding Cheerios in the oddest places for the next two years.)

The Ninth Month

Your baby is getting caught up in a mental and emotional tug-of-war: his increasing desire for independence versus his need for security, which he derives from your presence in a big way. The ultimate result is a strong emotion that experts call separation anxiety. Your baby literally becomes fearful of losing you, and he may begin to express major dismay if you so much as leave the room. Babies experience these feelings in different degrees, but most show some signs of it beginning about now and lasting off and on up until eighteen months of age. (Of course, some more reserved and shy personality types can remain clingy for years to come!)

Soon enough your baby will come to realize that when you leave him, be it for minutes or hours, you always do come back, but before that you may both have to endure a lot of wailing. If you're just out of sight doing chores or taking a quick bathroom break, leave the door open and talk to him from down the hall so he can at least hear your voice (believe us, your privacy left the building nine months ago). When you go out for longer periods, just try to be as reassuring as you can: "I'll be back in a little while; Nana is going to feed you your favorite dinner while I'm gone," or "I'm going to work now but I'll call and talk to you on the phone later this morning." One caveat about keeping in touch, however: Some babies may get upset all over again because hearing your voice reminds them that you're missing! If yours reacts in this way, you're better off just checking in with your caregiver instead. If hearing your voice is helpful to your baby, you can take advantage of technology in other ways: Make an audiotape of yourself reading stories that a caregiver can play, or a video of the two of you having fun that can be viewed in your absence. (Again, caveat: One of us here at *Babytalk* saw this strategy backfire when her baby wailed inconsolably at the sight of her two-dimensional mom.)

The most important thing you can do at this stage, however, is always say "good-bye" to your baby. It may seem easier to sneak out, but you will only make his anxiety worse. Be firm about going, reassuring that you'll be back, then hightail it out of there. The more drawn out you make your departure, the more worked up he's likely to get. And know that the vast majority of babies are just fine within a few minutes of a parent's leave-taking.

In contrast with all this angst when you make an escape, your baby may try to show you who's boss when you're around. Mealtime is one area where she may try to stake out her independence. Your child has probably begun to show distinct preferences for certain foods and flavors, and now she may also start to try to grab the spoon from your hands to feed herself. She may want to use her fingers to get the food to her mouth, and may also test gravity by flipping her bowl over or dropping things from her high chair. It only gets messier from here on out. Try to be patient and let her practice her self-feeding skills as much as you can tolerate—she may refuse to eat otherwise!

Not Crawling? No Problem

It's one of those skills that delight parents (until they realize how much trouble their baby can now get into because of it), but most experts feel crawling has little importance on the development scale. Some babies never crawl at all, and yet are soon able to pull up, cruise, and walk as well as their peers. And again, others concoct their own odd leapfrog, or belly- or bottom-scooting action, or crab-walk instead. There has been some concern in recent years that because of back sleeping and the resulting lack of tummy time, babies are not developing some of the muscle strength they used to have by this age, and thus are crawling less and later (along with rolling over and sitting up later, as we noted earlier in this chapter). In fact, more and more experts believe that crawling may be more critical than once thought. Crawling strengthens the hands, wrists and elbows since babies must bear their weight. But again, the majority of these babies still go on to reach their locomotion milestones in the end whether they crawl or not. In fact, anthropological studies of babies in other cultures who are worn all day in carriers and slings and often skip crawling as a result have demonstrated that these children are also timely in achieving their other gross-motor skills.

Thus, most experts still feel there's no need to sweat it if your baby skips crawling, and there is usually no mention of crawling on developmental checklists. But do all you can to give your tot the chance to move around. What *is* important is that your baby is interested in getting around some-how—and you're providing the opportunity for him to do so in a safe environment. Keeping him strapped in a high chair seat or confined to a stationary exerciser may be more convenient, but it can hamper your child's development if he spends too much of his day that way. Most older babies would protest at such confinement, but laid-back types might be content to not explore if you don't give them a chance. If your baby seems to be missing other milestones along with not crawling, bring it up with your pediatrician. But if he can sit independently, pull himself up, and bear weight on his legs, there's probably nothing physically wrong that's keeping your baby from doing a traditional crawl. On the upside, you'll probably have fewer rug-burned and scraped-up knees to contend with than other moms.

The Tenth Month

This month, playing takes on some serious importance. It was always a key to her learning, of course, but you'll notice that your baby doesn't just want to know what colorful, eye-catching toys are, but what they can do as well. He'll bang two blocks together, for example, or pound on a pot with a spoon. Nesting and stacking is fun, too, as he learns to take things in and out. You can practically see the wheels turning in your little mechanical engineer's brain as he experiments through play. It's fun to watch him when he's absorbed, but don't just sit on the sidelines—he's ready to learn a lot from social interaction, too. Clapping games and finger plays like "The Itsy Bitsy Spider" teach hand-eye coordination, for instance. "Pop Goes the Weasel" and "This Little Piggy" help promote vocabulary skills and drive home concepts such as anticipation and delayed gratification—something we're sure you have already learned.

Why crawl when you can walk? That's what your ten-month-old might say as she's pulling her wobbly body up to the coffee table for the umpteenth time. You can't blame her. She's had months and months of watching you glide effortlessly from one room to another, and now she wants a taste of the good life. Before walking, however, she may first begin to cruise, or walk while holding on to things. Watch carefully and you'll notice this skill evolve in baby steps, so to speak. First, your youngster will hold on to a piece of furniture and inch along while she slides her feet. Then she'll progress to picking up her feet and moving hand-over-hand. The final step before walking comes when she learns how to bridge gaps between pieces of furniture, going from, say, the coffee table to the sofa when they are only a few inches apart and she can grab one while still holding on to the other. She may even stand briefly by herself as she steps from one piece of furniture to another. The more confident she becomes in this skill, the less she will rely on her hands and the furniture for support. For some babies, walking is right around the corner, but others cruise for what seems like months before letting go. You can encourage your baby by positioning yourself at her level with your hands outstretched and saying, "Come to Mama." Your baby may giddily dive for you—then again, she may just give you one of those *Are you out of your mind?* looks and go back to her business.

And speaking of copping a 'tude, your little bundle of independence

VOICE OF REASON

"*No* is a power-packed word, quick on the lips, easy to say. Your child will hear you use this word often, and you will hear it from your child as well. It's necessary for a parent to say no to a child so the child can later say no to himself. But you need to strike a balance: If you rarely say no to your child, the few times that you do he'll disintegrate because he's not used to being frustrated. If his whole day is full of nos, he'll come to believe the world is a negative place. The real world will always be full of yesses and nos. When no is necessary, you can make it less dictatorial and more respectful by personalizing it with your child's name: 'That's not for Ashton . . .'"

—Babytalk *contributing editor William Sears MD, pediatrician, co-author of many books on parenting including* The Discipline Book, *and a father of eight.*

will discover the power of *no*. Where did she learn such a potent word? From you, of course. As your baby's mobility allows her to have frequent brushes with danger, you may have found yourself blurting "No!" more often than you ask "What day is it again?" To scale back the negative lessons, try to train yourself to say constructive things. It's not easy, but it's worth trying. For example, try this on for size: "You'll get a boo-boo if you touch that electrical outlet!" or "That's not yummy. That's a sock." Even if it seems mostly futile, she'll begin to get the idea. Your baby is also developing enough of a long-term memory to at least start to accept that certain areas or activities are off limits to her (though that doesn't mean she won't try to approach them now and then!).

Dare to Discipline

Yep, you heard us correctly: It's time to start thinking about disciplining that precious little angel. Not so much because he's purposely being naughty, but because his new skills make him a danger to himself. In fact, childproofing is one of the first forms of discipline: You're taking things away from him that he can't have, he just doesn't realize it yet. Starting to teach him the meaning of the word *no* is the next step, albeit a long, laborious one. You're going to have to say no about a gazillion-plus times before it's going to sink in, and by then he'll have figured out that it's fun to defy you anyway! Meanwhile, though your efforts will mostly seem fruitless, they will accomplish a few things, including sending your almost toddler the message that you disapprove of certain things, even if he's not exactly sure why. Here are a few gentle guidelines to get you started on the lifelong path of teaching right and wrong:

Limit your nos to as few as possible. At this stage, you could probably say no in every other sentence. The need to do so is a natural by-product of your baby's budding curiosity and blatant lack of common sense. One dad we know refers to toddlers (fondly, of course) as "legs with no brains." But constantly saying no is demoralizing—your baby will begin to think he can't do anything right—and the word will lose its effectiveness because he'll simply start to tune it out. That's why thoroughly childproofing (see chapter 8) is a smart move: Because your baby's environment will be safer, you will need to say no less often, and can limit it to the times when he's going to hurt himself, someone else, or do some real damage to your decor (get used to that).

Watch your language. We know you're not cursing at your baby, of course (at least out loud), but there is a politically correct language to discipline that has evolved for the better over the past two generations. And being new at this, you may not realize that *bad* and *punishment* are now akin to four-letter words in many parenting circles. While an odd slipup isn't going to harm your child emotionally for life, you do want to try to choose your words carefully. Many of us grew up hearing comments like "Why were you a bad girl for Grandma?" or "He's a bad kid—I don't want you playing with him." *Bad* is an easy description to fall back on, but it tells your child there's something inherently wrong with him when in fact it was his behavior that was "bad." It's better to say, "That was a dangerous thing to do," or "I like it when you do X instead of Y." The former explains what the problem is ("you'll get hurt"), and the latter gives your child an alternative that's preferable. Punishment is also the wrong approach because it's making your child pay for a misdeed that he probably doesn't even realize he did yet. On the other hand, discipline is about teaching the right things; it's got the potential to be a positive rather then negative experience when handled appropriately. Of course all this sounds like so much BS when you're dealing with a barely verbal baby, but the thing is, you'll get in the habit of doing discipline correctly from the get-go, and your baby will be learning from your actions and tone and expressions, even if she doesn't fully comprehend what you're trying to tell her.

Practice distraction as often as possible. Sometimes the best form of discipline is to simply swoop in when you see your baby heading for a no-no, gently turning her little body and attention in another direction. You can also avoid plenty of tantrums with this strategy, because your child will quickly forget just what it was she couldn't have when tempted by another fun choice.

Give him choices and therefore some control over the situation. Is he headed for the wall, crayon in hand? Instead of the usual "No, no, no!" try: "We can't color there, honey, but would you like to try this new Barney coloring book, or go outside with this bucket of sidewalk chalk?"

Don't expect too much. Much of the time, your child is going to turn around and try to do it again, whatever "it" happens to be. This will go on for quite some time. But he really is learning. Really. So keep at it.

THE TALKING TIME LINE

Although your baby won't say much during her first year of life (at least not in words you understand), her language skills begin to grow the minute she's born. Here's how the process unfolds.

Age: **Birth to three months**
What Your Baby Does: Your little sweetie is learning about voices by listening to yours. The coos and gurgles that emerge at the end of this period are her first attempts at imitating the sounds you make.
How to Help: Sing and talk to your baby often, but also keep other distracting background noises (the TV, radio) to a minimum so she can hear and focus on the sounds she's working on.

Age: **Three to six months**
What Your Baby Does: Your child is beginning to notice how people converse with each other, and wants to join in on the dialogue.

(continued on next page)

How to Help: When you talk to him, pause after saying something ("Would you like to play with this pretty red rattle?") so he has a chance to respond in his own language. If he tries to make the same sound as you, repeat the word for him.

Age: **Six to nine months**
What Your Baby Does: The vocalizations your baby makes are beginning to sound more like words now—*baba* and *dada*, for instance. She'll also express emotion in response to the tone of your voice, smiling if you are talking happily, showing distress if you are yelling or expressing anger.
How to Help: Talk her through her days: "Where did the puppy go? Oh, look, here's the puppy on the sofa," labeling and showing her what you're referring to as much as possible. Use a mirror to show her who she is: "Who's that little girl? It's Rachel!"

Age: **Nine to twelve months**
What Your Baby Does: His receptive language skills are exploding now; that is, he knows what you're referring to even though he can't repeat the words himself. He may scamper to the high chair if you say it's time to eat, or look around for a toy when you ask him where a favorite plaything is.
How to Help: Begin to label body parts ("nose," "eyes," "tummy," "toes"), spend more time reading books together and talking about the pictures, and teach interactions such as waving bye-bye and blowing kisses.

Age: **Twelve to fifteen months**
What Your Baby Does: Here come the words. Though the number an individual baby can say varies greatly at this stage—from one or two to a dozen or more—you can expect your child's spoken vocabulary to pick up speed during this period. Even when he can't say something, he knows how to tell you what he wants through gestures.
How to Help: Continue to label for your child, but also use more simple sentences so he can hear how to string words together. Respond enthusiastically at each new word development or attempt at communication.

The Eleventh Month

Up until this month, your little one has probably been making all kinds of chattering sounds, including *da-da* and *ma-ma*. But now there's a difference—she really is referring to the two of you! Don't expect to get top billing, though. She'll probably say *da-da* first, simply because the hard *d*-sound is easier to pronounce—some thanks we moms get after all we've been through.

This is just the beginning of what may be a burst of language over the next six months. Speak slowly and carefully to your baby, labeling everything in her world ("ball," "doggie," "toes") for her. Even though she probably won't yet repeat most of these words back to you, she is acquiring them in the form of receptive language (she understands the words you are using).

Don't be surprised if your baby also seems to come to you more often now for a hug or reassurance. Separation anxiety is at its peak because she's become so attached to you, and her quest for independence is scaring her a bit. Even during the course of her daily play, your baby will likely come back for brief refueling in the form of a hug or a touch or just to hear your voice. Peekaboo, while fun for all babies, is an especially good game for those children going though separation anxiety. It literally allows your baby to "practice" your disappearance for a few seconds at a time. Offer all the hugs and kisses you can to help her feel secure, but when you need to go somewhere, don't get caught up in a guilt trip. Stay firm in your need to leave and make sure your baby has some warm-up time with her babysitter if necessary. She'll be fine once you're out the door.

The Twelfth Month

The one-year mark is around the corner, and as far as your baby is concerned there's no looking back. Perhaps that's because she is busy trying to move forward using some combination of standing, walking, and stepping, with or without holding on. While some babies are adept solo walkers at this point, a great many others don't accomplish this milestone until thirteen or fourteen months, and some are as late as seventeen or eighteen. What is it that makes one baby want to get up and go and another content to stay put awhile longer? It's most likely a combination of physics and personality. There's a prevailing belief that bigger babies tend to walk sooner, but in fact, their very weight can keep them sedentary because it's harder for them to balance it all. Lean babies may actually be more agile. And a baby with a laid-back personality may be more cautious about letting go of whatever she's holding on to, while an adventurous baby takes off without even thinking about it. Rest assured that your baby will get there in her own good time. If you're eager, be sure to provide your baby with plenty of room and time to practice. Keeping her strapped in a high chair or corralled in a playpen, albeit safer, prevents her from building muscle strength and gaining confidence. And again, the right contraption at the right time, such as a toy your child can push while walking behind it, can do the trick. Go online to one of the baby retail sites and read the parents' reviews to see what might be the most intriguing for your reluctant toddler.

What happens after a baby takes his first step varies, too—some keep at it until they're experts practically overnight, while others decide it's not for them and don't bother to take another step for a month. Most are somewhere in between, of course, toddling around fairly confidently in about a week or two. Still, expect your baby to have a funny gait at first. His belly and backside will stick out, his legs will be bowed, his feet flat and plump, and his toes will turn in or out (some babies also walk on their tiptoes at first). This posture creates a wider base, and gives your baby extra stability as he learns to balance himself on two feet. Usually by about eighteen months of age all these quirks disappear, however, and your child will be strolling—or more likely running—full steam ahead. In the meantime, you can expect a fair amount of falling down, so stay close by your baby, and try to keep him away from hard surfaces as much as possible. That's not to say you shouldn't let him walk around outside, but a grassy yard is better than a concrete sidewalk, for obvious reasons. Keeping his legs covered in long pants is also a good idea; this way, when he does fall, he'll be less likely to tear up those tender knees.

If your baby seems uninterested in graduating to toddlerhood, it may well be that he's focusing on another type of milestone instead. He may be enjoying cognitive tasks like building and stacking and sorting, or concentrating on his verbal skills (a typical twelve-month-old may only say one or two words, or as many as twenty). It's not uncommon for babies to take a break in one area of development for a few weeks as they direct their energies to a different one. Some babies even regress a bit before a big developmental leap—wanting you to hold his baby bottle again even though he's been doing it by himself for a while, perhaps, or insisting on being rocked back to sleep in the middle of the night when you'd practically forgotten what that phase was like. Then after a few days or a week of being extra babyish, you suddenly have a toddler doing the Frankenstein walk everywhere! Or a Chatty Cathy who can't stop talking even in her sleep. That's when you realize the true meaning of the expression *One step forward, two steps back.* Your baby is experiencing the push–pull of wanting to be big, but also feeling safe being small.

Nevertheless, his burgeoning desire for independence will only increase as his first birthday draws closer. Your baby will be more likely to get mad when you tell him no or thwart his attempts at climbing or other risky behavior. He's got his own agenda, and while full-blown temper tantrums aren't quite the norm yet, he will increasingly want his own way. Lucky for you, distraction ("Hey, let's play with the train set now!") still works well when you need to protect him from his ambitions.

A fun new development you'll probably notice now is your baby's desire to imitate you. He'll attempt to comb his own hair (perhaps even insist on it!), position his diaper between his legs, or hold the receiver of his toy telephone up to his ear and "talk" into it. This is just the beginning of more and more real-life activities your tot will attempt—after all, he's growing up!

First Shoes: A Shopping Guide

Grandma has probably been criticizing you roundly for letting your baby go barefoot, but you've been doing the right thing for a prewalker (not to mention how annoying it is to keep up with all those socks that slide off every time you look the other way). The recommendation these days is to skip the footwear until your child is actually walking on those tender soles. He can better feel the ground and learn to balance without a layer of rubber separating his feet from the earth. (You need only resort to socks when warmth is an issue.) When the time comes to outfit those little tootsies, the recommendations have also changed. Forget those stiff white starter shoes that you probably wore and are now gold-plated on a plaque at you-know-whose. Here's what to look for in the shoe store instead:

A proper fit. Though it's tempting to allow for room to grow, novice walkers have enough challenges without slipping out of their shoes. The back of the shoe should be snug but comfortable. If his heel slides out easily, the shoe is too big; if the shoe pinches the heel, it's too small. The longest toe should be a thumb's width (roughly half an inch) from the tip of the shoe.

Careful measuring. Have the salesperson measure both feet. Most of us, babies included, have feet as much as half a size different, and you always want to buy shoes to fit the larger foot.

Flexibility. Shoes made entirely of rubber or plastic tend to be stiff and cause excessive sweating. Choose cloth, canvas, or leather, which stretch and allow a shoe to bend.

A boxy shape. Here's one tradition that's still around. The dimensions of the shoe should approximate the shape of your baby's foot, so choose square or oval shapes.

High style. High-top sneakers and soft leather ankle boots will stay on better than low-cut styles. But avoid such trendy styles as pointed cowboy boots, which can pinch tiny toes and restrict growth, or clogs, which look cute but fall off easily.

Rough and tough soles. Grooved rubber soles prevent a wobbly toddler from slipping. Try roughing up the soles of slick-bottomed shoes with sandpaper for added traction.

The Lowdown on Late Bloomers

It could be anything from a little-bit-limp muscle tone to a shy personality that keeps your kiddo sitting tight instead of crawling. Maybe your little one isn't talking because he's got older siblings conveying his needs ("Hey, Mom, Jack's diaper stinks!"). And it's possible that he's not outgoing with your in-laws because he doesn't really like them, either. Just kidding—but you get the idea: It's a unique combination of factors that motivates babies to reach milestones on time—or not. Usually there's no reason to worry, but to be on the safe side, here's a list of red flags you probably should bring up at your next doctor visit.

The Four-Month Mark

At the end of this newborn era, most babies are much more sociable and responsive than when they first crossed your home's threshold. Mention it at her four-month checkup if your baby is still not:

- Responding to loud sounds.
- Smiling at not just family members but other people she encounters as well.

- Reaching and grasping toys.
- Following objects with her eyes.
- Supporting her head on her own.
- Babbling.

The Eight-Month Mark

Between his four-month birthday and the end of the seventh month, your baby will change dramatically. He'll start out quietly sociable but still unable to move much. The next thing you know he'll be fully upright, boisterous, and able to get across the room in creative ways. Mention it to the doctor if by his eight-month-birthday:

- He still seems to have some of those quirky newborn movements like the Moro or tonic-neck reflex.
- His muscle tone doesn't seem right—it's either too stiff or too floppy—and he can't seem to bear weight on his legs (when you hold him in a standing position with his feet on the floor) or hold his head steady when you pull his body up by the arms to a sitting position.
- He's not cuddly or affectionate with the people who care for him, and doesn't show interest in being around people in general.
- Something seems amiss with his eyes: They consistently cross, turn in or out, or tear a lot, or he can't seem to follow an object with his eyes when you move it in front of his face.
- He does not turn to locate or otherwise respond to sounds.
- He doesn't actively reach for objects and still can't get them to his mouth (typically, everything is going into the mouth by the end of this stage).
- He hasn't reached physical milestones like rolling over or sitting up at the end of this period.
- He still has a lot of difficulty sleeping for any length of time at night.
- He continues to have colic or is frequently inconsolable.
- He does not try to attract your attention through actions or sounds.

The Twelve-Month Mark

Good-bye baby, hello toddler—maybe. By her first birthday, your baby may seem like a little boy or girl. Then again, she may still not have mastered many big-kid skills, as development continues to vary widely. You'll want to talk to your baby's doctor if:

- She isn't attempting much in the way of words. The typical just-turned-one-year-old may say two or three words recognizable only to Mom and Dad, or have a vocabulary of two dozen. But she should at least be babbling a lot.
- She isn't yet getting around efficiently, be it by crawling or cruising or walking.
- She shows no interest in interactive games like peekaboo or pat-a-cake, and doesn't search for objects that are hidden while she watches.
- She isn't pointing to objects or pictures or using gestures like waving or shaking her head no.

"WHAT NOBODY TOLD ME ABOUT MILESTONES"

"I worried that my son was never going to crawl. He finally started to do a crab-walk at eight months, but then was walking by nine and a half months. Then I wanted him to go back to not being mobile because it was easier and I missed my little baby!"

—*Brandy, Centerville, Maryland*

"With my daughter I was very nervous about milestones. She was born at twenty-eight weeks and even though I was told to expect her to be about three months behind, I wasn't prepared for it. I was mostly concerned about her gross-motor skills. She didn't sit up by herself until almost nine months old, but once she did that, she caught up to her full-term peers and then some!"   —*Lisa, Randolph, New Jersey*

"I had a preemie; my son was born seven weeks early. I always worried about him reaching milestones on time, even though his doctor told me some delays were to be expected. He started talking at six months and was always ahead of where he was supposed to be verbally, but physically he was consistently behind. He rolled over late, crawled late, didn't walk until he was sixteen months old. Now I see that he is not all that different from other kids, he has just always been cautious. He took his time learning these daunting skills, but when he did learn them, he mastered them right away. I should have worried about more important things, like what to cook for dinner!"   —*Kassandra, Austin, Texas*

"My daughter was very slow about her physical milestones. She didn't roll over until months after [the books I read said] she should have and didn't crawl until a week before her first birthday. She didn't get her two bottom teeth until eight months, and then didn't get any more until after she was one. Still, I knew she was very smart because she did everything verbal early. Friends with kids the same age would marvel at her language ability but I would be frustrated because she wasn't moving as well as their kids. But eventually she became as active as everyone else!"   —*Jennifer, Troy, Michigan*

"My daughter didn't cut her first tooth until she was thirteen months old. After a while of constantly thinking that whenever she was cranky she must be teething, I just gave up and stopped checking for teeth completely. I was really surprised when they did finally show up. I know milestones are exciting and moms look forward to them, but I think as a whole we obsess way too much."
                                                —*Lindsey, Springfield, Missouri*

"We were nervous that our baby boy was not going to reach his milestones on time. He was five weeks early, needed surgery when he was only twelve hours old, and had such severe reflux he was on three medications and required lots of sitting upright in his chair. We sure were surprised when he rolled over at only three months—before his perfectly healthy twin sister!"   —*Erin, Batavia, New York*

"I was worrying about milestones when my baby was still hibernating in my womb. I was worse still when he was born. He was my first, so I had no inkling when all these things were supposed to happen. As it turns out, my son did everything early and continues to shock everyone. Now all I have to worry about is how much sooner he'll be telling me that he knows everything and I don't!"
                                                —*Melissa, Long Beach, California*

"The most interesting thing I've found about milestones is the competition with other moms, and my mother-in-law especially. Of course her kids walked earlier, talked earlier, were potty-trained earlier, et cetera.

(continued on next page)

I understand moms who are contemporaries competing through their kids, but it has always stumped me that my mother-in-law competes with me!"   —*Denise, Hugo, Colorado*

"As twelve months came and went, we started to worry if our daughter would ever walk. Then our doctor pointed out that with us carrying her so much, she had no incentive to change! Once we realized what we were doing, we were able to help our little princess learn that being carried was not the only way to travel around her world."
                                       —*Samantha, San Diego, California*

"My oldest daughter didn't give us any time to worry: She was rolling over at a month, an expert crawler at six months, and walking by nine months. With our second, I prayed she'd put off a few of those mobility milestones just a bit longer, and lucky for me, she didn't walk until she was nearly twelve months old. Now our third is just about to turn four months and rolling all over the place, and I'm hoping she sticks to baby things a few months longer. Once you've been there, done that, you're much more aware of how fast this time goes, and less apt to want your baby to grow up. Unless there's a real problem, every baby will reach all these milestones, and it doesn't really make a difference when in the long run. Just try to enjoy your baby!"
                                       —*Kelli, Hellertown, Pennsylvania*

CHAPTER 6

In Good Health

Must-Know News on Vaccines, Baby Bugs, and Keeping Your Kiddo Well

Did you know that by becoming a parent, you have automatically earned an honorary doctorate in pediatric medicine? If not, let us be the first to say "Congratulations!" You have now joined millions of other neophytes who might have thought that thrush is a type of bird and roseola, a gay comedienne. The best part of garnering this imaginary MD is you didn't have to go through years of training or acquire many thousands in student loan debt. Of course, the worst part is that you didn't have to go through years of training. And now, baby in hand, you might feel just a smidge underqualified to be your child's CMO: chief medical officer.

Not to worry. We all feel that way, no matter how many children we have or how old they are. Even bona fide pediatricians aren't immune from feeling shaken when confronted with their own babies' first shots or bouts with fever. It's only natural. And while nothing will cure any of us from worrying about our limited ability to make everything all better, we happen to know a surefire prescription—seeing that we're honorary doctors, too—that can help lessen your anxiety while increasing your medical knowledge. First and most important, trust your instincts. You probably spend more time with your baby than anyone else and can decode clues that others may not even see. If you think something is amiss, don't hesitate to ask. By that we mean check in with your baby's doctor, not your girlfriend, mother-in-law, or the first person you meet at the playground. There are many medical myths out there when it comes to children's health, so go straight to your most trusted, qualified source. Second, read up on the latest thinking so you know what you can do from your end and what your doctor should be doing from hers (not all pediatricians are created equal). Of course you can find plenty right here and in the pages of *Babytalk* magazine, so keep us by your nightstand. (If you still crave more, make sure your sources are qualified; see page 205 for health Web sites you can trust.) It's not brain surgery, but being your child's CMO does take nerves of steel and lots of homework. Read on, dear Doctor.

The Road to Wellness

So you thought you ran to your ob-gyn a lot during pregnancy? Get ready to spend at least as much time with your baby's pediatrician. Your child will visit the doctor at least eight times in his first year of life, and that's just for well-baby checkups to make sure his growth is on target and to receive his vaccines to protect him from illness. Your pediatrician can also provide a wealth of advice on topics such as nutrition, development, sleep difficulties, and safety, as well as the expected healthcare. As a new parent (or even a seasoned one, because every baby is different), these checkups will be as exciting as a first date: You will look forward to them for days in advance because they will provide reassurance that your baby is doing well, and validation for your skills as a mom. If you have concerns, the answers you need will be forthcoming in most cases, or at least your doctor will put you on the right track to get further help for your baby.

Your baby's first exam will actually take place in the hospital right after birth, and your pediatrician will check up on him probably several times before you even leave the hospital. (That's why it was so important to hire your pediatrician during pregnancy—you want someone you trust to be on call for these first critical days.) What can you expect at subsequent checkups? The first one, which will take place within the first few days of your arrival home from the hospital, will be primarily to monitor your baby's vital signs, to check for weight gain and learn how well he's feeding, to see if you need any help breastfeeding, and to check for signs of jaundice (see pages 16–17 and 225–226 for more about this common newborn illness). Future checkups will then continue to follow pretty much the same familiar format. There will be lots of measuring: Your baby's height, weight, and head circumference will all be assessed and plotted on a percentile chart to determine where he stands compared with other babies of the same age and gender. Your doctor will probably show you where your baby lands on these graphs (ask to see it if he doesn't!), but don't be concerned if he's not in the 90th percentile. Unlike the SAT and other test scores you remember so well, bigger numbers don't add up to better babies. They simply mean that your child is, for example, of average weight or height for his age (with the 50th percentile being average), or a little smaller than average (more like the 35th or 40th percentile) or even quite a bit larger (in, say, the 80th or 90th percentile). What your doctor is trying to gauge by adding dots on a graph is that your baby's growth climbs *consistently* throughout the first year. A two-pound weight gain per checkup, for example, will result in a steady rise on the chart—providing you and your doctor with a reassuring exercise of connect-the-dots. If the line spikes up or dips down, however, your doctor may want to reassess what's going on. For instance, if your baby's weight gain drops (say he only gains one pound and falls from being in the 40th percentile to the 30th), it may indicate problems with his diet or his digestion. If he suddenly packs on the pounds (especially if his weight exceeds his height percentile), your doctor may need to assess what's going on. For instance, a baby in the 50th percentile in height and the 85th in weight may be in danger of becoming too heavy—a big concern of pediatricians in this day of epidemic childhood (and adult!) obesity rates.

After recording all the measurements, your pediatrician will then take a more hands-on approach at every checkup, conducting a physical exam of your baby's eyes, ears, nose, throat, genitals, and joints. He will listen to her heart and lungs through a stethoscope and check internal organs by pressing on her abdomen. Finally, he will discuss any recent illnesses, your baby's eating and sleeping habits, and other areas of behavior and development. Many pediatricians will also have you fill out a development questionnaire or verbally review your baby's progress with you, to track physical, cognitive, and fine-motor skills. If your doctor doesn't at least spend some time discussing your baby's developmental progress at each checkup, inquire as to why. Developmental assessment is an important part of your baby's well care, and it's probably worth changing physicians if yours is not vigilant in doing so.

Oh yes. One more tiny, very sharp point about these first-year checkups. Your baby will frequently receive shots. It's heartbreaking to see that squishy thigh pierced, but keep telling yourself it's for the greater good and you may stop weeping by the time you leave the office. If that doesn't help, the sheer number of times you will experience this scene (every checkup this year) may numb you to the pain. At the one-year mark, your baby may also be screened for lead exposure and anemia, which requires a blood sample. You won't be used to seeing this, so again, we remind you to remind yourself what a good mom you are for protecting your baby's health.

Because you will have so much to cover with your pediatrician at these checkups, it pays to schedule them for off-peak times so your doctor isn't in a rush. Avoid scheduling checkups for Mondays and Fridays, because that's when everybody with a sick child calls for an appointment—Mondays because the baby's been sick all weekend and they're worried, Fridays because something appears to be brewing and they need to get it checked out before the weekend. After-school hours are also prime time at the pediatrician, as are evenings and Saturday mornings so working parents don't have to take time away from the office. If you can, aim for Tuesday, Wednesday, or Thursday, and ask for one of the first morning appointments (by 11 AM the doctors are behind schedule!), or just after the office breaks for lunch, around 1 PM, because again you'll be the first appointment of that shift. It's also smart to arrive prepared with a list of questions so you use your time wisely and don't forget anything.

 YOUR BABY'S CHECKUP SCHEDULE

It's important that you like your pediatrician because you'll be seeing her every few weeks for the next year. Here is the usual schedule of appointments:

• A few days after you come home from the hospital (some doctors will suggest three to five days, but we recommend requesting a checkup about two days after you come home).
• Two weeks old.
• Four weeks old.
• Two months old.
• Four months old.
• Six months old.
• Nine months old.
• Twelve months old.
• Fifteen months old.
• Eighteen months old.

What to Ask during a Checkup

☐ What growth percentile is my baby in for height and weight? Is each percentile appropriate?

☐ Do my baby's eating habits seem normal for this age?

☐ Do my baby's sleep habits seem normal for this age?

☐ Does her development seem to be occurring at a healthy rate?

☐ What can I do to establish a secure, predictable routine?

☐ What kinds of reactions should I expect from the vaccines she's receiving today?

☐ May I have a record of the vaccines she is being given?

☐ What developmental milestones can I watch for between now and the next checkup?

Rate Your Pediatrician

As a newbie in the world of pediatric medicine, it's understandable and advisable that you defer to your doctor about your baby's health. But your child's doctor shouldn't just be someone who can fix things. Quality healthcare includes guidance and advice about practically everything, so you can avoid health problems and deal with developmental issues. In addition, finding an office that offers a pleasant environment, with a friendly staff, is not an indulgence. It can be the difference between a productive visit and a stressful one. Of course there will be hectic times—all types of businesses and services have their crunch days—but that should be the exception, not the norm. You should always feel free to voice any concerns and ask any questions. Keeping these points in mind, what kind of grade would your doctor get on the following test?

CHECKUPS

When you arrive for an appointment, how long do you have to wait to see the doctor:

☐ Ten minutes   ☐ Fifteen to twenty minutes   ☐ Thirty minutes or more

Best answer: Ten minutes or less.

How much time does your doctor spend with you and your baby:

☐ Fifteen minutes or less   ☐ Twenty minutes   ☐ Thirty minutes

Best answer: Each checkup should take a minimum of fifteen minutes, twenty to thirty is best.

When it comes to development, does your doctor:

☐ Have you fill out a questionnaire

☐ Verbally review the expected milestones with you from his own or a mental list

☐ Just ask if you have any concerns

Best answer: Your doctor should either fill out or verbally review a developmental questionnaire with you, taking time to explain the importance of things you may not think of, such as providing your baby tummy time or choosing toys that enhance fine-motor skills.

Does your doctor provide information in writing?

☐ Yes   ☐ No

Best answer: At well-visit checkups, your doctor should write down your baby's height, weight, and head circumference; preprinted forms with vaccine advice, and tips on feeding and sleeping are also often given to parents. And if your baby is ill, all medication instructions should be provided in writing.

OVERALL AVAILABILITY

Does your practice have a call-in hour when you can talk to a doctor most days of the week?

☐ Yes   ☐ No

Best answer: This should be standard procedure for any practice. During regular office hours, you should be able to relay your question to a nurse; if she can't answer it herself, she should talk to the doctor and get back to you within an hour.

Can you get in to see a doctor the same day your baby gets sick?

☐ Yes   ☐ No

Best answer: Seeing a doctor that very day is another must.

During off hours, does the physician on call get back to you quickly?

☐ Yes   ☐ No

Best answer: You should get a callback within an hour of contacting the answering service.

What to Believe on the Web

At some point in your baby's first year (and probably every year thereafter, too), you're going to have a nagging question about your baby's health in the middle of the night that won't be important enough to disturb your doctor, and won't be covered in any of the books next to your bed. That's when you'll do what every other red-blooded American mom would do: Google it. If you go to the right sites, you'll likely come away reassured, or at least with a plan for what to do next. But if you wander into a blog or a chat room, the exact opposite may happen. Fearmongering moms with radical or misguided advice may keep you from sleeping for the next week. Rule number one: Chat rooms are not fact rooms. If you hear a piece of information there or on a message board, check it out on a reliable site to be sure it's valid. You can generally count on a site that's affiliated with a reputable organization, such as the American Academy of Pediatrics or the March of Dimes, the government, a hospital, or university. It's also important to look for dates on Internet articles. Anything more than two years old may have fallen out of favor in the medical community. So when it comes to your baby's health and development, stick to these trusted Web sites:

> **Aap.org.** American Academy of Pediatrics at your disposal 24/7.
> **Cdc.gov.** Centers for Disease Control and Prevention's latest facts, figures, and advice on illness and immunization.
> **Zerotothree.org.** National Center for Infants, Toddlers and Families provides development information from some of the world's foremost experts.
> **Safekids.org.** Lists of baby product recalls and advice on protecting your child from injury.
> **Marchofdimes.com.** The March of Dimes provides a wealth of research and advice for expectant moms and mothers of preemies or infants with other health issues.
> **Webmd.com.** Smart, up-to-date health advice from doctors for the whole family.
> **Parenting.com/babytalk.** Straight talk for new moms—of course!

The Savvy Mom's Guide to Vaccines

You probably know that immunizations have become a somewhat controversial aspect of infancy. Ironically, that's probably because our vaccine program has been so successful that parents and even some grandparents don't remember the threat and very real toll of dangerous diseases like measles and polio. Many of today's school-age children haven't even experienced the chicken pox that had us itching as kids, thanks to the introduction of that vaccine a decade ago. The natural result is that society becomes less concerned and more skeptical about the need for vaccines. And as more people knowingly or accidentally skip them, outbreaks of forgotten illnesses have cropped up all over the country. In recent years, for example, we've seen a troubling resurgence of whooping cough, known medically as pertussis and prevented by the DTaP vaccine. High immunization rates are essential if we're going to keep these dangerous diseases from making a comeback. Unvaccinated children represent a threat to others as well as themselves. They can spread dangerous illnesses to other vulnerable members of the population, such as preemies, kids and adults with compromised immune systems, the elderly, and, yes, your healthy baby who has not yet received all of his own vaccines.

Occasionally, there is reason for concern about a vaccine, and your pediatrician should be the one to discuss that with you and help you make a decision based on your individual child. But blanket disregard for vaccinations in general, or a particular vaccine because of unfounded rumors, is not something we at *Babytalk* can condone. You'll find very few "shoulds" in the pages of *Babytalk,* because we support your right to raise your baby your way, as we keep repeating to what may be a tiring degree. But this is one of those instances—most of which involve your baby's health and safety—when we do insist you *should* do something. Your baby should sleep on her back, your baby should ride in a car seat, and, yes, she should get her vaccines, all of them, on time. We wholeheartedly support the AAP and every other child health advocacy group trying to provide vaccines to the entire population of children in this country, as well as around the world.

Now that we've made our point, we'll get down off our soapbox and admit that watching your baby being repeatedly stabbed with a needleful of germs just plain sucks. Then there are all those intimidating flyers you receive from the pediatrician to educate you about the potential side effects. As frightening as it can be to read, it's important to know that some babies do get a slight fever, a few bumps, or some soreness around the vaccine site, so you can be prepared to soothe her as necessary. But it's also important to know that it's very rare for a child to have a severe reaction to her shots, and that many of the fears about vaccines are unfounded. Because the vaccine myth machine is operating at full throttle these days, we're going to begin this section by dispelling some of the wild, weird, and just plain mistaken beliefs out there. Then we'll give you the inside scoop on what you really need to know about your baby's vaccine schedule: the what, when, why, and, yes, the side effects you and your baby may encounter—all in the name of a lifetime of good health.

Myth 1: My baby's immune system can't possibly fight off all the germs in the vaccines at once. This is a common reason parents cite for not wanting their babies to receive multiple vaccines at checkups, but experts say it shouldn't be a cause for concern. The typical baby's body is bombarded with bacteria, dirt, chemicals, and other immunological challenges every day in the food he eats, the air he breathes, the floor he plays on. Getting up to six shots at a time—a distinct possibility with the current immunization schedule recommended by the CDC (Centers for Disease Control and Prevention) and the AAP—is going to seem like a drop of water in the ocean to your child's immune system. The science shows it's safe for your baby to receive simultaneous vaccines or vaccine combinations, such as the five-in-one vaccine called Pediarix, which protects against hepatitis B, polio, tetanus, diphtheria, and pertussis (also known as whooping cough). Equally important, vaccines are as effective given in combination as they are given individually.

That said, if you *want* to separate your baby's vaccines, you have every right to do so. An excellent, fair-minded guide that lays out a plan for parents who want to vaccinate but have concerns about their particular baby is *The Vaccine Book: Making the Right Decision for Your Child,* by Robert W. Sears. MD, FAAP (Little, Brown, 2007), son of our contributing editor Dr. Bill Sears.

Myth 2: As long as other children are vaccinated, mine doesn't need to be. While it sounds logical, it's not. The ability of immunizations to prevent the spread of infection—known as herd immunity—depends on having a significant number of children immunized. To prevent a disease such as measles from spreading from child to child, 95 percent of them would need to have the vaccine. In reality, only about 75 percent of children under age two are fully immunized in this country, according to the latest figures from the Centers for Disease and Prevention. Why so low? More and more parents are claiming exemptions from vaccines for medical, personal, or religious reasons, and schools have to honor them. In certain states, Colorado being one of them, exemption rates are particularly high. As a result, children there are twenty-two times more likely to contract measles, for example. Herd immunity simply won't happen if these practices continue.

Myth 3: We don't really need vaccines anymore because these serious illnesses have pretty much disappeared. Guess again. The germs that cause the illness may still be circulating. Diseases can be brought here from foreign travelers, for instance. And again, herd immunity can be diminished as more and more people pass on vaccines in certain areas or communities. The incidence of whooping cough (pertussis) has been increasing since 1980; in 2003, thirteen children died of it in the United States despite the fact that their parents probably never knew anyone who had whooping cough when they themselves were growing up. As a result of the resurgence of pertussis, the Centers for Disease Control and Prevention recently recommended a pertussis booster shot for eleven-year-olds.

Myth 4: Vaccines can cause autism and other developmental disorders. This is certainly a frightening thought, especially to families who have a child or other relative with the disorder, but the notion has been repeatedly discredited. The idea that the combination MMR vaccine, which protects against measles, mumps, and rubella, could cause the serious developmental disorder of autism first surfaced about a decade ago. The fear has persisted because symptoms of autism become more apparent around the first birthday, which also happens to be when the vaccine is given. In reality, there have been more than a dozen studies proving that the risk of autism isn't any different if you get the vaccine or not. Indeed, we've learned much more about autism itself since the original idea made the headlines, including the fact that autism is very likely to have a genetic cause and be present at birth. But because a newborn's communication, social, and play skills are very limited, the signs of the disorder aren't always apparent until months later. Worries about a link continue in large part due to the widespread use of the Internet and the ability to easily transmit misguided and mistaken information. Autism is a frightening diagnosis to be sure, and it's understandable that affected parents would do anything to help their child's prognosis. That's also why it's all the more important to work with a team of trusted professionals who know how to separate science from conjecture.

There have also been similar fears about vaccines and the incidence of sudden infant death syndrome (SIDS)—but again, there are huge developmental changes going on in the early months of life. Just because a vaccine is given at the time something happens doesn't mean there's a cause-and-effect relationship. All that said, you do still have the right to request separate shots for your baby if you want, so discuss your concerns with your baby's doctor.

Myth 5: My baby might get the disease it's supposed to prevent. In the early days of vaccines, some did contain a live but weakened virus. Polio was one such vaccine, and a tiny fraction of the recipients—1 in 2.4 million—contracted polio from the immunization itself. But this type of polio vaccine was phased out in 2000, and other immunizations given today, such as meningitis and DTaP, contain killed vaccines—not live agents that could cause the illness. The exceptions to this rule are the MMR and chicken pox (varicella) vaccines, which do contain live weakened virus necessary to provoke an immune response. As a result, your baby may develop a slight fever and rash similar to the illness itself, but the symptoms will be much less severe than if he naturally contracted them.

Myth 6: Vaccines contain dangerous preservatives. Reality check: You should be more worried about the type of mercury in tuna fish sandwiches if you or your child eats them often. At the root of this particular myth is a compound called thimerosal, a form of mercury known as ethylmercury, which used to be included in vaccines to prevent them from being contaminated by bacteria. Now, we all know that mercury in large quantities is harmful to a child's brain development. But there are a number of reasons why you can discount this particular myth. For starters, worries about thimerosal prompted its removal from all but the flu vaccine back in 1999. You can ask your child's doctor for a thimerosal-free flu shot for your baby if you're worried, but you needn't be, which brings us to part two of our long explanation.

Since 1999, it's become increasingly clear that ethylmercury does not pose nearly the same health risks as the related substance, methylmercury, a dangerous metal found in the environment that's known to accumulate in the body. When researchers compared mercury concentrations in the urine, blood, and stools of children who got vaccines containing thimerosal with those of kids who received only thimerosal-free vaccines, all the children had mercury levels well below the EPA's most stringent public safety limits. So according to this evidence, even if your baby received a vaccine that contained thimerosal, there's scientific research proving that this wouldn't have caused any neurological problems after all. (Still, there's nothing wrong with requesting a thimerosol-free vaccine if you're really worried.)

In fact, your child will get her greatest exposure to mercury from two things we can't always control—the air we breathe and the water we drink—and one we can, the fish we eat. While not many infants are yet chowing down on high-mercury fish like tuna and swordfish, you will do well to limit your family diet's inclusion of this otherwise healthy food group as they grow, and watch your intake as well if you're pregnant or breastfeeding. The current Food and Drug Administration (FDA) recommendation is that it's okay for young children and pregnant or nursing moms to eat albacore tuna once a week, and fish that are lower in mercury (such as chunk light tuna, pollack, salmon, and catfish) twice a week. Shark, swordfish, king mackerel, and tilefish, which have high mercury levels, are indefinitely off the menu for women who are pregnant or may become pregnant as well as children. (It's not a bad idea for Dad to abstain, either.)

Myth 7: My baby can't receive her vaccines if she's sick at her checkup. Keep that appointment! While it sounds reasonable to think that a vaccine could make her already stressed immune system weaker still, it won't. Studies have demonstrated that having a mild illness doesn't hurt a child's ability to react appropriately to the vaccine. A low-grade fever, mild cold symptoms, or even a little diarrhea are no reason to postpone a vaccine, especially if the illness is on the way out. If your child is on an antibiotic for, say, an ear infection, you'll also get the green light. The general rule of thumb is to stick as closely to the vaccination schedule as possible, so that your baby will be fully immunized as soon as possible. Delaying one round of vaccines can have a domino effect—the next round has to be put off for the last missed set, and so on—or result in your baby getting a whopping number of shots at once. As we said on page 207, her little body can handle that, but it's certainly no fun for you to watch! So if you do need to postpone a vaccine for any reason, reschedule the appointment as soon as possible—don't wait until the next checkup, months later.

Myth 8: Chicken pox is a vaccine we can skip; I had it as a kid and it wasn't a big deal. It's true that chicken pox isn't a big deal for most kids. But sometimes it can be. Before the vaccine existed, many children were hospitalized each year with serious complications, including pneumonia and dangerous skin infections. Scratching can lead to the lesions becoming infected with staph bacteria, including necrotizing fasciitis—the "flesh-eating" bacteria. On rare occasions, children have died from chicken pox. Plus, now that the vaccine has been around a decade, less of the chicken pox virus is in circulation, so if your child isn't immunized against it, she may not be exposed until adulthood. And getting chicken pox as an adult is much more serious. As you probably know, if a pregnant woman contracts chicken pox, her baby may be born with birth defects.

Finally, on a lifestyle note, chicken pox is a relatively lengthy illness. The first symptom—fever—can last two days or so before any blisters appear. Then the child remains contagious until all the blisters have dried and crusted over, which is usually a good week. Chicken pox is highly contagious, so of course other unvaccinated siblings will follow suit when one brings it home, which can add up to an awful lot of sick, itchy, cranky, missed schooldays and workdays for parents. Now, that's what we call a big deal. Be on the safe side—vaccinate your baby for chicken pox.

Myth 9: Vaccines guarantee that my child will never get these diseases. As in the rest of life, there are no 100 percent guarantees with vaccines. Those made with live weakened virus, such as MMR and chicken pox, are the best, with about a 95 percent effectiveness rate. Vaccines made with killed, or inactivated, virus are less effective, in the neighborhood of 75 to 80 percent. So, yes, theoretically a child can be vaccinated against a disease and still get it. That's where the herd immunity comes in. There's less of a chance of these illnesses being in circulation, and less of a chance of your child being exposed, if everyone else is immunized, too. The more people in a community aren't immunized, the greater the risk to everyone who lives there as well.

Myth 10: It would be better to wait until children are older before giving them vaccines. There are three groups in our population who are most vulnerable to illness: the very young, the very old, and those people who have compromised immune systems due to other chronic illness. In other words, your baby needs his vaccines more right now than he will when he gets to be school age, or as an adult (unless he develops other health problems that weaken his immunity, of course). Consider this: Recently 300 children under age one in Wisconsin came down with whooping cough; 177 of them were less than six months old. Of these, half were hospitalized, and three died. That's exactly why vaccines are given at such a young age.

TAKING THE **OUCH!** OUT OF SHOTS

Soreness, fever, swelling, rash: Your doctor may call them "mild" reactions, but they can be a big pain to you and your baby. Here are some soothing ideas for before, during, and after vaccines:

Dose up beforehand. Pain relievers are more effective at preventing fever and soreness than reducing it, so ask your doctor about giving your baby an appropriate dose of acetaminophen or ibuprofen about an hour before your appointment.

Request a long needle. Studies show longer needles are associated with less redness and swelling.

Ask for a topical anesthetic cream, such as EMLA, that can be applied about an hour before an injection to numb the skin.

Employ soothing strategies. Let your baby nurse or have a bottle after a shot. Also helpful: a pacifier. And you can try swaddling your baby in a light blanket—most children under three months will find it comforting. Rocking your baby can help, too.

Your Baby's Vaccine Schedule

The following is a list of all the vaccines you can expect your baby to get in the first eighteen months of life.

What:	**Hepatitis B (HepB)**
When:	First dose at birth (most hospitals give it within hours of birth, except for preemies under 4.4 pounds who should wait until the one-month checkup); second dose between one and four months; third dose between six and eighteen months.
Why:	Protects against hepatitis B, a viral illness that can be passed from mother to newborn and can cause liver damage and death.
What to Expect:	About one in eleven babies will experience soreness at the vaccine site for a day or two; one in fourteen may have a mild

to moderate fever.
ceeds 100.4 degre
still under three
fever guidelines.

What: **Diphtheria, tet**
When: Two months, f
dose given betw
Why: Protects agains
which causes
ing cough.

What to Expect: About or
soreness at the injection si...
large knot (it can be as big as an egg), but medica...,
ered a mild reaction and nothing to worry about. (Call your
doctor if you're concerned anyway.) About one in three babies
will experience fussiness within three days. About one in ten,
fatigue or poor appetite. About one in fifty, vomiting.

What: **H. influenzae type B (Hib)**
When: Two months, four months, and six months, with a fourth
dose given between twelve and fifteen months.
Why: Protects against pneumonia and two life-threatening illnesses:
bacterial meningitis (an infection of the lining of the brain),
and epiglottis (swelling of the windpipe).

What to Expect: About one in four babies experiences redness, warmth, or
swelling at the injection site, and about one in twenty will
develop a fever over 101 degrees Fahrenheit.

What: **Polio (IPV)**
When: Two months, four months, and a third dose between six and
eighteen months.
Why: Protects against the polio virus, an infection of the central
nervous system that can cause paralysis and death.

What to Expect: Nothing; reactions are highly unlikely.

What: **Pneumococcal conjugate (PCV, Prevnar)**
When: Two, four, and six months, and a fourth dose between twelve
and fifteen months.

...inst recurrent ear infections (in fact, the rate of ear ...n children under two has plummeted since this vac-...s introduced!), bacterial meningitis, pneumonia, and ...remia, an infection of the bloodstream that can be deadly.

EGG ALLERGY ALERT!

If you've got a family history of allergies, you may have wondered about some vaccines containing eggs. You don't need to panic, or even worry, frankly: The risk to your baby is both minimal and rare. Here's what you need to know:

Which vaccines contain traces of egg? The MMR (measles, mumps rubella), the flu vaccine, and the yellow fever vaccine.

Why? These vaccines are cultured (grown) in chicken egg embryos.

How much? The MMR contains such trace amounts of egg protein that studies have shown even children with severe egg allergies are unlikely to have a reaction to it. The flu vaccine and yellow fever vaccines contain higher amounts.

Who's at risk? For the MMR vaccine, so few react to it that pediatricians don't even consider it a "contraindication" (medical-ese for a reason not to get it), even if you have family history of egg allergies or a baby with eczema (which can be a precursor to food allergies). One parent we know said her pediatrician suggested feeding her baby a whole egg before she received the vaccine to see if there was any reaction, but most of the other doctors we asked about didn't think this was necessary at all. The situation is different with the flu vaccine, which contains higher amounts of egg; talk to your pediatrician about whether you should have your baby tested first or even skip it if there are egg allergy concerns, particularly if your child has gotten a rash from eating egg in the past. The same goes for babies with eczema. And as for the yellow fever vaccine, your child isn't likely to be a candidate for it at all, unless you are traveling to tropical South America or Africa, in which case you should again discuss the issue with a medical professional.

What to Expect: One in four babies may experience redness or swelling at the injection site; one in three, a mild fever; and one in fifty, a fever over 102 degrees Fahrenheit. Some babies may also be fussy, be sleepy, or lose their appetite.

What: **RotaTeq**
When: Two, four, and six months.
Why: Protects against a viral illness, rotavirus, that causes severe diarrhea.
What to Expect: Side effects should be mild, but could possibly include fever, diarrhea, and/or vomiting. Since this is a brand-new vaccine (introduced in 2006), side effect statistics aren't yet available. However, it's being carefully monitored by the Centers for Disease Control and Prevention because a previous version of this vaccine appeared to have a connection between it and intussusception, a type of intestinal obstruction. Talk to your pediatrician about the most current recommendations when your baby receives her dose of RotaTeq.

What: **Pediarix**
When: Two months, four months, and six months.
Why: This new vaccine combines HepB, IPV, and DTaP, so your baby has to endure fewer shots.
What to Expect: It has a higher risk of mild fever than the individual shots.

What: **Measles, mumps, rubella (MMR)**
When: First dose between twelve and fifteen months, and a second dose not until between four and six years.
Why: MMR protects against measles, which can cause a rash, cold-like symptoms, pneumonia, encephalitis, seizures, and death; mumps, which can cause fever, swollen glands, and meningitis; and rubella (also known as German measles), which can cause a rash and fever, and is a major danger to a pregnant woman and her fetus.

What to Expect: One in six babies may develop a fever; one in twenty, a mild rash. Very rarely, there may be swelling of the glands in the cheeks or neck six to twelve days after the shot.

What: **Varicella (Varivax)**
When: One dose between twelve and eighteen months.
Why: Protects against chicken pox, a contagious illness that causes a blistering rash and, in serious cases, bacterial infection of the skin, pneumonia, encephalitis, and even death. Before it was introduced in 1995, this viral infection sent more than ten thousand U.S. kids to the hospital and killed about a hundred each year. If any adults in your family have not had chicken pox, they should get the vaccine as well (except for pregnant women). Chicken pox is a much more dangerous disease in adults than children.

What to Expect: One in five babies may experience soreness or swelling at the injection site; one in ten, a mild fever; one in twenty, a mild rash up to a month later (if so, keep your baby home— she may be contagious).

What: **ProQuad (MMRV)**
When: Twelve months.
Why: This new vaccine combines the MMR and varicella vaccines, so there's one less shot.

What to Expect: One in five babies may develop a fever over 102 degrees Fahrenheit, and one in fifteen may experience irritability or a rash five to twelve days later.

What: **Influenza**
When: Every year in the fall, from six months old to five years.
Why: Protects against the flu, which can be serious in infants and children with chronic medical conditions, as well as haemophilus type B, which can lead to pneumonia.

What to Expect: None; it's an inactivated vaccine, so your baby won't get the flu from it. You may need to have your baby tested or skip it if your baby has an egg allergy (or if you have a family history of egg allergy) or eczema, which is sometimes a precursor to food allergies (see page 214).

JUST IN CASE: SIDE EFFECT ALERT

Rarely will a vaccine cause enough of a reaction to warrant medical attention, but we still must warn you. Call your doctor if any of these symptoms occur:

- Your baby skips more than one feeding, vomits more than twice, or has diarrhea for more than a day—he could become dehydrated.
- Your baby develops a fever of 100.4 degrees Fahrenheit or more and is under three months, or 102 degrees Fahrenheit or above after three months of age.
- Your baby cries for more than three hours.
- After receiving his dose of RotaTeq, your baby develops blood in his stool or has a change in bowel movements (even if it's a few weeks after receiving the vaccine).
- Your baby's whole arm or leg swells up—this is considered a moderate reaction, but your doctor can tell you how to ease your baby's discomfort (if any) and may need to report the reaction to the CDC.
- Your baby has a seizure (a seizure itself is not considered a medical emergency, but you should have your baby checked out afterward).

Call 911 if:
- Your baby becomes very weak (for instance, she was able to hold her head up on her own and now can't).
- She has a very high fever.
- She has trouble breathing and/or hives.
- She develops hives, a fast heartbeat, or dizziness.

The No-Panic Guide to Infant Illness

When a nasty bug gets into your baby's system, he isn't the only one suffering ill effects. While you haven't contracted anything (yet), you and your partner will suffer more than a few panicked moments while trying to figure out what what's wrong and whether to call the doctor (just do it!), or how to use a rectal thermometer. And this is all on little or no sleep.

So from ones who have held feverish heads close to their chests, suctioned out mucus at 2, 4, and 6 AM, and been on the receiving end of projectile puke, let us give you this piece of advice: Do your best to relax. Repeat to yourself that this, too, shall pass, and this illness will help your baby build up his immunity. If that doesn't work the first time, no worries. You will have other chances to practice this year: On average, children experience between six and nine viral infections (colds, flu, stomach bugs) a year. Fortunately, maladies in the early months of infancy are usually few, but once the winter germ season rolls around, or your baby starts socializing with other tots, you might want to keep your doctor's number handy and wear your bulb syringe in a holster.

Most often, you won't need a doctor to tell you that your baby is coming down with something. Telltale signs such as a runny nose, cough, or extra-warm forehead will be obvious enough. Other times, however, the onset of an illness won't be quite as apparent. Your baby may seem "not quite right" but you won't be sure why, exactly. Your baby can't tell you if something is bothering her or what it is, so watch for these signs of illness: poor appetite for several feedings; unusual behavior such as whimpering or crankiness; and an excessive desire to sleep. If your baby doesn't fit this description, but you're still concerned, call anyway. It's your prerogative as a mom, and at no time does the motto "Better safe than sorry" apply more than when your baby's health is at stake. Your pediatrician knows this and expects this; if she doesn't, find a new doctor! Meanwhile, reading up on the common bugs that plague babies and their treatments will go a long way toward helping you and your baby feel better. Here, we'll get you started.

Fever Facts

The first symptom of many illnesses is likely to be fever—an increase in body temperature that, when measured rectally, is higher than 100.4 degrees Fahrenheit in a baby younger than three months, or 101 degrees Fahrenheit in a baby three to six months (see "How to Take Your Baby's Temperature," page 223). While doctors are fond of saying they do not

WHO SHOULDN'T BE VACCINATED?

- A child who has had a severe reaction—hives, low blood pressure, difficulty breathing, or shock—to a shot should not be given additional doses of that particular vaccine again.
- A child with a weakened immune system due to cancer or AIDS might not be given MMR or varicella, which are made from live viruses.
- Any child on long-term, high-dose steroids should not receive the live vaccines. But they're fine if your child takes inhaled steroids or uses oral steroids on a short-term basis.
- Children who are allergic to yeast, eggs (as we discussed on page 214), or some antibiotics may not be able to receive certain vaccines. Talk to your doctor about alternatives.

consider fever an illness itself, but rather a symptom that the body is trying to fight off illness or infection, most parents beg to differ. If your baby has a fever and nothing else (a fairly common reaction to the threat of a virus), she's still likely to act sick, which means hot, cranky, and more limp and lethargic than usual—though not necessarily bedridden. You know the difference for sure, and her behavior is likely to make you nervous and cranky as well. While the medical pros may not consider it serious, there's nothing like holding a live hot potato in your arms to make you start to question your capabilities. (The American Academy of Pediatrics must know we feel this way, because it has in fact given fever its own chapter in the bible *Caring for Your Baby and Young Child*.)

So while there are lots of fever rules about when to call the doctor (which we're going to get to in a minute), we know that no new mom in her right mind is going to let her baby lie around with any sort of fever without at least consulting a trained professional. You may get the brush-off ("give her some infant acetaminophen and call me again if she gets worse/it doesn't go down by tomorrow"), but at least you will have the peace of mind of knowing that you are following the advice of someone who knows *what they hell she's doing*.

Often enough, your baby's fever will simply subside in a day or two. This delightful occurrence means that your baby's body did exactly what it was supposed to do: fight off the offending bug. Other times, additional symptoms will follow—vomiting, ear pain, a rash—and you'll know you've got a bona fide illness on your hands, which your doctor will definitely need to assess. With luck, she will deem it worthy of a magical antibiotic that will have your baby feeling like her old self in twenty-four to forty-eight hours. We say this knowing full well that the medical community would pretty much rather give you anything than an antibiotic, because there are very real concerns about the world's population developing so much resistance to these wonder drugs that soon they will lose all of their marvelous powers. Of course that's a scary thought, and we shouldn't make light of it, but consider the other scary possibility: Your ten-month-old baby runs a raging fever of around 103 or 104 degrees Fahrenheit (actually, *raging* is higher even than that to an MD, but we all know we fall apart when our babies hit 102), you run back to the doctor something like three times in as many days, only to keep hearing, "It's just a virus that has to run its course," and you head back home again whimpering and quivering as much as your little one. At these moments, you won't really give a hoot about the rest of the world's population—you'll just want anything that makes your baby (and by default, yourself) feel better. So crazy as it sounds, there will be times when you will be glad when the problem is bacterial, and will result in an antibiotic that will make it all go away.

Seriously, though, when a baby younger than three months has any sort of fever, call your doctor ASAP (and have the rectal temperature reading ready); he will most likely want to examine your child to rule out any serious infection or disease. The degree recommendation as to when to seek medical attention increases with age: Between three and six months, call if the temperature is 101 degrees Fahrenheit or higher; after six months, 103 degrees Fahrenheit or higher. The other main concern doctors have about fevers is how a baby is behaving: If he's running a fever yet still alert, playful, eating normally, and otherwise tolerating it well, there's probably not much cause for concern. Conversely, if your baby is very cranky, lethargic, has little or no appetite, and is sleeping excessively, get thyself to the doctor. We have one caveat to add to this description, based on our cumulative years of motherhood: While a baby over three months with a temp of 100 or 101 degrees Fahrenheit may indeed "tolerate it well," we've yet to see any children at 102 degrees Fahrenheit or higher who weren't acting pretty darn sick!

STUFF YOU NEED IN YOUR BABY'S MEDICINE CABINET

Having to rush out to the pharmacy every time your baby starts to sniffle isn't pleasant, or practical. Keep these healthcare basics on hand so you are always prepared.

Equipment

❑ Digital rectal thermometer (mercury thermometers are no longer considered safe).

❑ Tweezers (for splinter removal).

❑ Nasal aspirator (babies can't blow their noses, so this allows you to do the job for them). Consider the Nose Frida, a newfangled gizmo from Sweden, that we admit sounds icky, but it's way more comfortable for your baby, which by default makes it less stressful for you. You position one end of a plastic tube against (not in) your baby's nostril, and then suck—yes, with your mouth—on the other end to extract the mucus. Wait—before you stop reading!—there's a filter on the baby's side of the hose that prevents the you-know-what from getting to your mouth. Check it out at nosefrida.com.

❑ Medicine dropper (but don't buy one—medicine droppers come in the package when you buy infant pain relievers, and most pharmacies will give you one for free with a prescription if you ask).

❑ Baby nail scissors and emery boards (to prevent him from scratching his face).

❑ Cotton balls and swabs.

❑ Selection of self-adhesive bandages, gauze pads, and bandage tape.

❑ Cold pack (kept in your freezer).

Medicines and preparations

❑ Infant acetaminophen drops and infant ibuprofen drops. For babies under six months, give acetaminophen for fevers and other aches, such as teething or vaccine discomfort. Infants older than six months can have ibuprofen as well. (In either case, talk to your doctor first.)

(continued on next page)

❏ Rubbing alcohol for cleaning thermometers or tweezers.
❏ Diaper rash ointment.
❏ Antibiotic ointment for cuts and scrapes.
❏ Hydrocortisone cream for skin rashes.
❏ Topical teething gel for teething pain.
❏ Petroleum jelly for lubricating rectal thermometers and soothing chapped skin.
❏ Saline nose drops.
❏ Oral rehydrating solution in case of diarrhea.

. . . AND STUFF YOU DON'T

- Syrup of ipecac. This used to be recommended to induce vomiting in the event of accidental poisoning, but experts now say some toxic chemicals can burn the esophagus and mouth if regurgitated, making the damage even worse.
- Baby or children's aspirin. Doctors strongly warn against its use under age twelve because it has been linked to Reye's syndrome, an illness that can cause liver and brain failure.
- Mercury thermometer. The mercury in it is a health hazard if it breaks.
- Ear thermometer. Rectal is better until age one.
- Baby powder. If it contains talc, that ingredient is dangerous to your baby's lungs. You can use baby powder with cornstarch, but it doesn't really serve any purpose.
- Infant cough and cold remedies. An FDA panel has recommended that these medicines be banned because of a lack of effectiveness and growing evidence that they may be dangerous. As of this writing, some manufacturers have voluntarily recalled their products, including Tylenol Infants' Drops Plus Cold, and PediaCare Infant Drops Decongestant. Until definitive action is taken, toss any single ingredient or multisymptom cough or cold (decongestant) medications you may have for babies and young children, and don't buy or use any such remedies you may still see on store shelves.

In the absence of other symptoms, fevers are typically treated with infant acetaminophen or ibuprofen (the latter acceptable after six months of age), extra fluids, and lukewarm baths. Always talk to your baby's doctor before administering any medicine, however. And never give your baby aspirin—even a children's aspirin—because it has been known to cause Reye's syndrome, an illness that could lead to liver and brain failure. Nor should you rub her down with alcohol, which can cause a coma. The fact is, keeping your baby dosed with acetaminophen or ibuprofen (according to your doctor's directions, of course) will often be all you need to do. These marvelous OTC products will seem to "cure" your child for the four- to six-hour period when they are in his system. Don't be surprised if he morphs from the aforementioned quivering heap of hot potato to the Energizer Bunny a mere twenty minutes after you administer the potion. Don't let this fool you; there's a good chance his fever will shoot back up and his energy level plummet as soon as it starts to wear off, until the bug has run its course. While it seems cruel to say, wait until the temperature does recur (and the manufacturer's directions say it's okay to administer more medicine) before giving him another dose. Your baby will also remain contagious until his fever breaks, so keep him away from other kids (sorry, no daycare center or playgroups, even on symptom-hiding medicine!).

How to Take Your Baby's Temperature

If you're dealing with a newborn, all those nifty new types of thermometers designed to make your life easier (the ear thermometer, the pacifier thermometer) will have to wait. The rectal thermometer is the gold standard of temperature taking for an infant six months or younger, because it's the most accurate—and any temperature in a baby this young could be serious, especially in the first three months. Later, when your baby is seven months and older, you can take his temperature with a pacifier thermometer, or take an axillary (under the arm) reading with a regular digital thermometer, but your pediatrician may still want you to confirm any temperature with a rectal reading as well. Ear thermometers aren't appropriate until after age one. At that point, you'll need to take your baby's temperature about three times and then average it, because ear thermometer readings can fluctuate.

Okay, we know taking a rectal temperature makes you squeamish—us, too. But it's actually very easy to do at this age. Here's how:

1. Apply petroleum jelly to a digital rectal thermometer tip (again, never use a mercury thermometer; they're no longer considered safe).
2. Lay your baby on his back on the changing table and lift his legs in the air as if you're going to change his diaper.

3. Gently slide the thermometer about half an inch into the rectum, then
hold it in place for two minutes, or until the thermometer signals that
it's done. (Note: There are some great new infant rectal thermometers
on the market that have safety stops and flexible comfort tips so you
don't have to worry about inserting them too far or causing your precious even an iota of discomfort.)

And here's an insider's tip: Rectal thermometers often stimulate baby's
bowels, so have some paper towels or wipes on hand in case you get a little
poop along with the temperature reading!

DO YOU NEED A DOCTOR?

Yes, if your baby has any of the following symptoms:

- Fever of 100.4 degrees Fahrenheit or higher in a baby three months
  or younger.
- Fever of 101 degrees Fahrenheit or higher in a baby three to six
  months of age.
- Your baby is unresponsive or sleeping excessively.
- She refuses to eat for three or four meals in a row.
- She's wetting fewer than four diapers a day.
- She has persistent vomiting and/or diarrhea for more than twenty-
  four hours.
- She has blood in her vomit, stool, or urine.
- She seems to be having difficulty breathing.
- She shows signs of ear pain (redness on an outer ear or cheek, cries
  when she's laid down) or has drainage from an ear.
- She has a rash accompanied by a fever.
- She has white patches in her mouth, which could be thrush (or the
  harmless Epstein pearls; see page 226).
- She has yellow- or orange-hued skin or eyes (which could be jaundice).
- She has discharge from her eyes, nails, navel, or genitals.

What to do during a sick visit. Begin by telling your doctor specifics about her symptoms: how long she's had a temperature and how
much it has changed since you began monitoring it; how her appe-

tite has been; whether there's been any change in elimination habits; her overall behavior (cranky, lethargic, tolerating the illness well). Then make sure you ask the following questions:

- Will my baby need any over-the-counter medications, and if so, how much and how often? Will there be any side effects—such as becoming overly excited or extra sleepy?
- Will my baby need any prescription medications, and if so, how much and how often? Will there be any side effects—such as becoming overly excited or extra sleepy?
- What kind of improvement should I expect in the next twenty-four to forty-eight hours?
- What symptoms would indicate that she might be getting worse?
- When should I call you again or bring her back into the office?

What's Up, Kid?

Infants experience a whole bunch of wacky-sounding illnesses you may never have heard of until you became a parent. They've been around practically forever, but unlike your garden-variety stuff, many of these maladies are unique to the under-three age group. That means in a few years you can forget about many of them (and you will, because you'll be distracted by other fun things like broken bones, sprains, stitches, or strep throat). Meanwhile, here's how to recognize and treat just what might be ailing your baby:

Illness: **Jaundice**
What It Is: A buildup of bilirubin in your baby's blood. Newborns typically have higher levels of this chemical, and their livers are not mature enough to process it. If the bilirubin levels stay too high for too long, damage to your baby's nervous system can occur.
Symptoms: A yellowish tinge to your baby's skin and the whites of her eyes during the first few days of life.
Treatment: Before you even leave the hospital, request that your newborn receive a blood test to check his bilirubin level (this procedure is standard in many places, but not always mandated, so you want to be certain your baby receives it). Then

see your pediatrician for another checkup two days after you go home. In fact, most doctors now offer this two-day check-up routinely to monitor jaundice because it's so common, and though yellow skin sounds obvious, it can look like a nice golden glow to a novice mom. If your baby's bilirubin levels don't get too high, your doctor will probably just continue to monitor your baby for a few days—jaundice frequently subsides without treatment. If the level is at the high end, however, phototherapy under special lights at the hospital may be necessary for a day or two to help break down the bilirubin while the liver matures.

Illness:	**Thrush**
What It Is:	A fungus infection in your baby's mouth due to an overgrowth of yeast, which thrives in the warm, moist environment. The presence of yeast in the mouth is normal, but for unknown reasons, sometimes too much develops and results in infection.
Symptoms:	Elevated white patches that look like cottage cheese on the inside of your baby's cheeks, tongue, or gums, or the roof of the mouth. If your try to wipe them away, the area will look raw and red and might bleed. Thrush may make nursing painful for your baby, and can actually spread to your nipples from your baby's mouth, resulting in (ouch!) painful, itching, and burning nipples, even when you're not feeding your baby. One caveat: There is a similar-appearing condition known as Epstein pearls (also sometimes called gingival cysts), which are harmless white bumps on the gums and roof of the mouth. As many as 80 percent of newborn infants have them, and they can be confused with thrush or emerging teeth. Epstein pearls disappear a few weeks after birth, and your pediatrician will be able to tell the difference.
Treatment:	See your pediatrician, who will prescribe an oral antifungal medication for your baby; you may also need to see your ob-gyn for a similar prescription of your own. A natural remedy you can also try (along with, not as a substitute for, a prescription) is acidophilus, a good type of bacteria the body needs that can eradicate excess yeast. It comes in powder form that you mix with a little breast milk to form a paste

you can put on the spots of thrush in your baby's mouth. You can also take it yourself in pill form. Acidophilus is available in most health food and nutrition stores.

Illness: **Respiratory syncytial virus (RSV)**

What It Is: This highly contagious infection of the lungs and breathing passages starts as a garden-variety cold, but can progress to more serious conditions such as bronchiolitis and pneumonia. RSV is the most common cause of hospitalization in infants; babies who are premature or who have congenital lung or heart disease are especially vulnerable to it. A preventive medicine called Synagis is often given to babies in these high-risk groups, so ask your doctor about it if your baby falls into that category. Synagis won't totally prevent your baby from contracting RSV, but it will help to lessen the severity if he does.

Symptoms: Runny or stuffy nose, sore throat, cough, fever, listlessness, and sometimes abnormally rapid breathing and wheezing.

Treatment: Initially, your doctor will probably recommend acetaminophen for fever, and use of a nasal aspirator, humidifier, and/ or saline nose drops to relieve symptoms. If the illness worsens, your baby may need bronchodilating medication (to open breathing passages). In severe cases, hospitalization may be necessary so your baby can benefit from a breathing machine until the infection subsides.

Illness: **Ear infection**

What It Is: Otitis media, as it is known medically, is a very common infection that is usually preceded by a cold. Most ear infections are caused by bacteria, but they can sometimes be viral in nature. Because of the tiny size and shape of the eustachian tube in babies and young children, congestion can drain into the middle ear, where the bacteria (or virus) builds up and results in a painful infection. Thanks to the pneumococcal vaccine (also known as Prevnar or PCV), recurring ear infections are becoming less of a problem in young children, because it protects against the main type of bacteria that causes them. Still, most children experience a few ear infections in their early years.

Symptoms: Congestion, fever, discomfort during feeding and sucking (on a pacifier, for instance), pain while lying down that interferes with sleeping, sometimes drainage from the ear.

Treatment: See your doctor, who will likely need to prescribe an antibiotic for your baby. (In children over age two, many doctors are now holding off on prescribing antibiotics, because research has shown that ear infections often subside on their own. Under two, however, doctors prefer not to take any risks.) She may also suggest an infant pain reliever until the fever and discomfort subside, which is typically about forty-eight hours after starting an antibiotic.

Illness: **Diarrhea**

What It Is: Loose, very watery stools that occur more than six to eight times a day (and more often than after each feeding, which is normal among breastfed infants). Diarrhea is usually caused by a viral infection.

Symptoms: Frequent loose, watery stools, which may be greenish yellow in color and also be accompanied by fever, vomiting, and irritability.

Treatment: There are no over-the-counter treatments for diarrhea that are appropriate for babies. If your baby has significant diarrhea, your pediatrician will probably recommend a commercially prepared electrolyte solution (such as Pedialyte) to aid in the prevention of dehydration (for more on recognizing and treating dehydration, see pages 233–34). Avoid giving your baby any sugary liquids such as fruit juice, soft drinks, Jell-O, or artificially sweetened beverages; anything too high in salt, such as canned soup or packaged broth; or too low in salt, such as water and tea. All of these choices can make diarrhea worse. If your solids-eating baby has been on an electrolyte solution for twelve to twenty-four hours (hint: Try the different brands if your baby rejects one) and the diarrhea appears to be decreasing, he can resume light eating; some pediatricians will recommend what is known as the BRAT diet—bananas, rice, applesauce, and toast. (These are all binding foods.) Cereal and yogurt are also good choices. Infants still exclusively on breast milk or formula would go back to their regular liquid diets.

Illness: **Vomiting**

What It Is: The forceful throwing up of stomach contents through the mouth. Many babies spit up small amounts after feedings. More persistent vomiting in the early months may be caused by a viral illness, or two other less common conditions. One is pyloric stenosis, a thickening of the muscle at the stomach exit that may require surgery. The other is gastroesophageal reflux (GER), a backing up of the stomach contents in the esophagus and throat, which may require some changes in feeding routine and/or medication.

Symptoms: Frequent forceful regurgitation, especially after eating, which may be accompanied by fever, lethargy, and abdominal pain. Dehydration can also occur as a result of vomiting.

Treatment: Notify your pediatrician. Vomiting due to a virus usually stops on its own in twelve to twenty-four hours, though you will have to be vigilant about preventing dehydration by giving your baby plenty of fluids. Notify your doctor if your baby has been vomiting more than twenty-four hours—or even before that, if you feel the need. It can be plenty scary the first time your baby has such an illness.

Illness: **Coxsackie virus**

What It Is: A viral illness, also known as hand, foot, and mouth disease, that tends to make the rounds in the summer and is transmitted by contact with saliva and feces. *How the heck is my baby going to come into contact with saliva and feces?* you're probably thinking. Why, the ever-popular baby pool, of course, because it's filled with leaky swim-diaper-clad bottoms. Theoretically the chlorine in the water should kill these germs, but every seasoned mother knows that this isn't always the case. If you're enjoying the sun with your little dipper, do your best to keep her from drinking the pool water—icky as it sounds, many do try!—or put toys into her mouth that have been sitting in the pool or handled by other kids (good luck!).

Symptoms: Fever, loss of appetite, irritability, and blistering on the hands, feet, and in the mouth. The fever may subside in a few days, but your child will still be contagious while he has blisters, which can last about a week.

Treatment: Your baby will probably act sick enough that you will contact your pediatrician, who will then tell you there's not much you can do but keep your baby comfortable until it passes, which can be anywhere from a few days to a week. Offer an appropriate dose of infant acetaminophen or ibuprofen, and soothe mouth sores with cold treats like ice pops. Avoid giving your baby salty or acidic foods such as orange juice—they may sting the blisters in his mouth.

Illness: **Roseola**

What It Is: A common viral illness that affects children under age three; outbreaks often occur in the spring and early-summer months.

Symptoms: A sudden onset of a high fever between 102 and 105 degrees Fahrenheit that lasts three days to a week and is accompanied by loss of appetite, crankiness, and sometimes a slight runny nose and cough. Your baby's eyelids may seem puffy and droopy, and she may also act a bit sleepier than usual.

Treatment: The fever will be high enough that you'll want to call the doctor, who will give you the usual advice—infant pain reliever, fluids, sponge baths—because he won't yet be able to officially diagnose roseola until the fever breaks. That's when a fine, lacy-looking red rash will begin creeping across your baby, beginning on her chest and spreading to her arms, neck, and face (sometimes it makes it to the legs as well). The rash may disappear in a day or hang around for a few. Happily, once your baby has had roseola, she'll become immune to it.

Illness: **Flu (influenza)**

What It Is: A highly contagious respiratory virus that can spread rapidly through communities between October and March. Flu germs are transmitted through the air by coughing and sneezing, and children are often especially vulnerable (along with seniors and anyone with compromised immunity).

Symptoms: Sudden fever of 101 degrees Fahrenheit or above; chills and shakes; extreme fatigue and lethargy; muscle aches and pains; a dry cough. After a few days, a sore throat and congestion usually develop, and coughs typically worsen. In contrast with the common cold, which produces a lower fever and less coughing, children (and adults) with the flu are much sicker overall.

Treatment: We don't need to tell you to call the doctor on this one—your gut instinct is going to compel you to do it anyway. Not necessarily because your baby's fever gets very high, but because it lasts so darn long and your baby is so darn miserable (plus, you will need a shoulder to cry on!). Your doctor will prescribe the usual doses of OTC infant pain reliever, lots of fluid, light meals, and bed rest (your baby won't be up to much else anyway) while the flu runs its course, in about a week. You will need to watch for secondary infections to develop, such as an ear or sinus infection, due to the congestion. Pneumonia is also a risk, so your doctor may have you bring your baby in as often as every other day while she is ill.

Decoding Your Baby's Coughs

There's nothing more maddening than lying in bed at night and listening to your baby hack, hack, hack. But coughing itself isn't an illness—it's a reflex to clear the airway; as a general rule, you don't want to suppress it. In fact, health professionals now warn against using over-the counter cough and cold preparations in children under age two because of the potential for serious side effects—see page 222 for more on this. Coughs usually clear up on their own—they just seem to be the last upper respiratory symptom to do so after an illness. Sometimes, however, coughing is a sign of something more serious that may need treatment. Here's how to tell.

What It Sounds Like: The bark of a dog or seal, sometimes accompanied by a high-pitched sound when inhaling

When It Occurs: Usually at night.

Other Symptoms: A cold, fever, hoarseness.

Possible Diagnosis: Croup—an inflammation of the voice box (larynx) and windpipe (trachea) that's usually caused by a virus, but can sometimes be associated with allergies. Croup tends to occur in the fall and winter in children under age three. Some kids are more prone to croup and tend to get it whenever they develop a respiratory illness.

What to Do: The traditional advice has been to take your baby into a hot
steamy bathroom so the moisture can help quiet the cough,
but a recent study found that steam didn't produce any significant improvement. Still, many doctors (and seasoned
mothers) continue to believe in this remedy for mild croup.
For one thing, the infants in the study had severe enough
croup that they were in the emergency room, so a steamy
bathroom may well help a cough that's not as bad. There's
certainly no harm in trying it (assuming your baby isn't having
such severe breathing difficulty that you should be calling 911
instead). You can also try taking her out into the cool night air.
If neither of these remedies quiets the cough, call your pediatrician. If your baby seems to be having difficulty breathing,
head to the ER or call 911 (depending on the severity) instead.

**What It Sounds Like: A pronounced deep, raspy cough that may be ac-
companied by rapid breathing; wheezing when exhaling**
When It Occurs: Constantly.
Other Symptoms: Lots of congestion, fever, irritability, lack of appetite.
Possible Diagnosis: Bronchiolitis or RSV (respiratory syncytial virus).
What to Do: Call your pediatrician.

**What It Sounds Like: A dry, hacking cough, that may be accompanied
by a high-pitched wheezing or whistling sound when your
baby exhales**
When It Occurs: Usually at night, but also may be triggered by exercising,
exposure to cold weather, or cigarette smoke.
Other Symptoms: Your baby may have a cold, too.
Possible Diagnosis: Asthma or reactive airway disease (a general term
used to describe a history of coughing or wheezing in young
children; the airway essentially overreacts to triggers such as
dust, smoke, or just a common cold).
What to Do: Call your pediatrician.

What It Sounds Like: Dry, irritating
When It Occurs: It may begin suddenly, any time of the day (though not
usually at night).
Other Symptoms: From none at all to difficulty breathing and wheezing.
Possible Diagnosis: Foreign object in the airway.

What to Do: Call 911 if your baby appears to be choking or having trouble breathing (see chapter 8, pages 299–306, for a detailed discussion of infant CPR and other ways to handle breathing or choking emergencies).

What It Sounds Like: Sharp, high-pitched, and spasmodic, possibly with a slight whoop at the end

When It Occurs: Develops after a week or two of common-cold symptoms.

Other Symptoms: Shortness of breath, drooling, bluish tint around the lips, exhaustion from coughing, vomiting.

Possible Diagnosis: Whooping cough (pertussis), a bacterial infection of the breathing passages. Your baby should have been vaccinated against whooping cough at two, four, six, and fifteen months, but if she wasn't, or hasn't received all four doses, she may be at risk.

What to Do: See your doctor right away; your baby will need antibiotics, and possibly hospitalization for oxygen and intravenous fluids. Whooping cough can be fatal in infants, so close medical observation is critical.

What Every Mom Needs to Know about Dehydration

When your baby's in the throes of a stomach bug, the biggest shocker is the mess—who knew such a little person could expel so much fluid from so many places? The biggest problem, however, isn't doing all those extra loads of laundry. It's the risk of dehydration, which can happen very quickly in an infant and cause a host of serious complications, and even death. Getting your baby the new RotaTeq vaccine can help ensure that this doesn't happen to her, because rotavirus—a viral gastrointestinal bug that causes severe diarrhea—is the single biggest cause of dehydration-related deaths in babies. The other important preventive measure is to keep feeding your baby. Alas, that means more laundry, because some of it will keep coming up (or out) until the bug runs its course, but a bit will stay, helping your baby retain enough fluid to keep her hydrated. The best thing to feed your baby if you're breastfeeding: breast milk, so continue to nurse, giving her short, frequent feeds. Formula-fed babies should pass on their usual bottles and drink an electrolyte solution such as Pedialyte instead, until the vomiting subsides. If your baby refuses to eat, get out a medicine dropper and give her two or three teaspoons of the electrolyte solution every fifteen

minutes. Meanwhile watch for these signs that dehydration could be setting in, and contact your pediatrician at the slightest inkling:

- Dry diapers are the first clue. Your baby should be wetting six to eight
  diapers a day (or from ten to twelve in the first two or three months);
  if you find one is still dry a few hours after a change, check in with
  your doctor. Can't be sure? Stick a tissue inside the diaper—you'll
  know when that's wet—but supervise an older baby since a grabbed
  tissue can become a choking hazard.
- A dry, parched-looking mouth, sunken eyes, a sunken fontanel (the
  soft spot at the top of your baby's head), and a lack of tears when your
  baby cries (after the second month, because newborn babies don't
  produce any tears) are all signs that moderate to severe dehydration is
  occurring. Get your baby to the doctor ASAP if she shows even just
  one of these symptoms.
- If your baby has been vomiting consistently for six hours or off and
  on for more than twenty-four hours, have her evaluated even if you
  don't yet see signs of dehydration.

Medicine Maneuvers

It's bad enough that your baby is sick—now you've got to figure out how
to get the medicine recommended by your doctor to go down and stay
down. Mary Poppins's strategy of a spoonful of sugar works wonders with
older kids, but when you're dealing with a baby who's not yet nimble
when it comes to chewing and swallowing, shooting a strange-tasting liquid down her trap presents a whole other set of challenges. Older babies
may like the flavor additives available at many pharmacies, especially that
perennial favorite, grape (go to flavorx.com for details). Beyond that, here
are some tricks and techniques to help relieve your pain.

Doctor's orders. The first thing you need to do is premeasure the correct
dose, then use an infant medicine dropper to either slowly drop the medicine into your baby's mouth, let her suck on the dropper, or squirt it
quickly back into the corner of her cheek. (Note: If your baby is crying,
the last approach may cause her to gag and spit it back out.)

   If your baby refuses to cooperate, mix the medicine with a small amount of
formula, breast milk, juice, or baby food (but not too large a serving; if your

baby doesn't finish it, she may not get all the medicine). If your baby spits out what seems like all the medicine, or vomits within five to ten minutes after you've administered it, repeat the full dose. (If the medicine stayed down for twenty minutes before the vomiting, you don't need to give it again.)

Then again, if only a little medicine rolls out and you think he got some, don't administer any more, especially if it's an infant pain reliever (it's easy and dangerous to overdose these). Finally, consider giving infant acetaminophen in suppository form, an especially good option for a vomiting baby.

Insider tricks. Not that we don't trust the docs, but sometimes we moms have a few ideas up our sleeves that happen to check out medically, too. First, run water on the dropper before putting the medicine into it; this will keep "sticky" liquids from adhering to the dropper itself and help ensure your baby gets the full dose.

If your baby hates the dropper, measure the medicine, pour it into a clean bottle nipple, and let him suck it through that (wet the nipple first, too).

Here are some other tricks to try: First, place your baby on her back on the changing table, then dangle a toy above her head. Her mouth will open while she watches the toy; you can administer the medicine while she's distracted. You can also try gently blowing into your baby's face as you give the medicine—it'll cause a natural swallowing reaction.

Finally, if your baby takes a pacifier, pop it in his mouth immediately after you give the medicine—it will make him more likely to suck and swallow, rather than spit.

"WHAT NOBODY TOLD ME ABOUT WHEN MY BABY GETS SICK"

"No matter how prepared I am when my son gets sick, I freak. To anyone else I look calm, cool, and collected, but I call the nurse's hotline at least once a day, especially if the symptoms change, and I do not sleep a wink! I am surprised by how helpless I feel, but when I call the office, I am always told that I'm doing everything exactly right. I guess all this fretting is just part of parenthood."

—*Melissa, Long Beach, California*

(continued on next page)

"After a bout of rotavirus, during which I managed to keep my cool, I freaked out when my son woke up barking like a seal at 2 AM and went to the emergency room. I could have saved a huge hospital bill by just calling the doctor instead. My advice to other moms: Always call, even in the middle of the night. That is what they are paid for, and they are used to it."   —*Tiffany, Garland, Texas*

"Chances are, it's probably not serious. If you live in a small town like we do, it really isn't an option to call the pediatrician after hours—the answering service just refers you to the emergency room. We've developed a repertoire of techniques that usually gets us through until morning, but if we feel that it's serious, we go."   —*Denise, Hugo, Colorado*

"At first I felt frustrated at my inability to keep my baby safe and healthy; that lasted for the first two or three illnesses. After that what really surprised me is that I had turned into my mother—the comforting, the waiting, the way I interacted with the doctor, the things I said to my husband about the doctor—all my mother. Not that it was a bad thing, just surprising."   —*Christy, Haltom City, Texas*

"It amazes me how uncertain I become, even though I am a well-educated, intelligent person. Images start flashing through my mind of all the serious diseases my kids could have instead of the simple bug they always end up with."   —*Kristin, North Ridgeville, Ohio*

"I consider myself a strong person. I don't like blood, but otherwise can hold my own in a stressful setting. Not so when it comes to my daughter. I am almost crippled at the sign of her distress, which is not the reaction I expected from myself. When she had an allergic reaction to food at nine months, I screamed so loud my husband heard me over the sound of his lawn tractor. Fortunately she has had only minimal injuries, but when she does, my husband ends up yelling at me to get myself together. I have more patience when she is sick, but after a point it gets to me and I cry. It breaks my heart to see my child in any other state than well."   —*Michele, Hainesport, New Jersey*

"I find it shocking that even when I am sick, too, I still somehow find the energy to do everything I can to soothe my baby!"   —*Kila, Keller, Texas*

CHAPTER 7

Feeding, Part II
Time to Chow Down on the Solid Stuff

Sometime after the first smile and before the first step comes the first solid food. Unlike most milestones, however, this is one whose arrival date you get to pick, which means you are prepared for once to create and capture the big moment. You set up the bouncy chair, you attach the bib, you get the cereal nice and mushy, you take out the tiny, rubber-tipped spoon you bought just for this meal, and finally you cue the videographer (your partner). So what happens? Your baby feels the spoon, pushes out his tongue, and his first meal slides down his chin instead of his gullet. You try again. And again. And again. By take fourteen, you realize that you can take a baby to mush but you can't make him eat.

No matter. You still count the meal as a milestone (he won't dance a jig for his first step, either), and you can still pronounce to your friends that your baby is now "on solids." If you're lucky, your gourmand will start relishing these exciting taste sensations and his new perspective of you as you foolishly make motorboat sounds and say "Open wide!"

What's next? After those first few bites of cereal, which occur between four and six months of age (there's more on how to tell when your particular baby is ready in the next section), you'll spend approximately six weeks introducing her to all the single-ingredient pureed "stage 1" foods in the fruit, veggie, and meat category, then move on to combination-ingredient meals ("stage 2") for another six weeks or so. Somewhere between eight and nine months, most babies are ready for chunkier textures in the form of "stage 3" foods, which also come in bigger jars for bigger appetites. You can begin to introduce finger foods, soft tiny tidbits, at the same time. Most babies continue this combination of chunky baby foods and finger foods until their first birthdays, and they're on a total table-food diet with the rest of the family not long after that. Throughout this whole process, your baby will continue to also drink plenty of breast milk or formula, which is still her primary source of nutrition until her first birthday. Here, the nitty-gritty on each of these stages.

Ready—or Not?

After months of nothing but a bland, round-the-clock liquid diet (yeah, we know breast milk is supposed to offer all kinds of tantalizing tastes, but you can't tell us it's the same as *coq au vin*), you'd think any baby would be thrilled to chow down on some real food. Not so. You may be bored out of your marbles with your little guy's never-changing menu, but your novice nibbler has just spent the past four to six months adjusting to a seismic shift in his concept of life, and now you're trying to rock his world all over again by taking away his most reliable source of satisfaction and security. What most novice moms don't expect to discover: Reality sometimes bites when it comes to helping your baby make the transition to a solid diet.

The fact is, most babies are at least a little bit reluctant to move on to the brave new world of solid foods. Who needs new tastes and textures when you've gotten used to months of lazy, soothing sucking? That devil-may-care attitude can make those first few feedings a challenge for both of you. Besides the sheer logistics—what to introduce first, how much, how often, avoiding allergic reactions, and trying to keep the inevitable mess to a minimum—you've got to get your baby to actually swallow the stuff. And that unsuspecting little mouth is likely to say, *Right back at you, Mom,* when you try to poke in a spoonful of mush. Take heart—and take it slow. Every baby is different, and while some kids may happily gobble up everything in sight, others may need more time to adapt.

Although many of our moms were spooning cereal into us at only a few weeks of age, the AAP now recommends waiting much longer, until your baby is between four and six months old. Most babies don't lose their tongue-thrust reflex—which causes them to push anything solid that enters their mouths back out—until between four and six months. (Kind of makes you wonder how Grandma got that cereal to go down our two-month-old traps, doesn't it?) The digestive system has also matured to the extent now that it can tolerate new foods, and your baby has spread out his feedings to the point that he can start falling into a more typical meal-like pattern—though he will continue to eat more frequently than you do. Your baby is physically ready, too: He will likely have full head control and be able to sit at least semi-upright with support.

There has also been concern that introducing any foods too soon into a baby's diet will contribute to the development of allergies. Research shows that babies fed cereal before three months of age had a greater risk of developing diabetes and celiac disease (a serious intolerance to wheat protein). Waiting too long can also backfire: The diabetes risk goes up again if a baby isn't introduced to cereal before seven months, and another recent study found that babies who weren't fed cereal until after six months were actually more likely—not less—to develop a wheat allergy. So what you're left with is a window of time between four and six months that is the best opportunity to introduce your little one to the solid stuff.

One more note on food allergies: They actually aren't that common, despite all the publicity they get. The average infant has only about a 5 percent chance of developing a food allergy. But because certain foods do cause more allergic reactions, most doctors warn parents to stay away from them for the first one to three years. If you've got a family history of allergies, there's greater cause for concern, since they tend to be hereditary. If either you or your baby's father suffers from asthma, eczema, hay fever, or food allergies, the risk that your baby will develop a food allergy goes up to between 20 and 30 percent. If both parents do, it increases to a whopping 40 to 70 percent.

Yet another reason for holding off on solids is that your baby will continue to enjoy the many benefits of breast milk as the main staple of his diet. That's really the prime motivation of the medical community, which has been recommending "exclusive" breastfeeding for the first six months of life for quite some time now. We certainly can't argue with that viewpoint, but now the delayed cereal/wheat allergy connection is complicating that recommendation a bit. Plus, far fewer women are still breastfeeding at six months than experts would like—about 36 percent according to the latest CDC numbers—and many of them may be supplementing.

All this adds up to one conclusion: There is no absolute best answer, no one D-day on the calendar of your baby's life. You two pretty much get to decide when during that four- to six-month window dinner should begin to be served. How can you be sure your dining companion is as hungry as you are to get started? One of the more obvious signs will be that your baby begins to mooch: Her eager little eyes watch every bite you take, as if she wants a taste. It's especially adorable when she opens her mouth as you take a bite, like a little bird waiting for her worm. Some moms find that their infants no longer seem to be satisfied with breast milk or formula alone because they cry for more when a feeding is done, want to eat more frequently during the day, or begin to wake up again for middle-of-the-night nips when sleeping through the night had been the norm. If your baby is bottlefeeding and her formula consumption has increased to a quart (thirty-two ounces) a day, that's yet another sign she's ready for something more substantial.

STUFF YOU NEED FOR FEEDING SOLIDS . . .

❑ Plastic bibs (with big pockets to catch drips).
❑ Baby spoons. (The kind with the soft-bite rubber-coated bowl are always popular, but so are heat-sensitive spoons with tips that turn white to prevent burning that tender tongue.)
❑ Plastic or melamine bowls or plates. (The kind with suction bottoms that adhere to the high chair tray can be handy.)
❑ An infant seat (until your baby can sit up well) or a high chair that reclines slightly.
❑ A high chair (once your baby can sit up).
❑ A lightweight, portable booster seat with tray (for feeding on the go).
❑ A splat mat to minimize cleanup.
❑ Several sippy cups (see pages 260–62 for how to choose).

. . . AND STUFF YOU DON'T

• Fabric bibs. Too hard to keep clean, and why increase your laundry?
• Silver spoons. You probably received one for a gift, but save it as an heirloom—many babies don't like the cold surface.
• Warming plates. Room temperature is just fine.

The Logistical Lowdown

Now that you're ready to begin, you've got to give some thought to the logistics of feeding your baby. First, where's your little chowhound going to sit? If he's closer to the four-month mark, a high chair probably isn't an option—he'll just slump forward or sideways—unless you have a model with a reclining seat. An infant car seat can work well because of the slight recline, or you can hold your baby upright on your lap. Don't use a bouncy seat unless you want food flying everywhere; it's hard enough to get those first bites in without your baby being in motion at the same time. Holding your baby on your lap for novice nibbling can also be a bit awkward, because that leaves you with only one free hand for wielding the spoon, wiping the dribble, and possibly prying that little mouth open (which may remain clamped shut the first few times). If this is your plan, you might want to enlist Dad or Grandma to do the holding (but bear in mind that the more people are involved, the more distracting it may be, too). Make sure your baby is wearing a real feeding bib made of plastic, because more is going to end up on him than in him. You'll discover soon enough that wipe-off plastic bibs are much easier to clean than the cloth variety, which are best saved for drool and wet burps.

Then there's the issue of timing. Though it may seem logical to you to begin with breakfast, this is not the best time to introduce your baby to solids. She's going to be ravenous in the morning, especially if she's been sleeping all night, and not in the mood to have something new sprung on her. Wait until the next feeding, around midmorning to offer her first bites. Midday after a nap, when she's rested and in a good mood, can also work out well. There are also two different schools of thought about when to offer the bottle or breast during the meal. Some say at first, to take the edge off your baby's hunger; others advise waiting until afterward, because she'll be less open to trying new foods if she's already partially sated. Each baby is different in this regard, so you're going to have to figure this one out for yourself. (See "The Fluid Factor" on page 252 for more on how much breast milk or formula your baby will continue to consume once she begins solids.) As for how often, most doctors recommend offering solids twice a day at first, and it's enough of a production that you won't feel like doing it more often than this anyway. Once your baby gets the hang of things and is eating more, you can add a third meal (probably between seven and nine months, depending on how early you started).

Again, bear in mind that whatever you spoon out is likely to be met with resistance at first. Some babies dislike the new textures so much that they cough and gag and even cry. Most certainly, they won't swallow much. Give your baby about a week to accept these first spoonfuls, and if it's not happening at that point, put your gear away and try again in the near future. Your baby will turn a corner when he's ready, most likely by six months. Meanwhile, there's no sense in making the whole experience a big negative in his happy little head.

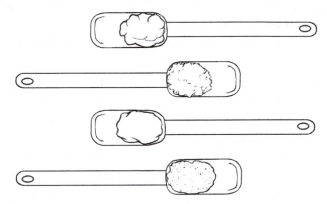

Figure 7.1a The average six- to twelve-month-old may eat only about a half table-spoon of each food group at a meal.

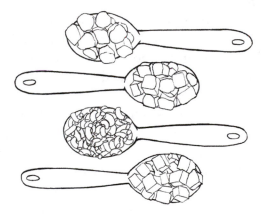

Figure 7.1b The average twelve- to eighteen-month-old progresses to more like a whole tablespoon of each food group per meal.

First Things First

Sounds like a lot to consider? There's more. You can't just pop open any old jar of baby food and spoon it between those little lips. There's a fairly organized method you need to follow, though some of the guidelines have been loosened up of late. Iron-fortified rice cereal is the most frequently recommended first food. Why? It's very nutritious, bland tasting, and can be thinned (with formula or breast milk) to an almost liquid consistency. The thinning also gives the cereal a taste to which your little one is accustomed. The term *solids* at this stage is really a misnomer; both baby cereals and first jarred foods are actually closer to liquids in consistency. Rice cereal is also free of gluten (a protein that can sometimes trigger an allergic reaction). And your baby's iron stores, which he's had from birth, are also beginning to deplete by this point, so the iron in the cereal is another important plus. All that said, there's been some acceptance recently of beginning with fruits and vegetables instead of cereal, because some doctors feel it may help babies develop a taste for those healthy, lower-calorie foods that can help prevent obesity down the road.

Regardless of what you ultimately start with (and your pediatrician can help you decide that), the introduction of new foods must be performed with care over several months. These first foods should always be smoothly pureed, single-ingredient, and introduced one at a time, waiting at least three days (and four to five isn't a bad idea) between new selections to make sure there is no allergic reaction. If you're buying commercial baby food (like the vast majority of us), you'll have no trouble determining which foods are appropriate: Manufacturers label them "stage 1" or "1st food" or something similar. Avoid combo (or "stage 2") items for now, because if your baby has a reaction, you won't know which ingredient caused it. (Also, their texture may be too much for your novice to handle.)

What are the signs of a food allergy? In most cases, they're fairly obvious:

- A skin rash resembling hives.
- Vomiting shortly after eating.
- Diarrhea within a few hours of eating.
- Blood in the stools.
- Breathing difficulty similar to an asthmatic reaction.

For the first few symptoms, check in with your pediatrician, who will likely tell you to just eliminate the offending food from your baby's diet for now. Chances are that down the road she'll be able to tolerate it just fine, but consult your doctor before you reintroduce it. In the case of breathing difficulties, call 911. Though it's pretty rare, a baby with severe allergies can go into anaphylactic shock, during which the trachea, larynx, and lungs all shut down, which can be fatal.

Such a severe reaction is typically associated with nut allergies, but there are a number of other highly allergenic foods you need to be aware of, especially if there is a history of food allergies in your family. These foods are generally not introduced into a baby's diet until after age one, and some physicians may counsel you to wait until age three if, again, there's a family history. Highly allergenic foods include:

- Egg whites.
- Corn.
- Spinach.
- Citrus fruits.
- Wheat.
- Shellfish.
- Peanuts and nut butters.
- Tree nuts (cashews, almonds, walnuts, pecans).

Two other foods that are off limits during the first year are cow's milk, because the fat and proteins it contains are difficult for a baby to digest, and honey, because it may contain the bacteria that can cause botulism, a serious form of food poisoning.

Now that we've scared the heck out of you, we'll get back to the day to day. Continue to work your way through the single-ingredient items until your baby has tried something from each of the groups successfully: fruits, veggies, meats, and assorted cereals. If you've got the brain cells, it's not a bad idea to keep a food diary, to help you remember what you introduced and when, since this is a fairly complex process.

Peas before Peaches? Who Cares!

It's an age-old question: Will introducing sweet foods first predestine your pumpkin toward a love of all things sugar-laden? It seems we moms don't really give a hoot if it does. We asked moms on Parenting.com/babytalk what their first choice was in jarred baby foods, and the more than fifteen hundred respondents overwhelmingly chose sweet varieties of fruits and veggies. And Mother may know best after all. After years of promoting blah first bites like green beans and peas, experts are finally conceding that it probably doesn't matter. For one thing, your baby may already have experienced plenty of taste sensations in breast milk. For another, all babies' taste buds are wired at birth with a preference for sweets. (So you really do have an excuse for those uncontrollable chocolate cravings.)

What was the first jarred food you introduced?

Bananas	27%
Sweet potatoes	19%
Apples	17%
Carrots	13%
Peas	9%
Squash	6%
String beans	5%
Pears	4%

Stepping Up to Stage Two

Once you've gone through the single foods and your baby has shown no sign of allergies, you can safely step up to the stage 2 jars: tastier combos like beef and carrots, or chicken and sweet potatoes. The equipment you need is still the same, but your baby will likely be ready for a full-size high chair by now if you've been using an infant seat. According to the nutritionists at Gerber (call them at 800-4-GERBER for good advice), your baby is ready for stage 2 foods when he can sit independently for half a minute or so, pick up and hold small toys (but not necessarily teeny-tiny things like Cheerios), and has tried the stage 1 foods to rule out allergies. He won't be allergic to the ingredients in stage 2 if he didn't react to them the first time around. If he did have a reaction, consult your pediatrician for future guidance (you probably already called her for advice when the reaction occurred); you'll likely have to avoid that particular food in your baby's diet for some time to come. By the way, both Beech-Nut (beechnut.com or 800-BEECH-NUT) and Gerber (gerber.com or its help line, 800-4-GERBER) have lots of helpful tips and feeding advice available on their Web sites or by calling their help lines, so don't hesitate to contact them if you have a quandary we've neglected to address.

Continue to serve cereal at least once, if not twice a day, for as long as your baby likes it. For instance, at breakfast he will probably eat cereal and a jar of fruit. Then you can serve cereal again at supper with a combination dinner (such as ham and sweet potatoes). Nutrition experts love baby cereal for its high levels of iron content, a much-needed nutrient in your child's diet. Iron is necessary for the production of blood hemoglobin, a red pigment that carries oxygen to the tissues and removes carbon dioxide (a waste material). Being women who shed blood on a monthly basis, we're all too familiar with what happens when we don't eat enough iron—anemia, which causes fatigue, paleness, and paper-thin fingernails, to name a few symptoms—and the same thing can happen to your baby. Severe anemia can cause real growth problems. Besides cereal, other baby foods, particularly those containing meats and green veggies, are also fortified with iron. And up until one year of age, if your baby is formula-fed, he will be drinking an iron-fortified formula, so all these sources should ensure he has plenty of iron in his diet.

How Much Is Enough?

That's the million-dollar question . . . for which there is no reliable answer. Unfortunately, there is no "average" we can give you, because babies vary so greatly in size. One who entered the world at ten pounds may be topping twenty pounds by now and polishing off two jars at a single meal. Another who began at six pounds may barely weigh fourteen, and may not eat as much over the course of a whole day as the former does at one sitting. Just like adults, size and appetites are seldom similar from one person to the next, yet both body types are bound to be equally healthy. While your baby is still getting breast milk or formula, which as you know are complete foods in terms of nutrition, the primary purpose of solids is to simply "practice" the art of eating. In fact, you actually don't want your baby too eat too much yet—it may hamper his hankering for that super-nutritious breast or bottle. Think of solids as an an appetizer before his main course of breast milk or fomula.

So if your baby rejects a meal now and then, or even what seems like an entire food group (no green veggies, or no meats, for instance), he's not going to develop any dietary deficiencies. Bear in mind, too, that even if he doesn't like something as a single food, he may eat it happily in a combo meal with something else. In fact, that's often the case with the single-ingredient meats, which as you can imagine are pretty tasteless. But pair up, say, some pureed chicken with apples, and the tables may turn. One final tidbit about likes and dislikes: It can take up to ten attempts to get a baby to accept a new taste or texture sensation, so just because he's not into that vegetable-and-barley dinner you thought looked so yummy the first or even fourth time you serve it, don't give up so easily. There's a good chance it will go down and stay down eventually.

Because you can also expect your baby's growth to slow during the second half of his first year, you should do your best to not obsess about how much he's eating, even if the ten-month-old next door has an appetite to rival your husband's. Most babies double their birth weight by four months, but only triple it by a year, so as long as your baby is growing at a steady clip, you can let him take the lead when it comes to quantity. To put things in perspective, babies between six months and one year of age need to consume about fifty calories per pound that they weigh. That means a seventeen-pound baby would need to consume about 850 calories a day, and that number includes both solids and breast milk or formula. Formula typically contains about 20 calories an ounce, so if he's drinking twenty-eight ounces of formula, that's 560 calories right there. You're left with room for between three and four jars of baby food (the little four-ounce size), plus a serving of cereal—not too hard to pull off, especially when your little one finds foods he really likes.

As for when your baby is full, he'll definitely set you straight if you pay attention to the signals. Most likely, he'll clamp his mouth shut, or even bat away the spoon. That's when you should put it down, so your child learns to pay attention to his own hunger cues, rather than cleaning his plate (er, jar) as we adults have fallen into the habit of doing.

Should You Go Organic?

In this age of culinary sophistication, with vegetable oil taking a backseat to extra-virgin olive, when we grill and sauté instead of shaking and baking, and goat's milk is preferred to cream cheese, it's no surprise that parents want their babies to have high-quality cuisine, too. Commercial baby food makers have responded by taking out the starchy fillers like tapioca once found in the baby foods we dined on, and whipping up healthier and trendier combos—for instance, organic "summer vegetable dinner" versus salt-laden "chicken noodle surprise." In fact, there are complete lines of organic baby foods from many major manufacturers such as Gerber and Earth's Best. Going beyond that is an entire cottage industry of freshly made, flash-frozen, organic baby foods. Some brands you have to order online; others are available in the freezer section of grocery stores.

Organic foods are popular because they (and the plants and animals they come from) are said to be free of pesticides, synthetic chemicals, dyes, hormones, antibiotics, and other additives. Are they really necessary?

That's a question best answered by your lifestyle and pocketbook. It's important to remember that nonorganic commercial baby food is also safe, nutritious, and convenient, not to mention more affordable. In fact, the ingredients used to make any type of baby food are held to a stricter growing standard than those fruits and veggies grown and sold to adults. Your baby will likely grow up plenty healthy eating the jarred foods found on grocery store shelves. If you want to splurge on higher-end products (and you will splurge, because these kinds of frills don't come cheap) and you've got the bucks, be our guest. Then again, putting that extra cash into a college fund may offer your child more benefit in the long run.

The other alternative is to make your own baby food, which some moms are inspired to do because they would like to save money as well as provide more nutrition. Again, both of these points are debatable. Ironically, concerns about unnecessary additives and pesticides often prompt parents to go this route, but unless you use organic produce, you can actually make things worse. That's because as we just said, regular produce is not held to the same growing standards as the produce baby food manufacturers are required to use. So buying all that organic produce can add up almost as fast as jars of baby food, not to mention the time involved in preparing homemade foods. If you want to try it anyway, here are some guidelines:

- Again, it's a good idea to buy only organic fruits and veggies, or those with a peel that can be removed before cooking.
- Wash all preparation utensils and storage containers in a dishwasher or very hot soapy water beforehand.
- Steam or pressure-cook raw vegetables and meats until they are soft enough to puree in a blender or food processor. Some ripe fruits, such as bananas and avocados, are soft enough to simply mash with a fork.
- Make large batches of baby food and freeze them in ice cube trays to create serving-size portions. Remove the cubes when frozen and store them in freezer bags so you only need to thaw as much as you need. Homemade baby food will stay fresh in the refrigerator for two days, or the freezer for about three weeks.

The Solids-and-Sleep Connection

It's a commonly held belief that starting solids helps babies sleep through the night—and one that experts love to dispute. The party line: Sleeping all night is a maturational development that just happens to occur for many babies at around the same time they are starting solids, which is between four and six months. Uh, okay. So there's no "direct link" as the research community would say. As moms, we can't help but wonder why you wouldn't sleep better with a full belly (we sure do). And wouldn't you imagine that cereal would "stick to your ribs," as the proverbial thinking goes, a lot better than a liquid diet? So, while there's no official connection, there's also no reason you can't hold out the hope that solids might help if you're still seriously deprived of your shut-eye. We asked moms what they thought of the issue in a Parenting.com/babytalk poll, and here's what they said. What shocked us most: all those babies younger than three months who are sleeping through the night (no way!).

When did your baby start sleeping through the night?

Before three months, and well before eating any solids.	44%
Between four and six months, but he/she still hadn't eaten solids.	15%
Between four and six months and right around the time when I introduced solids.	12%
Later than six months and well after starting solids.	7%
Help! My baby is older than seven months and still not sleeping through.	22%

The Big-Baby Syndrome

It's not your imagination: Babies today are bigger than ever before. In a recent Harvard Medical study of more than 120,000 children over a twenty-two-year period, infants from birth to six months of age had the greatest jump of all age groups "at risk" of being overweight: 59 percent. The number of already overweight infants increased even more, by a whopping 74 percent. What all this adds up to: If your baby is in a high percentile category for weight, but a lower percentile for height, then your pediatrician is likely to become concerned. Why is that once adorable baby fat getting a bad name? It's part of the overall obesity epidemic in our country, which has trickled down from adults to children in record numbers. Some experts believe the seeds of overeating are planted in infancy—or maybe even in pregnancy when moms pack on too many pregnancy pounds then give birth to oversize babies with oversize appetites.

Talk about confusing. The first and most important job for a mom is feeding her child, and we're supposed to do it on demand, as our babies' appetites dictate. So how can you be sure your pleasantly plump cherub won't turn into a tubby toddler, and an even fatter big kid? Here's the skinny on what you need to worry about—and what you don't.

Rumor: **Babies who are large at birth are more likely to develop weight problems.**

Fact: Not necessarily. Research shows that babies who are small for their gestational age (this generally refers to infants who weigh less than six pounds at birth, but are totally healthy in every other way) may be at greater risk because they usually have a higher percentage body fat. Conversely, infants who are in the 90th percentile for weight at birth have a greater proportion of lean tissue (they may simply have bigger bones and not necessarily a lot of excess fat). What you do want to watch: significant weight gain by about four months. In the first few weeks of life, weight gain is critical to get your baby off to a good start, growth-wise. Most infants drop ounces immediately after birth; losing as much as 10 percent of their body weight is considered normal. But by the two-week checkup, you want your baby to have at least gained back enough to be the same size he was at birth, and even a bit more than that is a good thing. If you're breastfeeding, it shows you're making enough milk, and your baby is consuming enough from his end, too, so don't start to stress about any of this until you get to the four-month checkup. Why then? Research shows that if a baby has started to gain excess weight by the four-month checkup, he is a bit more likely to be overweight later in childhood.

What You Can Do: Infants typically double their birth weight by four months of age, so if your baby was eight pounds at birth, he'll be expected to be around sixteen pounds at the four-month checkup. If your baby's weight is higher than what's expected at that point, discuss it with your pediatrician. It still may not be a big deal, depending on other factors—maybe your baby is also very tall or big-boned, for example. But while no one is going to tell you to put your baby on a diet, there may be other things you can do to improve the situation, such as providing a pacifier for those times when your baby still wants to suck after his tummy has been filled.

Rumor: **Formula-fed babies are more likely to get fat.**

Fact: There is definitely research supporting the fact that formula-fed babies tend to be heavier, but no one's entirely sure why. The composition of breast milk changes during the course of a feeding, with fat content increasing the longer the baby nurses, so it is possible that breastfed babies are consuming less fat overall. And the cow's-milk proteins found in formula are more concentrated than the proteins in breast milk, so that may add more calories.

What You Can Do: Of course experts say breastfeeding is best for many health reasons, including minimizing your baby's future chances of obesity. But we all know that not everyone can breastfeed, or will be able to keep it up for more than a few months, and we're not going to make you now think your baby is going to become a porker just because she's drinking formula. Many of our children here at *Babytalk* drank formula along with breast milk after a period of nursing, and we have no weight problems to report among them; in fact, most of us find getting them to stop playing and eat is a far bigger headache. See below for ways to keep your baby's formula consumption under control.

Rumor: **It's up to you to make sure your baby eats enough.**

Fact: Absolutely not. Your baby is perfectly capable of controlling her own food intake. That's one of the reasons breastfed babies may be leaner: They decide when they're tummies are full, and moms with no empty bottles to rely on simply have to trust their child's judgment. Research has also supported this fact: In one study, mothers who breastfed for six months or more were less controlling of their child's food intake at age one.

What You Can Do: Don't push your baby to finish that last ounce of formula or those last few spoonfuls in the baby food jar. Let her hunger dictate when and how much she eats. When your baby progresses to solid food, it's always a good idea to try to keep the mind-set that these first meals are for practicing, almost like an appetizer before her main course of breast milk. This will also keep you from becoming too anxious about whether she's eating enough or not.

When your baby is ready for finger foods, do your best to keep junk food, fast food, and processed food out of her diet. This is easiest with a first baby, of course, because there won't be older siblings to expose her to these delights, er, horrors. Our motto, here again, is that a few french fries or chicken nuggets now and then aren't going to kill anybody. But just like you wouldn't indulge in a bacon cheeseburger or death-by-chocolate dessert every day, neither should they. Everything will balance out if you also provide your child with plenty of opportunity for physical activity—meaning, don't keep her strapped in a high chair or stroller (too much anyway) when she could be crawling and exploring.

The Fluid Factor

You might think that once your baby moves beyond the exclusive breast or bottle stage, you needn't worry anymore about liquid intake. Guess again. For many moms, it continues to be an issue, and for a variety of reasons. *Should I substitute a solid feeding for a bottle feeding, or give both? When can I give up formula altogether? Should my baby be drinking juice?* These are just some of the confusing questions that will nag at and unnerve you. Fortunately, the answers are easy.

We've already told you that breast milk and formula will continue to be your baby's main source of nutrition even after solids have been introduced. So how can that tiny tummy have room for the same amount of liquid after a robust meal of pureed peaches and runny cereal? Believe it or not, most babies find a way to fit it all in. Once your baby is accustomed to solids, begin to delay offering the bottle or breast until about an hour after a meal. At this point, she can probably begin to play around with a drink in a sippy cup during meals—and we do mean *play*, because at first she'll do everything but put it into her mouth and drink from it. (For more advice on introducing a cup, see pages 260–62.) This way, your baby's tummy won't be as full. And she will no doubt still enjoy the nurturing aspect of her breast or bottle feeding and be eager to cuddle up with you for it. The one exception to this is that first morning meal. We mentioned earlier that you shouldn't try to introduce cereal to a ravenous baby who's been sleeping for hours, and that rule will probably hold true for a while. Nurse or give her a bottle first thing when she wakes in the morning, and her solid feeding a little later.

Of course there will be variations in how much babies of different sizes continue to drink after they are introduced to solids, but most do continue to consume about the same amount of liquid even after baby food has been added to their diet. If your baby's liquid intake seems to drop off, keep an eye out for a normal number of wet diapers (about six to eight a day). Dehydration is more likely to occur as a result of the diarrhea or vomiting that accompanies an illness, but it is possible that a baby who fills up on solids and doesn't take in enough breast milk or formula could also become dehydrated. Talk to your pediatrician if you are concerned.

One beverage you won't be serving for a while yet is whole milk. The AAP recommends that infants continue to receive breast milk or formula for the entire first year, because these liquids are more nutritious (cow's milk doesn't have enough iron, which is critical to your baby's health and development), and your baby's delicate digestive system is not yet ready for the harder-to-absorb cow's milk. When your baby reaches his first birthday, you'll be able to wean him from formula or breast milk to cow's milk, and at that point it will be important to give him whole milk, not reduced-fat or skim milk. Though most of the rest of the population—older kids and adults alike—is cautioned not to drink whole milk because of its high fat content, fat is critical to your baby's brain development for the first two years of life. (After his second birthday, it will be healthier to switch your baby to a lower-fat form of milk, but that probably seems like a million years away right now!)

How to Survive a Nursing Strike

Don't be surprised if your now solid-loving baby suddenly decides to turn up her nose at your nipple. What gives? It's not at all uncommon, now that your child has so many more taste sensations to choose from, and a world of activities beckoning (*No offense, Mom, but lying in your lap for twenty minutes is so not happening*). Don't panic; your baby probably isn't trying to totally wean herself just yet. She's still going to love those cuddle sessions at quieter times, and you may just need to rework your routine a bit. Help her graduate to a cup at mealtimes, for instance, and save nursing sessions for mornings, nap, and bedtime (see pages 260–62 for tips on introducing a cup). Also consider that a negative experience could be contributing to her reluctance. Something might be making nursing painful, such as teething or an ear infection, or you may be going through a stressful time yourself (a move, a new job) and she's protesting the disruption in her routine. The holidays are also a typical time for nursing strikes, because moms are usually overwhelmed with all they have to do (no kidding) and your baby can sense that she's not getting her usual amount of attention (as in *all me, all the time*). So before you pack up your breast pads, try these tricks to lure her back on:

- If you suspect it's teething, roll a nubby damp washcloth into a cigar shape, freeze it slightly, then use it to numb your baby's gums right before nursing.
- Consider the possibility of illness: If your baby's been congested, for instance, rejecting the breast may be a sign that an ear infection is setting in—sucking can increase the pain.
- Reconnect with your baby: Spend the next several hours devoting yourself totally to her—cuddle skin-to-skin, sit in a quiet room and rock, get in the bath and lay her on your chest.
- Get moving: Try getting your baby to latch on while strolling around the house. The combination of motion and soothing often does the trick.
- Lull her into latching on: Rock your baby until she's dozing or almost asleep, then moisten your nipple with some breast milk and slip it into her mouth.
- Usually you don't need to resort to bottles (unless you really want to). Instead express your milk and feed it in a cup, which is possible even with younger babies. When the cup doesn't fully satisfy her, chances are your baby will get the hint and be more likely to take your breast back.

The Third Stage: Transitioning to Table Food

By about nine months, many babies are hankering for some real food to sink those new teeth into. And it's not a moment too soon for you, either: Just as the constantly running faucet of your baby's liquid diet was getting old a few months ago, so, too, are all those tiny glass jars that have to be packed in gigantic brown grocery bags, lugged home rolling and banging together in the back of the minivan, then washed out and recycled. You'll begin this stage by adding chunkier baby foods to your child's repertoire. Usually labeled "stage 3" or "step 3," these foods come in bigger jars for bigger appetites. They have more texture than pureed foods so babies can learn to move food around in their mouth and mash it up a bit before swallowing. And if any of it does go down whole, it's not big enough to choke on.

How will you know your baby is ready to graduate to stage 3? Watch to see how his mouth moves when he eats. Rather than just slurping spoon-fuls down into his throat, you should see your baby's mouth working harder. He'll be moving food around, transferring it from side to side. You'll notice his jaw moving more, too, as he works on mashing things with it and with his tongue. A stage 3 baby should also be able to hold a cup independently, and he's probably trying to grab the spoon from you because he's interested in doing things for himself now.

To start, give your baby a lumpier version of a favorite stage 2 food and see how he handles it. For instance, if he couldn't get enough of a pureed stage 2 turkey and sweet potato dinner, introduce him to stage 3 turkey, rice, and garden vegetables with bits of veggies and rice to mash with his gums. At the same time your baby is gobbling up chunkier jarred food, you can begin giving him toddler biscuits or zwieback toasts with his meals or for a snack. They dissolve quickly in his mouth (making a really gooey mess!), and give him a chance to practice his self-feeding skills.

The other part of this phase is offering some finger foods—soft, bite-size table food—along with the jarred commercial stuff at each meal (so you're spoon-feeding him out of the jar and he's nibbling on finger foods himself between bites). You'll be able to tell your baby is developmentally ready for finger foods if he is becoming more mobile: crawling, pulling to a standing position, or even able to stand alone for a few seconds. These babies are also beginning to understand the meaning of cause and effect and use sounds or gestures to communicate (such as crawling over or pointing to the high chair when they want to eat).

Good choices for first finger foods include soft, ripe pieces of fruit or well-cooked vegetables—such as bananas, peaches, potatoes, or carrots—or well-cooked pasta, cubes of bread, and soft cheeses. To be on the safe side, all such finger foods should be cut into quarter-inch cubes—just about the size of fruit cocktail (remember that?) or a dime. For parents who are especially worried or especially busy (okay, that means all of us), major baby food manufacturers also offer pre-packaged sliced and diced bite-size foods, often labeled something like "pickups," "dices," or "table-teaching" foods.

The meat group is a trickier category when it comes to serving finger foods, simply because meats tend to be drier and chewier (it's fine to rely on the baby food varieties of meats until your child gets the hang of eating tougher textures). When you do offer meat from your dinner table, the key is to make sure it's ground and as moist as possible. Meat loaf is a good choice because it's moister than a hamburger. Of course that kid favorite, ketchup, can go along way toward making cubes of a hamburger more palatable! Gravy is another way to soften things up. When serving meatballs (which can be made from ground turkey for a leaner option), add a little mildly seasoned tomato sauce. Cooking a chicken or turkey? Boil those giblets—liver is a perfect soft meat for your baby and loaded with much-needed-but-hard-to-get iron.

Since babies are most comfortable with the familiar, proceed carefully with this new self-feeding process. Whenever you're introducing different textures—from pureed to mashed to chunks—introduce it in a food your little one already likes. For instance, if he loved pureed sweet potatoes or bananas, give him cubes of cooked sweet potato and ripe banana when he begins table foods so that the taste is the same even if the texture isn't. Don't forget about about dry cereal that easily softens up in baby's mouth (such as Cheerios or puffed wheat), and experiment with less-expected choices, too. Nutritionists recommend cooked sweet potato; ripe avocado; thin, shredded chicken or turkey; soft baked beans; scrambled eggs (made from the yolks only—whites are an allergy no-no); meat-filled ravioli; chunk light tuna packed in water; pancakes; waffles; and french toast.

Your inclination will be to offer well-balanced meals that include servings of carbs, proteins, dairy, veggies, and fruit over the course of a day—and that's certainly what you want to strive for down the road, after the first birthday, when your baby is no longer drinking formula or breast milk. But for now these liquids still remain your child's primary source of nutrition, so you needn't worry yet if he rejects a particular food group here and there. And again, don't give up on an item if your baby doesn't lap it right up; as we noted earlier, it can take up to ten attempts before a baby (or bigger child) accepts a new food.

Theoretically, life should get easier when your baby starts to eat the same food you do, but finger and table foods also add a new element of anxiety to your life: Am I feeding my baby enough, and is it the right stuff? After all, you're spending a good six to eight months or so transitioning your baby from a total liquid diet to an almost all table-food diet by somewhere between twelve and eighteen months, and frankly there are very few guidelines on exactly how much your baby needs. We've given you some, but you still will need to wean yourself from the security that comes with ounce markers on bottles and the clink of the spoon in the empty baby food jar, all while it looks like much of what you put on the high chair tray ends up on the floor. (Did someone look into a physics law for this? Because we're almost positive there is some scientific relationship.)

Your baby's calorie needs depend in large part on his size: As we've said, the rule of thumb is to consume fifty calories for each pound of weight for adequate growth. So now your bigger twenty-pound (or so) baby would need to consume about a thousand calories a day. Up until that first birthday, you've still got formula or breast milk to contribute to those calories and nutrients (typically, that now counts for about thirty-two ounces or 640 calories a day). When your baby reaches her first birthday and switches over to whole milk, then you can really worry. Okay, we're just kidding. You won't have to, but we know you probably will. Your baby's rate of growth will slow dramatically and she'll require less food—well, less than you expect, anyway. Your job at that point becomes providing healthy, delicious foods; it's her job to decide to eat them.

Meanwhile, if you'd like a sample menu for the average nine to twelve-month-old, you can find one from the American Academy of Pediatrics at aap.org. Personally, most of us here at *Babytalk* found that the AAP guidelines prescribed more food than our kids ate, yet they have continued to grow up healthy and happy, so don't panic if that applies to your baby as well. Along with the guidelines, remember your baby's size (a smaller baby may eat what seems like considerably less, for instance) and the fact that her appetite is going to fluctuate. She may eat more at one feeding, or over the course of one day, and less on another day. Also, the older she is, the more likely she'll be to consume the recommended amount.

So what is the supposedly "average" nine- to twelve-month old eating? Here's a very general idea:

Breakfast. A quarter to half cup of iron-fortified cereal; about the same amount of a fruit (either as a finger food or from a jar), or a scrambled egg yolk; half a cup of juice; four to six ounces of breast milk or formula.

Midmorning snack. Four to six ounces of juice; a quarter to half cup of yogurt, or about a quarter cup of cheese cubes, or a small whole wheat muffin with cream cheese; four to six ounces of breast milk or formula.

Lunch. A quarter to half cup yogurt (if you didn't serve it for a snack yet) or half a grilled cheese sandwich, cubed; a quarter to half cup of vegetables (from a jar or finger food); four to six ounces of breast milk or formula.

Afternoon snack. One teething biscuit or cracker; a quarter cup of diced cheese or meat; four to six ounces of breast milk or formula.

Dinner. A quarter cup of diced poultry, meat, or tofu; a quarter to half cup vegetables or fruit; a quarter cup of noodles, pasta, rice, or potato; four to six ounces of breast milk or formula.

Bedtime. Six to eight ounces of breast milk or formula.

Safer Swallowing: Choking Hazards to Avoid

As your child's diet expands, so, too, will the risks involved. Babies are far from being able to chew and swallow efficiently, so choking is going to remain an issue all the way up until about age four. While your baby is still learning to handle the most basic of textures, you need to carefully follow the recommendation that everything be soft, very ripe, well done (cooked to the point of being soft and gummable), and chopped into quarter-inch cubes (no bigger than your pinkie nail). Also keep in mind that when a baby is first trying finger foods, you should expect some gagging. Of course you should stay nearby when he's in this transition phase—just in case—but try not to overreact and scare him. Most babies pass through the gagging phase quickly, and as long as you are serving safe foods, you needn't worry too much. In addition, once your child begins to toddle, don't let him eat while he's running around. And never serve any of the following choking hazards to your baby or toddler, because they pose the most risk:

- Nuts or globs of peanut butter.
- Popcorn.
- Raisins and other dried fruit pieces.
- Seeds, such as sunflower or pumpkin.
- Hot dogs. (Some experts say they're okay if you first cut them into quarters lengthwise, then slice them into teeny cubes, but even so, they are chewy, so we prefer to reserve them for later.)

- Gum.
- Hard, gooey, or sticky candy like sour balls, marshmallows, jelly beans, and gummy candies.
- Raw veggies and fruits, such as carrots, celery, green beans, and apples.
- Whole grapes or cherry tomatoes (you can serve them cut into quarters or smaller).

A Fine Mess

Many babies are interested in finger foods between seven and nine months of age (the earlier they started solids, the sooner you will get to this stage), but it's still quite a challenge at this point for them to get the desired morsel to their mouths. Holding a chunk of bread, teething biscuit, or rice cake is one thing, because they can grasp it in their fists. But picking up smaller items—a cube of cheese or Cheerios, for instance—requires a close-to-perfected pincer grasp. Most babies don't develop this ability to hold an object between their thumb and forefinger until about nine months of age, and it can come as late as twelve months. Meanwhile, you can keep your wannabe self-feeder's frustrations to a minimum by giving her larger, soft chunks of food (think pancakes, french toast, rice cakes) that she can handle but that won't present a choking hazard. You can also help her spear smaller pieces with a baby fork then let her bring it to her mouth herself, and provide her with a spoon to wield at the same time you feed her the tough stuff. For instance, she can attempt to ladle yogurt to her mouth while you feed her the cubes of fruit she's struggling with. It's a messy time to be sure, but your baby's confidence will grow along with her appetite and fine-motor skills.

As much fun as this transitional third stage is for your baby, it's likely to be something of a headache for you. Up until now, you've probably had to deal with some icky green and orange stains on clothing or even the occasional cereal in the hair, but finger foods really fly. Long after you've cleaned off the high chair tray, you'll discover Cheerios and crackers crunching under your feet or some AWOL cheese cubes in the next room. And every mother has at least one photo with something like a bowl of spaghetti upside down on her baby's head.

Yes, the mess is supremely frustrating, but it's important to encourage your baby's attempts to feed herself. If you insist on holding the spoon, your baby may insist on not eating, setting you both up for a major food fight. Instead, prepare for the worst. If you haven't done so already, buy a splat mat (essentially an oversize bib that goes below the high chair). You can also buy plastic plates and bowls with suction cups so they can't be pulled off the tray and flipped over as easily (though your baby will eventually figure out how to do this, too).

When will your baby be big enough to feed herself on a regular basis? Around eighteen months is about average. Meanwhile, as she's is getting the hang of self-feeding, you can wield a spoon yourself to make sure something actually does go in—chances are she'll be so busy trying to get her own spoon filled and up to her mouth, she won't notice you slipping the other one in.

VOICE OF REASON

"Feeding themselves and their babies at the same time is a juggling feat most parents can't master—at least not gracefully, or without having to pop a couple of antacid tablets after every meal. So until your baby is a competent self-feeder, you might want to continue giving his meals separately. But that doesn't mean he shouldn't begin to sit in on some adult meals for practice in table manners and sociability. Draw his high chair up to the table, give him some finger foods, and include him in the conversation. But don't forget to reserve some late dinners for adults only to keep (or put back) the romance in your lives."
—Babytalk *contributing editor Heidi Murkoff in her terrific, must-read book* What to Expect the First Year

Baby Meets Cup

To hear the pediatric community tell it, even five months of age is not too soon to introduce a cup. The sooner your baby gets used to the idea that liquids can come from other sources, the thinking goes, the easier it will be to wean her off that bottle at the recommended one-year mark (see pages 265–67 for more on this bombshell). The earlier-the-better camp also insists that a baby will be more accepting of a cup at this young age, while more likely to throw it at you at age one, when her habits have become thoroughly ingrained and her disposition thoroughly obstinate. We can't argue with that. The challenge here, however, is that just because your baby is accepting of the novel new cup doesn't mean she can use it efficiently. So you've got more mess to contend with, and yet another new challenge at a stage already full of myriad transitions and feats to accomplish. Not that we mean to discourage you; your baby may take to a cup like, well, bread to butter. We just want you to know we understand if you don't get around to it right away. If and when you're game, here's some easy-to-swallow advice.

Choose the right cup. For a youngish baby, that probably means one with handles, or at least indentations on the side for gripping. A rounded, weighted bottom will help prevent spills because the cup will right itself when your baby knocks it around (which happens a lot). And as for a spout, those attached to their bottles may prefer a cup with a soft rubber nipple. There is also a style of cup out there known as "spillproof," which has a valve inside the lid to prevent liquid from flowing through unless it's being sucked out. These are a delight if you are averse to spills (and who isn't?), but some think these have drawbacks as well (see "The Spillproof Controversy" on page 263). For one thing, some babies don't like the fact that they have to work harder to get the liquid. For another, cleaning them is a bit of a pain; you have to disassemble the lid and valve and wash both pieces. And they're not totally spillproof: When your baby flings the cup across the room and it crashes into the wall (yes, this will happen), the valve may become dislodged and—voilà—sticky sweet juice everywhere.

Choose the right beverage. Which brings us to our next point. Start with water. Your baby may do more playing than drinking in the early weeks, so water is your safest bet until she really gets the hang of consuming the liquid. Then you can move to juice, breast milk, or formula as well.

Choose the right amount. A few sips of liquid are all that's necessary at first. More than that and you've just got more to spill if you're not going the spillproof route. Plus, it makes the cup heavier to wield.

Choose the right time. Don't try to introduce a cup when your baby is overtired, overhungry, or overthirsty. Offer it during a meal while she's in the high chair, somewhat sated, and in a good mood. Demonstrate it for her the first few times by holding the spout to her lips and dripping a few drops into her mouth. Plenty will roll back out, of course, so persevere slowly over a few weeks. Your baby will gradually become more and more comfortable with her cup, but you will still need to continue to breast- or

bottlefeed as well for up to six months, depending on how early you introduced the cup.

Avoiding Juice Abuse

Juice is another beverage we tend to think of as baby-friendly, but the
growing concern over childhood obesity has practically turned it into a
four-letter word these days, with health and nutrition experts pointing the
finger at sugary drinks. But let's face it: Babies and toddlers love juice, it
can be a convenient option for you, especially on the go, and there are
healthy varieties out there that can provide vitamin C and other important nutrients for tots who turn up their noses at real fruit. If you're careful
about what kind, when, and how you serve it, both you and your baby can
enjoy juice in moderation. Plan to pour with these guidelines in mind and
you won't be guilty of juice abuse:

- Wait to introduce juice until your baby has started solids, sometime
  after six months.
- Start with clear juices first (apple, pear, white grape). They'll be easier
  on your baby's tummy (and less messy when spilled for you!). Avoid
  citrus juices until after the first year.
- Only serve products labeled "100 percent fruit juice." Skip the varieties labeled juice "drink," "beverage," or "cocktail"—they may have
  zero nutritional value.
- Try to limit your baby's consumption to four to six ounces a day—this
  is the AAP recommendation all the way up until age six, but many
  moms we know say they find it hard to stick to that guideline. Just
  know that your baby will adore juice, and you'll have to be crafty
  about keeping her consumption at least somewhat in check (look at it
  as good practice for down the road, when she discovers soda).
- Dilute juice with water (about fifty–fifty) to minimize the amount of
  sugar your baby is getting. This is a great way to keep juice intake to
  (or at least near) the recommended maximum.
- Only serve juice in a sippy cup—drinking it from a bottle can contribute to tooth decay.
- Pass on the juice if your baby has diarrhea or is vomiting—the high
  carbohydrate count in juice can aggravate these conditions. Offer an
  oral rehydration solution, such as Pedialyte, instead. If she won't drink
  one brand, try another until you find a flavor she likes. Older babies

can suck on frozen oral rehydration ice pops, too, which they may like better than the drink.

- Finally, don't forget about water. If you teach your baby to like water, you can worry less about her filling up on juice to the degree that she's eating less at meals. She can even have fun filling her sippy cup at the sink herself.

 ## THE SPILLPROOF CONTROVERSY

Wait—you didn't know there was a controversy? We were shocked, too: What could be the problem with this fabulous invention that has saved many a carpet and sofa? Well, it turns out we've had several pediatricians mention to us recently that they don't like the spillproof sippy cups because the valve operation requires babies to perform the same sort of sucking action as nursing or drinking from a bottle. This means the baby is not learning to drink liquid in the normal fashion, and our goal should be to move the baby away from sucking, not prolong it. In addition, a baby-*cum*-toddler wielding a sippy cup full of juice all day long can get tooth and gum decay, and that's an easy habit to fall into when you don't have to concern yourself if the cup happens to land upside down somewhere and isn't discovered for a week (yes, this will happen as well).

Uh, okay, all this may be true. But just who do they think is cleaning up the resulting mess from a six-month-old with a free-flowing cup (some have lids but without that spillproof valve, as we all know, they leak like crazy)? Meanwhile, half of us still aren't yet getting a reasonable amount of shut-eye! And we've got babies still tethered to our breasts much of the day because we're trying hard to provide that optimum nutrition for as long as possible. Without a doubt, we deserve our spillproof sippy cups! So if you want to give your baby one, you go, girl!

Dealing with Picky Eaters

Sometime between the first and second birthday, you are likely to discover the true meaning of having a picky eater. Gone are the days of ounce markers and empty baby food jars. All you've got to gauge what your toddler is consuming is a messy high chair tray, an even messier floor below it, and an active kid who doesn't want to stop what's he's doing for anything as boring as eating. Welcome to the world of food strikes: As your baby heads into his second year, you will likely find it a challenge to feed him, because he's both more finicky and busier. And that's okay. He needs fewer calories now, because he's simply not growing as fast as he was only a few months ago. The rule of thumb for feeding a toddler is this: You provide healthy meals; he decides how much he's going to actually swallow. That's where your control ends, and you might as well get used to it—your baby will be exercising his independence in plenty of other ways, too.

Of course guidance is still available. You can find a sample one-year-old menu at aap.org, but again, we think this is a lot of food to expect a busy toddler to eat! Don't sweat it if some days (maybe many days) your toddler seems to only consume a fraction of what you offer. Or he wants to eat the same thing for a week straight. If he's really hungry, he'll really eat. Meanwhile, here are a few tips to keep in mind:

- Continue to offer regular, well-balanced meals, perhaps in smaller, less intimidating amounts. Remember, it can take many times before a young child will accept a new food. Don't give up too soon.
- Don't expect your child to sit still for long. Don't put him into the high chair until you have his meal ready, and take him out as soon as the food starts to fly. If he doesn't want to stop what he's doing for a snack, bring a healthy, minimal-mess snack to him—just stick around while he eats it so he doesn't start running and choke.
- Look for ways to sneak more nutritional ingredients into a serving: pancakes made with mashed banana; oatmeal with pureed baby food stirred into it; meatballs or meat loaf with spinach added to the mix; homemade breads with grated carrots or fruits in them. (We must mention one caveat about packaged foods, including baking mixes, however: Many bread, cake, or muffin mixes contain nuts and/or eggs, so check label ingredients carefully if your baby is still under one year, or even over a year if you have reason to be concerned about allergies to these ingredients.)
- Remember that toddlers get what they need nutrition-wise over the course of about a week, not a day. (So instead of RDAs—recommended daily allowances—for kids this age, why can't experts talk about recommended *weekly* allowances and relieve some of our anxiety!)

• Talk to your pediatrician about providing a vitamin supplement if you're really concerned.

Beefing Up on Iron

If your baby seems to be drinking less formula, or has passed his first birthday and moved on to whole milk, you'll need to get a little creative when it comes to keeping his diet iron-fortified. But don't panic—there are plenty of tasty places to find this mineral. The first is to keep feeding iron-fortified baby cereals until your kiddo starts to turn his nose up at them (try mixing with fruit or fruit juice to sweeten them up). Then start checking ingredient labels, and you'll find some unexpected sources. Many big-kid cereals, such as Cheerios (also a perennial finger-food favorite), are fortified with iron. Traditional oatmeal also has iron, and your child may find the chunkier texture more appealing than his variety; oatmeal doesn't have to be bland—try adding sugar and cinnamon, or mashed bananas.

You can serve sandwiches on whole wheat breads, which have more iron than white, and most little kids love pasta, which also is available in iron-fortified varieties. Remember red meat: Meatballs and hamburgers cut into bite-size chunks are good toddler treats. Beefaroni or spaghetti with meat sauce will give you a double dose of iron (from the pasta, too). Liverwurst is loaded with iron and softer to swallow than many other meats. And finally, don't forget that other source of protein, beans; soft, sweet baked beans will provide plenty of iron.

Saying Sayonara to Sucking

Weaning your baby from the bottle or breast is one of those events in life that reduces some moms to tears, while others feel like popping the champagne cork. Most of us probably feel a little of both, depending on which hormones are kicking at the time. The issue can also prompt a fair amount of guilt or anxiety about the right time and right way to wean. While the AAP recommends that you should breastfeed for a full year if possible, it also suggests that you can continue to nurse beyond the first birthday and for as long as Mother and baby both enjoy it. Meanwhile, the group is a little tougher on those moms who bottlefeed (which happens to be most of us by this point—only 17 percent are still breastfeeding at one year). Your baby will switch from formula to whole milk (cold turkey, no less) at his first birthday, and the AAP has a number of reasons why it feels you should be serving it from a cup, rather than a bottle. The biggest is tooth decay. Your baby has an ever-increasing number of chompers, and all that sweet liquid flowing across them can cause cavities. Babies who fall asleep with a bottle in their mouths while the stuff continues to drip across their teeth and gums as they snooze may actually experience rotten teeth and gums (a condition known as baby bottle mouth), so you shouldn't allow your baby to take a bottle into the crib with him. As you would imagine, super-sweet beverages like juice and chocolate milk also cause more tooth trauma than regular milk. Now, we all know kids who kept their bottles for two or more years and never ended up with teeth problems, but because it's our job to relay the recommendations, we did so. You, however, can decide what to do with them.

Another reason for weaning from a bottle is the fact that a one-year-old is now nutritionally dependent on his solid foods. Whole milk, while containing lots of healthy ingredients, is not a complete food as breast milk and formula were. So if your baby fills up on bottles of milk and juice, he may not be eating enough solids to satisfy his nutritional needs. Finally, keeping your baby on the bottle can keep him, well, a baby. We understand if you have mixed feelings about him leaving babyhood behind, but as the saying goes, you can't stop progress. (And hey, you can always have another if you miss your baby that much!)

So now that we've given you the thinking on why it makes sense to wean at a year, we have to 'fess up and tell you we know for a fact that not all moms do it. In a Parenting.com/babytalk poll, 53 percent of moms admitted that they didn't wean their baby off the bottle at one year of age. Half of those moms waited until eighteen months to make the switch to all sippy cups, all the time, and the other half delayed until age two or later. Yes, that also includes several of us *Babytalk* editors. It's not just that we love flouting authority so much. Breaking up with the bottle is hard to do—it's like breaking up with your first love in a lot of ways. You know you're no longer good for each other, but you enjoyed the romance so much, you hate to see it go. Okay, we're getting way too sappy (must be the hormone thing again). But the baby bottle, like Mom's breast, is about more than just nutrition. It's a comfort object that helps your baby relax and feel secure; plenty also use it to go to sleep. So taking away that bottle, especially at nap- and bedtime, means the added stress of coming up with a whole new routine for those parts of the day, no doubt with a lot of tears and trauma in the process.

Giving up the bottle also means you won't have it to rely on when you're out at the mall trying to finish your errands and your cranky baby wants out of his stroller. Some especially temperamental tots and their moms find a bottle gets them through lengthy car rides, visits from pesky old relatives who poke and pinch them, a Sunday church service, or sibling's school play when quiet is required. Suffice it to say, moms are dependent on their babies' bottles, too.

If your little one is headed for or past his first birthday and you both are still firmly attached to "ba-ba," you're not a bad parent. You can continue to rely on the bottle longer if you use it judiciously. The time will come when both of you know letting go is the right thing to do. Meanwhile, follow these tips to help ease the transition and protect his teeth in the process:

- After one year, reserve bottles as a wind-down for naps and bedtime and give your child a sippy cup to drink during meals and with snacks. If he's resistant, insist that he drink his bottle in your lap. When he gets down, the bottle goes back in the fridge. He may come to realize that he doesn't want to sit in your lap half the day when he could be playing.
- If your baby resists the sippy cup, look for a design with a soft, nipple-like tip. One to try: the Avent Magic Cup, which is also spillproof.
- The intrepid can try removing the spillproof valve from the sippy cup at first to make it easier for the baby to learn to suck from a cup. You can add it back once she gets the hang of it.
- Don't limit the cup to juice and water. Put breast milk or formula in it, too, so your baby realizes these beverages don't have to come from a nipple.
- When you reach the point that you're both ready to wean, you'll be in a better position for the transition if all you have to deal with is nap and bedtime. Help your baby give up the naptime bottle first, since nights tend to be the biggest deal. If your baby is used to rocking or sitting on your lap as part of her bedtime routine, she can still do so, only with a sippy cup of water instead. (The water won't do any damage to her teeth, and because it doesn't offer as much in the way of a taste sensation, it may also help her give up her before-bed beverage.) Keep all your other routines the same. The only caveat is if your baby has been falling asleep while sucking, you will both have to learn another method to get her to sleep. See chapter 3, page 93, for some options. Or you could also just stay with the bottle a bit longer. Believe us they all give it up eventually.

"WHAT NOBODY TOLD ME ABOUT FEEDING MY BABY SOLIDS"

"Don't be in a rush to start solids. They are a royal pain in the neck and once you get started, that's it. The key to solids is to get them on table food as soon as possible and feed them what you eat: mashed potatoes, carrots, well-done broccoli . . . lots of things on your plate can easily be served to your baby by about nine months. It will get you into the great habit of eating at the table together with your kids."

—*Meredith, Ridgefield, Connecticut*

"I wish someone would have told me not to put on a white bodysuit with the wonderful sweet potatoes and carrots—I learned that one the hard way!"   —*Arianne, Brooklyn, New York*

"I babied my oldest so much that he rarely experimented with anything new. Then, when he turned one year old he moved up into the older section of his daycare center, where they served him real lunches and snacks. I was surprised to hear that he didn't have any problem eating the unsmashed veggies, chicken, and other items. I had been missing out on feeding him so many different things, not to mention all the time I'd spent pureeing and pulverizing! Now that I'm on my third child I'm probably a bit too liberal on what he can and should eat, but at nine months he hasn't had a problem gumming anything I've given him. More importantly, he loves the variety and my life is so much easier knowing that he can eat mini versions of most table foods!"

—*Diane, Pensacola, Florida*

"I'd read it again and again but I wish someone would have told me—so maybe it would have sunk in—that it's perfectly normal to consider two bites as a success when starting rice cereal. We certainly ended up with more on the bib and clothes than in the baby. My second daughter was very resistant to eating rice cereal once we started with fruits and vegetables. I finally gave up, but then her grandma stayed a night and fed her breakfast. 'She won't eat that,' I told my mom. But like a true mother, mine came to the rescue, showing me to mix juice with the rice cereal instead of milk or water. My daughter gobbled down the rice cereal this way."   —*Jody, Claremore, Oklahoma*

"Nothing worried me more than the thought of my daughter choking when she started finger foods. She is a 'chipmunk' eater. She likes storing several pieces of food in her mouth at once. She had a mouthful of teeth at an early age. However, we had to remind ourselves that even though she had the teeth of a toddler, she still had the mind set of a baby and didn't fully understand the concepts of chewing or 'one at a time.'"

—*Lizzie, Villa Park, Illinois*

"My firstborn didn't eat solids until he was seven months, but by ten months he was chowing on sushi with wasabi sauce! So I certainly wasn't prepared for my daughter, Sadie, who is allergic to fifty-eight food proteins. It has made my diet (I'm still nursing) and her diet (she's just beginning to eat some solids) an adventure. I wish someone had told me that food allergies in infants can be something to really be aware of. Had it not been for my pediatrician, who worked overly hard to find out why Sadie was not thriving, we may never have found out the extent of her problem." —*Tara, Park City, Utah*

"No one told me that my babies might not be that interested in baby food. As a first-time mom, I ran to the store and stocked up on all organic (of course!) baby food. It was such a letdown when my twin girls really didn't act that excited to make the switch. So I tried table foods. I just chopped up whatever my husband and I were eating and that was all it took—they were hooked. I ended up giving a lot of my baby food to my neighbor!" —*Bethany, Wilmington, North Carolina*

"My daughter Sophia's favorite first foods were all orange—sweet potatoes, carrots, squash. She ate so much that she turned a shade of orange herself! Too bad it's not a good way to get a quick and cheap tan for Mommy!" —*Andrea, Byfield, Massachusetts*

"The only problem I had with solids was people telling me I should start earlier. I heard story after story how it was going to be so hard if I didn't get going. Not true! I started my son on solids when my pediatrician recommended and he ate like a champ, didn't refuse anything, and has not developed any allergies. I thought I could do homemade but I soon realized Gerber and Beech-Nut were my best friends. With all the trials of motherhood I'm glad eating isn't one of them. Now, if I could just get him to do the dishes . . ." —*Melissa, Long Beach, California*

CHAPTER 8

Babyproofing and Beyond
The No-Panic Guide to Safety and (Eeks!) First Aid

Watching your newborn blossom from a helpless blob of love to a strong-necked and strong-willed bundle of curiosity, you are no doubt filled with pride and awe. If you have your wits about you, you are also filled with fear. When it comes to babies with bodies that are seriously out of proportion with their level of understanding, free will isn't just seriously overrated, it's downright dangerous. So when yours gets it into his big, top-heavy head that he should crawl, cruise, toddle, or do anything other than take the nap you so desperately need him to have (a good three-hour-long snooze would be about right most days), you may actually find yourself pining for the days of crying jags and all-night feed-a-thons. Okay, maybe we're exaggerating. But once mobility arrives, you're in for a big change from the early months when your questions were simpler, like "Is he breathing?" "Is food going in and coming out from different places?" and "Where are those #$%* doughnuts!" One thing remains the same, however: the deep desire to keep your baby safe, healthy, and happy. Unfortunately, as he hurtles through the second half of his first year, he becomes increasingly active and a threat to himself. From about six months on—if your baby is an early crawler, or even just incredibly creative at scooting his little body around—the world is no longer a pretty mobile dangling out of reach. It is a sphere of endless intrigue that calls out to your fledgling Christopher Columbus, *Come on! Check me out! I probably taste pretty good!* This brave new world presents a host of potential hazards, however, and guess who gets to make sure her explorer doesn't fall off the face off the earth? You got it.

Now that we've pushed your panic button (and we had the nerve to call this a no-panic guide!), we're going to do an about-face and tell you to relax. Seriously. The upside is that you're not the only one charged with this job. Fortunately, the babyproofing industry has become so sophisticated that there's a gadget to keep virtually everything but your free time protected. We can't promise you'll be able to get the toilet lid unlocked in time yourself, but at least your baby won't be able to play in it (oh, yeah, you're in for that). There's also a bevy of sanitizing and safety aids for when you're on the go and need to use "public facilities" (somehow that term never sounded nearly as creepy when you were the only one in the stall, did it?).

If that doesn't reassure you, just keep reminding yourself (Grandma will no doubt do it for you if you forget) that when you grew up there were no car seats, no childproof safety caps on medicines, no smoke alarms or carbon monoxide detectors, and no toilet lid locks. Babyproofing consisted of accordion gates and barred playpens that were often more hazardous than what they blocked. So instead of losing your mind worrying, comfort yourself with the thought of how lucky you are to have both the gadgets and the good sense to read about how to keep your baby safe.

One more caveat: We usually make it our policy to not hammer you with "shoulds": You *should* do this, you *shouldn't* do that. This chapter, you're going to find our advice much more by-the-book than usual. We apologize for the preachiness, but when it comes to your baby's safety, you really *should* follow the rules.

Safety at Home

It's true that some babies seem to hit the world running, doing everything earlier than expected, while more laid-back types take it slow. But no matter what type of baby you have, one thing is certain: He will invariably roll, reach, crawl, or cruise when you least expect it (and when you're farther than two steps away to catch him). So rule number one in the world of babyproof prep is that even before your child starts rolling over (usually between four and five months), you'll need to start thinking about babyproofing his environment. This first involves conducting a room-by-room check of potential hazards by seeing the space as your baby does: Get down on the floor and crawl around to see what's at your child's eye level. This is easily done in the nursery or wherever you spend time on the floor playing with your baby. As for the rest of the house, um, we have to confess that not all of us did the official whole-house crawl. And we realize you may not, either (no offense). So at the risk of being overprotective (not that there's anything wrong with that), we're going to take the liberty of pointing out virtually everything that might be hazardous. Then we suggest that you make a copy of our babyproofing shopping list (see page 283); head for your nearest baby superstore or home center retailer, or go online to a baby gear Web site (see "Surfing for Safety," page 285); and stock up on the protective gadgets you need.

Rule number two: Outfit your home immediately. Okay, once again, we confess that only a couple of us followed through on this one, and some of us are even finding safety gewgaws in our junk drawers to this day. So just in case you're not completely anal-retentive about completing tasks, we suggest instead that you first tackle some of the harder items, like cabinet locks and safety gates, which involve drills and screws and endless patience. Later, when you've stopped cursing and had some ice cream, you'll feel refreshed and ready to pop in outlet covers or stick on table-corner cushions. And for the rooms you haven't gotten to yet, there's a very simple solution: Close the door. You want to take more precautions than this eventually, of course, but it sure works in a pinch—at least until your baby figures out how to stand up and turn the knob.

In addition to considering the basic room-by-room guidelines, you've also got to take into account your own family and lifestyle. Say you've got older siblings with toys that can be choking hazards—or a collection of Ming dynasty porcelain. Then it's time to think about putting things out of reach by either reorganizing your space or putting up safety barriers. You could use safety gates to close off the bigger kids' bedrooms or play-rooms, or slap on those nifty plastic doorknob covers that keep your baby from turning the handle for another inexpensive way to keep forbidden rooms off limits. Would you prefer to keep your living room a toy-free, adults-only zone? Close it off with a gate (there are now extra-long expandable versions for more open living spaces), or make your nursery one giant playpen by putting a gate on that doorway and putting your baby inside it (assuming all hazards have been removed, of course).

What your baby gets into will also depend in large part on his personality. Some of our kids were highly entertained by unrolling toilet paper, which meant about two years of keeping it out of reach or the threat of going everywhere with it stuck to our shoes. Meanwhile, another mom we know was able to keep houseplants right on the floor and crystal on the coffee table, and her son never touched the stuff. It's enough to make us seriously resentful (until we consider the fact that she also had to deal with five months of colic, so we won't complain). As your baby gets bigger and becomes more mobile, you may start to notice that certain dangerous objects are irresistible to him. Maybe it's a pen, or maybe it's a penny, or maybe it's poop. Whatever his weakness, you'll probably learn to spot it before he does. But no matter how quick your reflexes, you also can't be everywhere at once. So don't forget to conduct frequent look-arounds and quiz your friends about any cool new gear or ideas they may have discovered in the world of baby safety. Meanwhile, we'll help you get started by providing this basic babyproofing blueprint. You'll be well on your way to a home, safe home.

Some things can wait, others, not so much. Here are the must-fix, must-remove, must-destroy objects that are present in virtually every household.

Dangling details. Certain window blind cords are strangulation hazards, and tablecloths are also risky business. Your baby can grab the edge of the tablecloth and pull it off, along with everything sitting on top of it, like breakable dishes and hot foods and beverages; the injury possibilities are endless. One of the easiest things to do is simply forgo tablecloths for now (place mats are easier to clean off anyway). As for window blinds and shades, some products made before 2001 have a dangerous double-loop cord design, or the cord may be too long or may not have a locking mechanism or a tie-down device to keep the cords in place. For these products, you can order a free retrofit kit from the Window Covering Safety Council (WCSC) by calling 800-506-4636 or going online to windowcoverings.org. Window cords on coverings made after 2001 are safer, but still need to be kept out of your baby's reach. Move cribs, beds, furniture, and toys away from windows, and keep cords as short and high up as possible. If you are redecorating, consider investing in the newer cordless window products, especially in your baby's bedroom and rooms where she spends most of her time.

Engaging electrics. Cover electrical outlets and secure excess electrical cords along the wall or bind them up with a specially designed spool or holder. You're better off spending a bit more on outlet covers, which replace the complete outlet plate with a safety plate, rather than using separate plastic plugs. If your baby is determined enough, she can work the plug out of the socket, pop it in her mouth, and potentially choke on it. Consider an outlet strip cover for your computer system, too (babies love to crawl under desks), and buy extension cords with locking plug covers.

Frightening furnishings. Unstable furniture pieces such as heavy bookcases or media stands should be anchored to the wall because they may topple over if your baby tries to pull herself up or climb on them. Cover coffee and end tables and fireplace ledges with corner guards and padded strips (don't worry—all this stuff is for sale at your nearest baby super store or home center, as well as online; turn to page 285 for a listing of Web sites). Keep breakable knickknacks and any decorative objects that can be disassembled into small pieces well out of reach. It's also a good idea to move furniture away from windows; a curious climber could scale a sofa or table and then fall out the window. Finally, throw rugs can be a tripping hazard, so you might want to pack them away for a while.

Stairways to trouble. Block off the top and bottom of all staircases with safety gates. But not just any gates. You *must* use the type of gates that fasten to the wall with hardware for staircases—pressure-mounted gates can cave in or be dislodged by an enterprising child if not properly secured. And *never* use accordion-style gates, even if your mom still has your old one in the attic; they can entangle clothing and fingers as well as pose a strangulation hazard (the top V-shape can literally entrap a kid's head—lovely thought, isn't it?). Finally, if balusters on staircases, decks, or porches are more than three and a half inches apart, buy railing guards (usually made of mesh) so your baby won't get stuck in between or fall through them.

Window wisdom. When you open your windows for fresh air, if possible, do so from the top down so that your child can't fall out. Some states require window guards on windows above ground-floor level; if you live in a multistory apartment building, you definitely don't want to be without them. When choosing window guards, be sure to opt for removable ones that can be taken down in the event that you need to escape from a fire. It's also a smart idea to put decals on sliding glass doors to keep unsuspecting crawlers from smashing into them (many an adult has been known to walk into a clear glass door, too!).

Fireplace facts. Let's face it—no matter how cozy or romantic, having a fire burning with a mobile baby or toddler at home is a serious risk. If you just can't resist, it goes without saying that you should never leave your baby unattended in a room with a fire burning, and install a screen and hearth gate in front of the fireplace. When not in use, keep the fireplace doors locked (a mesh safety belt or removable cabinet lock threaded though handles can often do the trick) or put a gate in front of it: Your baby can also climb into the fireplace and feast on leftover soot and ashes.

The Kitchen

It's probably the room where you spend the most time, which means your baby will, too. Unfortunately, dangers abound here. One study found that, not surprisingly, one-year-olds were at the highest risk of getting hurt in the kitchen. A stove is an obvious hazard, but it may not have occurred to you that active babies can pull over hot dishes, tug on electrical cords attached to coffeepots, or get into cabinets that house blenders or food processors with sharp blades. Plus, a primary behavior at the end of the first year is imitating you—and just look at what you're doing here: wielding knives, handling hot skillets and breakable dishes, running water in the sink. In short, don't skimp on precautions when it comes to the kitchen. Here's what you need to do:

- ☐ Install locks on lower cabinets (below the counter) that are your baby's level.
- ☐ Keep matches, sharp tools, knives, cleaners, and liquor in cabinets that lock; better still, store them in locked cabinets well above your baby's reach.
- ☐ Unplug countertop appliances after use and tuck the cords away from counter edges—your baby can grab the cords and pull the appliances off the counter, potentially landing on him.
- ☐ Try to use only the back burners of the stove, and turn pot handles toward the back. According to research, one of the most common causes of scalding was a child reaching up and pulling a pot of hot water off the stove or other elevated surface.
- ☐ Keep the dishwasher locked. Your baby could open it and crawl inside, or pull out dishes, break them, and cut himself. Only fill the soap dispenser right before you turn the dishwasher on so your baby can't get into it—dishwasher detergent is caustic and can burn your baby if ingested.

☐ Install refrigerator and oven locks. If your baby can open these appliances, he could burn himself or choke on something he finds in the fridge, not to mention crawl inside and become trapped.

☐ Use knob covers on the stove (so he can't turn it on).

☐ Always test food that has been warmed in a microwave for heat and steam before giving it to your child.

☐ Store your kitchen garbage can and recycling in a cabinet with a child lock.

☐ Don't position the high chair near a counter or table that will allow your baby to reach dishes, appliances, or other problematic doohickies. Always use the safety belt on the high chair.

If your baby will tolerate it, the safest thing to do is put him in the high chair while you're working in the kitchen and keep him busy with a finger-food snack or some toys on the tray. (Okay, we admit to using DVDs as well.) Positioning a playpen or activity center in the room are other options, but never use a walker in the kitchen—it may allow your baby to reach a hot stove or other dangerous object. (Frankly, we think you should never use the kind of walker that your baby sits in and propels himself around, period. See chapter 5, pages 180–81, for more details about why they're both dangerous and useless. A stationary exerciser is okay, of course, and stand-and-push-from-behind walking toys are okay, but the latter aren't meant for the kitchen, either.)

The Bathroom

The second most dangerous room in your house is probably the bathroom, and while you can keep the door closed when you're not in it, your baby will be following right along every time you need to use it. There's simply no telling what trouble your baby can concoct while you're brushing your teeth. To be safe:

☐ Install toilet lid safety locks.

☐ Set your water heater no higher than 120 degrees Fahrenheit or install anti-scald devices on all faucets.

☐ Use a nonskid mat in the tub, and put a faucet cover on the tub faucet to avoid bumped heads.

☐ Lock all cabinets with medicines, toiletries, and cleaning products. Even better: Put them in a cabinet that's out of your baby's reach, and lock them as well. You think we're nuts? Just wait until the day you blink and then see your little acrobat on top of the toilet tank reaching for the medicine chest.

- [ ] If your bathroom isn't carpeted, put down a rubber-backed bath mat. Wet feet and a wet floor is a slippery combination. Toilet lid covers are also not a bad idea; if your baby slips and hits his head, at least it will cushion the blow a bit.
- [ ] Unplug appliances such as hair dryers and put them away (out of your baby's reach) right after use. Never leave a curling iron or other hot hair appliance on to warm up in a bathroom your baby has access to—we guarantee he will find it.
- [ ] Pass on bathroom cleaning products that don't get rinsed away, such as toilet sanitizers that get released into the bowl after each flush, or shower fresheners that you spray on and leave there when you're finished to prevent soap scum buildup. They may make it easier to keep your bathroom clean, but if your baby decides one day to play in the toilet when you're not looking (we know it's gross, but it may well happen—see the "Toilet Trauma" box below for how to handle it) or crawl into an open shower stall, he could eat the poisonous cleanser, or perhaps rub it in his eyes if it's on his hands.

TOILET TRAUMA

You've got your back turned putting away towels when suddenly you hear the sound of splashing, only to whip around and see that your busy baby has pulled himself up to the toilet, lifted the lid, and discovered a new wading pool. Ick! Fortunately you've caught him before the worst-case scenario—he could have fallen in headfirst and drowned—but you also can't help thinking about the gross factor. Is he going to come down with some horrible virus now? Theoretically, he could. While urine is relatively sterile (so don't worry too much about your baby peeing in the bathtub), feces is full of germs that can cause illness, and those germs can live on toilet surfaces long after the offending stuff has been flushed away. But before you panic, the usual prescription is to just wash your baby off carefully with soap and water. There's probably only a need to swallow your pride and call the doctor if your baby has come into contact with actual stools at the same time someone in the house has recently been ill with a stomach virus or diarrhea, or if your child has a weakened immune system. So just wash his hands like crazy and go buy a toilet lid lock, pronto!

The Nursery

There's nothing more innocent seeming than a nursery, sweet and pretty and pure. Yet dangers lurk here, too, even in furnishings designed especially for a baby. Here's what you need to know:

☐ Your baby's crib is the only place where he will spend a significant amount of time alone. It's imperative that it be as safe as possible. Any new crib you buy will meet current safety standards (the government regulates the manufacturing of cribs). However, older cribs (built prior to 1991) can be quite dangerous. You need to make certain even recently manufactured hand-me-down cribs are safe, and we have to caution against using any type of crib that can be described as "antique" or even just "old." Ditto for a crib whose history can't be traced. See "Crib Concerns" on page 279 for more specifics on how to ensure your baby's crib is as safe as it can be. You also need to place the crib away from a window, and avoid hanging any wall decor near it that your baby may be able to reach and pull down on himself.

☐ Your baby's changing table can be the source of lots of problems once she starts to roll over. Some of us at *Babytalk* opted to quit using it altogether from about six months on, and simply changed our babies on a carpeted floor with a portable mat or a towel underneath—you can't fall from there! When you do use a changing table, it should have a safety strap and high sides; if the table doesn't have high sides, then at least the pad should. In 2006, a new recommendation came out advising that separately sold changing table pads have contoured sides and a nonslip surface, so look for these features if you're buying one. Always use the safety strap, and never leave your baby unattended even with it on. Though you want to have all of your baby's toiletries—diaper rash ointment, wipes, lotions—within *your* reach for diaper changes and dressing, you need to be sure they are out of *her* reach, so she doesn't accidentally get them in her mouth or eyes. Don't position the changing table near a window, and put a soft rug with a no-slip pad underneath below the table in case the worst does happen and your baby falls—at least she won't land on a hard surface.

☐ If you use a diaper pail, make sure it's closed securely at all times. If you can position it out of your mobile baby's reach (perhaps inside a closet with a knob cover on the handle so she can't open it), that's even better. If you opt for a diaper disposal system, you'll have less of a problem—these are harder to open.

☐ Avoid unsafe toy boxes. Store toys on shelves or in a child-safe toy box. The best models have spring-loaded hinges to prevent the lid from slamming shut on your baby's hands. You can also remove the lid altogether. Airholes or other types of ventilation are important as well, in case your child climbs or falls in and becomes trapped.

☐ Install a working smoke detector near the nursery, and make sure to change the batteries twice a year (when you change your clocks). See page 307 for more advice about where to install smoke detectors in your home.

☐ Use only "cool" night-lights that don't get hot.

☐ Put a child-finder decal from your local fire department on your baby's nursery window.

CRIB CONCERNS

The things that can go wrong while a baby is alone in his crib are enough to keep you in nightmares for years: He can fall out, become entrapped, or smother, to name a few. For that reason, crib safety advice is twofold: You need to make sure the item itself is properly designed, and then you need to use it correctly. If you buy a new crib, look for the seal of the Juvenile Products Manufacturers Association (JPMA) to be sure it meets safety regulations (any new crib currently being sold in the United States should, but check anyway). Here's what else you need to know:

Inspecting a used crib

• The slats should be no more than two and three-eights inches apart so a baby cannot become trapped between them.

• There should not be any cutouts in the headboard or footboard (your baby's head could become trapped in them).

• There should not be any corner posts; your baby's clothing could get snagged on a corner post and choke him.

• Make sure that the wood is smooth with no splinters and no peeling paint.

(continued on next page)

- A crib made prior to 1979 may have been painted with lead paint, which can poison your baby if he gnaws on it, not to mention other safety issues, so again, please just don't use an old or antique crib.

Using *any* crib

- Remove and destroy all wrapping on new crib mattresses (it can be a suffocation hazard). If you put a mattress cover on it, make sure it fits snugly. Zippered covers are the best option
- Make sure the mattress itself fits snugly into the crib—you should not be able to fit more than two fingers between the mattress and sides or ends of the crib.
- When your baby is a newborn, it's easiest to position the mattress at the highest level, but begin to lower it as soon as he can sit up so that he can't fall out. By the time your child learns to stand, the mattress should be in the lowest position.
- Crib bedding in the early months should be minimal—a sheet to lie on is all your baby really needs. Pillows and comforters are suffocation hazards and may contribute to SIDS, and even a blanket poses an unnecessary risk. There are cozy zip-up sleepers or PJs that will keep him warm. (If you do use a blanket, the AAP recommends tucking the ends snugly under the mattress on both sides and at the end of the crib.)
- Make sure the drop side(s) of the crib are raised and locked in place when your baby is inside.
- If you use a crib mobile, make sure it's securely attached to the side of the crib and too high for your baby to reach and pull down on himself. Remove it when he's big enough to sit up.
- Never put any stuffed animals or other toys in your baby's crib; they pose a suffocation risk.

Bumper pads are another controversial element. While these items were initially intended to prevent a baby's arms, legs, or head from becoming entrapped in the slats, cribs have been redesigned so that the space between the slats is narrower and this risk is eliminated. And it's not likely that a baby is going to bang herself into the slats hard enough to hurt herself. Nowadays some experts have come to feel crib bumpers may actually be a hazard because they reduce airflow (possibly allowing your baby to rebreathe carbon dioxide) and may pose a risk of suffocation. When your baby is young and unable to move around during sleep, positioning her in the center of the crib well away from the bumper pad should suffice. Once she can roll around, however—which can be as soon as four months—many experts recommend removing the bumpers, so it begs the question, are they really worth buying in the first place? (Crib bumpers are not exactly cheap.) In fact, safety experts have long recommended removing crib bumpers when babies get big enough to stand because they can climb on them and fall out of the crib. For now, the decision is yours, but expect to hear more about this controversy in the future. In some states, there are movements under way to eventually outlaw crib bumpers in childcare centers.

Don't Overlook the Toy Box

They seem so innocent, designed to delight and educate, but the wrong toys at the wrong time can also be a danger to your child. The biggest risk to babies and toddlers is choking, of course. But an overeager little guy can also climb on an older sibling's or cousin's bike or skateboard and go flying, too. (We're sorry to say one of us has also been there, done that, resulting in an emergency trip to the pediatric dentist.) You never know what will appeal to your fledgling daredevil, so know the biggest risks and take precautions now.

The good news: If you carefully adhere to age guidelines and don't allow your baby access to toys made for children over three years old, she'll have much less of a chance of choking. However, there are toys for sale out there that do end up being recalled because they're later found to be choking hazards, or your baby could be visiting somewhere and discover an irresistible—and inappropriate—toy belonging to another child, so keep an extra-vigilant eye on her in other families' playrooms. When all is said and done (so far, anyway), the best advice is probably this: Always remember the toilet paper roll rule—if the item can fit through one, it's a choking hazard—and for bigger items, anything you wouldn't put in your own mouth shouldn't go into your baby's, either. Things to watch for include:

> **Small parts** on stuffed animals or dolls, like eyes made of buttons, that can be pulled loose.
> **Cords or strings,** which can wrap around a baby's neck and strangle him.

Giveaways. Toys sold or given away at a carnival or fair and in vending machines may not be labeled as choking hazards, may be painted with lead, may be . . . oh, who are we kidding, just skip these risky things.

Balloons. Never let a baby or toddler play with a balloon unattended. In fact, experts say children shouldn't have balloons all the way up until age eight, but go to any birthday party and you'll see how cavalier people are about this advice. Balloons are pretty much everywhere in our world, it seems. But they really shouldn't be—if your baby puts a piece of popped balloon in her mouth, she can easily choke. If you can't resist balloons, spring for the higher-priced Mylar instead of the traditional latex variety.

Beware the pretty (and pain-in-the-butt) packaging. Shrink-wrap and all those plastic straps and bolts are choking hazards, too.

Damaged goods. Throw out (or repair) broken toys. Look for ripped seams on soft toys, where small parts could be exposed; splinters or chipped paint on wooden toys; rust on outdoor playthings.

Hazards Even Paranoid Moms Forget

Now that we've told you all the usual danger zones, we've got a few more to add. Some may or may not apply to your particular home or decor, and there are probably more items no one will think of until a near accident occurs. Still, here are a few other warnings to keep in mind:

Blanket chests. Some models can lock automatically, suffocating a child who might have climbed inside. One manufacturer, Lane, will provide a new lock for free for models made prior to 1987; call 888-856-8758 for more details. Old-fashioned toy boxes may also entrap a child who climbs or falls into one and then isn't strong enough or able to lift the lid.

Button batteries. In our world of ever-shrinking technology, these tiny batteries can be found in everything from musical greeting cards to handheld electronic games. Even if a child swallows one without choking, the electrical currents can damage the esophagus. If you suspect your child has swallowed a button battery, get him to the emergency room immediately.

Doorstop tips. The rubber tips of metal spring doorstops (attached to the door) are a choking hazard.

STUFF YOU NEED FOR BABYPROOFING . . .

❑ Lower cabinet and drawer locks.

❑ Stove knob covers to prevent your baby from turning on a burner.

❑ Oven lock.

❑ Toilet lid locks.

❑ Tub spout cover.

❑ Corner guards and edge bumpers for coffee tables and raised fireplace hearths.

❑ Safety gates (the hardware-mounted style for the top and bottom of staircases).

❑ Railing netting or plastic guards (if you have an open railing).

❑ Furniture straps, brackets, or other hardware that can be used to attach any heavy furniture to the wall.

❑ Outlet plate covers (not the plugs, which come out too easily).

❑ Power strip covers.

❑ Window blind cord wraps (or cut cords short, or replace them with shades).

❑ Window guards (if your windows don't lock securely).

❑ Doorknob or lever-style handle covers for any off-limits areas.

❑ Smoke and carbon monoxide detectors (one on each floor, near the bedrooms).

. . . AND STUFF YOU DON'T

We can't think of anything, because we don't know where you live or how curious your child is. Maybe you live in a ranch and don't have a staircase, which would negate your need for a gate. Bottom line: Assess your needs and then implement them. And by all means, don't take any notice of others who may wonder if you are overdoing it. When your baby is at this death-defying age, there is no such thing.

Garbage. From bottle caps to cotton swabs, trash contains myriad choking hazards. Keep garbage cans inside of cabinets with safety latches.

Lamp oil. Never put decorative lamps containing oil where your child can reach them. He could accidentally ingest the oil, or spill it and create a fire hazard.

Magnets. Someday you'll need them to post all that school artwork on the fridge, but for now, skip them. They can easily fall or be pulled off by curious little fingers and then make their way into your baby's mouth.

Old freezers. Some freestanding chest freezers made prior to 1971 can trap and suffocate kids. There aren't many still in existence, but if you or someone you know has one, you need to learn how to disable the latch so it can be opened from the inside. For details, go to the Web site of the Association of Home Appliance Manufacturers: aham.org. Or better still, just get rid of the old freezer.

Paper shredders. A new must-have with all the worries about identify theft, these inexpensive and low-tech appliances can cause devastating injuries to curious little fingers. It's best to store them both unplugged and out of reach. It also goes without saying, but we're saying it anyway because your older child will beg: Never let a child use a paper shredder, even with adult supervision.

Plants. Plenty of houseplants and flowers are poisonous, including ivy, holly, peace lily, philodendron, hyacinth, daffodils, and paper whites. (Ironically, one plant long believed to be poisonous, the holiday favorite poinsettias, actually are not.) Ask your local nursery for a list or go online to poison.org. Even nontoxic plants aren't truly baby-friendly, because your child can pull off the leaves and put them in his mouth.

Plastic bags. Any type of plastic bag can pose a suffocation hazard if your baby puts it over his head—and that's what they all seem to do. Ditto plastic wrap from the dry cleaner.

Toothpaste. Too much fluoride is harmful. Your baby doesn't need to brush with any toothpaste yet (it's not recommended until after age two). If your baby gets hold of yours, call the National Capital Poison Center (800-222-1222) for advice if you suspect he may have swallowed more than a pea-size amount of it.

Vitamins. Even one can be an overdose for an infant, so treat them just like medicine and store them out of reach.

Wicker. Bits of sticks and branches commonly break off wicker baskets and laundry hampers, and even more durable painted or lacquered wicker furniture may wear to the point that this happens, so watch for loose pieces that your baby could choke on. Better yet, avoid wicker furnishings in your home until your child is bigger.

Whew! Let's see, did we forget anything else that's dangerous? The air perhaps? Okay, we're kidding, and we know that reading this can be a one-way ticket to freak-out town, but laying it out in black and white is just one of those big good-for-you pills that every mom needs to swallow for her baby's sake. (We find it goes down easier when tucked inside a Twinkie.) Okay. Deep breath. Are you ready for more scary but necessary info? Then read on, Macduff.

Do You Need a Babyproofing Pro?

It sounds a bit extravagant, but some parents feel it's worth every penny to hire a professional childproofer. If you can't spare the time, can't even hang a picture without help, or have twins and triplets who are difficult to keep up with, you may feel it's worth the investment, too. The business has become so popular that it shouldn't be hard to find a babyproofing pro if you live near a city. Word of mouth is always the best reference, but you can also locate a childproofer in your area by calling the International Association for Child Safety at 888-677-4227, or go to iafcs.org. Before you hire someone, ask about the childproofer's training and if his work is insured. You'll also want to check references. Fees can range from $250 to more than $1,000, including supplies.

SURFING FOR SAFETY

Many babyproofing products can easily be found online or in catalogs, while your little one is snoozing safe and sound in her crib. Here are some resources to start with:

- One Step Ahead, onestepahead.com, 800-274-8440.
- The First Years by Learning Curve, learningcurve.com, 800-533-6708.
- Safety 1st, safety1st.com, 800-544-1108.
- Perfectly Safe, kidsstuff.com, 800-837-5437.
- KidCo, kidcoinc.com, 800-553-5529. This company makes kits that let you use any gate with wrought-iron or other tricky railings. It also manufactures a toilet lock that automatically resets when the lid is lowered.

Have a Baby-Safe Holiday

Your baby's first holiday season is a special one, for reasons your may not have thought of: Traditional decorations such as Christmas trees, menorahs, and mistletoe turn merrymaking into risky business. That doesn't mean it can't be enjoyable, however. Here's how to deck your halls wisely:

Stress-free trees. Make sure real trees are as fresh as possible—a shower of pine needles when it's shaken is a bad sign—so they don't create a fire hazard. Artificial trees should be labeled "fire-resistant." Don't put breakable ornaments or those that look like food (your baby may think he can eat them) on low branches where he can reach them. Double-check that any lights are in good shape (no frayed cords or broken bulbs) before putting them on the tree. Secure the tree to the wall or ceiling so it can't be pulled over. And always keep a close eye on your baby when he's near the tree.

Presents perfect. Buy age-appropriate gifts (toys for kids over age three will be a choking hazard for your baby), and double-check that relatives do, too. (Grandma may not remember what's okay, what's not.) Then supervise your baby while she's opening them—wrapping paper, bags, ribbons, and bows can be both suffocation and choking hazards. (Don't worry. You'll probably be taking her weight in photographs, so we think you'll be attentive.)

Plant pointers. Many of the season's traditional blooms—mistletoe berries, holly berries, English ivy, Jerusalem cherry, Christmas cherry, and amaryllis—are downright poisonous, so keep them out of your baby's reach and mouth. (Contrary to popular opinion, poinsettias are not poisonous, though you still wouldn't want your baby gnawing on one!)

Candle caveats. Don't place a lit menorah or holiday candles within your baby's reach or on a tablecloth—he could grab the end and pull them over, causing a fire. It also goes without saying, and yet again we're saying it: Never put a lit candle on a Christmas tree.

Party pitfalls. Be vigilant about keeping toxic alcoholic drinks, hot drinks, and appetizers (nuts, candies, raw veggies, hard cheese cubes, popcorn) that can present a choking hazard away from your baby.

Living Peacefully with Pets

You loved your little Fido or Fifi for years before your baby came along, and you probably never imagined you'd feel any differently when your family expanded. But all the fuss over a new baby can be a big adjustment for a pet who's been enjoying squatter's rights. Her nose is out of joint, yet you've got a baby to protect. And even when time goes by and you think everything is hunky-dory, suddenly your bigger babe sees tails for tugging and pet food bowls for flipping, trying even the most patient pets.

If you haven't had a pet before, but thought that you'd like your baby to have a fuzzy pal, you might want to hold off. When researchers analyzed the medical charts of children bitten by dogs between 1994 and 2003, they found that when a new pet is brought home to a house with a child under age five, the child is more likely to get bitten. Babies under age one were most vulnerable, and the breeds most likely to bite children were German shepherds and Dobermans. Still, plenty of pet-loving parents co-exist peacefully with dogs, cats, and young children by taking some precautions. Here's how to pull it off.

Before-the-baby basics. Think carefully about your pet's current lifestyle and how that might change when you bring the baby home from the hospital. If Mom is the one who always takes Rover for walks, for instance, Dad should start doing some of the strolling so it doesn't seem obvious to your pooch that you've dumped him for that little interloper who's suddenly appeared. Perhaps an older sibling can learn to take over some pet-care chores, like filling water or dinner bowls. Or if you know Grandma will be coming to lend a hand for a few weeks, schedule a few playdates with her and your feline friend, so he gets used to having her in the house and preparing his meals. And by all means, if your pet has anxiety issues or a tendency toward aggressive behavior, now is the time to consult a veterinarian or animal behavior specialist. All pets will need to learn some baby manners, such as staying on the floor beside you unless you specifically invite him onto your chair or lap. Finally, taking your pet for a medical checkup is a must—you need to be sure he is up-to-date on vaccines and doesn't have any health concerns that will complicate your chaotic new life.

Role-play with your pet. Invite over a friend with a baby—but be vigilant about supervising your pet during this visit if she's not used to being around children, so she can experience the sights, sounds, and smells of life with an infant. At other times, pretend with a baby doll: You can carry it around the house, push it in a stroller when you take your dog for a walk and snuggle it against your breast as you're watching TV together in the evening to demonstrate everyday babycare for your pet. You can even introduce your pet to the sounds of baby life with a clever CD called *Preparing Fido* (available at preparingfido.com) that features sounds such as a baby crying, the motor of a mechanical infant swing, and the gentle creak of a rocking chair. Playing lullaby music around the house is another good idea, or put on an infant video such as the Baby Einstein series now and then so your pet can watch babies and their behavior on TV.

Get acquainted gradually. Send home a baby blanket from the hospital prior to your newborn's homecoming so your pet can sniff her new "sibling's" scent. When you both arrive home, hand the baby over to Dad and spend some quality time with your pet first—she'll have missed you while you were away. Then invite her to "sit and stay" with the two of you, rewarding her with a treat when she does as you ask. This will build positive feelings toward the baby for her. Conversely, if you exclude or banish her to another room, she may become resentful of the baby.

Be smart about supervision. Obviously you want to keep bird cages, fish tanks, hamster habitats and the like out of your baby's reach. But even under the best of circumstances—your more mobile pet appears to love your baby and vice versa—you should never leave the two of them in a room alone together. Don't permit your dog or cat to get into the crib, infant seat, or Pack 'n Play; install gates if necessary to keep him away from off-limits areas. Your dog or cat may simply be trying to cuddle or play with your baby, but he can't possibly know his own strength, and your baby, as she gets bigger, won't realize she can hurt your pet by poking his eyes, for instance. It will be a long time before either family member understands such boundaries, and once again it's up to you to make sure they aren't crossed for the foreseeable future (read: years).

The Most Common Accidents and How to Prevent or (When That Doesn't Work) Handle Them

By now we've probably scared you out of your wits, and of course we apologize for that. But our intentions are good: The better you understand the risks and accept the idea that babies aren't the most reasonable human beings, the more carefully you'll watch over your child. (Why would she want to taste the bottom of your shoes or try to touch her eyeball? Repeat after us: because she can.) That's why toddlers between one and three years of age have the highest injury rates in all of childhood. Even sadder: Infants have higher rates of accidental-injury-related deaths than older children, particularly from suffocation, drowning, falls, and motor vehicle occupant injury, according to Safe Kids Worldwide.

Now that you've done your best to babyproof your living environment, it's time to read up on what the most common injuries are, additional ways to prevent them, and how to treat them if, God forbid, they occur. While it's sure frightening to think about, by arming yourself with the right knowledge, you'll be better able to remain calm and help your child—maybe even save her life. We're going to tell you everything you need to know to do that, but don't stop at reading what we have to say. The very best preparation is to take an actual emergency first-aid class. Parents and caregivers who enroll in these classes learn hands-on the proper procedures for infant CPR (cardiopulmonary resuscitation), older child and adult CPR, and emergency choking procedures. To find one, contact your local hospital, or a local chapter of the American Red Cross or American Heart Association. You can also go online to redcross.org. If you learned CPR awhile ago, you should also know that the American Heart Association and the American Red Cross issued revised guidelines in 2005 that put more emphasis on chest compressions. Read our updated directions on pages 303–5, and consider taking a refresher course. Keep an eye out for further updates in the news as our understanding of the most effective lifesaving methods for children and adults continues to evolve.

Accident: **A fall**

What Happens: For infants between one month and one year of age, the most common accident in this age group is falling—from places like furniture (changing tables, beds), stairs, shopping carts, or playground equipment. Once your baby begins to crawl and cruise and walk, falling down will literally become an everyday part of childhood, and the majority of these instances will result in nothing more than a few tears and maybe a scrape or a bruise. Just check out the legs from the knee down of a typical toddler and you'll know what we mean. Then there are the more dangerous falls: a walker that rolls down the steps with your baby in it (see "Be Wary of Walkers," page 180, to read up on more reasons why we don't like them), or the newly minted climber who attempts to scale the ladder-back chair in the dining room only to end up on the ground with it on top of him.

This is the beginning of the stage when you literally can't let your child out of your sight, and it goes on for several years. (Again, for taking this parenting pill, we suggest a Twinkie.) You simply can't imagine what your child will think of. One of us (who shall remain nameless) looked out the kitchen window to see her one-year-old on top of the table on her outside deck only inches away from the railing, which was about ten feet above ground level. The deck had a safety gate at the top of the stairs, and she mistakenly thought he was just fine out there in what constituted a big outdoor playpen. Fortunately, she got to him before he went over the side. Unfortunately, the same adventurous child a few weeks later figured out how to unbuckle the seat belt of his stroller, tried to climb out, and landed on the back of his head on his aunt's stone patio; he went to the ER to get the gash stapled together. So with that in mind, here are some preventive measures. If your child is injured despite your best efforts, try not to berate yourself too much—it happens to all of us.

How to Prevent It: The first order of business is to learn never to turn your back on your baby while he is on a changing table, the examining table in a doctor's office, a sofa, an adult bed, or any other type of furniture. It's also not a good idea to put an infant seat or bouncy seat up on a table. Even young babies can wiggle and squirm enough to flip these unsecured devices over, and if they're high up, the momentum can propel them right off the table, too. (Don't listen to Grandma: Your baby will not catch cold if his bouncy seat is on the floor!)

In addition:

- Keep the crib sides raised and firmly secured. Once your baby can pull up, remove bumper guards because he can use them as a step to help him lean over and consequently fall out the side.

- Do not allow siblings to carry a baby unless they are mature enough to do so safely. When closely supervised, young children can hold the baby while seated in the middle of your bed—if either of them topples, they'll still land safely on the mattress.
- Make sure hardware-mounted gates are installed at the top and bottom of all stairways (don't forget about stairs on outside decks). They should open away from the stairs, not into them, and of course you need to keep them securely closed at all times. (We know one dad who was horrified to find his ten-month-old daughter swinging from an open gate at the top of the stairs!)
- Place operable window guards on all windows above the ground floor, and keep furniture away from windows. If you have double-hung windows, open them from the top down for fresh air.

How to Handle It: What to do in case of a fall depends on the injury that may have been incurred.

Head injuries: Most head injuries, though scary, are minor. If the injury is indeed mild, your baby will remain alert and awake after the incident. She certainly may cry, but it should last no more than ten minutes, and will probably be even briefer. If there's a bruise or swelling, apply an ice pack or cold compresses. A cut that appears deep or long, or is bleeding significantly, may require stitches; head to the ER if necessary. Otherwise, you can treat it yourself by washing it with soap and water and applying an antibiotic ointment such as bacitracin, then a snugly adhering bandage (you can skip the bandage if it's going to get stuck in her hair). A minor head injury may sometimes cause a headache or even an episode of vomiting. If that's the case, we know you're going to want to call your pediatrician (we would) for another opinion, though there's a good chance she'll be just fine. Either way, watch your baby for the next twenty-four to forty-eight hours to make sure she doesn't get worse: She vomits again; becomes very sleepy or lethargic; becomes very cranky, which could indicate a severe headache; or seems off balance or confused. Very rarely, internal bleeding could occur. A bonk on the head may result in a mild concussion, which won't cause her to pass out, but she may seem a little dazed. Call your doctor for reassurance and monitor her as outlined above.

You'll know you have a more serious issue on your hands if your baby loses consciousness after a head injury, even if it's just for a few minutes. This is referred to as a classic concussion, and though it doesn't necessarily mean her brain has been damaged, its functioning has been disturbed. Call your pediatrician for further evaluation even if she quickly resumes consciousness. If your child doesn't awaken after a few minutes, she needs immediate medical attention, so call 911. While you're waiting for help to arrive, take the following steps:

- Do not move your child unless you absolutely have to (for instance, if she's in danger of falling farther because she's on a ledge). If you must move her, take care to avoid bending or twisting her neck, which could make the injury worse.
- Check to see if she's breathing and if not, perform CPR (see pages 303–5 for instructions).
- If she's bleeding severely from a wound, place a clean cloth over the wound and apply direct pressure (see pages 293–96 for more on cuts and wounds).

Back or neck injuries. If your baby has fallen and you believe she may have injured her neck or back, do not attempt to move her or you may cause more serious harm. Call 911 immediately, tell them what you suspect, and wait for help to arrive.

Broken bones. You would think a broken arm or leg would be obvious, but that's often not the case. Infants and young children have such pliable bones that they can break in a way that's known as a greenstick fracture—the bone bends like a green piece of wood that tears away on only one side of the stick or, in this case, the bone. The bone may also buckle on one side, but not actually separate. And even if it breaks all the way through, the bone may not be displaced, so you won't necessarily be able to see the break without an X-ray (this is known as a simple fracture). To check for a break, gently press along the length of the bone—if your baby winces or cries at a certain spot, it might be a fracture. Other signs: swelling, bruising, tenderness, limping, and, of course, obvious deformity. Sometimes a bone is broken even when the child can move the limb. If in doubt, always call your pediatrician. One more caveat: Though it's appropriate for older children, you shouldn't apply ice to a suspected fracture in an infant or toddler: The extreme cold can make the injury worse.

Though traumatic and guilt producing for you, these early-childhood fractures are usually fast healing and typically just need to be kept immobilized with a cast for about four weeks while the fractured area grows back together on its own. In fact, your biggest issue will probably be keeping your active baby from daring feats while wearing a cast. It will make you crazy when you see him climbing or running, but try to relax. Even if he falls right on the injured appendage again, the cast will protect it from further harm!

For more complex breaks in which the bone is protruding through the skin, or the arm or leg is badly twisted, try not to move the injured area. Call 911 for an ambulance to properly transport your child to the hospital, and do your best to keep him comfortable while you wait for help to arrive. Avoid giving him anything to eat or drink, or pain relievers, because they may interfere with other medications if surgery is necessary.

Cuts and scrapes. Most boo-boos are but an everyday fact of childhood. The sight of blood for some little guys and girls is often more stressful than the pain of falling down. Usually just cleansing the injured area with a little soap and water, then applying a dab of over-the-counter antibiotic ointment and a bandage to protect it (and this is more psychological than medical in many cases), plus a good dose of TLC, is all that's necessary. Skip antiseptics and iodine: They'll sting and don't really help much anyway. If the scrape contains a lot of dirt, or even a tiny bit of gravel, glass, or some other sort of scary debris that you can't remove, a visit to the pediatrician for a more thorough cleaning is warranted. Besides providing his expertise, the physician can also apply a topical anesthetic so the cleaning won't hurt your baby.

If a cut goes deeper than the skin surface and into the tissue below, it's known as a laceration and may require stitches or other treatment. To stop the bleeding, apply direct pressure to the wound by covering it with a clean cloth or a piece of gauze and holding it firmly over the cut. Almost all lacerations will stop bleeding in five to ten minutes with this type of pressure. Try not to keep peeking at the injured area while you're applying the pressure—the most common mistake—because it will just prolong the bleeding. If for some reason the bleeding still won't stop, call 911 for help, but don't try making a tourniquet or tying off the injured area unless you have been trained to do so—you can cause more problems if you do this incorrectly.

Once the bleeding has let up, if you're calm enough to handle things or you have someone on hand to help you, cleanse and bandage the wound as described above, then call your pediatrician about the next step. You can also proceed directly to the ER, but some wounds may be treatable in the doctor's office—a more pleasant experience for both you and your baby. As a general rule of thumb, lacerations that are deeper than the skin and/or more than half an inch long will probably need stitches, staples, a butterfly bandage, or a type of glue (more on these options shortly) to help minimize scarring and avoid damage to underlying muscles, nerves, or tendons. (Even smaller cuts on the face may be better off stitched; consult your baby's doctor if you're at all uncertain.) Still, as long as you've got the bleeding under control, you don't need to panic. Being seen soon is best, of course, but the time frame for stitches and the like to keep scarring to a minimum is actually within eight hours of the injury. One of us mom-editors with especially accident-prone children has a favorite plastic surgeon who instructs her to come over to his office (after reporting to the ER first for insurance reasons), where he does the sewing in a relaxing plush suite with a very nurturing nurse at his side—again, far better than the chaos of the ER for your child and yourself.

Speaking of plastic surgeons, their skills are a must for any stitches on the face, so demand that one be called in if that's where your baby's injury is. Not every hospital or doctor's office will mention this option, so be aware of your right to ask. Most insurance plans will cover the cost of a plastic surgeon or other specialist for an emergency, but again, you've got time to call your particular insurance carrier's general hotline to double-check, so don't let anyone pressure you into making a quick decision on this. Any ER doctor will probably tell you that he's qualified to stitch a child's face, and technically he would be, but that does not mean the results will be as good! A caveat from one of us: After many hours in the ER with a crying baby boy, a *Babytalk* editor let the attending doc do the stitches rather than wait three hours more for the plastic surgeon. She feels the scar—half hidden in her son's eyebrow—gives her little man character. We all do what we need to do.

Fortunately there are a few modern-day options for treating lacerations that are a bit less traumatic than stitches. Wounds to the head that are covered by hair and won't be visible can literally be stapled together. It sounds harsh, but it's a much faster procedure than stitching, and your child won't feel the staples after they're applied. You will need to have the staples removed about a week later, however. A terrific new skin glue called Dermabond is another option for some lacerations; it literally holds the wound together as it heals, then sloughs off on its own, so no removal is necessary. It can't be used in certain spots, however, such as near the mouth—the moisture will keep it from adhering for a long enough time. Finally, a special super-adhesive type of bandage called a Steri-Strip, or a butterfly bandage (which looks just like it sounds and is designed to hold cuts tight as they heal), may be another option for lacerations that aren't too deep.

Once you get the injury sealed up, you'll just have to

spend about a week keeping an eye out for infection (redness, swelling, pus) and sweating every time your baby attempts a physical feat that could reopen the cut. If the worst happens, however, know that you are not alone. Your doctor will likely recant tales of other tots who ripped open their stitches even sooner than yours. And remember the one of us who is oh-so-familiar with the plastic surgeon? She has a child who needed stitches near his eye from slipping out of his dad's hands after a bath and catching the corner of the bathroom vanity *while he still had two staples in the back of his head from a fall five days earlier!*

 ## AVOIDING PLAYGROUND PITFALLS

There's nothing more fun for little crawlers and climbers than being let loose on the local jungle gym, and it's a real treat for you to get out of the house and chat up some other moms. But when your baby is just beginning to get his sea legs, you've got to be extra careful. Keep these playground safety tips in mind:

Small-size equipment. Never let your baby on any slide or climbing structure more than a few feet high; the farther he falls, the worse the injury.

Separate play areas. Tot equipment should be in a section away from where the older kids play so your little one isn't in danger of getting plowed down by the big guys.

Safe surfaces. All playground equipment should have either sand, pea gravel, wood chips, or rubber cushioning underneath to prevent injury from falls. Believe it or not, grass is not an appropriate surface.

Sandbox smarts. Stay away from sandboxes that contain any kind of litter; while ingesting a little of the grainy stuff won't necessarily hurt your baby, bacteria that may have accumulated from insects or animal droppings could.

Serious supervision. You know it, but it's always worth repeating: Don't let your child out of your sight for a second.

Accident: **Potential drowning**

What Happens: Water is a kiddie magnet. Most babies and young children love to play in it wherever they can find it, including bathtubs, toilets, sinks, buckets, and pools. And it doesn't have to be deep to be dangerous—it's possible for your baby to drown in less than two inches of water in mere minutes. Why? Babies and toddlers are top-heavy; they fall in headfirst and then can't lift themselves out. They also don't know how to hold their breath so they panic and inhale water, causing them to suffocate. Once babies begin to sit up on their own, the risk of submersion injuries and drowning in the bathtub really skyrockets, probably because parents mistakenly think they can right themselves if they fall over. The cardinal rule to remember: Just because a baby can sit up doesn't mean he can be left alone, even for a second in a shallow tub. And don't count on a bathtub seat or ring to be a lifesaving device. It's convenient, but it won't save your baby from drowning. (See "Should You Use a Baby Bath Seat?" on pages 298–99.)

How to Prevent It: Take the following precautions:

- Never leave an infant or toddler alone—even for an instant—in or near a bathtub, bucket of water, toilet, or other body of water. Always stay within arm's reach of your child if she's near water.
- Do not allow your baby any unsupervised access to the bathroom. Keep the door closed and a plastic knob cover on the handle to prevent her from turning it.
- Put toilet lid locks on all the toilets in your house.
- If you have a pool or a hot tub on your property, make sure it's surrounded by a locked four-sided fence that's at least five feet high. An alarm (which goes off if a child falls in) and a pool cover are also smart ideas.
- Parents, caretakers, and pool owners should learn CPR and have in the pool area both a telephone and U.S. Coast Guard–approved rescue equipment, such as a ring buoy or throw line and reaching pole.

How to Handle It: Take the following steps:

- As soon as you pull your baby from the water, check to see if he's breathing on his own. If he's not, immediately begin CPR (see pages 303–5 for instructions).
- If someone else is with you, that person should call 911. If you're alone, perform CPR for two minutes, then call 911. Bring your child to the phone with you and resume CPR after the call. When he begins to breathe on his own, he will most likely vomit the swallowed water, and this is a good sign.
- Once paramedics arrive, they will continue CPR and give your baby oxygen. Your baby will likely need to remain under medical observation for the next twenty-four hours to determine if there was any damage to his respiratory or nervous system. A child who spent only a brief time under water may well recover fully, but a baby who was deprived of oxygen for longer may suffer damage to his heart, lungs, or brain. Contact your pediatrician when you get to the hospital and your baby is under medical supervision.

SHOULD YOU USE A BABY BATH SEAT— OR NOT?

Most parents are thrilled when their babies are big enough to graduate to a real bathtub and sit in a handy seat—it's so much easier than trying to hold and bathe a slippery, squirmy tyke in an infant bathtub. But if you've heard anything about the baby bath seat controversy, you might be nervous about using one. You don't have to be if you're very careful, according to experts at Safe Kids Worldwide, a nonprofit organization working to prevent accidental childhood injury. Back in 2000, a group of safety organizations, including the Consumer Federation of America, petitioned the Consumer Product Safety Commission to ban bath seats. The AAP and Safe Kids Worldwide were not among them, however, because they've taken the position that bath seats can be useful when used carefully and properly. In response, the CPSC chose instead to add a warning label to the seats, and manufacturers have redesigned them to be more stable and have more suction. Unlike the controversial baby walkers, which pose a safety risk and have no inherent value beyond entertainment, bath seats do help parents hold slippery babies. You just have to be very vigilant about watching your child while in one—as you should in any situation involving water. After all, if your baby was wearing a flotation device in a swimming pool, you still wouldn't walk away and leave her unattended, right? Well, bathtub rings are not safety devices, and bathtubs are not safe places, even though they contain much less water than a pool. Here are more guidelines to ensure your baby has a splashingly good and safe bath time:

- Never, ever leave your infant's side, even for a minute, whether she's in a bath seat or not. "Within arm's reach" is the recommended distance.
- Don't multitask—talk on the phone, put away bath towels—while you're in the bathroom with your baby.
- Use as little water in the bathtub as possible. About an inch is enough to clean your baby and allow him to have fun splashing.
- Stop using the seat as soon as your child attempts to climb or wiggle out of it, or becomes too big to fit comfortably in it.

Accident: **Choking**

What Happens: Your baby's natural curiosity will lead him to explore many things with his mouth, chewing on pretty much anything he can pick up with his newly perfected pincer grasp, even if it tastes yucky (or is poisonous—see pages 310–13). Not surprisingly, choking becomes the main hazard toward the end of the first year and remains at the top of the list up to age three, depending on how strong your baby's oral tendencies are. Even if he doesn't seem to put as much in his mouth as other tots, you never know when something will motivate him to do so. Infants can choke on objects they encounter on the floor, such as dried hard pieces of food, toy parts, coins, pen caps—you name it. To make things worse, the smaller diameter of their airways and gastrointestinal tracts makes them more prone to choking than older kids and adults.

How to Prevent It: Take the following precautions:

- Keep plastic bags, balloons, small, hard foods (see chapter 7, pages 258–59, for a list of foods babies can choke on) as well as small objects away from your baby.
- Put any object you're uncertain about through the toilet paper roll test: If a toy or toy part can fit through here, a child under age four can choke on it. (Food, however, needs to be even smaller. Again, see chapter 7 for guidelines on cutting up foods to avoid choking.)
- Do not let your child run or play while eating.
- Do not put anything around your baby's neck. Remove drawstrings from all her clothing. Keep cribs away from windows that have cords from blinds or draperies—they can also strangle her. (Cutting the loop at the bottom of the drawstring will eliminate the danger.) It's also a good idea to keep anything with an electrical cord away from the crib. Not only can the cord be a strangulation risk if your baby should pull it into the crib, but she could also be electrocuted if she bites it.
- Keep laundry hampers away from the crib as well. Some clever kids have managed to pull off the top and drag the dirty clothing into the crib—a suffocation hazard (not to mention potentially gross, depending what's on the dirty clothing!).
- Follow age guidelines on toy packaging; toys stating that they are for ages three and up only are almost always a choking hazard.

How to Handle It: Babies may gag and wheeze when a drink "goes down the wrong way," or even because they've just tasted something unfamiliar, and this is normal.

If your baby starts coughing but is still able to breathe, stand by and just let her keep coughing. Anything else—like sticking your fingers in her mouth to remove the object—might make the obstruction worse.

If she doesn't cough up the object, her cough begins to weaken, and/or her breathing becomes more difficult, you need to take action. You'll know it's a true choking emergency if your baby is unable to talk or make normal sounds or if her face turns first a bright red and then blue. This situation requires immediate first aid. If someone also is present, that person can call 911. If you're alone, try to relieve the obstruction as described below, making one or two attempts. If you're unsuccessful or your baby becomes unconscious, then call 911. As we noted before, bring the baby to the phone with you and resume CPR after making the call.

If your baby cannot breathe and is unable to cough or cry take the following steps. Be as gentle as possible; her organs are fragile.

1. Give your baby five back slaps. To do this, first position her facedown and head-down on your forearm, with your hand supporting her head and neck and her legs straddling your arm. Lower her onto your thigh, keeping her head lower than her chest. Then use the heel of your free hand to give her five firm, rapid slaps between her shoulder blades. (If your baby is too large to hold this way, you can lay her facedown over your lap instead, with her head lower than her trunk and firmly supported.)

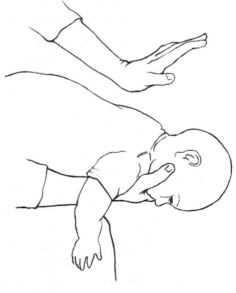

Figure 8.1 The traditional Heimlich maneuver is too forceful to perform on an infant. Instead, hold your baby head down and facedown (like a football) on your forearm. Then deliver five back slaps between his shoulder blades with the lower end of the palm of your hand.

2. Give five chest thrusts. If she still cannot breathe, rotate her so that she is faceup on your opposite forearm with her head lower than her chest (or lay her on her back on a firm surface). With your free hand, use *only two fingers* to give five chest thrusts, depressing the breastbone one-half inch to one inch. (The correct position for your fingers is in the center of the breastbone just below the nipple line.)

3. If your baby still can't cough or breathe, continue to repeat five back slaps and five chest thrusts until the object is forced out, she starts to breathe on her own, or she becomes unconscious. Call your doctor even if your baby seems to be fine; she will still need to be evaluated.

4. If your choking baby becomes unconscious, deliver two rescue breaths. (See "How to Save Your Baby's Life," beginning on the next page, for the complete CPR technique.) If the breaths do not go in, the airway is probably blocked. Tilt your baby's head farther back, lift her chin, and give two more rescue breaths. If the breaths still do not go in, give thirty chest compressions depressing her breastbone one-half inch to one inch. (The correct position for your fingers is in the center of the breastbone just below the nipple line; don't remove your fingers from your baby's chest between compressions.)

5. Look for a foreign object. Open your baby's airway using the tongue-jaw-lift technique (also called the head tilt/chin lift technique): Position her on her back on a firm surface, then tilt her head back just enough so that her chin is lifted, while also pushing down on her forehead with your other hand to move her tongue from the back of the throat. Opening the airway in this manner may allow your baby to breathe on her own. If it doesn't, look in the throat for a foreign object or piece of food. If you can see one, sweep it out with your finger (the smaller the finger, the better). *Do not stick your finger or anything else in your baby's throat if you cannot see the object she is choking on.*

6. Give two rescue breaths. If your baby's chest still does not rise, continue the cycle of giving thirty chest compressions, looking for a foreign object, and giving two

rescue breaths until help arrives. If you've successfully removed the object from her airway, check for signs of life
(breathing and movement), including a pulse.

HOW TO SAVE YOUR BABY'S LIFE WITH RESCUE BREATHING AND CPR

Your baby may stop breathing or her heart may stop beating for
many reasons: drowning, poisoning, suffocation, choking, smoke
inhalation, a traumatic injury such as a car accident, or an infection
or illness. Signs that your baby is in need of rescue breathing (mouth-
to-mouth resuscitation) or CPR include:

- Unresponsiveness with no evidence of effective breathing.
- Blue lips or skin with no evidence of effective breathing.
- Drooling or difficulty in swallowing accompanied by trouble
  breathing.
- Extreme paleness.

Check for other signs that he is breathing: Is his chest moving up
and down? Can you hear him take breaths if you put your ear over
his mouth? Determine if he is conscious or not by tapping him and
shouting his name. He is probably unconscious if he doesn't respond.
Ask someone to call 911, or, if you are alone, call for help after you
have attempted rescue efforts for two minutes. If possible, bring the
baby with you to the phone while you continue to give rescue breathing or CPR.

Step 1. Lay your baby faceup on a firm surface. Tilt his head back
and lift his chin to open the airway. Check for signs of life (breathing and movement) for just a few seconds.

Step 2. For an infant (under one year), place your open mouth over
his entire nose and mouth, forming as tight a seal as possible. Blow
two slow rescue breaths into your baby's mouth, providing enough
air to cause his chest to rise slightly. For an infant, this is about the
amount of air it takes to puff out your cheeks—blowing excess air
won't help.

(continued on next page)

If your baby's chest *doesn't* rise

- Retilt his head and give two more rescue breaths.
- If the chest still doesn't rise, his airway may be blocked, so you're going to need to follow the procedure for removing the obstruction described on pages 301–3 (in the interest of saving you time, we'll repeat it here): Place two fingers in the center of your baby's breastbone, about one finger width below the nipple line. Give thirty quick chest compressions, depressing his breastbone between one-half and one inch. (Don't remove your fingers from his chest between compressions.)
- Then tilt his head back again and check for an object in his mouth. If you see one, sweep it out using the smallest finger you can manage.
- Give two more slow, gentle rescue breaths.
- If your baby's chest still doesn't rise, repeat the pattern of giving thirty chest compressions, checking for an object in his mouth, removing it if visible, and giving two rescue breaths until the air goes in.

If your baby's chest *does* rise

- Check for a pulse on the inside of your baby's upper arm (on the bone in between the bicep and the tricep muscles).
- If a pulse is present but he doesn't appear to be breathing, continue to provide rescue breaths at a rate of about one breath every three seconds (twenty per minute), removing your mouth between breaths. After about two minutes, check for a pulse again. If you can still feel it, but your baby is still not breathing, give one breath every three seconds and check for a pulse about every two minutes.
- If there are no signs of life or a pulse, tilt your baby's head back with one hand to open the airway. Administer thirty chest compressions, followed by two rescue breaths.
- Repeat the cycle of thirty chest compressions and two breaths until you see signs of life or are too exhausted to continue and another adult or a trained responder is now available to take over.

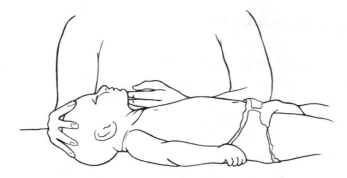

Figure 8.2a Lay your baby faceup on a firm surface with his head and chin tilted up.

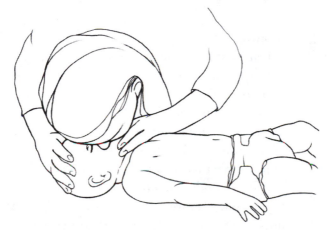

Figure 8.2b Form a tight seal over his entire mouth and nose with your mouth. Blow two slow rescue breaths into his mouth.

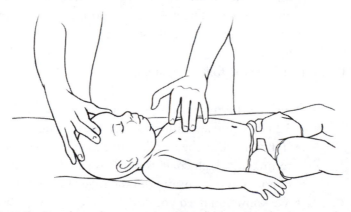

Figure 8.2c Give thirty chest compressions, alternating with two rescue breaths, until he begins to cough or breathe on his own or help arrives.

A PRODUCT WE LOVE: CPR TEDDY

Here's one stuffed animal that may someday come to your and your baby's rescue. Just press on the hand of this lovable bear and he'll talk you through the process of both infant and child CPR so you can hone your skills right at home—and before you need them. A red heart on the teddy's chest shows you exactly where you should be compressing, and if you're doing it correctly a green light on the bow tie flashes. CPR Teddy comes with an instructional DVD ($60; cprteddy.com).

Accident: **A burn**

What Happens: When someone mentions a burn injury, fire raging through your home is probably the first thing that pops into your mind. But it can take a lot less to harm your baby's precious soft skin. Burns from hot liquids, steam, or even a bathtub faucet are far bigger threats. A baby, whose thinner skin burns at a lower temperature and more deeply than an adult's, can suffer third-degree burns in a few seconds when the water temperature in the bathtub or sink is above 120 degrees Fahrenheit. And if a fire does occur, your baby is also at greater risk than you because her small body will succumb to deadly smoke and fumes from toxic combustion products much more quickly as well. The good news: Both fire and burn injuries are easily prevented by taking just a few simple precautions.

How to Prevent It: Take the following steps:

- Set the thermostat on your home's hot-water heater to 120 degrees Fahrenheit to prevent scalding.
- If she's in the kitchen while you're cooking, keep your baby secured in a high chair as much as possible. Turn handles of pots and pans away from the edge of the stove.
- We know you need your caffeine (because we practically mainline the stuff, too), but be extremely careful with any hot beverages. Don't drink them while you're hold-

ing your baby—a squirm at the wrong time can result in a serious burn to one or both of you. And if you're walking around with a hot beverage, make sure your baby is in full view so you don't trip over him (which can hurt him in more ways than one). You might also want to get a cup with a lid to minimize any spills. And even if your cup o' joe is on a table or counter, be vigilant about not leaving it on the edge where your baby can pull it over. Skip the tablecloth, too, because again, he can yank it, and everything sitting on it can fall down on him.

- Don't overlook the hazards of cooking on an outdoor grill. Your baby may be able to get a nasty burn on his hand just by touching a closed lid or other hot area of the appliance, so don't let him near a grill while it's in use, and for about an hour after it's turned off so there's plenty of time for it too cool down. (We're sad to say we know this firsthand; one of our children touched a hot grill just after her first birthday. It happened so quickly that her still-guilt-ridden parents were standing right there and didn't even realize it until she started screaming.)
- Install smoke detectors throughout your home. Experts recommend that there be a smoke detector on each level of your home, especially positioned outside the bedrooms and near the kitchen.
- Have working fire extinguishers in your home. Keep one designed for grease fires in or near the kitchen (these will be described as specifically for kitchens on the label). Remember, too, that fire extinguishers are for use only on small localized fires; if you've got one that's larger or spreading rapidly, get out of the house as fast as you can and call 911 or your local fire department (if you have the number handy).
- If you smoke, do not smoke in bed, and properly dispose of butts and ashes.
- We've said this before, but keep electrical appliances and cords out of your child's reach.
- Erect barriers around space heaters, woodstoves, fireplaces, or kerosene heaters. Even better, try to avoid using them altogether if your baby is around.

- Check your heating system at least once a year to prevent malfunctioning, carbon monoxide (a toxic gas that
  can occur when appliance such as furnaces or stoves
  malfunction), and fires. Install carbon monoxide detectors outside bedrooms and near the kitchen. For more
  on carbon monoxide poisoning, see page 309.
- Avoid sunburn by keep young infants (under six months)
  out of direct sunlight. Use shading, sunscreen, and hats
  when outdoors.

How to Handle It: There are three different degrees of burns. A first-degree
burn is the mildest (though it's still painful) and simply
causes redness and maybe some swelling of the skin; second-
degree burns also cause blistering and more severe swelling.
The worst burns, third degree, result in whitening or char-
ring (blackening) of the skin and damage to deeper layers.

   If your baby gets any type of burn:

- First, soak or run cool (not cold) water over the injury
  long enough to bring the temperature down and relieve
  the pain. The exception to this rule: electrical burns
  (from, say, an outlet). In the event of an electrical burn,
  just cover the injury with a dry clean cloth or gauze and
  call 911. Electrical burns may cause serious harm even
  when they seem minor on the surface.
- Do not apply ice to the burn, or any other home remedies such as butter, grease, or powder—they can all
  make the burn worse, cause infection, and generally
  make it harder for the doctor to treat the injured area.
- Remove any clothing near the burn, unless it's sticking
  to it. If that's the case, cut away as much of the clothing
  as possible around the burn.
- For serious burns or those that cover large areas, call 911,
  because they can cause breathing difficulty, fluid loss, and
  impair the body's ability to regulate its temperature. Administer mouth-to-mouth resuscitation if necessary while
  you wait for help to arrive (see pages 303–4).
- If the burned area is small but blistered and/or oozing,
  cover it lightly with sterile gauze and immediately seek
  medical attention—at your doctor's office if it's open, or
  the ER otherwise.

- Always seek medical attention for any type of burn on the hands, feet, face, or genitals, where the skin is thinnest and susceptible to more damage.
- For chemical burns, flush the area with large quantities of cool water, remove any clothing that may still have the chemical on it, and call 911. Chemicals can be absorbed into the rest of the body and hurt your baby in other ways.
- If the burn isn't oozing, cover it with a sterile gauze pad. The usual advice is to consult a doctor if redness and pain continue for more than a few hours; an appropriate dose of infant acetaminophen or ibuprofen will also help keep your baby comfortable. Frankly, however, we know you're probably going to want to call the doctor even if the burn seems minor (you may be in more pain than the baby is), so go ahead and pick up the phone, girlfriend!

 CARBON MONOXIDE ALERT

Carbon monoxide (CO) is a colorless and odorless gas that is a natural by-product of burning wood, gas, oil, charcoal, or kerosene. It only becomes a danger when there's too much of it in the air—and then it can kill you and your family. Making sure that any fuel-burning appliances (furnaces, ovens, stoves, gas dryers) are working properly by having them inspected annually at the beginning of each heating season will help ensure that carbon monoxide poisoning does not occur in your home. These appliances should all vent fumes outside, not in your home, whenever possible. And always open a window whenever you use an unvented fuel-burning appliance. Other ways to avoid CO poisoning include:

- Never use a gas stove to heat your home.
- Never use a charcoal grill indoors.
- Don't let a car or other vehicle idle in a garage attached to your home (even if the garage door is open).

(continued on next page)

- Don't sleep in a room with an unvented gas or kerosene space heater.

   Despite these precautions, it's still essential to install carbon monoxide detectors in your home (one on each floor and near the bedrooms): There's no other way to tell that levels are getting too high, unless you begin to experience the physical symptoms of carbon monoxide poisoning, which include headaches, nausea, dizziness, confusion, shortness of breath, and fainting. For infants, who are especially susceptible because of their high metabolic rate, that may be too late. Pregnant women and their fetuses, the elderly, and those who are anemic or who have a history of heart or respiratory disease are also especially vulnerable. Because carbon monoxide poisoning impairs the body's ability to transport oxygen through the bloodstream, it can cause brain damage, permanent injury to the lungs, and even death. If your carbon monoxide detector goes off:

- Check to see if anyone in your home is experiencing symptoms. If they are, get them out of the house immediately and go to the emergency room. If someone is available to help you, have that person open the doors and windows, and turn off combustion appliances (any fuel-burning appliances such as furnaces, ovens, stoves, gas dryers, kerosene lamps, and space heaters) before leaving the house.
- At the ER, tell the physician you suspect CO poisoning. A blood test can confirm this if it's done soon after exposure has occurred.
- If no one in your household is experiencing symptoms, ventilate your home by opening doors and windows anyway, turn off potential sources of CO, call your local fire or police department, and ask them to come and check your home (they will likely tell you to evacuate it ASAP until they arrive and inspect the situation).

Accident: **Poisoning**

What Happens: Accidental poisoning is a major threat between one and two years of age. Of course it can happen even earlier, too, as soon as babies develop the ability to get pretty much anywhere they want but remain clueless about what might be dangerous (despite all those burgeoning brain cells allegedly forming intricate connections in their little minds). You know to lock up obvious poisons like pesticides or bleach, but plenty of other household substances also pose a serious threat, from laundry detergent to plant fertilizer to leftover wine in your refrigerator to the perfume or nail polish that may be sitting on your bedroom dresser as you read this chapter. Even innocent-seeming art supplies may contain lead, mercury, or other dangerous chemicals. (Buy only those labeled with an ACMI— Art & Creative Materials Institute—nontoxic seal.)

And despite the Posion Prevention Packaging Act of 1970 requiring child safety caps, medicines continue to be an all-too-common form of poisoning. Those tough-to-twist caps can't work if they aren't used; many grandparents find these lids just as difficult to take off as toddlers do, so they opt for easier containers. Or how about those clever little travel containers that have a pill compartment for each day that Grandpa may pack in his suitcase when he comes to stay so he doesn't have to bring his entire medicine cabinet? No childproof lid there, unfortunately. Not that we want to knock our loving grandparents—it's just that they're typically not as vigilant as you are. They don't have to think of these things on a daily basis. And you can lecture your parents and in-laws plenty, but bear in mind that even if they don't say it, they're probably still thinking, *Yeah, sure, we raised you without all this crap and managed not to kill you in the process.* A nod of the head does not necessarily guarantee a changing of the ways, so you can never really afford to let your guard down around Grandma or Grandpa.

The consequences of ingesting a poisonous substance aren't pretty: Household cleaners can permanently burn and scar the mouth, throat, and esophagus; overdosing on medication can lead to breathing problems, coma, and death. Here's how to make sure it never happens to your child.

How to Prevent It: Take the following precautions:

- It's not enough to just install child locks on cabinets that contain toxic substances—they should also be stored up high, out of reach and out of sight (because clever little climbers have been known to scale amazing heights when they see an intriguing object).

- Keep the number of the National Capital Poison hotline (800-222-1222) near your home telephone and programmed into your cell phone.
- Buy only medications (over-the-counter and prescription) with child safety caps, and keep them in these containers. If you want a smaller container for travel purposes, make sure it has a safety cap as well.
- Never store medicine or other toxic products in other containers, especially food or drink containers.
- Discard outdated medications and prescriptions that go unused after an illness.

How to Handle It: Assess your baby's reaction.

If you suspect your baby may have ingested a toxic substance and he is unconscious, not breathing, or having convulsions or seizures, immediately call 911. You need emergency services right away.

If your child may have ingested a toxic substance but he doesn't have the above symptoms, immediately call the poison center hotline: 800-222-1222. This is a national number that works night and day anywhere in the United States. You will be connected to the closest regional center, and they will dispatch emergency personnel if it is deemed necessary. Have the substance container or label in hand so you can give any details about it that the emergency personnel may request. (If you don't know the poison control number, call 911 instead.)

- Do not administer any treatments unless you are instructed to do so by a poison center authority; they may make the situation worse. For instance, activated charcoal was once commonly recommended because it minimizes the absorption of poison, but it can also be accidentally inhaled into the lungs, so it's more dangerous to attempt to use it on your own. And syrup of ipecac used to be recommended to induce vomiting, but that can be the wrong thing to do if your child has swallowed a caustic substance; vomiting it back up can cause further damage to the mouth, throat, and esophagus.

- Do not give your child anything to eat or drink before calling the poison hotline.
- Do not attempt to "neutralize" the poison with substances such as lemon juice or vinegar, or attempt any other home remedy you may have heard of.
- Administer rescue breathing or CPR if necessary.
- Remove any clothing that may have the poisonous substance on it. If the substance is on the skin, rinse it off with lukewarm (not hot) water.
- If the substance is in the eye, flush the eye with lukewarm water for about five minutes, then call the poison center (bottled saline solution can also be used to flush the eye). You will likely need help doing this because you will have to hold your child's eyelid open while you pour a stream of water across the nose and into the inner corner of the affected eye. Don't use any eyedrops or other eye medication until instructed to do so by a poison expert.
- If toxic fumes are present from the substance, get your child out into the fresh air.

Safety Out and About

If we've done our job, right about now you might have the urge to take your baby and run screaming out of that danger trap known as your home. Before you do, however, we'd ask that you take a moment to read further, because we have even more feel-good advice to share. This time, come with us as we take you through the hazards that lurk outside your door and how you can prevent or deal with them. Good times. (Hey, we're only doing this so that you can fully enjoy your freedom whenever you actually have the opportunity to take an outing. We know you'll thank us later—maybe when the nightmares stop.)

Car Seats

Since most places, save New York City, require a car to go practically anywhere, we'll start with car seat safety. First step: finding the best car seat for your baby. Second step: using the car seat correctly, because it ain't much good if it's not. While infants are required by law to be secured in car seats when traveling in passenger vehicles virtually everywhere in the United States, some 572 babies under one year old were still killed in traffic accidents between 2001 and 2005, according to the National Highway Traffic Safety Administration (NHTSA). While some of those deaths resulted from babies traveling unrestrained, others were in car seats that were being used improperly. What's a nervous parent to do? For starters, shop wisely, then be vigilant about following installation and usage instructions for your baby's particular model of car seat. Also, watch online for recalls issued by the U.S. Consumer Product Safety Commission (cpsc.gov).

Now, while we can't tell you exactly which car seat to buy, we can tell you which *not* to buy. Not ever. Never buy a used car seat at a garage sale or accept a hand-me-down model from a friend or relative. You won't know for sure whether such a seat was ever recalled, or ever in a crash, which can hamper a seat's ability to do its job (for more on how to know if you can continue to use your own seat if it's been in a crash, see pages 318–19); and you may not get the manufacturer's instruction manual, so you can't be sure you're installing or using the seat properly. If cost is an issue for you (and let's face it, that means most of us!), you're better off saving money by borrowing a stroller, high chair, front carrier, toys, clothing—almost any other baby items but a car safety seat (the same goes for a crib—see pages 279–80 for important safety concerns about your baby's bed).

And just for the record, a higher price tag does not make for a safer seat. It makes for added features and options, which may make the seat model easier or harder for you to use. And if it's harder to use, you may not use it correctly. Try out all the features in the store before you buy; even better, if it's possible, have a friend who owns the model you're interested in come over and let you try to install it in your own car with her baby in it. That way you can see how easy—or not—it is to handle right in your car. Here's what else you need to know to protect your precious cargo.

Choose the right car seat for your baby's age and weight. There are three basic types of car seats. The first is an infant seat that can only be used facing the rear, and holds newborns and babies up to about twenty or twenty-two pounds, with a five-point harness to secure them. You may find some less expensive models that have a three-point harness, which is acceptable, but we think five-point is best, and many safety experts agree. The second style is what's known as a convertible seat and can be used rear-facing for infants, but also forward-facing for babies who are older and larger (typically up to forty to fifty pounds). Convertible seats may have a five-point harness or an overhead bar shield (a padded tray-like shield that swings down over the baby's head and buckles between her legs). To accommodate the very different sizes of a newborn and a toddler, these seats can be adjusted in a variety of ways: the shoulder strap entry points, the seat belt path, and the level of recline. Still, a tiny baby can seem to get lost in such a big seat, so many parents prefer infant seats for the first year if they can afford both. The third type is what's known as a combination seat and cannot be used rear-facing, so it is not an option until your baby is older than one and weighs more than twenty pounds. These seats can accommodate heavier toddlers up to about fifty pounds, and some convert to booster seats—a safety seat that works with a regular shoulder-style seat belt—for children who exceed the height or weight limits of a car safety seat harness. (Booster seats are designed for children under four feet nine, and up to about eighty pounds, who have outgrown their child safety seats but are still too small to be properly secured by a standard seat belt. They're now required in thirty-eight states, and some experts are pushing for this to become a nationwide law—not a bad idea as far as we're concerned.)

Whichever model you choose, newborns and babies up to one year of age must ride in a rear-facing infant or convertible car seat both until they reach their first birthday and weigh at least twenty pounds to minimize the risk of spine injury in the event of a crash. Infants who are younger than a year but weigh twenty pounds or more should continue to ride in a rear-facing convertible seat, or an infant seat designed for higher weights, until they reach that first birthday. If your baby turns one and still weighs less than twenty pounds, keep her in that rear-facing seat until she hits the twenty-pound mark. Only when a baby reaches both guidelines—at least one year and at least twenty pounds—do you turn that car safety seat to face the front.

Another good rule of thumb: Your baby should remain rear-facing until reaching the maximum weight for the car seat, as long as the top of her head is an inch below the top of the seat back. Forward-facing seats for toddlers over age one and more than twenty pounds should then be used until the child reaches the seat's weight limit or the tops of her ears reach the top of the seat back.

A special note about premature and small infants: You need to take special care when transporting your baby in a vehicle. These tiny babies are especially in need of snugger fitting infant-size seats with low-weight limits of five pounds or less, as well as five-point harnesses; shield-style harnesses could cause harm to a small baby in the event of an impact. In addition, the position of recline can sometimes compromise a small baby's ability to breathe. In fact, some premature infants may need to be transported in a car bed lying on their backs. (You can find one at angel-guard. com.) Insist that the hospital staff observe your baby in her car safety seat— an AAP recommendation for all preemies and low-birth-weight newborns— to ensure she will be safe in a semi-reclined position before transporting her home from the hospital. (For more advice on the special needs and challenges of parenting a premature infant, see chapter 11, page 381.)

Make sure the car seat is properly installed. It's not enough to just have the right car safety seat; you've got to make sure you get it into your particular vehicle exactly right or it won't be able to do its job. Sadly, that's a task that's easier said than done. The NHTSA estimates that car safety seat misuse may be as high as 73 percent, and infant seats are just about the most difficult type to install because they have to be at a certain angle or your baby's head can fall forward and cut off his airway. To make sure that this never happens to your baby, follow the manufacturer's directions exactly, then double-check for these rules:

- If your baby reaches the weight limit for your model infant seat (typically twenty pounds) before his first birthday, use a larger convertible car seat in a rear-facing position.
- The best spot for the seat: the center of the backseat. Never put a car seat in the front passenger's seat, because the air bag could crush the baby if it inflates. Keeping the seat away from doors is also a good idea in the event of a side-impact crash.
- Make sure the seat won't move more than an inch from front to back or side to side. If it does, you need to tighten the seat belt that's holding it in place. The best way to do so: Put your knee in the seat and lean your whole body weight into it while a second person fastens the seat belt snugly.
- Check the gauge on the side of the safety seat to make sure it's sitting at a forty-five-degree angle. If it's not, there are a few ways to level it off, including positioning a rolled-up towel in the crack where your car's seat and back meet. You can also get one of those foam swimming noodles and cut it to the right size; it will mold to the shape of the seat, and it won't come unrolled as a towel might. However, before attempting either of these remedies, check your car manufactur-

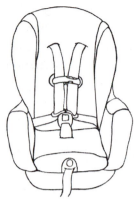

Figure 8.3a Car safety seats with five-point harnesses have straps over your baby's shoulders, each hip, and between the legs.

Figure 8.3b Rear-facing car seats should sit at a forty-five-degree angle (the wrong position can interfere with breathing). Most models have an indicator gauge that shows the seat is positioned at the safest angle.

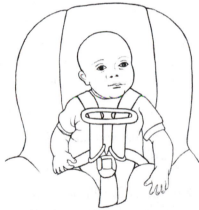

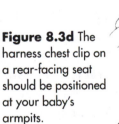

Figure 8.3d The harness chest clip on a rear-facing seat should be positioned at your baby's armpits.

Figure 8.3c Position harness straps in the slot closest to or just below your baby's shoulders.

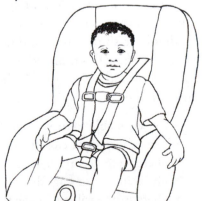

Figure 8.3e When your baby is big enough to graduate to a front-facing car seat, the harness shoulder straps should be positioned in the slots at or just above his shoulders.

er's directions, and also consider going to an NHTSA-certified inspection station for assistance in doing it correctly. To find one near you, go to the Web site, nhtsa.gov and enter your zip code. These trained experts will install your car safety seat and give you a lesson in using it correctly. (You won't have to go far; many local fire or police stations offer this service, as well as auto repair shops.)

- Check your manufacturer's instructions for the correct handle position. It should usually be in the up or closed position (behind the baby's head), so your baby's head doesn't hit it in a crash (some models can only be installed this way).

Finally, make sure your baby is correctly placed in the seat. When your baby is fastened in the seat, do the following:

- Check that the harness straps are sitting in the slots at or just below your baby's shoulders. Move them into the appropriate slots as your baby grows.
- Try to insert your fingers between the harness straps and your baby's chest when the straps are fastened. The straps should be as snug as suspenders, with no slack between them and your baby's chest.
- Check that the chest clip is positioned at your baby's armpits—not on the abdomen (too low) or in the neck area (too high).

Still uncertain? Again, we can't emphasize enough that you should consider going to an NHTSA inspection station for assistance.

What to do if your car seat is in a crash: One of the cardinal rules about car safety seats has always been "Replace a model that's been in a crash," but that thinking is beginning to change. There are indeed instances when you can go on to use your car safety seat after an accident; recent studies have shown that child safety seats can withstand the impact of a minor crash without affecting their future performance. How can you tell if your crash was minor? The accident must meet *all* of the following criteria:

- You were able to drive your car away from the scene of the crash.
- The vehicle door closest to the child safety seat was not damaged.
- There were no injuries to any of the occupants of your vehicle.
- The vehicle's air bags did not deploy (open).
- There is no visible damage to the car safety seat itself.

If you're still not sure what to do, have the seat examined at an NHTSA inspection station near you. Need to replace a damaged car seat? Talk to your insurance representative; some policies will cover the cost of a replacement seat.

Safer Strolling

Next to his car safety seat, your baby will probably spend the most time outside the house sitting like a king in his stroller. Much more than just a seat on wheels, today's stroller models can be as deluxe as some new luxury cars, and that can be a pretty cushy thing. Before you plunk down big bucks for the baby buggy version of a BMW, however, consider that riding in a stroller is about more than the perks—these babies come with safety caveats, too. For starters, you want to be sure you have:

- A model with a wide base to prevent tipping over.
- A seat belt with a crotch strap. A chest harness isn't a bad idea, either.
- Brakes on at least one wheel; two is even better.
- A locking mechanism to keep the stroller from collapsing when open—and make sure it's in the locked position before you deposit your baby into the seat.
- A basket that is below or behind the seat, down near the wheels. Baskets or bags that hang off the handles can cause the stroller to tip backward.

Then, when you're out and about, keep these smart moves in mind:

- Don't fold or open the stroller unless your baby is a safe distance away—he could get his fingers caught in the hinges.
- Always buckle your baby up.
- Don't allow strings, straps, scarves, or toys to dangle over the side—they could get caught in the wheels.
- Don't let your baby lean over, either—he could tip it over.
- Be careful about hanging shopping bags, pocketbooks, or coats off the handle—these, too, can cause it to tip. (We know you'll need to at times—we've all done it—but be sure to remove everything before you take your hands off the stroller or it may topple with your tot inside.)
- Never take your baby stroller on an escalator while your baby is sitting in it—always use an elevator instead. If there is no other option, re-

move your baby from the stroller and hold him in one arm, the folded stroller in the other, while you ride the escalator (of course, if you have another adult with you, he or she can hold the empty stroller instead).

Shopping Cart Concerns

It's a simple fact of life: Moms need to go to the grocery store. Where else would we get all those diapers, wipes, cans of formula, and jars of baby food? You could have them delivered, of course, but unless you're the wife of Donald Trump with a little Barron to raise, that's a bit pricey for most of us to do on a regular basis (splurge now and then, though, if you need to!). Which means there will be times when we have to go with baby in tow. While some hip grocery store chains have tried to make it easy on us by adding special close-to-the-store parking spots for pregger moms-to-be and those with small children, and others have added cute mini carts for preschoolers to push on their own—along with carts with side cabs and racecar seats for toddlers—there remains the ages-old question: What to do with an infant and his particular seat? The AAP has further complicated this dilemma by issuing a new warning about the dangers of shopping carts, motivated by a high number of injuries to children under the age of five caused primarily by falls from or tipping over of the carts. Their advice: We should pretty much avoid putting our children in shopping carts if at all possible. Deep down we know they're right, of course, and we have always been nervous about the scenario of infant seats precariously plopped on the metal bars (even though manufacturers design them to clip on); about the ickiness of germs left behind in the seats; and about the risky combo of worn-out safety belts and wiggly kids. It all begs the question, of course, *how are we supposed to get our shopping done?* Here is our best advice.

There are ways to avoid shopping carts: When your baby is still young enough, put him in a front carrier or a baby sling while you shop.

You might also get someone to accompany you to the store so one of you can push the baby in the stroller and the other can push the cart of groceries, or you might leave the baby home with Dad, Grandma, or another caregiver. (Of course this is the ideal all the time if you can get away with it! After all, it's not like you need him on hand to tell you which brand of cereal he prefers . . .)

If you need to put your baby in a shopping cart, keep the following in mind:

- Don't place an infant seat on the top of the shopping cart. If you need to keep your baby in one, put the entire seat down into the basket. This limits the room you will have for your groceries, of course, so save your big shopping orders for times when you can go to the store alone.
- If you put your baby in a shopping cart seat, make sure the safety belt is secure, and never leave him alone in the cart. Don't let him lean over the side of the cart, either.
- Never allow your child to ride in the basket of the cart unrestrained or to stand up in the cart (good luck with that one—they all attempt it, of course!).
- Don't allow an older child to push the cart with a younger child in it, or ride on the side of the cart. (Good luck with this latter one, too—you might as well start perfecting your hollering muscles now.)
- As soon as your baby is big enough, allow him to ride instead in a safer style of cart with the lower-to-the-ground seats (such as those styled to look like little cars)—but make sure he's safely strapped into this seat as well.
- Patronize stores that offer these safer styles of shopping carts, or that offer supervised in-store play areas while parents shop. Avoid stores that have poorly maintained shopping carts (such as broken safety belts), so that all store chains will be encouraged to offer family-friendly and child-safe service (power to the parents!).

"WHAT NOBODY TOLD ME ABOUT WHEN MY BABY GETS HURT"

"What has blown my mind is how my children can take a fall and still keep going. I remember hearing that little kids know how to fall—they just go limp so they can absorb the impact. Adults, on the other hand, tend to tighten up and try to brace, which is where most of the injuries come from. The first time my daughter fell was when my husband put her on the couch and turned away. She rolled right off and onto the hardwood floor. She cried, but my husband practically became hysteri-

(continued on next page)

cal. I had to take the baby into the other room until he could calm down because he was upsetting her! She was fine, and has been with all her other falls as well, including two tumbles down the stairs (one on each of our watches). Now we're really good about putting up the gate! What I try to keep in mind is: (a) Stay calm—your child is going to be hysterical so she needs you to help her feel safe again; and (b) your kids will fall no matter how careful you try to be."

—*Kristin, North Ridgeville, Ohio*

"While I was lifting my son out of the bathtub, he slipped out of my arms and banged his left eye on the tub. His eyelid cracked and was bleeding heavily. I quickly grabbed a washcloth, put it under cold water, and held it on his eye until the bleeding wasn't heavy. Then I dried him off, threw on his clothes, and went to the emergency room. The doctor there told me that if the cut was anywhere else on my son's body, he would need three stitches, but it was too hard to stitch the eyelid. I needed to keep it clean until it healed. I was very proud of my response. I was calm and didn't panic. I feel that if I would have, my son wouldn't have been as calm as he was and the bleeding wouldn't have stopped as quickly as it did. Nobody ever mentioned that when your child is hurt, you do everything possible to help him and you know exactly what to do."   —*Daniela, Land O'Lakes, Florida*

"When my husband tripped and dropped our then eighteen-day-old twin boys down our staircase I stayed focused and calm, but he started to lose it while we were driving to the hospital. He kept repeating, 'I hurt the babies,' and started to cry. I was able to calm him down by telling him that right now all that mattered was getting us safely to the hospital. While we waited in the ER, I continued to assure him that it was an accident and that the boys would be just fine. When I finally had a moment to step away from my husband to call my parents, I was able to let my emotions out. I was incredibly sad and worried but I didn't want my husband to see how upset I was, for fear that he would feel more guilty than he already did. Things turned out just fine. Despite falling down nine stairs, their swaddled little bodies were perfectly cushioned. The only injuries they had were minor skull fractures, which have now healed. The doctors tried to comfort us. They told us this type of accident is common for new parents and there is no reason to feel guilty. I'm sure these accidents are due to sleep deprivation. I wish I would have known just how mentally and physically unstable you are when you're sleep-deprived."

—*Chris, Richmond Heights, Missouri*

"Once when I was changing my little guy I turned around from getting a diaper and saw him gleefully waving a bottle of ear-pain medication in one hand, the ear dropper in the other. My heart stopped as I realized that the bottle had ended up on the table during a sleep-deprived midnight session of tending to his ear infection; I'd neglected to notice it the following morning and must have also forgotten to close the bottle properly. I literally ran the eight blocks to the nearest hospital, since a cab would have been slower. Emergency workers took him right away and kept him under observation for several hours. They asked me piles of questions I agonizingly couldn't answer: How much was in the bottle? Could you tell if he ingested any? Once he got a clean bill of health, the head E.R. doctor told me what I had just discovered: One minute babies are quiet little lumps lying there minding their own business on the changing table, the next thing you know, they have figured out how to launch themselves into trouble six ways to heaven." —*Graziella, New York, New York*

"When my son was a year old, he woke up early one morning and without making a sound he climbed out of his crib, went into our bedroom, found my makeup bag, and helped himself to tasting all of my makeup, including drinking an entire bottle of liquid foundation! When I awoke and found him, I immediately called Poison Control. They assured me that he would be all right and at worst, the makeup would just give him a tummy ache!" —*Jessica, Portland, Tennessee*

"When my little boy was about ten months old and running everywhere I had a close call. We were headed out the door for my husband's afternoon rugby game when I smelled wood stain. I just thought the smell was wafting from one of his recently finished projects. I opened the window, turned the corner, and there in front of me

(continued on next page)

was my angel covered from chin to belly in wood stain—it looked like he drank it. Well, 911 was never dialed so quickly. They connected me to Poison Control, where I was told to have him drink milk. He did. They dispatched the fire truck, sirens and all. Needless to say, everything was okay. After piecing it all together, my beaver-toothed son had not drunk any stain at all, but instead used his little teeth to pry off the lid. When the lid popped off, the stain got on his chin, cheeks, and down the front of his shirt. Scary, yes. Lesson learned, you bet! I spoke to my husband about the proper way to store items and I, too, keep a more diligent eye out. I did wish I had had the direct Poison Control number available—and now I do."

—*Christy, Haltom City, Texas*

"I had been a nanny for a number of years and worked with many different families. But nothing had ever prepared me for the time my one-year-old son took a header into the brick platform our woodstove sits on. I was folding clothes and literally watched it happen in slow motion, right in front of me. He laid there for a split second and for a moment I thought it wasn't that bad. By the time I got to him and saw his forehead, I was shocked. It looked like a tiny, precise triangle was cut from his head exposing his skull. I carried him into the kitchen and called, of all people, my mom! I knew he had to be taken to the doctor and I needed someone to come stay with my (then) six-week-old daughter. By the time I pulled into the pediatrician's parking lot, the wound had long since stopped bleeding but still required a few stitches. He was no worse for the wear, and a week later pulled out his own stitches while we were out shopping! I won't deny that it was definitely frightening. And everyone kept telling me 'It's always so much scarier when it's your own kids' but I had never had any kind of emergency with anyone else's kids, either! I had been trained in CPR and first aid, but when your turn is up, it's up, whether you're ready or not!"

—*Liz, Keizer, Oregon*

"My son had two horrible falls both before his first birthday—one on Thanksgiving and one on Christmas. The first fall was off the bed. I left the room and left my son with his dad. Daddy forgot all the times he heard not to leave the baby alone and next thing I knew I heard a crash. I raced to the bedroom, leapt over the bed in what seemed like a single bound, and found my son eyes wide open, upside down, and his neck in a seemingly twisted position. I truly thought he was dead. Then he cried a terrible cry, but I was overjoyed to hear it. I picked him up not even thinking about head/neck stabilization. He had a bump on the head, which I applied a cold rag to. (I wet small washcloths and store them in the freezer for teething and accidents because I've realized children don't sit still for an ice pack.) I watched his behavior for sluggishness and anything out of the ordinary but he was fine. The second time was pretty much the same thing except this time he was cruising and Daddy fell asleep. My guy fell. Same response: frozen washcloth, lots of love, and vigilant eyes. I keep a wide array of medical supplies in the house and take a compact first-aid kit whenever we are out. I still get chills when I look back on my son's first Thanksgiving when I thought I'd lost him."

—*Melissa, Long Beach, California*

"Upon the birth of my second child, a few friends of mine came over to visit us. One of my friends, who doesn't have children of her own, had a complete brain fog and dropped the new baby. More specifically, the baby slid off her lap headfirst and landed down between my friend's legs and the side of the couch (so her fragile head and neck were unsuccessfully supporting the entire weight of her little body). I quickly rescued my baby from my friend, did a quick check-over to make sure she was okay, and then kept an eye on her to make sure there was no change in her condition. There was no need to make a bigger deal out of it than was needed. My one peeve: My friend cried nonstop pretty much until she left. It was my baby! I thought I should be the one consoled, not the other way around!"

—*Sonja, Jasper, Georgia*

CHAPTER 9

The Stuff of Motherhood
Great Gear Guaranteed to
Make Your Life Easier

Remember when your favorite Saturday-afternoon activity was trolling the mall for the latest trends in fashion and home? Now here you are, looking forward to an outing perusing designer receiving blankets instead of four-hundred-thread-count duvets. And you're going to snuggle with your *other* significant other instead of the one you once held dearest "till death do you part" (what's his name again?).

So in the world of the new mom, pink and blue are the new black and brown. Needless to say, shopping the baby center stores can eventually wear down your mind and run up your credit cards. But that's only if you don't know what you need. While you won't escape the first year without buying a ton of molded plastic—from car seats to outlet covers—you can make the most of your time by narrowing your list to items that you truly require.

There's certainly no disputing the fact that's there's some really great baby gear out there. In fact, most of it is just amazing, and your haywire hormones will soon lure you into making many an impulse purchase (try not to shop alone, if you can help it). If you're a first-time mom, there's a good chance you'll acquire much of your gear at a baby shower. That's an advantage money-wise, naturally, but actually a bit of a disadvantage because there's so much you don't know about your baby and your own preferences yet. Even if you choose the products yourself by registering, you can't yet be sure they're exactly what you need. One fact to remember is that you definitely don't need all this gear before your baby arrives. Delay purchases such as high chairs, stationary exercisers, umbrella strollers, and childproofing gear for down the road; you won't clog up your closets, and you'll have a little experience under the belt (or shall we say the elastic waistband of your "transitional" pants?). Hint to shower guests that you'd love some gift cards for bigger baby needs (trust us—in a few months there will be something new and improved!). Also, some products are only useful for a very short time, so you may be able to get away with borrowing them instead (we'll let you know which are good candidates).

Finally, you need to think about how a product would fit in your home, with your lifestyle, and, last but not least, with your baby's personality. Depending on where you live—big-city condo, rambling farmhouse, or something in between—some features may be worth splurging on and others, a waste of money. Likewise, some babies will be happy in a swing, drifting off as soon as they start moving, while others wouldn't give a hoot even if the thing came with a nipple-mobile. Those babies refuse to rock for even the amount of time it takes to throw in a load of laundry. Obviously, we can't tell you what your baby will like, but after road-testing the latest and greatest new gear, we can give you some inside tips on what may suit your needs.

STUFF YOU NEED IN YOUR NURSERY

Let's start with the obvious, and the not quite so. Many traditional nursery items you really can live without, and some, though still available everywhere, are even considered hazards in this safety-conscious age. Meanwhile, other items you may barely notice are absolute musts. Here's what no nursery should be without:

- ❏ A safe crib (see chapter 8 for what this truly means).
- ❏ A new, firm mattress. Used mattresses have been linked to a higher incidence of SIDS.
- ❏ Fitted sheets (about 4).
- ❏ Sheet protector. Look for one that sits on top of the sheet and attaches to the corner posts for speedy midnight cleanups.
- ❏ Sleep sacks (again, about 4, to minimize your daily laundry).
- ❏ Dirty clothes hamper.

(continued on next page)

❑ Diaper disposal system or diaper pail (many parents prefer the first).
❑ Rocking chair (gliders are the preferred style—down the line, you won't have to worry about little limbs getting rocked on).
❑ Dresser (a changing pad on top is a great space saver if the dresser is designed for this purpose).
❑ Toy storage of some sort (cubbies, bins, and carts with wheels can be more convenient than traditional immobile toy boxes).

. . . STUFF YOU MAY LIKE . . .

❑ Baby monitor (see pages 337–38 for the scoop on why we think you could skip this).
❑ Musical mobile (can be a great, inexpensive soother for the early months, but remove it as soon as your baby can roll over).
❑ Separate changing table (if you've got the room and the money to really do it up).
❑ Glow-in-the dark clock (to time those wee-hour nursing sessions).

. . . AND STUFF YOU DON'T NEED

• Quilts, comforters, loose blankets—they're not safe, so why spend your money on them? You just need a couple of blankets for stroller rides on nippy days.
• Bumper pads—a hazard once your baby can roll over, so again, why bother?
• Crib skirt—pretty, but that's about it.
• Lamp. If you have a ceiling light and a night light, you'll do fine.
• Ottoman. Nursing stools are cheaper and can be more comfy anyway.
• Diaper stacker—they have to be refilled and, once in a while, washed. If you can't bear a diaper package lying around your perfectly decorated nursery, stick it in a drawer or closet instead.
• Sleep positioner. Though these were devised as safety devices, it's now believed they could instead be hazards.
• Teething pads for crib rails. The plastic covers on the side rails usually do the trick.

Big-Deal Gear

Car Seats

We gave you the lowdown on car seats and safety back in chapter 8 (see page 313 for the beginning of our treatise on that), and frankly, that should be your main priority when it comes to making the right purchase: Does the seat suit your particular vehicle, and do you understand how to install and use it properly? (Before you buy, there's a terrific Web site you should check out: carseatdata.org. This lists which brands of seats are compatible with specific makes and models of cars. It's not exhaustive, but it's extensive enough that there's a good chance it includes your vehicle.) Here are a few other considerations to mull over.

Must-haves. We really like infant seats, but if you're on a budget, it's fine to use a convertible seat (see pages 314–16 for a detailed description of the types of car safety seats) from the start. Infant seats, though, fit newborns best. The semi-reclining position of an infant seat provides better head and neck support for a young baby (though some convertible seats do have an easy-to-use reclining option). Also, an infant safety seat plays a dual role by working as an infant carrier, too, and when you've got a sleeping baby to move, that function can be handy. (Reality check: Once your baby gets to about fifteen pounds, these things are pretty darn tough to tote around.) If you decide to go the convertible route, make sure you get a five-point harness; they're safest for little ones. Also, the lower the lowest harness slot is, the snugger the fit will be for a newborn. Carseatdata.org, which we mentioned above, also provides measurements for many brands of car seats.

What you don't need. Other products come with plenty of gizmos, gadgets, and features that you can do without, but for a car seat the situation is a bit trickier. Anything that will make your baby safer is necessary as far as we're concerned, and so is anything that's going to keep him comfy and content, so you can keep your focus on the road. In a nutshell, buy the best car seat you can afford and scrimp on something less critical. We do have to give you a word of warning, however, about accessories such as neck pillows, boot- or bunting-like covers, attachable toys, and the like: The National Highway Traffic Safety Administration recommends that you not buy any of these unless they come with the seat, or the manufacturer has designed them specifically for your model, because of the risk that they could interfere with proper functioning or come loose and fly around the vehicle if you stop short or crash.

High Chairs

More than just a seat in which to eat, the high chair is frequently used as a sort of entertainment center during meal prep and while the rest of the family is dining—your baby will always enjoy being at the dinner table with the gang, even if he's done chowing down himself (at least until he starts walking). Just give him a sippy cup and some Cheerios to gnaw on, or a few blocks, plastic spoons, or stacking cups. Here's some more food for thought on the best high chair for your house.

Must-haves. Most important: a safety strap and the center post (sometimes called a crotch post). This post should be attached to the seat rather than the tray, since your baby will be more protected from falls when you remove the tray to take him out. Also, you want a tray that's easy to lift off with one hand. If you are borrowing a high chair, check with the manufacturer or cpsc.gov to see if the model meets today's safety standards. And if you're thinking of using an old high chair from your own baby days, think again. It probably doesn't have a good restraint (or any restraint), and it may have sharp edges, a wobbly base, or some other hazard you won't discover until it's too late. Old isn't charming when it comes to baby gear.

Not so necessary. Before you shell out for wheels, adjustable heights, or a reclining feature, talk to moms with slightly older babies. Did they really wheel their high chair around and need to make it higher or lower? A reclining seat will let a young baby hang out at your level while you eat your sandwich or do the dishes, instead of being down on the floor in a bouncer. But while he's likely to be happier being able to see you, it will be unsafe to feed him solids in a reclining position (he can choke), so once he's really eating in his high chair you won't be using this feature anymore. And while a toy tray can be a sanity saver with a fussy baby, you can also just use your own toys.

Space considerations. If you've got a tiny kitchen, a compact high chair is key. If you need to put the high chair out of the way after every meal, and have the will to bother, look for a model that folds up. Try it out in the store to see how easy this feat really is. (You also want a locking mechanism so you don't need to worry about it folding up on your baby while he's in it.) Another handy option is a feeding seat—a legless high chair of sorts; you just strap it to a kitchen chair. They're inexpensive and great space savers for tiny kitchens or apartment dwellers. You can also pack your feeding seat in the trunk when you're going on vacation or to Grandma's for the day.

Neat freak finds. Feeding a baby beyond the liquid stage is a seriously gooey undertaking. One feature to lessen the mess that comes with some high chair models is a snap-off tray that covers the larger tray and fits in the dishwasher. Avoid high chairs with lots of crevices that will be tougher to clean, and definitely opt for a vinyl, wipe-off seat pad. There are wipe-off splat mats out there, too, for positioning under the high chair to catch UFFs—unidentified flying foods—which will be common for quite some time to come. Then again, unless you're often feeding your baby in a carpeted dining room, it's just as easy to wipe the gunk off a kitchen floor as it is to clean the mat.

Strollers

Like cars, some strollers look flashy and classy, but what still matters most is how smoothly they ride (for the baby) and drive (for you); how easy they are to fold and unfold; and reclineability—younger babies (under six months) need to be able to recline fully for back support, and older babies for napping. Beyond that, you've got to consider your budget and where you live. It's not hard to get an idea of which models are best—just look around your neighborhood. Those moms have already figured out what works (or doesn't), so check out what they're pushing. Here are the key features in a nutshell:

City slickers. You'll want a model that folds fast if you're dashing for a bus or taxi; is lightweight enough to get up and down train-station steps or apartment-building staircases; but is also durable enough to handle curbs and potholes. Because your stroller will be your baby's primary vehicle, weather protection is essential. Look for a model that comes with a rain cover (which also saves sweet skin from snow and wind exposure) as well as a "boot"—a warm covering for little legs. If your preferred stroller model doesn't come with these accessories, don't fret; you can buy them separately, and they won't be that expensive. A cushy amount of padding is also important, since city babes can spend substantial amounts of time on their tushies and you don't want them to get cranky in a crowd.

Suburb dwellers. You've got another specific set of needs if you spend your time strolling a leafier neighborhood and traveling in a car instead of on mass transit. You'll be hauling your stroller in and out of your trunk multiple times in the same day, most days, so you want it to be lightweight (seventeen pounds or less), and a cinch to fold and unfold with as few levers and latches as possible. It's also a huge help if you can attach your car seat to the stroller. There's nothing more annoying than having to transfer a sleeping baby from a car seat to a stroller and waking him in the process. The original invention of this type, the "travel system," is now widely available, but ironically it's not always the best choice. These systems comprise a stroller and infant seat sold together. When your baby is small, he can ride in the car seat that attaches to the stroller. Later, you just use the stroller. It sounds good, but the accompanying car seat may not be the best one for your car (of primo importance), and the stroller may not have all the features you really want. Travel system strollers also tend to be more cumbersome than other strollers, so many parents ditch them, opting instead for a more compact model for the toddler stage. We vote for a stroller base that lets you attach a car seat to it. Kolcraft's Universal Car Seat Carrier works with any infant car seat, and has a nice large basket, tray, and cup holder, all for a very reasonable price. Keep it in your trunk for those times when your little guy has nodded off, and use a more cushy "home on wheels" type of stroller for roaming the neighborhood or all-day outings. And speaking of trunks, consider the size of yours and how compactly a particular stroller folds up. Can you fit the stroller and your groceries? Believe it or not, some big minivans can barely hold both. A compact-folding stroller is worth the extra money, all other things being equal.

One other feature you might appreciate is a big basket for shopping booty or toting gear to siblings' activities or the local swimming pool—but be sure it's accessible. Some baskets look gigantic but are completely covered up when baby is reclining for a nap, for instance.

Adventure lovers. If you plan on taking nature walks or jogging, or you live in a semi-rural area, you need a stroller model on the rugged side of the spectrum. Many such moms, and even those who just like the look, opt for three-wheel strollers. There are two basic types. Those that are meant for actual jogging will have a locking front wheel, hand brakes, and wrist straps; these are pretty pricey, so unless you're a serious athlete you don't need one. Then there are the three-wheel all-terrain models that are your basic SUVs of the stroller world. Features such as big knobby wheels and shock absorbers will keep your baby snoozing over bumpy paths. You'll want front wheels that swivel on all-terrain strollers. Inflated rubber (pneumatic) wheels offer the smoothest riding whether you're on a mountainside or a cracked and broken city sidewalk. However, you will need to keep an air pump in your trunk because, yes, you can get a flat! And while you can use all-terrain strollers for simple errands and other day-to-day stuff, don't forget that they are wider than other strollers and may not easily wend through store aisles.

Size matters. If either you or your partner is especially tall or petite, look for an adjustable handle height to preserve your back. Tall people also want to avoid bruised shins, so try out the stroller to be sure the design allows you plenty of leg room for longer-than-normal strides.

Cribs

We gave you lots of crib advice to consider back in chapter 8 (see pages 279–80) to ensure your baby's safety. We'll say it one more time: Do not buy or borrow a used crib if you don't know the brand, date of manufacture, and model number. Armed with that information, you can check cpsc.gov for possible recall information, and the manufacturer's Web site for assembly and use details. It's wise to be judicious about what you borrow; your sister-in-law's two-year-old crib is probably fine, for instance, but pass on the garage-sale find. (And getting a new mattress is a must.) When it comes to brand-new models, every crib must meet the exact same safety standards, regardless of price, though some manufacturers do more than the minimum testing. In addition, there are some bedding amenities you may or may not want.

Must-haves. Beyond the essential safety features, durability is key. Give the floor model in the store a good shake to be sure it feels sturdy, not flimsy. It's hard to imagine, but by the end of infancy, your baby will be using his crib as a trampoline. And don't neglect to check out the casters (wheels): Metal will be stronger than plastic; a wide design is better than narrow.

Not so necessary. You don't need to pay extra for a crib that adjusts to more than a couple of mattress heights. High (for newborns) and low (for whenever your baby starts sitting up) is fine. One drop side is typically enough, so you needn't splurge on a model that drops on both sides; chances are the other side of the crib will be up against a wall anyway. You do want to be sure the drop side operates quietly and locks securely. You'll lower it to get your baby out, and keep it in this position so you can smoothly deposit him in the crib while he's sleeping, then raise it back up; if moving the railing results in a loud grate or squeak, you're in trouble! If you and your partner happen to be tall, you may get away with a basic crib model and skip the cost of drop sides altogether, but most parents prefer this feature. You also don't need to splurge on an under-crib drawer unless you're seriously hurting for storage space. The drawer has no top, so whatever is in there gets dusty fast. Finally, furniture sales people are big pushers of convertible cribs that become youth beds (a bit shorter and narrower than a twin), or full-size twin beds, or even a twin and a full-size bed after that, so you can get the most bang for your buck. Beware of this sales pitch. These are very pricey pieces, and while they may make sense for some families, you should think about how many children you will be having and how soon. A second baby will need a place to sleep, too, so converting your crib to a bed may not make sense if you've then got to buy another crib. You may also need to buy a conversion kit—which can cost as much as $200. Ultimately, buying a crib you can use for two or more babies, and then bigger beds as necessary, may be the most affordable option.

Changing Tables

Most novice parents think changing tables are a must, and any nursery picture will certainly convince you of that—there the changing table always sits, right next to the crib and lots of other pretty pink or blue extras. We've got news for you: You and your baby can live without one. One of our editors has had three children and never once owned a changing table. She bought a cushy foam changing pad with four sides that attached with hardware to an existing dresser, and several washable changing pad covers. She used this for the first four or so months with each of her children until they were increasingly squirmy and getting close to rolling over, then packed up the changing pad. At this point, she kept a set of the necessary accessories—a vinyl changing pad, wipes, diaper ointment, and a toy or two—in her family room, her bedroom, and her baby's nursery (out of reach of the baby, of course), and simply changed her kids on the floor wherever they were in the house. She never needed to buckle them up or worry about falling. And it was less of a production than dragging them away from a favorite plaything and up to the nursery. What started out as an effort to save the cost of purchasing a high-ticket dresser/changing table combo actually became the safest and easiest alternative for her.

If you must have one, keep in mind that stand-alone changing tables—those pieces of furniture that are essentially a table with a few shelves below—are pretty useless in the long run. And cheaper models often don't appear that sturdy—a potentially serious problem with a big, wiggly baby who doesn't want to be changed. A better investment is a combination changing table and dresser, which can be used for clothing long after your child is out of the diaper stage. These designs can be found in attractive children's furniture collections, but expect to shell out big bucks for them (maybe Grandma will treat!).

Smaller Stuff You May (or May Not) Love

Front carriers

These are a personality purchase: Some moms can't live without 'em; others never take the tags off. Metro moms who are hoofing it a lot usually find them pretty useful, and they are a smart way to avoid putting your baby into a risky or germy shopping cart when he's little, as we discussed back on pages 320–21. Front carriers can also be great for soothing colic—studies show that babies worn this way cry less, probably because they tend to nod off from the swaying motion and lull of your heartbeat so close to their little ears. Front carriers can also be useful for getting around airports and train stations, because your hands are free to drag luggage and the like. The negatives: Yeah, your hands are free, but you can't (and shouldn't) try to cook, clean, or bend over to pick up toys while wearing one. Mall crawlers who drive everywhere may find that car seat/stroller combos are more useful—not only do you have an easier time transferring a sleeping baby, but you also have that basket for packages. Still, if you love to walk around the block sans stroller, then go ahead and get one. Just remember that the life spans for these are short, too: While manufacturers often claim front carriers can accommodate children up to thirty pounds, your aching back will be begging you for mercy long before your baby gets this big!

Slings

Slings drape your baby across your body, and can be adjusted to hold her in a lying-down position, or more upright. If you think you may like babywearing, you may want to give it a try. This is one of those love-'em-or-hate-'em propositions: Some moms break a sweat just trying to get them wrapped on correctly, but plenty of others find them indispensable in the early months. They can be ideal for newborns, when front carriers seem just a little too big, and breastfeeding becomes a much simpler proposition. It usually takes a few tries to get the knack of putting on a sling and actually wearing it—many moms report feeling like their baby is going to fall out at first—but practice does make perfect. The higher your baby sits, the better for your back. If you're really having trouble, considering buying a DVD from Tummy2Tummy.com; it'll show you how to properly wear all the different brands of carriers. It also helps to get one of the new styles with stretchy, strong fabric. You can splurge on one of the luxe silk numbers favored by celebs if you've got, oh, $160 lying around. Otherwise, consider the Maya Wrap Sling (mayawrap.com), a much more affordable option that draws raves for its ease of use and comfort.

Figure 9.1 Front carrier.

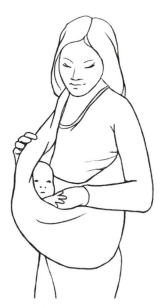

Figure 9.2 Sling carrier.

Another clever, related product is the Slurp & Burp, which gives you some privacy while nursing, while also allowing you to view your bambino as she dines. It goes on over your head, sort of like a tube top, and keeps you, but not your baby, covered up. It even has a built-in burp cloth. It comes in lots of fun colors and prints, and, as of this writing, is the only breastfeeding cover-up on the market with this unique design. Find out more at slurpburp.com.

Backpack Carriers

If your pre-baby lifestyle included long Sunday-afternoon hikes, there's no reason that has to change. Once your baby hits about the six-month mark and can sit up on his own, he can ride in a framed backpack carrier. Obviously, you want a model that's lightweight, so choose one with an aluminum frame. And a kickstand comes in handy, too, allowing you to sit the carrier on the ground so you can get your baby in and out easier. Some of these carriers have more accessories than your car: sunshades, rain hoods, attachable diaper bags, adjustable seats, and packs for your own supplies are all available. As with so many baby items, the more

Figure 9.3 Backpack carrier.

perks, the higher the price. This type of baby transport is popular with dads, so many of the top models are made with him in mind. A notable exception is Sherpani (sherpanipacks.com or 720-214-2194), whose line is especially designed to suit a woman's body. Other good companies to check out in this arena are Kelty (kelty.com or 800-423-2320) and Tough Traveler (toughtraveler.com or 800-GO-TOUGH). Keep in mind that these are serious pieces of gear, and prices often top $200. Unless you are a truly outdoorsy type, however, you can take a pass on one of these.

Monitor

If you live in a home with an upstairs and downstairs, say, or an especially long ranch-style home where the bedrooms are indeed far from the kitchen, you will probably make use of a monitor. Otherwise—and we know you probably won't listen to us if it's your first baby—we'll tell you straight out: Save your money. You will hear your child crying. Trust us. And if you still don't believe us, consider borrowing a monitor until you figure it out for yourself. The newest technology can run you close to $100, and if you've got cordless phones and wireless Internet connections you may need to spring for one of these high-end models or risk a lot of static and interference: The other signals can get in the way (so much for a "smart" home). One thing we do like a monitor for: you can go in the yard for fresh air while your baby naps inside in his crib, and hear him when he wakes up and cries. An inexpensive model can allow you to do this.

Swing

Lots of babies love these, but some outright hate them. If yours is the former, however, a mechanical swing can be a real lifesaver. You won't be sure about your gal's opinion until you plop her in one, so consider borrowing this item, if possible, or test-drive a friend's or store model. One thing we can say for sure: Swing prices have gone through the roof in recent years as multiple speeds, music, motion, and toys have all been added to create a complete sensory experience. (Actually, it seems to us that all this stimulation could make a sensitive baby go manic, so bear that in mind, too.) Another option you won't need: the ability to hold a baby beyond the usual twenty to twenty-five pounds. Babies this big are going to be mobile, active, and mad as you-know-what if you try to strap them into a swing! You'll find their usage drops way off—and probably stops altogether in plenty of homes—once your baby hits the crawling stage.

Bouncy Seat

Most moms can't imagine life without their bouncer. Their usefulness is short-lived to be sure; they supposedly hold babies up to about twenty-five pounds, but there's a very good chance you won't use it that long. Still, those early months are a high-need time, and this little product is

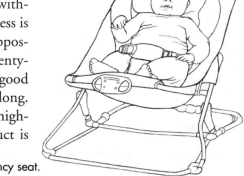

Figure 9.4 Bouncy seat.

practically an extra pair of hands—plus very lightweight and portable. Of course, you can spend close to $100 for some models, but here, too, the simplest model is really all you need. The baby's wiggling and flailing movements make basic bouncers rock aplenty, and that's what actually does the soothing. If your budget won't allow for them, you can certainly take a pass on the vibrations, sounds, and toy bars.

Stationary Activity Center

We're going to give you the thumbs-up here, with one caveat: You don't need to spring for the deluxe model with all kinds of toys attached (just plop a few favorite playthings on the tray instead). A simple padded seat that swirls, bounces, and rocks is all your baby really needs to have fun. (However, we wouldn't tell you to stop a friend or great-aunt from buying the loaded model.) This clever product will most likely buy you loads of entertainment time from about five or six months (when your baby can at least sit with support) until she starts walking. Babies almost universally love these seats, and you can sit nearby and do all your bills while she's happily entertained. Of course, as with all other confining contraptions, you have to be careful not to overuse a stationary activity center. As we noted at the beginning of this chapter, your mobile baby also needs plenty of time to crawl and explore, for both his mental and physical development. Some baby experts we know and love are not fond of these devices

because they keep babies from actually seeing their legs and thus getting the brain signals about what needs to occur to make the device bounce or spin. We, however, prefer to focus on the positives, including their safety as compared with other baby gear, so we're going to say go ahead and just use your judgment about how much time your baby spends in the stationary activity center. That may not be too tough to figure out: Most of

Figure 9.5 Stationary exerciser.

our children, in fact, were plenty vocal about when they had had enough! (And if anyone out there thinks of a shorter generic description than "stationary activity center," by all means let us know!)

WE ASKED, YOU TOLD

What's the one baby gear item you couldn't live without? More than sixteen hundred moms dished on Parenting.com/babytalk about the equipment that saves their sanity, lowers their stress level, or just gets them through the day because it keeps the kiddies content. When you're deciding just what to plunk down your hard-earned cash for, consider what other BFFs wouldn't want to be without:

1. Swing. Yeah, we know we said not all babies like them, but when they do, they can be lifesaving fuss-busters!
2. Bouncy seat.
3. Stationary activity center.
4. Nursing/propping pillow.
5. Baby monitor. (Maybe these moms have bigger houses than us, or are sounder sleepers.)
6. Stroller frame that holds a car seat.
7. Front carrier.
8. Play mat.

The Dirt (No, We Don't Mean Poop) on Diaper Bags

Happily, the majority of diaper bags don't look like the frumpy pastel satchels of old. We say *happily* because whether you're used to toting designer handbags or equally stylish knockoffs, switching to an ugly duckling tote (adorned with the pale yellow variety) is just depressing. Blame designer maternity clothes, but we care what our diaper bags look like now.

Still, basic utilitarian advice continues to apply: Bigger is usually better (though not always—read on), and darker, wipe-off fabrics are always a plus. But what matters most is what's inside the diaper bag. A plastic or vinyl changing pad is a must, and if you can score a bag with a wipe-down interior, all the better. You'll also want lots of pockets to tuck tiny items such as pacifiers, baby spoons, and crackers. There should be a place to put bottles and sippy cups and interior pockets to keep wipes and diapers segregated from food and toys. In addition, there are a few other personal preferences you'll want to consider.

First, do you want to bother with a purse? Some moms want to keep their stuff separate, and you may need to if you're a working mom who needs a BlackBerry with you at all times, or a place to stash expense receipts so they don't end up next to a smushed banana. Other moms may just need room to lug eyeglass cases, makeup, cell phones, and the like, or prefer not to so totally give their identity over to their child that they don't even have a bag to call their own. If you do want to skip the purse, however, you'll want to opt for the larger diaper bag, which will have several separate compartments—or at least a couple of zippered pockets—to keep your stuff in a different corner from your baby's. Otherwise you never will find that favorite lipstick.

Do you drive most places? If so, we have a nifty idea for you. You can greatly reduce the size of your diaper bag by keeping an all-purpose baby backup tote in your trunk. Store the just-in-case items in your car: an extra change of clothes, sweater, or jacket for when the sun goes down on an all-day outing, a bottle of infant pain reliever, bandages for boo-boos, an extra toy or two, half a dozen diapers and a jumbo pack of wipes just in case the poop suddenly becomes more prolific than usual, an extra jar or two of baby food—you get the gist of this. Thus the diaper bag you lug on your shoulder or in your stroller basket can be quite small—a diaper, a bottle, a bib or burp cloth, a few wipes in a zip-top bag, a snack, a toy—if you know the emergency supplies are right outside in the driveway or parking lot. In fact, you might even be able to fit it all in that purse you didn't want to give up.

Consider keeping two bags packed. Some outings are longer—a big family party for a special occasion or holiday, a sibling's swim meet or class field trip you volunteered to chaperone, an afternoon roaming around an outdoor antiques show on a summer day. Others are quite quick: a dash to the mall for a new pair of sneakers, a checkup at the pediatrician, a Sunday church service. You don't need to bring everything you own all the time, so why not keep two prepacked bags, one big, one smaller, with just the essentials, and grab whichever one you need at the time? You won't be unnecessarily encumbered, and you will get to enjoy the smug feeling of being oh-so-organized (for this little aspect of your life at least).

WHAT TO PACK IN YOUR DIAPER BAG

In the first six months

- ❑ Diapers.
- ❑ Wipes (in a portable case or zip-top plastic bag).
- ❑ Changing pad.
- ❑ Plastic bag for dirty diapers.
- ❑ 2 burp cloths (one for drying off that tiny tushie; one for messes).
- ❑ Bottle, water, powdered formula (if you bottlefeed).
- ❑ Nursing pads (if you breastfeed).
- ❑ Pacifier (if your baby uses one).
- ❑ Hat (to shield your baby from the sun in warm weather, and keep him warm in cold weather).
- ❑ Extra one-piece outfit (with feet in cold weather).
- ❑ Favorite toy.

In the second six months

- ❑ All of the above, plus:
- ❑ Baby food.
- ❑ Spoon.
- ❑ Feeding bib.
- ❑ Finger-food snack (such as Cheerios).
- ❑ Baby-safe sunblock.

Vacationing with Your Baby

Have long days and sleepless nights left you dreaming about a week at a family resort, or perhaps a visit to Grandma's (so someone can take care of you for a change)? Good idea—but realize that it won't be the same relaxing experience you had in your pre-baby days. Vacationing with a baby is one of those damned-if-you-do-and-damned-if-you-don't deals. On the one hand, you really need a break from your everyday routine, be it babycare 24/7 or juggling the demands of a job and a family. On the other, you've got to pack more than you thought possible (and you'll still forget that favorite toy), figure out how to travel so it won't disrupt your baby's routine too much (because a tired and cranky travel partner is a nightmare that there are no real words available to describe), worry about safety issues at your destination, pray that your baby doesn't get sick, and, yes, try desperately to release your stress. As one of our husbands once declared while sitting on the beach: "This is no vacation—we still have to do all the same things for these kids we do at home!" That pretty much sums it up. Then again, the operative word here is *beach*. You will be doing those same babycare things at a lovely sun-filled resort, perhaps, or a cozy mountain ski cabin, or maybe at your parents' while your saintly mother whips up your favorite childhood meals and takes the baby for strolls as you catch up on *Desperate Housewives*. And there is nothing more adorable than watching Dad and his daughter in an itsy-bitsy teeny-weeny bikini with rolls of baby belly pooching out over the top as they attempt to sculpt the world's most fabulous sand castle (one of the many skills fatherhood seems to suddenly bring out in men). Or how about having fun making snow angels with your mini cherub, who's as comically round as he is tall clad in all that winter-weather padding? Family vacations are the stuff of holiday cards for a good reason: Parts of them do indeed make for amazing memories. Try these travel-savvy tips to make the most of your maiden voyage.

Don't plan a trip before you and your baby are somewhat in sync. You need to be recovered from your delivery, and your baby needs to be feeding well and primed with at least the first two months' worth of vaccines. If there's at least a little bit of a routine evolving, you'll have a better idea of what to expect (read: no colic or gastrointestinal issues). And while a getaway sounds like a good idea before your maternity leave winds down, you may be better off working toward getting acquainted with your new caregiver and figuring out how to pump and store breast milk.

Schedule road trips, airplane flights, or train rides during naptime if possible. A sleeping baby can make air travel substantially easier on everyone. If you're going to be driving a long distance, plan to stop frequently. Your baby may not be able to stretch his legs quite like you, but he will need a break from that car seat, and you will find it much easier to feed him when you're not in motion. In fact, it's not safe to take your baby out of his safety seat to nurse while the car is moving, so unless you're capable of some amazing contortionism, you'll pretty much have to get out of the car for breastfeeding breaks.

Avoid peak travel times. The fewer germs your baby is exposed to, the better, especially during winter months when airplane cabins are full of sick people breathing the same air. Be especially vigilant if your baby was a preemie or has a medical condition, such as a heart problem.

If you're on an airplane and find yourself seated next to an obviously sick passenger, ask to have your seat changed. (Trust us: The other passenger won't mind a bit.)

Consider the safety seat issue carefully if you're flying. You probably know that by far the safest way to travel on an airplane with a baby is to buy him his own seat, bring along his car safety seat, and secure him inside. You probably also know this is big bucks, and it's a royal pain to lug a car seat through an airport. We'll let you make the final call on this one. Do know, however, that once your baby reaches twenty-two pounds, $75 will get you a device known as CARES, a lightweight harness that the Federal Aviation Administration has approved for children between twenty-two and forty-four pounds. It's a simple system of straps and buckles that wrap around the seat back and loop through the lap belt. You can order it at kidsflysafe.com.

Avoid traveling when your baby is sick. If your baby has an upper respiratory infection, stomach virus, or diarrhea, consider postponing your trip. We'll bet money that she'll get worse as soon as you leave home, not better! Seriously, infants can become dehydrated faster when flying. If you do go, get the name of a pediatrician either before you leave or once you're there.

On an airplane, prepare for uncomfortable ear pressure during takeoff and landing. (Your baby has teeny ear tubes.) Use a pacifier or offer a bottle or your breast; sucking can usually relieve the sensation.

STUFF YOU NEED FOR TRAVELING WITH A BABY . . .

The expression *packing light* does not apply to you anymore. You can minimize your freight, however, if you stick to this list:

❑ Stroller.

❑ Front or back carrier (if you use these items at home).

❑ Car safety seat (or rent one along with a car). If you're not going to need a car seat at your destination, set it up before you go that whatever taxi takes you from your airport to your hotel or Grandma's has a car seat. Any reputable company will accommodate you.

❑ Travel bed or Pack 'n Play with two sheets (spit happens) or better, see if you can rent or borrow one at your destination (you almost always can). Nearly all hotels have portable cribs. If you're staying at Grandma's, research places nearby that rent these and other large infant items. One to try: babiestravellite.com.

❑ Enough diapers, wipes, formula (in whatever form you prefer), and baby food to get you to your destination and through the first day there.

❑ Changing pad.

❑ Burp cloths and/or cloth diapers.

❑ 2–3 changes of baby clothes for each day you'll be gone (less if you'll have access to a washing machine).

❑ Appropriate outerwear: jacket, snowsuit, winter hat, or sunbonnet and bathing suit cover-up.

❑ Feeding utensils: bottles, sippy cups, spoons, bowls, bibs.

❑ Sample sizes of baby soap (it can double as shampoo) and diaper rash ointment.

❑ Sunscreen (if your baby will be outdoors, including winter, when she can get sunburned from the glare off the snow).

❑ Medicine: infant acetaminophen or ibuprofen (for babies over six months), teething gel, and a thermometer.

❑ Plastic bags (to store spit-upon clothing, dirty diapers, and so forth, until you get to your destination or a garbage can).

(continued on next page)

❑ Pacifiers (if your baby uses one).

❑ Finger-food snacks for the ride.

❑ Entertainment: a favorite book, toy, or music CD.

❑ Camera or video recorder!

❑ Agreement with your spouse that you aren't automatically blamed if something for the baby doesn't get packed.

. . . AND STUFF YOU DON'T

- Large supplies of diapers, baby food, or formula. Bring just enough for the first day or so and buy when you get there; give Grandma a shopping list and have her stock up before you arrive; or go to jet-setbabies.com and have these supplies and more shipped to your destination so they're waiting for you. Sure, this last one feels like a splurge, but you deserve it. And isn't a vacation supposed to be a bit more luxurious than your everyday life?

- Going to visit friends or relatives? You may be able to borrow gear like strollers and play yards from them, which is a huge help, so investigate such options beforehand.

- Going to a family-friendly hotel or resort? Most will rent you the above gear and save you the hassle of lugging it along. The same often goes for privately rented beach houses or ski cabins. Some landlords are baby-savvy these days and provide such amenities with their rentals; with others, not necessarily. (Again, you can rent them from babiestravellite.com.)

CHAPTER 10

What's Up with You?
Time to Think about Mom (for a Change)

Do you know why mothers of older children and grandparents are oh-so-fond of saying that you should treasure every moment of your baby's first year because "it all goes by so fast"? Because they're not *in* "it" anymore! For them the baby stage is long gone, and the farther they travel from it, the fuzzier the memories become, until one day they swear that their first year with their children passed like a glorious bright comet in a clear night sky. And guess what? Someday you'll have the same memory and annoy many a new mom by making the same comment.

For the moment, however, you wouldn't think of making such a remark because you are in "it," which is why you may feel like time doesn't pass as much as stretch and contract like a rubber band. A two-hour nap can feel like a two-minute commercial break, but the same amount of time can lengthen like a string of pulled taffy when it comes at the end of an afternoon with little napping and not much sleeping the night before. Then there are the moments when you don't know how much time has passed because you are busy containing a diaper explosion that rivaled Mount St. Helen's last rumble, which happened just before the dog threw up or the dishwasher overflowed massive amounts of suds because you were so sleep-deprived you accidentally put the wrong soap into it, which was right before your best childless friend from college called to tell you about her new boyfriend booking them a fabulous cruise of the Greek Isles. No, those few hours between, say, late afternoon and dinnertime when dear old Dad is going to sail through the door and rescue you from the doldrums/chaos/insanity of your new-but-getting-old-fast life most definitely do not always seem to go by fast. Or maybe you're a working mom watching the clock tick, tick, tick in slow motion from 3 PM to 5 PM until you can rush home for your fix of baby love that you so desperately miss during the workday, no matter how fulfilled you are by your job. Simply put, everyday life as a new mother is far from everyday, even when it is.

Complicating this intricate new concept of time is the fact that there is so much else about your life that is changing at warp speed: your body, your emotions, your career, your role as wife and lover. Nothing, it seems, is the same as it was pre-baby, or even close. Not that that's necessarily a bad thing. But it is a confusing thing. By the end of your baby's first year, and possibly much sooner, you will have gotten comfortable in this new skin of yours, figuratively and literally. Along the way, however, you'll need some support. The best place we think of to get it is at Parenting.com/babytalk, where you can connect with plenty of other new moms sharing both their gripes and glee. We want you to join us in this never-ending discussion, and get much more than milk off your chest. Meanwhile, we're going to give you some out-of-the-starting-gate advice about the new you, physical, emotional, sexual, and professional. Read on, girlfriend.

Whose Body Is This, Anyway?

It's not like you didn't expect this. Surely every already minted mom you know foretold the truth when you were pregnant: Your body will never be the same. Well, duh. You had something weighing roughly between five and ten pounds doing somersaults in it not so long ago, plus lots of fluid and extra blubber, and you knew your skin wasn't made of rubber. Yet here you are, astounded that there's so much more to consider than poundage and stretch marks. There's a good chance you're avoiding the bathroom mirror when you step out of the shower (assuming you can even pull that off). If you're lucky enough to drop the postpartum pounds relatively quickly (which we would define as in the neighborhood of six months, not the six weeks that celebs like Angelina Jolie and Gwen Stefani seem to pull off), there are likely to be other changes still staring back at you, including the following:

Your breasts, which can range from Playmate-style voluptuousness to deflated zeppelins, depending on how long you manage to nurse and what their size was to begin with. Some women enjoy their newfound cleavage while breastfeeding; others find them a leaky, annoying load to bear.

Your waist, or shall we say the lack of one? Even when you lose the weight, your waistline will most likely disappear, surrounded as it now is by stretched-out skin that only liposuction can possibly repair (which, for most of us, means we're stuck with it for life). Bizarrely, you can even weigh less than you did before you were pregnant yet still not fit into those favorite old jeans because of the shifting sands.

Your feet. Everyone told you they could get larger during pregnancy, but for many of us, they also never go back to their original size. Bones don't bounce back when they've been victimized by forty or so pounds resting on them for a trimester or two. Thus, some favorite strappy sandals and devilish heels may go the way of those aforementioned pre-baby jeans. Of course a great new pair of shoes in your new size will make acceptance much easier.

Your legs. For some lucky women, the tiny spider veins of pregnancy will all but disappear when the extra load is lifted from your legs. Bigger, bulging varicose veins are another story. Varicose veins tend to be hereditary and are a big deal for some women, not so much for others. If you are afflicted by them, you will now know the real reason Capris have remained in fashion for decades, and it has nothing to do with Audrey Hepburn. Sure, you can have varicose veins treated by a dermatologist, but just like many cosmetic fixes, the results tend to be temporary. A cheaper alternative is to camouflage them with a tan-building moisturizer or easy spray-on color. We like Sally Hansen's Airbrush Sun (sallyhansen.com) which comes in two formulations, one for the body and another for the face.

Your skin. What can we say? You knew stretch marks were an inevitable by-product of pregnancy, but probably not to the extent of one *Babytalk* reader, who described hers as "a topographical map of Western Europe." There is some good news, however: Many stretch mark do fade into silvery streaks—think of them as badges of honor that match your earrings! Meanwhile, if you discover an effective treatment, please share it with us at letters@babytalk.com.

Down there: Officially known as your pelvic floor or perineum, this area bore the brunt of pregnancy, labor, delivery, and recovery (like we need to tell you that). Side effects range from incontinence (hopefully just occasional, such as every time you sneeze or laugh for the rest of your life) to diminished sexual pleasure. The remedy, which you've also been told a gazillion times before, is to do frequent Kegel exercises: Squeeze the muscles you use to stop the flow of urine, hold them there for ten seconds, then release. Do this exercise ten to twenty times in a row, about three times a day, for maximum results.

We'll stop here, although there are also myriad other teeny, tiny changes you may or may not experience, from blotchy skin to thinning hair to an achy back as your muscles and joints return to normal (late-pregnancy hormones actually help them loosen up to prepare for birth). In many ways your body will bounce back, even if it's not quite the same as it was. You will get used to this new incarnation of your physical self (much like you get used to getting by on less sleep), and your partner will probably notice all this so little that he will look at you quizzically when you whine about it, just as he does when you can't choose between paint shades or some other subtle aesthetic detail of life. Basically, he's going to see your body as pregnant or not pregnant, and love it as much as ever.

Losing the Weight

Now that we've gotten the postpartum anatomy lesson out of the way, let's talk about what you really want to know: when and how to lose that weight (and still enjoy your cake, too!). Umm, well, remember all that other diet advice you used to adhere to before you were a mom-to-be? Tips like watch your portion size, exercising regularly, enjoying everything in moderation, lose the pounds slowly to really keep them off? Guess what? We're going to tell you all the same things, all over again. The recommendation to lose the weight slowly is even more important if you're breastfeeding, because you have to eat not just well, but actually consume more calories than usual, in order to make enough breast milk for your hungry little bambino. Here are some common misperceptions and the reality about postpartum weight loss:

Rumor: **You should be back to your normal weight by your six-week checkup.**

Fact: Except for the very rich and/or very insane, this is total crap. As we noted before, six months is a more realistic goal. However, you can probably count on dropping much of the actual baby weight—the twenty pounds comprising your actual baby, placenta, extra fluids—by your six-week checkup. What will likely remain are the fat stores your body needs for breastfeeding, and those extra pounds that resulted from pregnancy cravings. Women who didn't gain more than the recommended amount during pregnancy will obviously have less to lose, and those who resume exercise sooner are also more likely to have an easier time. P.S. We cannot tell a lie: Several of us gained forty-plus pounds while preggers. We've all lost most of the flab, and so will you.

Rumor: **You can't begin exercising if you're breastfeeding.**

Fact: False. While running a marathon or training for a weight-lifting competition would be ill advised, you can certainly begin light workouts once your milk supply is well established (usually by around four weeks). Prior to that you also want to be careful, because your body is still healing. Women who have experienced surgical births may also need to wait a few weeks longer, and should consult with their doctors about beginning an exercise regimen.

Rumor: **Breastfeeding will help you lose weight faster.**

Fact: This is true, but with some caveats. Your metabolism will burn additional calories by producing breast milk, but you also need to consume a few more calories (about 350 to 500 a day) to help make the milk, and the actual act of breastfeeding requires copious amounts of sitting around. The end result is that some women find that nursing melts away pounds, while others can't seem to shake them until they wean their babies. Typically, the longer you nurse, the more weight you will lose from it, because you are also able to become more active and less tied to your rocking chair. And we don't have to tell you that if the extra calories are coming from salads and whole grains, as opposed to plates of fettuccine Alfredo, that's also going to help in the weight-loss department.

To get you off on the right track, here are some general guidelines. Of course you should check with your healthcare provider before beginning an exercise program, to be sure your body has healed from childbirth and to discuss any particular dietary concerns you might have. You can also go to Parenting.com/babytalk for more ideas on meal plans and exercise routines.

Exercise. In general, most women can resume a fairly vigorous (jogging, pilates classes, strength-training) exercise program by about six weeks postpartum, or eight weeks if you've had a cesarean or otherwise complicated delivery. Before that, however, you can do plenty of light exercise almost from the day you come home from the hospital. You can begin right away with Kegels to help your pelvic floor return to normal (though plenty of us never bothered and we're doing just fine). By the end of the first week, you can do some light stretching of your leg muscles, pelvic tilts, head and neck rolls, and push-ups. Walking is another great form of aerobic exercise that you can even do with your baby in the stroller, weather permitting, by about the second or third week, when your lochia (postpartum menstrual flow) begins to lighten up. The main thing you need to remember here is that if your bleeding increases suddenly (when it seemed to have been lighter for a few or more days) and becomes bright red again, that could be a sign that you're exerting yourself too much physically and need to get off your feet.

Now for the reality check: We know you are still going to be exhausted six weeks after giving birth, and exercise is one of the last things you'll have on your mind, somewhere near sex and cleaning out the linen closet on your postpartum priority list. In fact, you'd probably rather write thank-you notes for baby gifts than do tummy crunches (or have sex). So while the above advice is in every new-mom bible and magazine article out there, we confess it was a lot later than six weeks when we all began to exercise again. A *lot* later. A select few of you may have the gumption early on, but if you don't, we won't tell.

Diet. After nine months of eating with abandon (we know you did), *diet* is truly a four-letter word. The good news is that if you're breastfeeding, you've got another good excuse why you can't start one—or rather, why you can't start a serious weight-loss diet. You can, however, start a healthy-eating, nutritious-milk-making diet. Breastfeeding moms need to consume an additional 350 to 500 calories a day to maintain their milk production. Still, that's only twenty-two to twenty-five hundred calories a day for the average woman. If you get those calories from nutrition-packed fruits, veggies, whole grains, fish, and lean meats, you really can eat an awful lot of food—plenty to fill that mummy tummy. And sticking to the lower end up of that calorie range, along with some consistent exercise, will help you maintain a gradual, realistic weight loss of about a pound a week.

BABY IN ONE HAND, DINNER IN THE OTHER

One of the many facts of new motherhood almost no one seems to mention is the challenge of feeding yourself. Sure, there are plenty of tips on how much and what you need to make the optimum amount and quality of breast milk, melt away postpartum pounds, and maintain the maximum level of energy on almost zero sleep (we're guilty, too, as you just read), but how in the heck do you get food to mouth when you are always either holding your baby, changing your baby, feeding your baby, pushing a stroller, or lugging an infant carrier to and fro? Even eating wearing a front carrier or a sling is overrated unless you don't care about dripping salad dressing on that delicate little scalp (and plenty of times you will indeed be too hungry to care). Well, we've got some ideas for you. Check out these nutritious nibbles you can literally eat with one hand:

Frozen "pocket" sandwiches. Pop them into the microwave, then into your mouth.

New-wave nuggets. Save the chicken variety for the kids and pick up some frozen veggie nuggets, or spring or egg rolls, for yourself.

Less-mess wraps. Skip the drippy dressings and use hummus, yogurt, or bean dip as a tasty spread instead. Buy mini tortillas, add prepared grilled veggies and goat cheese or chicken (cut into bitesize pieces), and keep them rolled and ready to grab in your fridge. Try also wraps with muenster or mozzarella and tomato.

Yogurt. No spoon needed if you opt for the drinkable smoothies or the type in tubes that you just squeeze (so what if they were invented for preschoolers?).

Snack bars. Not all granola bars are created equal, however. Look for Bellybars (nutrabella.com) and LUNA Bars (lunabar.com), both of which were created with a mom's nutritional needs in mind.

Quick snacks. Hard-boiled eggs, string cheese, baby carrot sticks, and dried fruits pack plenty of protein, calcium, and other healthy nutrients when you need sustenance on the run. Dip them into some hummus, yogurt, spreadable cheese, peanut butter, or salsa to tickle your tongue even more.

One-hundred-calorie snack packs and chocolate bars. You'll need a treat sometimes to keep you going, so stock the house.

Of course it's also easy to overdo it and consume too many high-calorie fried and sauce-laden dishes, which will keep you in transitional elastic-waist pants for months to come. We know you know what's smart and what's not when it comes to food choices. And again, Parenting.com/babytalk has lots of great meal plans and smart snacking ideas, so check that out. Otherwise, watch your portion sizes, don't neglect to treat yourself to desserts or a glass of wine now and then so you don't feel totally deprived, and focus on these important nutrients that will boost your energy, help your body heal, and keep that mother's milk flowing:

> **Protein.** Aim for sixty to seventy grams a day from lean red meat, fish, chicken, beans, and eggs.
>
> **Calcium.** Consume twelve hundred milligrams a day in the form of milk, yogurt, cheese, and spinach (or take a supplement).
>
> **Iron.** You need eighteen milligrams a day and can get it from lean red meat, fortified grains, cereal, or a supplement.
>
> **Folic acid.** Continue to consume what you needed for pregnancy, which was four hundred micrograms a day, and can be found in fortified cereals, orange juice, and prenatal vitamins (which you should be continuing to take anyway if you're nursing).
>
> **Choline.** This little-known nutrient will help restore some of those lost brain cells that have been affecting your memory since pregnancy! Aim for 425 milligrams a day, which can be found in egg yolks, steak, beef, liver, or a supplement.

The Carriage versus the Marriage: Can They Cohabitate?

Yes, if you accept the fact that there's a new meaning of *normal*. That doesn't mean you both won't be happy—it'll just be a different kind of satisfaction (and in the long run a better kind, but we don't want to get all gushy). When it comes to keeping your postbaby marriage intact, the lifestyle variables just don't matter. You can get an easy baby or a case of colic from hell, a great sleeper or no-way napper. You two may still feel like you're on your honeymoon or you may have been together so long, you can't remember a time when your sweetheart wasn't part of your life package. Maybe you have mostly child-free friends or lots of other new parents to commiserate with. You can choose to go back to work or stay home. Any way you slice or dice it, the end result will be this: Your marriage (or partnership or commitment or whatever style relationship you have with the other parent of your baby) is going to go through a period of adjustment. The telling moment may come when you cross the delivery room threshold, or six months later. But trust us: It will come.

Postbaby marital upheaval isn't just the stuff of playground lore—there are actual statistics to support it. One popular marriage guru found in his research that after the birth of a first child, couples typically experience eight times as much conflict as before, and two-thirds of them undergo a drop in marital satisfaction. But don't call the divorce lawyer just yet: This marriage can be saved! You just need some hard-core advice for overcoming the eruptions that are the result of that precious little interloper you both adore—despite the havoc she has wreaked on your household.

The Power of Love

Having a deep appreciation for each other also goes a long way toward helping new parents overcome stress, the experts insist. The accepted theory: Even happy couples are going to argue, but they still have a fondness and admiration for each other that wins out during bad times. They make a conscious effort to know and understand everything about each other—from their aspirations to their annoyances. And they maintain a sense of fairness and equality in their relationship, which, when it comes to babycare, means sharing everything from diaper duty to laundry loads to night-time feedings. If you have to, sit down and divvy up the duties in a way that works for both of you. Say you stay home and he works—who should be the night watchman? Both of you, because you do work all day even if you don't leave the house. Okay, technically you can nap. You probably don't take advantage of that nearly as often as you should, and if he wants clean underwear, your partner will recognize the fact that he's still got to spell you a few nights a week once he gets home from work. Do you both head out the door in the AM? Then you've both got to take a shift, plain and simple. Take this approach with your new responsibilities and tensions may still mount, but they will remain more manageable.

How to Fight the Good Fight

Sleepless nights, diaper explosions, misplaced pacis—sometimes new parenthood can feel like month after month of nothing but stress and upheaval. Since you can't take it out on the baby, sometimes you truly do have to take it out on each other. We can tell you this tension is likely temporary, but unfortunately, we can't give an ETA on when the negative emotions will begin to ebb. That depends on many factors, from your child's sleeping habits to family finances to your work schedules.

Why is the tension so unavoidable? Because the presence of a baby magnifies everything, whether it's anxiety and exhaustion, or love and lust (okay, maybe not that). So, for example, if you were always ticked off by your husband's habit of leaving his gym bag by the front door, you might really freak when you trip over it and almost drop your precious bundle. Now consider the bigger issues, like living on a tighter budget or meddling mothers-in-law, and it's understandable how they can grow from molehills to mountains seemingly overnight.

What to do about your mother-in-law may remain unsolvable for a while, but we can help you shrink some of the lesser problems down to a more manageable size. Begin by asking yourself what the most stressful issues are (your lack of sleep, the bills, his gym bag) and simply talking to your partner about them. Be prepared to listen to his laundry list as well, because he will surely have one. Sometimes just venting about the fact that you're both overwhelmed and desperately seeking sleep helps, if only by preventing the resentment from escalating.

You're going to probably blow your top now and then, of course, but aim to have effective discussions more often than not. Avoid accusing ("You're never available—you always put the office first!") and frame your complaint gently ("Some days I'm so lonely. I really miss the time we used to have together."). Even when your spouse says something that seems insensitive to you ("Hi, honey! What's for dinner?"), try not to get defensive or nasty: "Are you kidding me? Do you think I had time to cook you dinner? And why should I? Your belly's getting bigger than mine was when I was pregnant!" We know you're going to be too pissed to give the typical therapists-recommended response: "Gee, honey. It hurts my feelings that you don't recognize how demanding my days are. I wish you could appreciate the fact that I just don't have the time to cook like I used to." (Of course you really feel like saying, *Dinner? I can't even brush my #&?@!!%# teeth!*). You can, however, attempt to make your point a little more productively, perhaps with a bit of humor or sarcasm: "Dinner—that's a laugh. I hope your day was better than mine!" For those times when you do snap, apologize and move on: "Okay, I lost it. Your belly's not quite that big. But try to remember these days at home alone with a baby who only catnaps and screams unless I pick him up are no picnic."

And once you've cleared the air about what's pulling you apart, be sure to find some time to bring up what binds you together: your beautiful bambino. Talk about the ways that he inspires you and how much love you feel for him when you see him in your husband's arms, for instance. These pep talks may sound superficial, but they are essential reminders to both of you that though your bickering matches are temporary, the love you have for your baby is everlasting (you'll certainly get no argument there).

What's Sex Got to Do with It?

Pretty much everything, whether you're doing "it" or not. We all know that in the early stages of parenthood, sex is low on most couples' to-do lists. Okay, for most moms, that is. When will your libido come back to life? It could be six weeks, six months, even a year, particularly if you're breastfeeding. Why? Two reasons: estrogen and fatigue. The first drops and the second spikes, leaving you with little desire and even less energy. Your husband could be George Clooney covered in chocolate and you still may not notice him.

Still, sometimes you've got to make an effort (remember what we said about fairness). Dad might be sympathetic to your plight, but he's not dead, and he still needs some, uh, affection. When we surveyed more than fifteen thousand new moms and dads about their postbaby relationship, 50 percent of the dads said they felt sexually neglected. Believe it or not, while you feel most emotionally attached to your baby right now (like 62 percent of our moms), he still feels most connected to you (62 percent of the dads). At first they understand how tired you are, but after that, many men say they begin to wonder if their wives are just using it as an excuse. This could be just paranoia on their part, but then again, it doesn't take a rocket scientist to figure out that the longer you two avoid intimacy, the tenser your relationship is bound to get, and those fears can turn into a self-fulfilling prophecy. Don't let that happen: Just like you drag yourself out of bed to answer those wee-hour wails, you can drag yourself into bed now and then for a little nookie. Try to remember that sexual intercourse is more than a "treat" to him: It's also how the male species stay emotionally connected to their soul mates. So forget your worries about your still-lumpy belly, the spit-up and sweat-scented aroma that now surround you, and the fact that you may practically sleepwalk through the, er, relations. He'll be so happy to have you back, he won't even notice.

We also know just how rough it is to muster up that energy. With the baby stuck to you all day long, getting covered by all sorts of bodily fluids, the new moms we polled (56 percent of 'em) said that when their husbands reached for them at night, it just felt like "one more demand" on their bodies. So keep in mind that you really can also have a happy, satisfying, intimate relationship with your partner without making love as frequently as you used to. (There are plenty of ways to physically give each other pleasure that don't involve going all the way—we're sure you can figure them out without a how-to from us.) Don't be overly ambitious; just begin with something like a relaxing couple massage and see where it takes you. And mark your calendar, if necessary, to be sure you don't let more than a month go by without going all the way—that's about the bare minimum any marriage can endure. Later you can aim for weekly love fests.

Rethinking Couple Time

The other challenge is that even when your libido begins to come back to life, the chances of actually finding some privacy when the urge strikes are often slimmer than your pre-pregnancy waistline. Even a few hours each week can go a long way toward helping you connect (or reconnect). Ways to carve out couple time:

- Put the baby to bed an hour or so early.
- Get up before your bambino and have a quiet breakfast together.
- Meet for lunch once a week.
- Pop in a DVD and let it entertain your baby for half an hour in the evening while you two catch up (and don't feel guilty about it!).
- Take plenty of opportunities to give each other hugs, kisses, or compliments. It will help you both feel intimate—even when the baby's screaming in the background.

Working Out the Work Issue (Because It Will Be an Issue Whether You Choose to Work or Not)

Regardless of what you once thought about the entire working-mom versus stay-at-home-mom question, your perspective may change—many,

many times, in fact—once you actually have your baby in your arms. Going back to work is so much easier said than done for many women, yet others who secretly thought that that they would quit working during maternity leave are sometimes equally surprised to find that they miss their jobs, their co-workers, and the predictability of their previous lives. The point is, there's just no telling how you'll ultimately feel, so it's often best to just keep an open mind during your pregnancy. The exceptions: knowing you have to work for the income or benefits, or knowing the cost of childcare will outweigh your paycheck so you might as well stay home for now.

You've probably also heard tell of the Mommy Wars, a clever little term coined by our out-of-control media (okay, that means us at *Babytalk,* too, but we prefer to think we're more rational than the typical ranting reporters of cable-news shows). In case you've been on another planet for the past decade, this phrase refers to the fact that stay-at-home moms supposedly feel working mothers are cold, selfish, materialistic, and neglecting their children, and that working mothers think the stay-home crowd are overinvolved, Martha-esque throwbacks to the era of *Father Knows Best* who can't make it in the professional world so they are micromanaging their children instead. Sounds pretty nasty, doesn't it? We agree, and we also think it's mostly BS. We *Babytalk* moms count our stay-home neighbors among our closest friends, and know the feelings are mutual. And some of us are freelancers, which means we do a lot of our writing and editing on a part-time basis from home offices so we have toes stuck in both ends of the job pool, so to speak. Take it from us: Most moms are more interested in comparing their kids' poopy diapers than their career choices. We all simply do what's best for our families in terms of these lifestyle choices, and that includes every angle: our children's well-being, our own personal sanity, our financial needs, and our marriages. We're thankfully in an era where we can make almost any lifestyle choice work, despite what the media screams at us about the latest studies and statistics, and we all just do our best and mostly get along. (Yes, there are the more obnoxious members of your mommy group to contend with, but there are those types in every stage and walk of life.)

Meanwhile, you need ideas and answers, strategies and solutions for managing it all. Much of this book so far has been devoted to handling the day-to-day of life with a baby, so we're going to turn our focus now to those of us who return to work and how to handle all that. Most importantly, finding the right childcare and making it work for you and your baby. Even if you have your baby in some form of childcare already, you may not be totally happy with it, so we want you to know what other options you have. You will hear that consistency is critical, so don't bounce that baby around to a different setup every month. But we want you to know you can and should make a change if your current situation isn't working. Your baby will cope with the transition just fine, especially if he's going to be better off with a new, improved caregiving arrangement. Let's take a real-world look at your options.

The Daycare Decision

So you're headed back to work. Where can you find a clone of yourself who will love and care for your baby as much and in the same way? Nowhere. But your baby will benefit from other people in her life who love her differently, and yes, she will still love you just the same. Before you roll your eyes or start gagging, we're not just trying to pacify you here. It's all sappy, but true. Children benefit from the understanding that there are different people who can meet their needs, and different styles of feeding and playing and nurturing. Your partner doesn't do things with the baby exactly the way you do (much to your chagrin), yet you've learned to trust him to change a diaper and buckle up the car seat (sort of). Yes, choosing another person—or several if you're going the group care route—to watch your baby while you work is one of the toughest decisions you will face in the foreseeable future. But you can and will do a good job of it. So try to tune out the fact that there's a (slight) chance someone else may witness your baby's first steps or hear her first words (she may well save them just for you!), along with those truly frightening reports of daycare center dangers and abusive au pairs. Most caregivers do the job they do because they love their charges and will be happy to respect your wishes on how to care for her. And research shows that even young infants can thrive in a high-quality childcare situation.

You have three basic choices.

Option 1: Daycare centers. This arrangement is essentially organized group childcare, in which children are usually divided up into several age groups—typically infants, toddlers, and preschoolers—since their needs are different at each stage. There will be at least several, if not quite a few employees, depending on the overall size of the facility. Ideally, however, there will be smaller subgroups within each age range, and the same two or three staffers will be the primary caregivers for your baby. You'll also want to find out if the caregivers have been trained in child development or education, or are working toward such credentials (the entire staff doesn't have to be, but some should).

Some daycare centers are part of large franchises; others are privately owned stand-alone businesses. Either way, they must be licensed and meet state-mandated health and safety requirements. (You can contact the National Resource Center for Health and Safety in Child Care at 800-598-5437 or nrc.uchsc.edu to learn your state's standards.) Centers can also be accredited by agencies such as the National Association for the Education of Young Children (NAEYC). To find an accredited center, visit naeyc.org, but rest assured that any center that has voluntarily applied for and been awarded this accreditation is going to be boasting about it; it's also a good sign they take the quality of their care seriously.

There are a number of advantages to larger group daycare centers, one of them being that they are always there. You won't have any last-minute crisis if a caregiver gets sick, quits, or needs vacation time or personal leave, as you would with a one-on-one in-home caregiver or a smaller family daycare arrangement (we're going to give you more details on those options shortly). If you have just one child, the cost of group daycare is certainly more affordable than one-on-one home care, but if you're paying for two or three children, the bill can really escalate.

Another plus is careful routine and educational activities. As you already know, predictability in day-to-day life is a terrific way to help your baby feel loved and secure. Because larger centers must be organized and efficient in their care, this is practically a guarantee at a well-run operation. And more than one mom having trouble getting her baby into a napping routine at home has benefited from the strategies employed at daycare centers. As your baby gets bigger and has more alert playtime, he'll

"WHAT NOBODY TOLD ME ABOUT BEING A WORKING MOM"

"I went back to work when my twins were four months old. It was not a hard decision since I love what I do and we could not financially afford for me to stay home. I don't think I could; I'd go insane! The

(continued on next page)

most challenging part of my decision is the fact that many of my girlfriends are stay-home moms. I don't know how they do it, but I do feel a twinge of guilt when they talk about their day at the park. But I also know that I can give my children just as much love and attention as they can—it just can only be on certain days of the week. My husband fully supports me and since he works from home, we are a pretty relaxed household and feel lucky that we get to spend time with the kids as well as work our full-time jobs that we love!" —*Shana, Nashville, Tennessee*

"I went back to work after my first son was born, but I switched from full-time to part-time. It was a great decision! I get to enjoy a mini workweek (three days) of accomplishment in the workplace, not to mention the relative peace and quiet of sitting at a desk all day. Then I have two great weekdays of being a stay-home mom with my kids, and then we have our weekend as a family. The biggest challenge is getting my two little sons and me out the door on my workday mornings, but I can't complain—I have the best of all worlds!"

—*Erin, West Hills, California*

"The most challenging part of the decision to continue working was finding daycare and adjusting to the cost. My daughter is in two different places during the week: Grandma watches her two days free of charge, she goes to an in-home daycare two more days, and I work from home one day a week. I find that working out of the home actually helps me to cope with being a mom. I have a challenging job that I love, plus it's a way to get out of the house each day and recharge. I am able to spend three days a week all day with my daughter, so I don't feel that I'm missing out on anything. If I didn't like my career, my decision might have been different, but the income my job provides is essential." —*Michelle, Maple Grove, Minnesota*

"I knew I would go back to work. I knew I would be tired, and I am, always. But I am not surprised. I wake between 5:30 and 6 AM and cannot get myself into work before nine thirty. I've already been awake for four hours before I've even started work! I get home between six and six thirty, get dinner ready, feed the children (my husband and I often forgo dinner or scrounge about after). I clean the kitchen, try to do some laundry (I cannot believe how much time I spend folding clothes!), get the kids to bed. Then I read about five minutes before I fall asleep around ten thirty or eleven, and hope no one wakes up until after I've gotten myself together around seven! I have not watched more than ten minutes of TV since I returned to work from maternity leave after my second child was born."   —*Jill, Watertown, Massachusetts*

"I went back to work—I really had no choice since I'm the primary breadwinner at home. But I also knew that I would not be able to handle being at home full-time. I enjoy my job as a social worker and really need the stimulation and contact with friends and co-workers. Yet it is a constant struggle to feel as though I am doing 'enough.' My house is never as clean as I would like it to be, and that 'working mother's guilt' means that I often let my daughter get away with more than I probably should. My husband is great about helping out, but I am still the one who keeps track of just about everything, so I spend a lot of mental energy between work and home. Luckily I am able to stay aware of when I'm getting too stressed with it all and can take a conscious and deliberate step back to regain perspective. That's why it took until February to take our holiday decorations down!"   —*Kristin, North Ridgeville, Ohio*

be exposed to fun educational playtime activities like sing-alongs, puppet shows, painting, and block building, much like you'd expect at preschool. Good daycare centers often even have large indoor play spaces with climbing gyms, slides, and ride-on toys for physical play on inclement-weather days.

What else? We've seen centers that offer monthly family get-togethers including outdoor barbecues or pizza parties with clowns and the like, so parents can get to know one another as well. And when your baby is big enough to really socialize, he'll have a ready-made group of playmates.

Of course the downside to other kids is germs. No matter how clean the facility or fastidious the staff, baby germs are difficult to contain, because (as you know) little ones are nothing if not moist. And they don't mind drizzling their drool or any other bodily fluid on any toy or kid within reach. This means that your baby will contract more run-of-the-mill colds and stomach bugs, as well as secondary infections, than her stay-at-home peers. The upside to this is that a daycare child is going to develop immunity to garden-variety illnesses faster than a more sheltered child, so by preschool she will suffer fewer sick days. In short, illness is inevitable once kids start hanging out together anyway, so it's nothing you should beat yourself up over—just be sure you have good backup care arranged: a grandma close by willing to come over as needed, or, if you work in an office, a sympathetic boss who lets you work at home when all else fails. Some centers have strict policies about keeping sick kids home; others are more lax. The latter situation is ideal when yours is the one with the fever, but you want to make sure the sick children are cared for in a separate area than the healthy ones (or your well baby will get unwelcome germs, too).

Other issues you'll want to look into:

- How do they handle hygiene? For all the above reasons, you want to be sure changing tables are kept away from play and eating areas, caregivers use gloves when changing or wash their hands constantly, toys appear to be cleaned frequently, and care is taken to make sure children don't accidentally pop someone else's pacifiers, bottles, sippy cups, and the like into their own mouths. In general, the place should be clean and well maintained. Not that there won't be toys scattered about after a busy afternoon, and spills are going to happen, but there should be plenty of evidence that the staff are keeping things as clean as possible.
- How do the staff handle disciplinary issues? These may not loom large for your baby yet, but eventually behaviors like hitting, biting, and taking toys away from another child will happen, and you'll want to be comfortable with the way they're handled, whether your baby is the culprit or the victim.
- What are the rules about drop-off and pickup times, and will they mesh with your work schedule? Are there additional fees for late pick-ups (this is a common practice)?
- What's the vacation policy? Many centers require a monthly fee, and you must pay it in full—even when you take a vacation—to maintain your child's spot at the center. We know it seems unfair, but it's pretty much the norm and worth it for a quality daycare center. And look at it this way: The facility probably couldn't maintain the same standard of quality if parents just popped their kids in and out at will; they need a guaranteed income, too. Another caveat: Good daycare centers often have waiting lists, which is why, if you know this is the route you are going, it's smart to begin investigating your options before you even have your baby.

- Are you able to visit anytime? There should be an open-door policy if a center has nothing to hide.
- Are nursing visits encouraged and accepted if you work nearby? Will they handle pumped breast milk appropriately if you plan on providing it?
- How many babies are there per caregiver and per group? This is a state-mandated guideline, but it's usually in the neighborhood of one adult to every three children under twelve months; the preferred group size is no more than six infants. In other words, babies should be divided up into consistent groups of six, with two caregivers devoted as exclusively as possible to each group; there will be days when a caregiver is sick or out on vacation so a substitute will be necessary, but the same people should care for your child most of the time.
- Are the staff loving, responsive, and playful with the babies?
- What is the staff turnover rate? If it seems the caregivers are coming and going frequently, it may not be a pleasant place for them to work, which also means it may not be a pleasant place for your baby to spend his days.
- Check references. Ask for phone numbers of parents who have or are using the center; their comments can be very revealing.
- Perhaps most importantly, how do you feel after visiting the center? Do you walk out excited about the possibility of your baby being cared for there, or uncertain it's the right thing to do? When it comes to choosing childcare, your gut feelings may speak louder than anything else.

Option 2: Family childcare. In many ways, this is like a daycare center on a smaller scale, if you're lucky. It's group care provided by another mom right in her home and can be a happy medium between a high-priced nanny and a larger, more impersonal center. The caregiver may watch only your child and her own, or she may take in several and even have other helpers on her staff. Advantages of this kind of care include a warm, home-like environment; possibly more flexibility in scheduling for you; less exposure to germs, since there are fewer children overall; more individualized attention for your baby; and probably more affordable rates, since the caregiver has less overhead.

Still, there are disadvantages to this arrangement as well. It's best if the caregiver has formal training beyond raising her own children (some don't); there should be backup if she or her children get sick or take a vacation (sometimes there isn't); and family daycares should still be licensed (some aren't), otherwise there's no one policing their health and safety practices or ensuring the recommended adult-to-child ratio. At a minimum, there should be no more than six children to one adult, and no more than two charges under age two. Licensed family daycare centers may offer benefits such as CPR training (depending on state requirements), and you will be able to fund the cost through a flexible spending account (if your employer provides that benefit).

Again, your gut feelings play a very important role. You know if you feel good about what seems to be going on: Your baby makes a reasonable transition when you drop her off (perhaps some tears, but no fits) and in a clean diaper, well fed, and well rested when you pick her up. But if the place is in surprising disarray at the end of the day; you find soggy diapers on her butt more than just occasionally (everyone has a bad day now and then); the other children appear to have snotty noses and hacking coughs more often than not; and the caregiver is frequently on the phone, on the computer, or otherwise occupied—well, what you see is most likely what your baby gets.

Other issues to consider:

- How much TV or DVD time is allowed each day? We all fall back on the boob tube at some point in the day, but it shouldn't be the main form of entertainment.
- Will the caregiver provide lunch and snacks? If so, are they healthy and safe?
- What sort of play area do the children have—is it safe and separate from other living areas of the home?
- Are there outdoor activities?
- What is her disciplinary style, and are you comfortable with it?
- Is there structure to the day, including snacks and naptimes?
- Does she do any educational activities with the children, such as reading, block play, and sing-alongs?
- How does the caregiver handle personal matters—such as needing to take one of her children to the doctor? Does she have backup help to cover for her while she's gone, or will she be bringing your child along?
- If she will be driving your baby places, is the car in good condition, and can you provide her with or does she have a safe and appropriate-size car safety seat? Does she balk if you ask to check her driving record?
- And again, what's your gut instinct? Do you feel good about your

baby being cared for in this environment—or is it a far cry from the home you would run?

Option 3: In-home care. For many parents, a one-on-one caregiver who comes to your home seems like the ideal, and certainly it can be. These nannies may live in or come and go each day, offer the most convenience for you (you only have to get yourself out the door each morning), and provide an optimum environment for your little one, who receives lots of affection and attention in familiar surroundings. However, this is by far the most expensive option, and there are plenty of things that can go wrong if the situation isn't carefully monitored.

First off, where will you find your own personal Mary Poppins? Au pairs—young women from foreign countries eager to live in the United States—can be found through agencies (see pages 370 and 444–46 for resources) and are often more affordable than older, more experienced nannies. But their youth also may make them less reliable and less skilled; most are able to remain in the country for only a year, too, so you and your baby will have to adjust to annual change. And because you provide room and board, you will have the au pair in your life 24/7.

Agencies also can help you find a traditional in-home caregiver who has more training and goes home at the end of each day (look in the phone book under "childcare," or see our resource lists on the pages noted above). You may also be able to find one yourself (and avoid a placement fee) through word of mouth, local advertising, a local college, community groups, or your doctor or hospital. You will have to conduct face-to-face interviews, so give yourself plenty of time. Since this person will be alone with your baby most of the time, you want to be sure you're comfortable with her childrearing and discipline philosophies, and that she has the appropriate childcare skills, including an understanding of proper nutrition, attentiveness to cleanliness and good hygiene, the importance of routines, knowledge about choking hazards and other safety issues, CPR training for emergencies (you can arrange this for her; see chapter 8, page 289, for information on how and where), and how to make your baby's days fun and stimulating. You may want to set some ground rules about what she should be doing when the baby's awake versus sleeping, so he's not spending more time with the Baby Einstein bunny than getting the one-on-one attention you're paying for. Reliability is also key. You need a caregiver who's on time, doesn't take too many sick days, and isn't steaming at the ears when your train is late. Finally, what will you do for backup when the sitter is sick or on vacation?

Another important detail: You'll need to check for references carefully. We've all heard horror stories from other parents or seen them on the news, and while they are rare, it makes sense to do your homework before bringing a person into your home. When a former employer gives a couched comment like "We just decided we needed a change," recognize it for the code that it really is: Something was wrong but we don't want to go into detail about it. Even when you get glowing references, it's not a bad idea to do a background check to make sure the sitter hasn't been involved in any unsavory situations or, heaven forbid, criminal activities. And as with a family daycare provider, you'll want to be sure your nanny has a safe driving record and a safe vehicle, because she'll most likely be bringing your baby places. (In fact, you might consider getting her covered under your insurance policy so she can drive one of your vehicles.) An advantage to using an agency is that its staff do all this background work for you as part of the fee.

Finally, once you've found what you hope is the next best thing to you, put your agreement in writing with a contract listing her responsibilities, schedule, pay, holidays, vacation days, and sick days. Of course you're going to be concerned about expense, but put yourself in her place when it comes to benefits: The best bosses are going to offer paid vacation and a certain number of sick days (you can base these issues on your own work place's policies). It may well be worth it to keep happy a sitter whom both you and your child feel good about. All this goes a long way toward preventing resentment or misunderstandings and promoting goodwill on both sides.

Six Steps to Smart Care

1. Start your search early. If you're considering family childcare or center daycare, you may need to sign up even before your child is born—the good ones often have waiting lists. If you plan to hire an in-home caregiver, begin looking at least six weeks before you return to work.

2. Interview carefully. Whether you are interviewing a potential nanny, a family childcare provider, or the director of a daycare center, remember: Actions speak louder than words, so observe how a candidate responds to your baby as well as how she answers your questions. Revealing interview questions include:

- What do you like most and least about working with children?

- How long have you been working with children as a childcare provider?
- Are you (and your staff) CPR-certified? If not, will you be willing to take a class if I arrange it?
- How do you feel about parent visits?
- How do you discipline?
- What do you think babies need most?

3. Keep it legal. If you choose care in your home, remember: The Nanny Tax isn't just for politicians. If you're caught paying someone off the books, you'll pay steep back taxes, interest, and penalties. In addition, paying your caregiver legally provides her with Social Security and unemployment benefits, and, as with other types of childcare arrangements, allows you to use a flexible spending account and claim a child and dependent care tax credit. For details, call 800-829-1040 and ask for IRS Publication 926. (We won't kid you—hiring a legal nanny can require a ton of paperwork. If neither you nor your hubby is good at this sort of thing, pay your tax preparer a little extra to manage all the forms for you.)

4. Arrange backup care. Inevitably, childcare plans fall apart from time to time—your sitter gets sick or quits, or your baby runs a fever and can't go to daycare. Since you may not always be able to take time off work when this happens, have an emergency backup plan ready. Can you call a nearby relative or stay-at-home friend? Does either your or your spouse's employer offer emergency childcare? Is there a local nanny agency that provides short-term, in-home sitters for emergencies? Some centers also offer "sick care" for occasional use and keep contagious kids in a separate space from healthy ones. Look in the phone book under "childcare" to see what's available in your area.

5. Ease the transition. Visit the center several times with your baby before leaving him there on his own so he can become familiar with the setting, and you'll feel more comfortable with the program. If you hire a nanny, have her start during your last week home, so she and your baby have time to become acquainted, and she can get to know your home and your routines.

6. Keep in touch. Once you're back at work, check in regularly. Set up a convenient calling time, such as during your baby's nap. When you return home or pick your baby up, ask the caregiver for a summary of her day:

How long did she nap? What and when did she eat? Was she cheerful or fussy? If pickup time is hectic for group care providers, ask for a log of your baby's meals, naps, diaper changes, and overall mood.

WHERE TO TURN FOR MORE HELP

Nannies: International Nanny Association, nanny.org, 888-878-1477.
Au pair care: aupairusa.org.
Daycare centers: Child Care Aware Hotline, childcareaware.org, 800-424-2246.

Working at Home: Dream Job or Nightmare?

Actually, it could go either way, depending on your setup. It sounds ideal: keeping a paycheck and a foot on the career ladder while not having to leave your baby, pump breast milk, or spend a lot on clothing or commuting. But here's the catch: You still need childcare. You will have to be available to your boss, colleagues, and clients by phone or e-mail, and can't carry on a conversation with a crying baby in the background. And while all those gadgets to entertain him are handy for ten minutes here and there, they aren't going to get you through an eight-hour workday. In addition to arranging childcare, you also need to have the self-discipline to stay focused on your work when other household tasks beckon (folding laundry can suddenly seem like fun when the alternative is a spreadsheet). To ensure that working at home will work for you, consider the following:

Set a strict schedule. If you will still be working for your current employer, you'll likely need to spend some time in the office. Set aside certain days for meeting there or with clients, and others for being at home. If you're going to be self-employed, you'll need to be firm about staying at your desk and reserving errands for lunchtime.

Get equipped. Make sure your home computer can handle all the graphics, spreadsheets, and other assignments you handled at your office. Invest in fax machines, wireless networks, and whatever else you may need to stay connected. Consider your work space, too: Sitting at the kitchen table is fine for a little catch-up work over the weekend, but you can't spend an entire workday there without getting a backache. Get yourself a good desk, chair, and lighting.

Stay connected. If you're telecommuting, e-mail colleagues frequently from your home office and return phone messages ASAP, so they imagine you at your desk, not playing with the baby. Check in with your boss every day you're working at home, and when you're in the office, go out of your way to mingle and keep up with office politics, scuttlebutt, and the like, so you stay in the loop.

Hire help. Squeezing in calls to the office at naptime on maternity leave is one thing, but you can't get away with it for long. The day of your big deadline, your baby will come down with an ear infection or refuse to take a nap. Even with a sitter on hand, you'll still have the benefit of being able to breastfeed during the workday, enjoying the extra time with her you would have spent commuting to work, and squeezing in other little visits here and there. You'll also be less stressed about getting everything done. And that truly is a blessing.

"WHAT NOBODY TOLD ME ABOUT BEING A STAY-HOME MOM"

"After working for five years and being very career-driven, I decided to become a stay-at-home mom after the baby. The most challenging part is adjusting from a nine-to-five job to a 24-hour one. With a baby, work starts as soon as they wake up and it doesn't end when they fall asleep. There are chores to be done, nursing when they're little, and putting them back to sleep when they wake up at night. Still, I think it's a bit tougher for working moms because they have to deal with office stress, then they switch to mom-mode when they go home. I cope with chocolates and ice cream and a hot, relaxing shower. Having a very supportive husband who will take over the kids when he gets home is a big help, too." —*Melody, Hackensack, New Jersey*

(continued on next page)

"I made the decision with my husband to stay home long before we ever had children. I actually left work at twenty-eight weeks to enjoy some 'me' time before the baby came, and am so grateful. We aren't rich by any means but we had already learned to live on one salary so my leaving work wasn't such an ordeal. The biggest challenge about staying home is the fact that we moved and I lost my mommy network, and haven't yet found new friends. It's good that my daughter and I enjoy each other's company so much, because most of the time it's just us right now." —*J. J., Shoreview, Minnesota*

"I always wanted to stay home with my children, but after working for fifteen years, this was a big transition because so much of my identity was wrapped up in the different jobs that I held. My biggest challenge has been trying to identify my new job description. When you work outside the home, your job performance is clearly measured and your job description is specifically defined. As a stay-at-home mom, I feel like I wear so many hats that it is impossible to measure how well I am doing in any area."
—*Tara, Chattanooga, Tennessee*

"I did all of it! I stayed home with my son until nearly his first birthday, at which point I seriously needed some adult interaction or I thought I would lose my mind. So I went to work full-time and put him in daycare. Then I missed my son and felt guilty, so I cut back to part-time and worked it out with my hubby's schedule so we each watch him and don't have to put him in daycare. And after considering how much money we were spending on daycare, I'm just about breaking even working for twenty-four hours a week instead of forty, and so far staying much more sane!"
—*Erin, Auburn Hills, Michigan*

"Being a stay-at-home mom after working the grind in Washington, DC, has been a nice adjustment. I have to continue to stay plugged in with current events, alumni functions, and my old working friends. Once-a-month lunches in the city help keep my mind in check . . . and remind me that I love not riding the subway each day!"
—*Andrea, Vienna, Virginia*

"I decided to stay home after I had my baby, but after six months I craved adult interaction, missed working, and just didn't know how to reach out to other new moms. At the same time, I did not want to work full-time because I wanted to treasure moments with my family; working and taking care of a newborn is a really hectic schedule. So, I decided to do something I had wanted for a long time instead: go back to business school. This has allowed me to spend quality time with our little guy without the pressures of a full-time job and made scheduling a little more convenient." —*Sujatha, Edison, New Jersey*

"I found changing from a career person to a stay-at-home mom was one of the single most humbling experiences in my entire life. Managing a staff of a hundred people was easier than managing this one baby on her own terms. I cherish every moment I've had, but it's also dumbfounding how being a full-time mom changed me. My priorities were new, the material I read was new, the thoughts in my head were new, my long-term and short-term plans were new, even my sleep schedule was new. I try to get time for myself by jogging and biking either by myself or with the kiddies in tow."
—*Jody, Claremore, Oklahoma*

Managing All Those Emotions in Motion

Whatever work/life/home style you ultimately choose for yourself and your family, you will be confronted with two unavoidable emotions: guilt and envy. You'll be working and feel guilty and afraid you are spending too little time with your child. Or you'll be staying home and feel guilty that you're bored or that you miss going to work. Much of this comes from the popular perception that no matter how much we do for our children, no matter how devoted we are, it's never enough. Unfortunately, this idealization of motherhood undermines us all. If we have no other identity beyond "supermom," we're bound to get lonely or frustrated or overwhelmed—then we feel like the worst mothers in the world because we're not enjoying our lives and feeling fulfilled like we think we should be. And the resulting guilt complex doesn't help anyone but the snack-food industry.

The other evil twin dragging us down is envy. Because we're trying to live up to a mythic mommyhood, we can't help but think that there is someone else who is doing more or doing it better. It's inevitable, for example, that just when you decide to switch from breast to bottle, you will run into nursing mothers everywhere you turn. When you stay home and are pinched for cash, you will notice working moms in fabulous clothes and perfectly highlighted hair, headed off on vacations to Disney World that their babies will never remember. If you go to work, you will look out your car window on the way and see svelte stay-at-homes pushing jogging strollers through the park with their giggly little charges in tow. Or you'll go green at the gills when, rushing to a meeting with clients, you pass a group of moms comparing development notes over coffee at an outdoor café while their babes nap in slings or strollers next to them. These scenes are unavoidable, but if you're smart—and we know you are—you'll heed this pearl of wisdom: Put on your blinders. The proverbial expression *The grass is always greener on the other side of the fence* is never so true as it will be at this point in your life. Believe us, no one has the perfect setup. Stay-at-home moms have been known to cry in their lattes because their husbands are working longer hours to make up for their missing paychecks, and working moms often wish they could trade their highlights for finger paints. It's part of being human. We want what we don't have and sometimes don't appreciate what we do. So we're sorry to say that guilt and envy won't disappear. When you're a mom, they'll always be waiting in the wings, but there are ways to prevent them from completely stealing your show.

Baby Breathers Every Mom Needs

Let's get one thing straight: Even though you are now someone's mother, and that someone depends on you to stay alive, you don't need to be focused on your baby like a laser beam every minute of the day. He's not going to lose IQ points if you let him zone out on an overhead play gym or a Teletubbies video once in a while so you can paint your toenails or check out your favorite blog. This is not neglect; your baby needs to learn to occupy himself, so you are actually teaching him a skill. And let's be frank: You have to take care of yourself if you expect to take care of your baby. This is why God made bouncy seats and swings and stationary exercisers: to put your baby in them so you can go about your life, even if it's a Saturday and you're trying to make up for lost time from your workweek. You still deserve whatever you need to do to give you that get-up-

VOICE OF REASON

"Lists are a new mother's best friend. First thing in the morning, jot down a list of what needs to be done, in three categories: chores that must be taken care of as soon as possible; those that can wait until later in the day; and those that can be put off until tomorrow, or next week, or indefinitely. Assign approximate times to each activity and don't forget to cross off completed tasks for a satisfying feeling of accomplishment. Though organizing your day on paper doesn't always mean that everything will get done on schedule (in fact, for new mothers it rarely does), it will give you a sense of control over what may now seem like a completely uncontrollable situation. Plans on paper are always more manageable than plans flying frenetically around your head."
—Babytalk *contributing editor Heidi Murkoff in her highly recommended book* What to Expect the First Year

and-go. We'll give you a few postpartum months to get your act together, of course, but there's simply no reason that a once vivid, energetic, intelligent woman needs to permanently morph into an overwhelmed, exhausted, distracted shell of her former self simply because she has a child and maybe a job that comes with a paycheck as well. You should and you must take the time necessary to retrench and rejuvenate your mind, body, and all those other inner workings that make you feel good about yourself. As your newborn grows and matures, so, too, will your confidence and ability as a mom. Just think how amazing you are physically and mentally to be pulling all this off. Your body produced another human being, for gosh sake, and now you're doing a pretty darn good job of keeping that achievement going. Okay, enough lecturing. Here's a painless, two-part prescription and some ideas on what to do with it.

1. Build some me time into your day. You need at least half an hour, and preferably an hour, a day (yes, *each and every day*) to read a book, vent in a chat room, exercise on a treadmill, watch a TV show without interruption, paint, blog, or whatever is it that can make you focus your energy on something other than your baby. This is not an impossible task: You can do it while your baby naps, or while your partner gives her a bath, or while you're sitting on a train, book or laptop in hand. Just don't do anything in the allotted time frame that has to do with the baby (or anyone else who's dependent on you, for that matter). Other possibilities: Try meditation (studies show it reduces stress); go hiking; clean out a junk drawer (it's a chore, but one that makes you feel good).

2. Build an evening (or afternoon if that works better for you) out of the house once a week sans baby. Once your baby can go more than two hours between feedings, we want you to seriously think about joining a reading or scrapbooking group; taking a yoga or cooking or quilting class; going shopping (but not for the baby!); getting into nature by hiking or going jogging on the beach; or meeting some girlfriends or colleagues or—here's a novel idea—your husband for dinner. We're sure you can think of something you'll enjoy.

TWENTY THINGS YOU SHOULD NEVER FEEL GUILTY ABOUT

We could probably come up with about two hundred things to not feel guilty about, but then we would just feel guilty about never feeling guilty at all. This list will give you the general idea of what kinds of not-exactly-maternal feelings are within limits, and what child-care chores you can cheat on now and then.

1. Wanting to stay home with your baby.
2. Loving your job.
3. Hating your husband now and then.
4. Still not wanting sex way, way, way after your six-week checkup.
5. Not reading to your baby as much as all the experts say you should.
6. Introducing a bottle as soon as you get home from the hospital (even though you're not sure your milk supply is established yet) so you can get some sleep.
7. Supplementing with formula at *any* time.

8. Lying to the other women in your mommy group about how long your baby sleeps at night (but you will get more sympathy if you tell the truth).

9. Not keeping up with all the milestones you're supposed to be recording in your baby book.

10. Never even starting the baby book.

11. Saying, "Great idea—I'll try it!" to your mother-in-law's advice when you have absolutely no intention of giving it an iota of thought once she walks out the door.

12. Telling your partner you're going to the doctor for a checkup when you're actually going for a massage, pedicure, or to have your hair highlighted (it's not like he's going to notice anyway).

13. Paying cash for your massage/pedicure/highlights so he won't discover the credit card charge.

14. Refusing another mom's invitation to a playdate because you can't stand it that she can leave crystal on her coffee table and toilet paper on the rollers and her baby doesn't bother any of it.

15. Feeling a twinge of delight when the above mom's baby still isn't saying any words and yours has a vocabulary of six!

16. Putting on the Baby Einstein DVD for the third time before lunch so you can apply some makeup because that cute landscaping guy is due to come by and cut your grass sometime this afternoon (just because you don't want to have sex doesn't mean you're dead).

17. Wanting to spend Mother's Day alone instead of with your family.

18. Going to visit your parents for the weekend because you know they will insist on doing everything for the baby and your mother will cook all your favorite foods for you. (Grandmothers can spoil their own children as well as their grandchildren.)

19. Napping when the baby naps even though he's nine months old.

20. Driving your baby home from the mall with poop in his diaper because the bathroom is all the way at the other end and you know he couldn't care less anyway.

Learning to Live with the Little Green Monster

No, we don't mean Kermit the Frog; nor did we forget that Elmo is red and Barney, purple. We are referring to the little green monster that rears its ugly head every time a mother whose life seems better than ours happens, for whatever reason, to pop into our temporarily vacant heads. Whether it's the sleep deprivation, the haywire hormones, those lingering postpartum pounds, the lack of control we suddenly have over our day-to-day existence, or any number of further reasons, perfectly clever and competent women can turn into desperate housewives, employed or not, as soon as they're inducted into Club Mom. After all, if you're ever going to feel uncertain, or insecure, it's going to be when everything is new and you don't have any experience to fall back on. And even women who have logged mommy time can have trouble staying the course: keeping the house clean, working, cooking dinner every night, and acting perky to boot. For most of us, envy is inevitable, whether we feel it or are the object of it (yeah, seriously, we mean you). There's a good chance you can name someone who reminds you of several of the following characters.

The Martha mom. It's hard not to notice her: She's the one whose baby never has a drop of pureed sweet potatoes on her romper, and her playroom looks like a photo in the Pottery Barn catalog. She's also able by some manipulation of the time-space continuum to get showered, styled, manicured, and made up daily. Of course anyone can prepare for company by shoving stuff under the bed and in the closet and throwing on a streak of lipstick, but one of us had the nasty experience of dropping by a Martha mom's apartment unexpectedly and finding it immaculate then, too, despite two children residing there. Needless to say, our colleague never went back to this "frenemy's" home again (definition of *frenemy:* one who is both a friend and an enemy for reasons only you can appreciate). But as the old saying goes, you never know what's really going on behind those closed doors. While these moms may be able to win a proverbial "Tidy Bowl," their superiority might just go down the drain if we got to really know them. One mom who's a frequent contributor to *Babytalk* told us she used to berate herself every time she visited a friend's spotless home, until the woman confided that her husband was Attila the Household Hun: She was literally afraid he'd blow up if he found a ring around the bathtub or a favorite shirt unwashed. For all you know, the object of your envy could be popping Prozac by the handful to combat her supermom anxiety. And her baby may be zoned out in front of the tube all day while she cleans instead of playing with him.

The gifted child's mom. You know you wouldn't trade your child for anyone else's, yet wishing your kid could be more like the baby next door is an envy pit that swallows many a new mom. Even babies you've only heard about in online message boards can incite real envy, and who knows if what those moms are boasting about is even the truth? Certain milestones will hit home, including the biggies like crawling, walking, and talking, even though they usher in a more challenging era of care. Then there's sleeping through the night. One mom told us she couldn't even stand to be around moms whose babies were good sleepers, as if she had somehow failed in her parenting ability when a lot of it is pure luck.

When you love your baby more than yourself, why envy another person's child? Perhaps because in some sense, you view your baby as extension of yourself; it's like you're losing the race against this little person who isn't even potty-trained. It can also make us feel like we're doing something wrong: We can't even get the bedtime routine right, for instance, or can't control the nagging fear that lack of language is due to too much boob tube and not enough mommy-baby interaction. Crazy concepts, we know, but they occur to many a mom from time to time.

The bombshell mom. Thanks to the likes of Cindy Crawford and Elizabeth Hurley, nothing trips the envy wire as surely as a svelte new mom. Comparing your body with someone else's is as idiotic now as it was in seventh grade, but it's also just as natural. Like puberty, motherhood transforms a woman's body, which can make her acutely aware of it. Add to that the fact that our culture continually heralds celebrity moms who can fit back into their skinny jeans a few weeks after delivery, and it's easy to understand why many moms feel like they don't measure up. But size 4 envy is really part of a larger desire to regain control over your appearance. Indeed, seeing mom out and about with clean hair and makeup leaves others scratching their heads in disbelief. Rather than stress because you're still as zaftig as a Rembrandt painting (and a work of art to be admired, at that), try to focus on the little things: fitting a shower into your day; getting out of the house in clean clothes before the baby spits up on them. In time, the need for transitional pants will diminish along with the challenge of getting around to makeup. You may never regain the exact same shape you once had, but you will be able to look awfully good if you put your mind to it. And if you don't, well, you've got plenty of excuses.

The truth is, no matter what you think you can surmise from a mom's outward appearance, you still have no way of knowing what's really lurking under her skinny duds, including envy-destroying stretch marks and cellulite. Carefully chosen clothing can still hide those postpartum tummy rolls that we all know nothing short of liposuction can cure. As for insta-thin celebrity moms, remember that they have access to personal trainers and nannies to watch their babies. And if they don't get back in shape, their rippled buns will be splashed across the pages of tabloids; at least there's no *Fat Actress* reality show in the future for the rest of us.

The know-it-all mom. Like those children born to be intellectual or athletic whiz kids, some women seem born to be, well, perfect mothers, with the immediate answer to every cranky spell, sleepless night, food jag, or earache. They not only know what they "should" do—be it breastfeed with grace and skill or put their baby down when he's drowsy instead of sleeping—they actually manage to do it. One of our friends was humiliated when she complained to a mom friend that she couldn't get her baby to stop whining. Like Mary Poppins, her friend plopped down on the floor with the cranky kid and had him laughing in about two minutes. And our bud was left wondering, *Why didn't I think of that?*

The underlying message in all this is that everyone mothers in a different style; it may not be your thing to do a lot of floor time, and that's okay. Your own way of showing love and affection is precious to your child, and will evolve over time right along with him. For instance, one of us discovered child's play was much more fun for her when her son turned five and the two of them really got into building some incredible LEGO projects together. And whatever form of envy happens to be plaguing you, there's bound to be something you have or do that other moms don't. Not in size 6 jeans? The fact that you've made it to size 12 signals serious progress to onlookers in 16s. Even sagging breasts hoisted up in a push-up bra look good to the woman who promptly deflated back to her A cup. That job that limits your time with your baby may sound like a euphoric escape to the stay-at-home mom of three down the block (no one screaming in the background every time she picks up the phone!). Your friends may think you're organized because you have time to bake when they have no clue about the sky-high piles of laundry being ignored down in your basement. But if you don't care, then why should anyone else? That's the perspective that will get you through the good nights and the bad, and see that dirty glass in the sink as half full instead of half empty.

CHAPTER 11

Special Families, Special Needs

Real-Life Advice for Parents of Premature Babies and Infants with Medical Issues

One of the lapses of logic that happen with the onset of parenthood—and there are many—is that there are millions and millions of new moms populating the earth, and every one of them can't help thinking, *No one knows what I'm going through!* Those are frustrating and lonely times, but most of us can muddle through long enough to call and chat with a girlfriend or spouse, or read a reassuring passage in a baby book until we calm down. For those of us caring for premature or special-needs babies, however, the road to reassurance can be infinitely more difficult to find. Indeed, unless you know someone who has taken the same path, you'll be hard-pressed to find it on the usual parenting maps.

Even if someone is kind enough to put their hands on your shoulders and turn you in the right direction—usually by providing reams of brochures, medical articles, and Web sites to peruse—you still may feel lost, not to mention angry, frustrated, or excruciatingly sad. The reason? Because neither babies nor parents thrive on facts alone, and just being taken to the right road doesn't mean you will be able to navigate it. All moms with new babies need both emotional and logistical support. And if you have a baby with a disability, or one who was born prematurely, you are particularly desperate for facts and friendship.

In addition to the usual difficulties of recovery and learning to care for your child, you may have to deal with endless medical tests—which may or may not be conclusive—procedures, hospitalizations, health insurance paperwork headaches, setting up appointments for early-intervention evaluations and therapies, as well as exacerbated marital or financial stress. When you're heading up the already steep curve of parental learning, these added layers of ice can make any mom develop a deep sense of injustice—followed quickly by a deep sense of guilt, anger, depression, or all three. And while we can't eliminate these feelings for you, we can help you strap on the climbing gear you'll need to become your baby's best advocate. Once outfitted with knowledge *and* support, you can take your first steps forward and eventually scale the mountains of medical information, logistical labyrinths, and emotional eruptions (yours and your family's) you'll confront during this first year. At some point down the road, you may even have a moment to notice a spectacular view—the one of yourself and your beautiful and very special baby.

Babies with Disabilities

All of us daydream about our babies: whether they'll look like our side of the family, whether they'll be the lead in the school play, or whether they'll grow up to be a doctor, lawyer, or both. What never occurs to us is whether or not they will have disabilities. Not that the thought doesn't pop into our heads. The idea of physical or mental problems is a specter rattling around every parent's brain. It's just that it is so frightening, we shove it into the *that can't happen to me* closet of our gray matter. The fact is, it can happen to *anyone,* and does happen more than most parents realize.

Most disabilities fit into three broad categories: physical, genetic, and chromosomal, although they often overlap. Physical abnormalities are quite common and include defects of the organs, such as a septal defect (a hole in the heart), or structural problems, like cleft palate. According to the Centers for Disease Control and Prevention (CDC), among the most frequently seen defects are congenital problems with the heart, which affect roughly one in every one hundred to two hundred babies. (See pages 392–99 for more physical disabilities.) Some of these disabilities require one or more surgeries to repair the damage or reconstruct the malformed tissue. And once corrected, some of these abnormalities have no effect on a child's later physical development. Indeed, you'd be surprised to know how many of the kids you see running and playing at a schoolyard underwent corrective surgeries as babies. We know that won't diminish the fear you'll experience when your baby is being prepped for the operating room or monitored for post-op complications, but we hope you will get some comfort in knowing that you and your baby have lots of people in the same lifeboat.

The second group of disabilities are linked to genetic abnormalities, which are passed from parents to children. Untold numbers of problems stem from out-of-whack genes; untold because while researchers may suspect that certain disabilities are inherited, most cannot be pinned without any doubt on Mom and Dad—so that's one less thing to feel guilty about. Each of us receives our unique mix of genes from both parents, and these thousands and thousands of markers form the blueprint of our physical and biochemical systems. Some of the resulting traits are obvious—our hair color matches our mom's, for example—while some are not—maybe no one has blue eyes in your family except you. The ones that seem to show up out of nowhere may come from recessive genes (those that are not dominant in either parent), which is why parents without any impairment can have a child with a disability. There are now genetic tests that can tell parents as early as the first trimester whether or not their child is a likely carrier of a disease, but it may or may not be related to what was handed down from you and your spouse. Disabilities that are conclusively linked to the parents' genes include sickle-cell anemia, Rh disease, cystic fibrosis, and muscular dystrophy.

Finally, there are chromosomal abnormalities, which happen when there is a defect in the number or structure of the chromosomes that reside in every cell. Normally, a person receives an equal pair of chromosomes from a mother and a father: Every sperm and every egg brings twenty-three chromosomes to the fertilization party, with the final tally being forty-six chromosomes within each cell. Sometimes, however, a problem occurs during cell division, and the resulting sperm or egg has too many or too few chromosomes. One of the most common disabilities caused by a chromosomal abnormality is Down syndrome, which according to the March of Dimes occurs in 1 of every 1,250 births to women at twenty-five and increases to 1 in every 100 births by the time they reach forty—and the risk continues to rise with age. In the case of Down syndrome, an extra copy of the "number 21" chromosome is transferred, thus giving the baby three copies (called a trisomy) instead of two. If your baby has Down syndrome, he may have low muscle tone (a floppy body), a thick tongue and neck, some degree of mental retardation, and a susceptibility to infections as well as other health problems. He may also be incredibly happy and loving, and with early intervention—both medical and educational—he may join other babies his age in most normal playtime activities. Other chromosomal abnormalities include trisomy 13 or trisomy 18 (extra copies of the number 13 or number 18 chromosome), which are less common than Down syndrome and result in more severe mental retardation and physical defects, or disabilities caused by defects in the so-called sex chromosomes X and Y. Boys normally have an X and Y chromosome, while girls have two X's. One in approximately six hundred to eight hundred boys, however, have two or more X chromosomes in addition to the Y chromosome. Called Klinefelter's syndrome, it causes them to produce lower amounts of testosterone as adults and can be treated with hormones. As common as these and other disabilities are, it's staggering to consider that many babies suffer not just one problem but multiple disabilities (for example, babies with Down syndrome often have heart problems or digestive difficulties), and that there are untold numbers of disabilities and their variants that exist but aren't publicized or perhaps even yet identified.

One disability that defies general categorization is autism. In fact, this disability is not one problem but a range of impairments encompassing many problems, including differences in cognitive aptitude and social difficulties. The real name is autism spectrum disorders (ASD), and, as you might guess, the large number of symptoms associated with ASD makes it particularly difficult to diagnose. Recent advances in understanding what ASD comprises, however, have enabled physicians to sometimes detect it as early as eighteen months. And promising research and continued interest by parents and scientists may push the age back even further. If your baby is not imitating sounds by five months or responding to his name or babbling by ten months, or if he engages in repetitive unusual movements or behaviors or avoids eye contact around the year mark, you should talk with your pediatrician. We realize that all of these symptoms may seem vague in the extreme, and might apply to any number of problems that have nothing to do with ASD. But again, spending every waking moment (and some half-asleep ones) with your baby may give you some insight as to what constitutes "unusual behavior." As always, when in doubt, contact your pediatrician and follow up with a specialist if necessary. As with many other disabilities, the effects of ASD can be tempered by early diagnosis and therapy.

Why Me? Why My Baby?

Although advances in prenatal screenings can now pinpoint when many of these defects occur—at conception or during pregnancy, for example— the reasons *why* they happen often remain a mystery. The American Academy of Pediatrics estimates that a large number of disabilities stem from unknown causes, though the usual suspects are genes or environmental factors, such as infections or exposure to toxins when the baby is in the womb. Genetic testing has come a long way toward predicting the possibility of certain diseases that can result in a disability, and parents can also educate themselves on how to eliminate toxins from their surroundings and their diets during pregnancy. But even with these precautions, there is often nothing you can do to prevent your baby from being born with a disability.

This bears repeating: It is very likely that you had *nothing to do with your baby's condition*. To say this, of course, we have to assume a couple of things. First, we assume you tried your best to have a healthy pregnancy. This doesn't mean you had to be perfect while pregnant—none of us is. Rather, most days you tried to do your best. Second, we assume that you have absolutely no control over your genes and that you didn't stay up late one night writing your baby's genetic code for submission to a higher power. If these assumptions are correct, then once again let us say that it is very likely you had *nothing to do with your baby's condition.*

Will our saying this alleviate your feelings of responsibility? We wish that were the case, but no. You may always feel pangs of guilt—that if you just hadn't tripped up the stairs one day or if you hadn't married a certain someone you could have prevented your baby's condition. The only thing we can say is that guilt does not have to overshadow your daily life, particularly if you can tap into a support system to help you through that first year. Whether it's a physician, a therapist, a family member, or a friend, reaching out for help can keep your life in perspective and your guilt in check. (More on this later.)

Some disabilities are mild and common while others are severe and rare, but all require attention, whether through medical intervention, physical therapy, or home-based care. Thank goodness we live in the twenty-first century when disabilities are no longer considered stagnant conditions or societal taboos. Doctors are now armed with new diagnostic tools ranging from auditory screening for newborns to improved therapies for babies with sensory integration problems (see chapter 4, page 145). In addition, there are early-intervention and physical therapy options that can advance a child's motor and cognitive development well beyond what was previously available. In short, the future for disabled kids and their parents has never been brighter.

Getting a Diagnosis

The first step to gaining a sense of control is to determine a proper diagnosis of the disability. Thanks to a battery of prenatal tests, some parents know the specifics during pregnancy, allowing them time to prepare and inquire about services or treatments, while others have an obvious and easily confirmed disability diagnosed soon after delivery. Some parents, however, find out weeks or even months after leaving the hospital. How can it be that you can show up for weeks and weeks of well-baby visits before learning that all is not well? Quite simply, unless your baby exhibits blatant signs of a disease or defect, she may look and act like all other newborns. She may eat, sleep, and poop with abandon, so the first perfunctory visits with the pediatrician may not reveal anything amiss. Still other parents receive a diagnosis soon after delivery, but the degree of severity is not revealed until much later. No matter which of these matches your situation, you can expect to watch your baby go through lots of blood tests or other diagnostic procedures. And each time you will experience an agonizing wait for the results.

It's at this stage when you are hit full in the face with the depressing fact that while medical science has made incredible advances, it still may require a lot of detective work by both the doctors and the parents to figure out what's the matter with your little love. Once again, it's your baby's constant companion—namely you—who is often the first, and sometimes only, person who catches a glimpse of something being "not quite right." Especially if you're a first-time mom, though, it's difficult to feel secure about your new instincts. On the one hand, experts like us tell you not to get uptight because there is a wide range of "normal," and on the other your gut instinct is yelling at you to pick up the phone and call the doctor already. It's an incredibly tough decision, but it is possible to clear your head if you remember this pearl of wisdom: You don't have to be absolutely sure about what you see. Think about it . . . even trained medical professionals have to make educated guesses—*very* educated guesses, but guesses nonetheless. And even if a diagnosis is determined, how the disability will play out over time is often, well, anyone's guess.

So consult with a professional if you have any inkling that something is wrong.

In terms of spotting disabilities, there are a few warning signs that you should always bring up with your pediatrician: If your baby's body is excessively floppy or rigid; if he continually arches his back, can only use one side of his body, or cannot sit up by eight months (possibly indicating a muscle tone problem); or if he does not respond to your voice unless he sees your face (possibly indicating a hearing problem). In addition, if your baby has recurrent pneumonia, a chronic cough, or is easily bruised from crawling, bring it to your doctor's attention immediately. Because the effects of many disabilities can be drastically lessened with therapy or medical treatments, time is of the essence. Also be sure to ask your pediatrician—if you didn't do so at the hospital—what screenings your baby had, and ask if there are others that may not be mandatory but are important. Newborns in forty-five states and the District of Columbia are now given mandatory hearing screenings before they leave the hospital, for example, but many experts agree that all children should be tested. When in doubt, just follow this ironclad rule: If you think you need to call your pediatrician for a consultation, then you need to call your pediatrician for a consultation. It's as simple as that. And if you continue to notice a problem, pester your physician for a follow-up or ask for a referral to a specialist. In fact, demand a referral to a specialist. You've got the right to do so.

Making a Plan, Moving Forward

Once you have been given a diagnosis or at least have an idea of the area of impairment, you may be consumed with an overwhelming urge to solve the problem or to just make it go away. Some parents throw themselves headlong into medical textbooks and consult teams of doctors and therapists, while others who are perhaps overwhelmed with other family responsibilities or financial burdens may back away and allow the pediatrician to determine a course of action. And as experienced moms of special-needs kids can tell you, neither reaction is totally right or wrong. The best path, say moms who have been there, is one that allows you to take care of your baby's needs without losing a grip on your life. Even if you devour all the literature you can get your hands on or call your doctor every day, for instance, you aren't guaranteed to completely understand the disability or know what the best treatment will be for your child. Don't get us wrong: You don't want to be passive about your baby's health, and being informed and as involved as is practical is essential. But it's also necessary to realize that caring for a baby with a disability is an ongoing *process*. One that changes, sometimes for better, sometimes for worse. And as one mom of a now-four-year-old with special needs tells us, accepting this will ease your anxiety and allow you to focus on your baby—indeed, to get excited about your baby—for the person he is at any given moment. We realize that it may be impossible to reach this elevated state of awareness, particularly during the first year when you're desperate for solutions and filled with anxiety about the future (feel free to yell out loud at this book: "Oh yeah? Why don't *you* accept it!"). But we're not putting this out there to tell you everything will be okay or that you should feel grateful. We pass it along knowing that you may actually find solace knowing that it is within the realm of possibility to reach a level of acceptance of (read: not resignation to) your baby's disability.

Well before this happens, though, you will simply want to understand what is happening with your baby. The good news is that you can expect a lot of hand-holding from specialists, social workers, and government agencies to explain medical terms (though you will soon become surprisingly literate on that front), set up appointments for evaluation and any necessary therapies, as well as steering you through follow-up care. Again, if you don't think you are getting enough help, don't hesitate to call your local department of health or pester your pediatrician. They may also be able to offer tips on dealing with your insurance to make sure that you are either covered or can receive free services. In fact, all states offer free services for babies with disabilities, usually through the Department of Health & Human Services. Check your state's Web site or go to the national Web site at dhhs.gov.

In addition, you can contact your local Social Security office to apply for Supplemental Security Income (SSI), a federal Social Security cash benefit available to a disabled individual who has financial need. A parent's income is used to determine eligibility for all applicants under the age of eighteen. Recipients of this benefit also receive Medicaid.

The type of therapy you pursue depends, of course, on the type of disability your baby has. A baby with hearing loss, for example, may benefit from a hearing aid (children as young as four weeks can be fitted with one) as well as help from a speech-language pathologist and an early-intervention specialist. For babies with profound sensorineural hearing loss (when the hair cells in the inner ear cannot detect vibrations or neural impulses are not transmitted to the brain), a cochlear implant may be an option for kids as young as twelve months.

For babies with Down syndrome, on the other hand, surgery may be the first step (to fix a heart defect, for example), and then physical and occupational therapies would follow to improve muscle tone and cognitive abilities. Trying to sort out all that you should be doing isn't easy, but in many cases—specifically those that concern life-threatening defects soon after delivery—the medical choice is a foregone conclusion. For other problems, you can count on plenty of informed advice from physicians and other parents in your situation.

Being Your Baby's Advocate

It's one thing for us to declare that early intervention is vital for the health and future development of your special-needs baby, but it's quite another to make sure that it happens. That's because most often the person in charge of getting your baby what she needs is you—her frequently overwhelmed, overtired, and overjoyed mother. But how the heck are you supposed to be your baby's advocate when you've just learned to spell her disability (no doubt, by typing it into a search engine)? Well, we'll tell you. Or better yet, we'll let moms who have been there do that. Many we've spoken with say it's essential to elect a point person for every task. It takes Herculean efforts to keep medical records and directives from different physicians organized, for example, so it helps if you can put one person in charge of coordinating your baby's care. This can be your pediatrician or a specialist or even you or your spouse. (FYI: Doctors tell us that they also appreciate having a point person, as it helps them avoid miscommunication with the family and other physicians.) In time, when you are settled at home, you may also want to start keeping track of everything by making binders or files for different categories, such as hospital bills or physical therapy instructions. Moreover, you will want to put together a small binder filled with emergency information and medical history to take along anytime you go with your baby on trips.

As we mentioned before, doctors are your best source for preliminary information, whether it's a pediatrician, a neonatal intensive care unit (NICU) doctor, a pediatric neurologist, or another specialist. And according to moms we spoke with, you should milk that source for all she's worth. Whether or not a doctor will welcome all of your questions or take your concerns seriously is another story. Again, don't discount your instincts. The gut is a marvelous barometer for condescension or derision. And when you have a baby with a disability, it's essential to feel comfortable with her doctor. We don't mean that she should be your best friend—just your best doctor. For example, you should be able to call her with concerns without feeling like you've walked in on her during a dinner engagement. Her responses should be professional and never dismissive. A good physician is worth her weight in co-payments if she can tactfully weed out non-issues without making you feel silly for bringing them to her attention. Bottom line: If you feel an issue needs to be pursued further or that you would like a second opinion, don't hesitate to follow through. You will not hurt a doctor's feelings, you will not be considered a "crazy mom" by other physicians, you will not be accused by anyone of being anything other than a caring, concerned mother (particularly by us). And if you are, pardon our French, that person sucks. Feel better? We hope so.

Come to Your Own Emotional Rescue

Receiving the news that your baby has a disability, no matter how mild or severe, can be devastatingly brutal. It doesn't matter if it's a complete surprise, if you always suspected something might be wrong, or if you have the nicest ob-gyn in the business delivering the diagnosis. The instant you hear it, everything you took for granted about your life and your future becomes unmoored, including all of those daydreams you harbored. How does a parent recover? Some parents throw themselves into finding out all they can about the disability, others seek second, third, and fourth opinions, while still others may rely on friends and family for support with the logistics of daily life. No matter what course of action a parent takes, however, all can expect to face an oppressive grief.

It may come cloaked in sadness, in anger, or in guilt, and it may seem impossible to jettison. One mom we know who has identical twins with cerebral palsy says that it's nearly impossible to describe her experience, but one thing she has no trouble explaining is that grief is not a onetime deal. You don't "go through it" and then suddenly find yourself blessed to be on the other side. It's a constant companion that may or may not decide to ruin any given day. Another mom with a child who had a cochlear implant says that no matter what emotions you feel, particularly in the early months after the diagnosis, you can expect them to be incredibly intense and raw, and you shouldn't be surprised if you cry or lose your temper. Every day. You may even feel guilty for feeling grief at all, because as the mom of twins tells us, part of the grief is selfish—you are grieving for what you won't be doing in the future. We're passing on this bit of wisdom because it's important to realize that feeling grief is not the same as feeling rejection for your child. Indeed, it may be necessary to grieve for an imagined future before you can embrace the real one lying before you.

Experienced moms and experts will also tell you that it's essential to reach out to family and friends. Those first days and weeks after delivery are exhausting for every mother, but if you have a baby with a disability you can count on shouldering a much larger workload. Not only do you need to take care of your baby and yourself, you need to direct her care, find out what medical interventions may be necessary, talk with specialists, and deal with insurance paperwork, not to mention breaking the news to family and friends. To tackle all of this without losing your mind, make sure you do three things: delegate, delegate, and delegate some more. Even if you were operating on eight hours' sleep, you would feel overwhelmed with the avalanche of tasks dumped in your lap. So do yourself a favor and spread out the weight of your burden to those you trust.

Relationships

To state the obvious, caring for a baby with a disability is a tremendous adjustment for your entire family. You can expect everyone to have different reactions to the news, and like your own, those reactions may change any given day, or hour, or minute. It's only natural and, therefore, only fair that you should allow everyone their feelings. But you may wonder why you have to be fair. Why is it your job to field insensitive comments from a friend ("At least he can breathe and eat on his own . . ."), or explain your choice of medical therapy to your in-laws, or try to coax your spouse to show more affection to his baby, or listen to him complain about his stress when you're ready to put your fist through a window? Well, we're here to tell you that none of this is your job. In fact, allow us to help you clarify your terms of employment as Mom: You take care of yourself. You take care of your baby. And you do your best to care for your spouse and keep your relationships on track. You are *not* supposed to take care of everyone. And as amazing as you are, you can't be all things for all people.

Of course, you cannot shut yourself away from everyone (as tempting as this may be sometimes), but you can learn to focus your energy, your empathy, and even your anger on certain people and issues that might produce positive results, and simply ignore the rest. Trusted friends and family, for example, may have the best of intentions, but simply don't know what to say or do. It's not your job to give them a script, but your reaction can provide them with cues on what to do or say next time. From indicating that you don't have time to cook due to all the visits to specialists (which might get you a much-appreciated lasagna) to flatly stating that it is not helpful to hear that you should feel grateful or that God only gives you what you can handle (which will stop them from going that route again), you can let people know what's appropriate. They may never understand what you are going through and may continue to say idiotic things, but at the heart of it, they probably want what's best for you and your baby, so do your best to let them know what that is and walk away. And if someone just doesn't get it, remember that taking care of that person is not your job.

One person you certainly don't have to make understand is your spouse. He probably knows better than anyone else what you are experiencing, and so he may be your best helpmate. Or, he may not. As we've said, everyone reacts in his own way, and your husband's way may not jibe with your own, so you can expect your marriage to waver under the strain of a new baby—in fact, we don't know anyone who during that first year looked at her spouse with undying love every day. (Sometimes she can't look at her spouse at all.) But regardless of ups and downs you experience, you and your husband need to reach a common understanding of how you are both feeling and what aspects of your baby's care either of you should handle. He may not want to talk about things—and how many men do?—but that doesn't mean your spouse isn't interested in his baby's well-being. It could be that he doesn't see the point of talking—and how many men do?—and what he is really after is a sense of control, of being able to solve the problem. As we've mentioned, this may not be possible. However, your husband may be able to spearhead aspects of his baby's care, such as tackling the insurance paperwork or contacting specialists for appointments, which may take away some of the helplessness he feels. Whatever he takes on, be sure to remind him that you are each other's best source of solace, and that if the relationship suffers neither of you can give your best to your baby. If you find, however, that communication is becoming more difficult, you may want to consider family counseling, even if you are the only one who agrees to attend in the beginning.

Common Disabilities

Disability: **Autism spectrum disorders (ASD)**
What It Is: A group of developmental disabilities impairing social interaction, communication, behaviors, and learning.

Who Has It: The Centers for Disease Control estimates that 1 in 150 kids have ASD. It is more common in boys than girls.

What Causes It: No one root cause, but studies point to genetic links.

Common Treatments: A variety of therapies, depending on the area of impairment. These may include special education, speech-language therapy, physical and occupational therapy, and applied behavior analysis (ABA), which uses a system of rewards to teach an autistic child new behavioral skills. Another commonly used therapy is known as Floortime; here, a child is first engaged with toys or other items she likes and then guided toward more complex interactions.

Where to Turn: The Autism Society of America, at autism-society.org; Autism Speaks, autismspeaks.org; 212-252-8584, and First Signs, firstsigns.org.

Disability: **Cerebral palsy (CP)**

What It Is: A group of chronic neurological conditions resulting in compromised muscle control and coordination, which can make the child appear either stiff or floppy. CP also causes learning, communication, and sensory problems.

Who Has It: Two to three babies per thousand have CP. Premature babies are thirty times more likely to develop CP than full-term babies.

What Causes It: Damage to or a disorder of the brain either before, during, or, rarely, after birth.

Common Treatments: A physician determines the type of CP and creates a plan of physical therapy to improve motor skills and muscle tone. In some instances, surgery or medications are deemed necessary; as the child grows, he may use a walker or wheelchair, and enhance his communication through a computerized device. He may need early intervention, special education for learning issues, and language therapy.

Where to Turn: United Cerebral Palsy (UCP), ucp.org, 800-USA-5UCP (872-5827); Children's Neurobiological Solutions (CNS) Foundation, cnafoundation.org, 866-267-5580; Children's Hemiplegia & Stroke Association (CHASA), chasa.org, 817-492-4325.

Disability: **Cleft lip or cleft palate**
What It Is: When the upper lip and/or roof of the mouth do not grow together.
Who Has It: About five thousand babies a year in the United States, with the condition being more common in Native Americans.
What Causes It: No one knows for certain, though studies point to both genetic and environmental causes, such as maternal illnesses, smoking and alcohol use, and deficiency of the B vitamin folic acid during pregnancy.
Common Treatments: One or more surgeries before eighteen months to repair the separation. More surgeries may be necessary as the child grows. Preconceptual and prenatal folic acid (four hundred micrograms or more) will reduce risk of cleft lip and palate up to 75 percent.
Where to Turn: Cleft Palate Foundation, cleftline.org, 919-933-9044; Cleft Advocate, cleftadvocate.org.

Disability: **Clubfoot (metatarsus varus)**
What It Is: A deformity of the foot or both feet, ranging in severity from a foot that points inward (metatarsus), which may not be detected until the child starts walking, to a foot that is twisted to both inward and downward (equinovarus).
Who Has It: One in four hundred babies.
What Causes It: Usually, no specific cause can be identified. In a small number of cases, prenatal illness, drugs, or genetics are thought to be the culprit. In others, brain, nerve, or muscle diseases in the baby are thought to contribute to the development of a clubfoot.
Common Treatments: Manipulation, casts, or surgeries directed by an orthopedic surgeon.
Where to Turn: March of Dimes, marchofdimes.com, 888-663-4637; American Academy of Orthopaedic Surgeons, aaos.org, 847-823-7186.

Disability: **Cystic fibrosis (CF)**
What It Is: A disease that changes the glandular secretions, causing in some cases excessive salt in perspiration and possible thick secretions in the lungs or bowels, or the inability to digest protein and fat.

Who Has It: Approximately one in sixteen hundred Caucasian babies, one in seventeen thousand African Americans, and rarely in Asians.

What Causes It: Cystic fibrosis is an inherited disease. Both parents must be carriers of the gene that causes CF for their baby to have it.

Common Treatments: Close medical supervision, daily respiratory therapy to clear mucus from the lungs, medications to prevent and treat infections and improve food absorption.

Where to Turn: Cystic Fibrosis Foundation, cff.org, 800-344-4823; cysticfibrosis.com.

Disability: **Down syndrome**

What It Is: A chromosomal abnormality that often causes mental retardation and is marked by physical traits including a low muscle tone, a large tongue, a short neck, and smaller ears, as well as other birth defects.

Who Has It: One in 733 births.

What Causes It: Most commonly, an extra chromosome passed from either the mother or the father gives a child forty-seven instead of the usual forty-six chromosomes.

Common Treatments: Early-intervention therapies to improve muscle tone and cognitive abilities, and surgery to correct heart abnormalities. Special education after three years is usually needed.

Where to Turn: National Down Syndrome Society, ndss.org, 800-221-4602; National Association for Down Syndrome, nads.org, 630-325-9112; National Down Syndrome Congress, ndsccenter.org, 800-232-6372.

Disability: **Hearing loss**

What It Is: The decreased ability to hear sounds.

Who Has It: Three to four in every thousand newborns.

What Causes It: In 90 percent of cases, there is no known cause, although genetics, toxins, infections, or other illnesses in the pregnant mother are believed to play important roles.

Common Treatments: Assessment by medical experts to determine services needed, hearing aids, speech or language therapy, or surgery.

Where to Turn: National Center for Hearing Assessment and Management, infanthearing.org; Alexander Graham Bell Association for the Deaf and Hard of Hearing, agbell.org, 202-337-5220; Starkey Hearing Foundation, sotheworldmayhear.org, 800-769-2799; Gift of Hearing Foundation, giftofhearingfoundation.org, 617-661-4327.

Disability: **Heart defect**

What It Is: Any abnormality affecting the structure or function of the heart, which may occur in conjunction with other congenital problems such as Down syndrome.

Who Has It: About 1 in 175 babies.

What Causes It: The sheer range of heart problems discounts one root cause. It has been linked to genetic abnormalities as well as environmental toxins and prenatal infections such as rubella.

Common Treatments: Medications and one or more surgeries, sometimes started before the end of the first year.

Where to Turn: American Heart Association, americanheart.org; Congenital Heart Information Network, tchin.org, 215-627-4034.

Disability: **Hypospadias**

What It Is: An abnormal location for the opening of the urethra in boys, either just off center or on the underside of the penis.

Who Has It: One to three every thousand baby boys.

What Causes It: There is no known cause.

Common Treatments: One or more surgeries to reconstruct the urethra (often using the foreskin of the penis) and create a new opening.

Where to Turn: The Society for Pediatric Urology, spuonline.org, 978-927-8330.

Disability: **Fetal alcohol syndrome**

What It Is: A group of symptoms, including low birth weight, physical deformities, damage to the nervous system, and compromised learning and behavioral abilities.

Who Has It: One in 750 births.

What Causes It: Alcohol consumption during pregnancy, especially chronic or occasionally excessive use.

Common Treatments: Physical or occupational therapy, speech-language therapy, special education, behavioral treatments.

Where to Turn: National Organization on Fetal Alcohol Syndrome, no fas.org, 202-785-4585; Centers for Disease Control and Prevention, cdc.gov/ncbddd/fas.

Disability: **Klinefelter's syndrome (XXY syndrome)**

What It Is: A chromosomal condition that adversely affects male sexual development.

Who Has It: One in every five hundred to a thousand males.

What Causes It: An extra copy of the X chromosome, which is not inherited but a random result of an error during cell division (nondisjunction).

Common Treatments: Hormone injections beginning after a boy is eleven or twelve years old.

Where to Turn: Klinefelter Syndrome and Associates, genetic.org, 888-999-9428.

Disability: **Muscular dystrophy—Duchenne or Becker**

What It Is: The muscular dystrophies (MD) are a group of more than thirty genetic diseases characterized by progressive weakness and degeneration of the skeletal muscles that control movement.

Who Has It: Between four hundred and six hundred boys are born with Duchenne or Becker MD in the United States each year.

What Causes It: Duchenne MD is the most common form and primarily affects boys. It is caused by the absence of dystrophin, a protein involved in maintaining the integrity of muscle. Onset is at between three and five years old, and the disorder progresses rapidly. Children with Becker MD (which is very similar to but less severe than Duchenne MD) have faulty or not enough dystrophin. There are different congenital (present at birth) forms of MD, as well, though these are more rare, and they may affect both cognitive development, with degrees of mental retardation, and/or muscle strength.

Common Treatments: Physical therapy, respiratory therapy, speech therapy, orthopedic appliances, and corrective orthopedic surgery. Drug therapy may include corticosteroids to slow muscle degeneration, anticonvulsants to control seizures and some muscle activity, immunosuppressants to delay some damage to dying muscle cells, and antibiotics to fight respiratory infections.

Where to Turn: Muscular Dystrophy Association, mda.org, 800-344-4863; Muscular Dystrophy Family Foundation, mdff.org, 800-544-1213.

Disability: Pyloric stenosis

What It Is: A thickening of muscle that narrows and blocks an area of the stomach (the pylorus) leading to the small intestines, causing forceful vomiting.

Who Has It: One in two hundred boys; one in a thousand girls.

What Causes It: No known cause.

Common Treatments: Surgery to cut the thickened muscle and relieve the blockage.

Where to Turn: March of Dimes, marchofdimes.com, 888-663-4637; Centers for Disease Control and Prevention, cdc.gov: American Pediatric Surgical Association, eapsa.org.

Disability: Rh disease

What It Is: A condition in which antibodies from the mother attack her baby's blood during pregnancy or during labor and delivery.

Who Has It: Four thousand newborns in the United State each year.

What Causes It: If a baby inherits her father's blood type and it is incompatible with her mother's, her mother's antibodies will consider the baby's blood type foreign and attack the blood cells in the fetus.

Common Treatments: Prenatal shots, if the condition is diagnosed during pregnancy, or a vaccine can be given within three days of the birth. A complete blood transfusion (called an exchange transfusion) for the baby shortly after birth may be necessary.

Where to Turn: March of Dimes, marchofdimes.com, 888-663-4637.

Disability: **Sickle-cell anemia**

What It Is: A disorder that affects hemoglobin, a protein that enables red blood cells to carry oxygen to all parts of the body, causing them to "sickle" or become crescent-shaped and die prematurely. Those affected are more vulnerable to infection, episodes of severe pain, and swelling of the feet and hands.

Who Has It: One in five hundred African American newborns and one in a thousand to fourteen hundred Hispanic American babies.

What Causes It: A mutation of the gene that produces hemoglobin, which is inherited from both parents.

Common Treatments: Iron supplements directed by a doctor; frequent checks of iron levels; medication or hospitalization to relieve pain; and sometimes full blood transfusions.

Where to Turn: Sickle Cell Disease Association of America, sicklecelldisease.org, 800-421-8453; Sickle Cell Information Center, scinfo.org, 404-616-3572; National Heart, Lung, and Blood Institute Information Center, nhlbi.nih.gov, 301-592-8573.

Disability: **Spina bifida**

What It Is: A congenital abnormality in which the spinal bones fail to close during gestation, causing damage to the development of the spinal cord and sometimes brain.

Who Has It: One in two thousand births.

What Causes It: No known cause, though heredity is thought to play a role. Preconceptual and prenatal vitamin supplements with folic acid (four hundred micrograms per day or more) lower the risk of spina bifida by 75 percent.

Common Treatments: Surgery within the first few days to close the opening in the spine. Later surgeries may be necessary to drain fluid buildup on the brain (hydrocephalus) or correct physical abnormalities of the hips, knees, and feet. Medication for bowel and bladder control.

Where to Turn: Spina Bifida Association of America, sbaa.org, 800-621-3141.

"Our son failed the birth screening for hearing and I remember a nurse saying to me, 'Your baby is deaf. Get ready for deaf school.' And I just broke down. I remember running to call my husband on the phone and freaking out, telling him that our baby was deaf. We called a specialist to make an appointment, but they kind of said not to worry because 90 percent of newborns fail their hearing screening. So we were optimistic, thinking 'Okay, he's probably fine.'

"Initially I think we were in a kind a denial. Everyone is so supportive or politically correct, no one is going to tell you, 'Gee, your child seems verbally delayed.' People kept telling me, 'Einstein didn't talk until he was four.' If I heard that once, I heard it a thousand times. When we went for a follow-up we were told that our son could hear in one ear, which was a relief. Then one day in the park when my son was twenty-one months old, I met a woman who had a child the same age as mine. We were talking and found out that we delivered in the same hospital, on the same day, within hours of each other. While we were talking a helicopter flew overhead and I saw that her child was upset by the commotion and lots of other kids were as well, but my son was sitting there happily playing.

"After that, we got a CT scan and I remember a nurse told me, 'Your boy's in trouble,' and when I asked why she said, 'You'll see.' It turned out that he was profoundly deaf in both ears. After that it was like I went through a period of mourning, because the baby I thought I had was gone—that feeling hit me at the strangest times. Soon, my husband and I started researching online and had to make a decision whether our child was going to be in the deaf world or if we were going to try the cochlear implant, and we decided to have the surgery done. Now our son is three and doing very well."

—*Dimity, New York, New York*

"We were told something could be wrong with one of our twins fourteen weeks into the pregnancy. My doctors decided as a team that it was actually necessary for our babies to come early because they knew our son would probably need surgery. When they were delivered at thirty-five weeks we found out that our son's stomach and small intestine were not connected (our daughter was fine). There was little time to process what was going on. Surgery didn't cross my mind until we were told by the NICU that he would have to have it as soon as the doctors could perform it. I couldn't hold him and didn't get to see him until twelve hours later and five minutes before his surgery. Signing off on something that could take my child and knowing that if I didn't he would die anyway was horrible. To make matters worse, my husband was home with our two oldest. Luckily my mom and grandmother were with me. They made sure my daughter got to be with me as much as possible and thankfully she could go home with me.

"He spent twenty-six days in the NICU. It was a crazy month. We live about forty minutes away from the hospital so someone would make the nightly trip to see him. We met a lot of wonderful parents who were going through something along the same lines and it helped to talk.

"The thing that surprised me the most was how much I fell in love with this little baby that had all these tubes coming out of him. He was mine and I loved him no matter what he looked like. At the same time you just say a prayer whenever you can in hopes that heaven above would let you get to know this little baby.

"Our lives have completely changed. Having three healthy kids and one sick little baby is hard. There have been many ER trips; we had to learn about a feeding tube, keep track of between five and ten medicines at a time, see doctors up to five times a week, and learn that there a lot of very uneducated people in this world (including our own family members). Our son is smaller than his twin and it is pointed out on a daily basis to us (like we don't know). Sometimes the comments are more than I can bear. It hurts enough to go through everything we have gone through. We just try to remain positive and hopeful. We have the best doctors in our town and they (and their staff) have made sure he gets the best care. We have great friends and the majority of our family is great (they ran out and got flu shots without us even having to ask!). We have no idea if our son will ever be off his medicine and he has a very difficult time eating food right now. Only time will tell what's going to happen with him."
　　　　　　　　　　　　　　　　　　　　　—*Erin, Batavia, New York*

(continued on next page)

"When I found out I was pregnant with my third child, it was old news: been there, done that, or so I thought. Little did I know that I was in for the ride of my life. At seven weeks I had my first ultrasound and that evening my doctor called me to tell me that I was being put on modified bed rest. The placenta was not fully attached to my uterine wall, so I was bleeding into my uterus and there was a huge chance that I could lose the baby. Suddenly I couldn't play in the park with my other kids, then five and two, or pick up my two-year-old, or even stand long enough to cook a meal.

"By seventeen weeks I had a complete placenta previa and the doctors also thought they saw a problem with the baby's brain. We learned she was a girl, and I ended up in the hospital with preterm labor. The doctors tried different medications, which weren't stopping my contractions. I was twenty weeks and three days into my pregnancy. The doctors tried a last-ditch effort to stop my labor and put me on magnesium sulfate. Within four hours my contractions stopped. The doctors, however, were undecided on how far they should go to save my baby. One doctor actually told me that this was my body's way of trying to rid itself of an imperfect fetus, and I should let them take my baby and go home and take care of my other kids. I chose to fight for my daughter's life.

"The next fourteen weeks were spent on complete bed rest, with a few trips to the hospital thrown in for more episodes of preterm labor, and twice-weekly doctor visits and biweekly ultrasounds. From the ultrasounds, we learned that our daughter had a cyst in her brain that would possibly need to be shunted after birth, and also had a very small head—the growth of her head was five weeks behind the rest of her body. The doctors were also still unsure as to whether or not the portion of her brain that they hadn't been able to find was there. We were told these things about our unborn daughter, but we were never told to prepare for a special-needs child.

"At thirty-five weeks and two days' gestation, she was born weighing four pounds, eleven ounces. I was allowed to hold her for a minute or two before she was whisked away to the NICU. Because I was bleeding heavily, it was seven hours before I was stable enough to be moved and able to go to the NICU to see my brand-new baby girl. I was crying hysterically because all I wanted was to be with my baby, and I had sent my husband with her so she wouldn't be alone. The nurse went down to the NICU and took a photo of her for me, and my mom stayed with me trying to calm me down, but worse than not being with my new baby was also not knowing if she was okay.

"When I finally got to see her, she was hooked up to all these tubes and wires, and had an IV for nutrition. And she was so *small*. But she looked okay. She thrived in the NICU. When I went home from the hospital without her, I cried. I even got up in the middle of the night that night and drove back to the NICU because I couldn't stand being away from her. It just didn't feel right to come home without my baby. She was in the NICU for ten days, and on the day before she came home, a Friday, she had an MRI done to check on her cyst, and to see what was *really* going on with her brain. I was positive that everything would be fine. She was doing much better than the doctors had expected already, and she took to breastfeeding like a champ.

"Because it was a Friday afternoon when her MRI was done, the results weren't available until after the weekend, but she was doing so well they let us take her home. Ignorance is such bliss. Her two-week checkup was scheduled for the following week, and it was there that we learned the results of her MRI. Our perfect-looking little angel had lobar holoprosencephaly, or HPE for short. HPE is a very rare birth defect in which the brain does not completely divide. Our pediatrician even had to look up the diagnosis in one of her medical books when she told me. When I did more research, what I found was absolutely terrifying. A lot of the information out there is very out of date, and I was sure that my baby had been given a death sentence. One article I read even said that most children born with this defect, if they survive birth, usually die within one year.

"Doctor's appointments were made, and we were referred to pediatric specialists including a pediatric neurologist, the closest of which was three and a half hours away from the town where we live. We were referred to all kinds of services for children with disabilities. While I dealt with all the appointments and the day-to-day care for our daughter, my husband went into denial. He refused to even talk about what was going on; for him if he didn't acknowledge it, it didn't exist.

"Slowly we learned more about HPE, and that our daughter was lucky to have one of the mildest forms of the disease. There was even a

(continued on next page)

chance that she would be able to walk and talk, which according to a lot of the previous research I had done was highly unlikely. The information I had found painted a bleak picture of a child who would be a vegetable. But my 'vegetable' is eight months old now, and already doing more than most doctors ever thought would be possible. Her brain is partially fused, and some parts are missing. She has a feeding tube placed permanently into her stomach, has spastic cerebral palsy; we have to watch her fluid intake and output to make sure her sodium levels aren't too high, and we have to test different levels in her blood fairly regularly. She has four different medications that she takes daily, some of them multiple times each day. She also cannot tolerate large amounts of formula at one time, so she is on a continuous slow drip of formula through her feeding tube. If the power goes out, it's a crisis for us. If the temperature gets too hot, or too cold, it's another crisis. When she was two months old, we had a problem with our air-conditioning system breaking—on a weekend that it was 117 degrees! We had to take the baby to different family and friends' houses every day and night to avoid her having seizures.

"But despite everything, she is also a beautiful happy child. Even when she is horribly sick she grins and laughs. She knows who her parents and siblings are, and she's even starting to say 'Dada.' She has a favorite color—red—and a favorite blanket—her fleece one with the frogs on it. She hates being ignored, and loves to be held. And cleaning out her ears gives her a look of enraptured bliss over her face that is just too sweet and adorable.

"Yes, my life has changed; now it revolves around doctors' appointments, hospitalizations, and therapies, just as much as it revolves around cleaning, paying the bills, and spending time with my older kids. But my special baby shows me every day what true joy is. She shows me how to fight, and inspires me to reach for more than I am already capable of. She inspires me, and I am her voice. I have learned to fight for what she needs. If someone tells you no, you just have to ask again, a different way until they aren't saying no anymore. Most of all, my daughter has taught me to look at her and not see her disabilities, but to see her *capabilities*. And I wouldn't trade a minute of the joy I have had having her in my life to change her into a 'normal' baby. She could never be normal, she's extraordinary!"

—*Raina, Redding, California*

Preemies

As any parent can tell you, a successful transition to mommyhood depends a lot upon preparation: being able to wrap your mind around the fact that you will be a mom. For most of us, it takes the full nine months (sometimes a full nine more) to feel comfortable making the leap. Unfortunately, not all of us have the luxury of a forty-week gestation. Indeed, one in eight babies in the United States arrives before the thirty-seventh week (the official cutoff separating premature and full-term newborns). And according to a 2006 report, the high number of preemies indicates a real trend, with the number rising 30 percent in the past twenty years. Part of this consistent uptick in premature births may be traced to the rise in fertility treatments, as well as an increase in the average age of new moms, both of which are more likely to produce multiples—and multiples are more likely to be born premature. While some premature births can be linked to causes such as maternal illness or infection, half of all early arrivals have no known cause.

The great news is that thanks to recent medical advances, a preemie arriving as early as twenty-eight weeks and weighing at least two pounds, three ounces, has an amazing 95 percent chance of survival. Moreover, according to a Harvard University study, many preemies can "catch up" to their peers thanks to early-intervention therapies, with preemies who received extra help throughout their first three years achieving similar test scores at age eighteen as those who were born full-term. As any mom of a preemie will tell you, however, surviving and thriving may involve months and months of medical care. A study from Massachusetts General Hospital in Boston found that even mildly premature infants (those born between thirty-five and thirty-seven weeks) are more prone to developing jaundice, low blood sugar, breathing problems, and infections.

Whatever the week of delivery or however many medical complications develop, the quick shift from being an expectant mother to full-fledged one can be jarring, particularly if there was no prior warning that you would have an early delivery. We all feel confused to some degree, of course. But if you're a parent of a preemie, the adjustments go well beyond the mundane tasks of trying to get enough sleep and changing your C-section dressing. You may have to cope with making the NICU your home away from home as you conduct a vigil at your baby's isolette—often he will have to stay until he reaches his original due date, which is well beyond the day that you are discharged. You may be pumping breast milk around the clock, waiting around for permission to hold your baby or change his diaper, fielding phone calls in the middle of the night to ask permission to administer yet another blood transfusion, or coming to terms with disabilities. And then there is the daily trial of keeping it together while you watch your tiny fighter struggle to grow and thrive.

As one mom of a preemie tells us, it's no banal cliché that you will go on a roller-coaster ride of emotions. It's a pure fact. One day you'll feel positive about your baby's health—certain that you will be going home soon—and the next you're being told that your baby needs more observation and you can't stop crying. Or you'll be so tired of sitting by your baby's bedside but racked with guilt the minute you leave to take a break. There is only one feeling that you can expect to remain constant every day: the feeling of helplessness. Unlike other new moms on the maternity ward, you might not able to act on impulse and pick up your baby, hold him, feed him, or change him without a nurse's okay, and even if your baby is progressing there is always the chance for complications to arise. You'll get the daily or hourly updates and may experience dread and relief over and over again. It's no wonder that many moms of preemies say that they have trouble feeling like "real" moms until well after they bring their babies home. Of course they *are* real moms, but that fact can feel far removed from the truth of their daily emotions.

So once again we'll say that while information is essential—learning as much as you can about your baby's condition can only improve your ability to care for him—you need to gather emotional support as well. Obviously your partner, family, and friends will want to be there for you, but sometimes they can't give you what you need, either because they, too, are reeling from the experience or because they simply don't know what to do. That's why it's incredibly important to reach out to other moms who are in the same situation or who are one step ahead of you. (Your local hospital or your baby's team of specialists should be able to put you in touch with a support group. You can also check out our list of Web sites on page 411, many of which offer chat rooms for parents who need advice and emotional support.) These are the parents who will speak your language— one that includes words like *bronchodilator, intubation,* or *CPAP* (continuous positive airway pressure)—and they may even be able to enhance your vocabulary with words they learned while caring for their preemies. They may also be able to help you figure out how to clear logistical hurdles, such as how to extend your maternity leave or ask for time off from your job, how to keep on top of insurance claims, or, if you have other children, how to keep their daily lives on track while you go back and forth from the hospital. It's also just nice to find a person who knows what you're experiencing, and who doesn't have to be coached about what to say or how to act. With all the complicating factors, from medical to emotional, learning to be the mom of a preemie can be painfully slow. And while we can't speed up the process, we can help you prepare yourself for the experience. Here's what you need to know.

Life in the NICU

The first time you walk into a neonatal intensive care unit, you may be overwhelmed by the strangeness of the place: the dim lights, the softly beeping monitors, the intricate webs of wires at every isolette (incubator), the teams of nurses attending to their charges. And, of course, you may be disturbed by the fact that one or more of the teeny-tiny lovelies housed there belongs to you. The sight of your baby may also take you by surprise, particularly if he was whisked away soon after delivery for emergency care.

In addition to being incredibly small—some babies can fit into the palms of their parents' hands—your baby may appear scrawny and his skin translucent and wrinkled, all because he hasn't developed a critical layer of fat. This is also why your baby may need to stay under warming lights. And because normal reflexes have yet to develop, your newborn may seem inactive, but rest assured he is expending energy. Much of it may be spent on breathing, which—depending on how small he is—may be extremely labored. He may also seem very quiet, because his immature lungs aren't ready to deliver a full-throated cry just yet. The most disconcerting sight, however, is all the medical devices that may be connected to your child. He may be under a plastic hood, have a feeding tube in his nostril and stomach, and have monitoring wires taped to his body. But believe it or not, over time even this aspect will become familiar.

With each visit you will acquire a degree of comfort in the NICU, even as your fear for your baby's health remains a constant companion. Soon you will know the nurses by name and by which shift they work, as well as the neonatologists on staff. You'll also learn which nurse will welcome your requests to hold your baby and which will be annoyed. You'll even become used to your baby's small size. As one mother tells us, after spending months visiting her baby in the NICU, she would be startled when she saw healthy, full-term babies ("they looked gigantic!"). You should expect help from the nurses as to when and how you can touch your baby—and if no one volunteers, be sure to ask! They may show you how to massage or change him without dislodging any wires or how to lift and hold him, and you may receive tutorials on how to do infant CPR. None of this familiarity alleviates the desire to get your baby the hell *out* of the NICU. But at least knowing how to navigate your way around can make you feel more in control of your experience.

Family and friends can also peek in, even if they can't visit your baby in the NICU every day. Many hospitals offer a video visiting service, allowing those invited to log on and see pictures of your beautiful baby. Or you might want to upload shots of your baby to a photo-sharing site and give friends and family a password to access it (examples include caringbridge.com, flickr.com, kodakgallery.com, and shutterfly.com). Keeping your family connected not only gets them acquainted with your baby, but also allows them to understand a bit more of what you and your husband are going through. Another way you can reach out to your circle of support if you feel up to it is to have a good friend organize a small baby shower. If you delivered before you could enjoy one, you may feel that you missed your chance, but it's never too late to get a gift. It can be a small affair—and obviously, you'll only want to do it if you feel comfortable setting up the new nursery before the baby arrives home.

Nourishing Your Baby, in Body and Soul

You may not know how to run an IV, attach an endotracheal tube, or even be able to pronounce *endotracheal,* but you can bond with your baby, whether it's by holding him skin-to-skin or taking an active role in feeding him. It may not be the experience you imagined—in fact, we can tell you that it won't be—but it can be a positive one for both of you. And just in case you skipped the first ten chapters of this book, let us tell you that neither breastfeeding nor bonding skills magically fall into any woman's lap no matter when she delivered her baby. (Truth be told, the flip side is often true: She learns them both by the seat of her pants.) The difference with being a preemie mom is that you are bonding despite extended physical separations or, in cases of critically ill babies, almost complete isolation. Add to that the different nutritional concerns for premature babies and their difficulty or inability to feed from a nipple, and it may seem like breastfeeding and bonding are reserved only for mothers of full-term babies. There are major roadblocks, to be sure, but many can be overcome with the proper medical guidance, a supportive husband or friend, and a whole lot of steely maternal will.

Even if you haven't thought of nursing or thought it was impossible, your doctor may urge you to pump anyway. Babies who arrive before the thirty-week mark will not have developed a sucking reflex and therefore cannot be successfully placed on the breast. A preemie can be fed pumped milk through a nasogastric tube, however. Experts agree that a mother's breast milk is the best balance of nutrients a baby can receive as well as the most easily digested and most conducive to absorption of essential fats. In fact, research has shown that mothers who delivered early actually produced a milk higher in proteins and calories for the first few weeks. For some moms, however, breastfeeding may not be their choice or even possible, in which case a baby formula made specifically for premature babies is the best option.

Once you figure out what to feed your baby, the question is how. If you decide to breastfeed, a trained nurse or lactation consultant can help you get started, and depending on your baby's condition you may be able to hold and feed him. You may have to wake your baby to feed, as preemies sleep more than other newborns and easily get tired, or you may have difficulty achieving a good latch because he has a weak sucking reflex. Dr. William Sears recommends easing a premature baby onto the breast, using what he calls the "compress-and-stuff" method. With your thumb on top of your breast and your fingers underneath it, you compress the breast, touch it to the baby's mouth to get him to open wide, and then gradually ease the areola into the mouth.

If you are pumping, the hospital will provide you with a pump and store your milk, labeling it and putting it into a refrigerator until feeding times. (For the scoop on the best way to preserve your precious milk, see chapter 2, pages 70–71.) Don't worry if you don't notice any milk for a few days—as that's perfectly normal. In the beginning, your body will only produce colostrum, a yellowish substance filled with antibodies and nutrients. You may literally be giving a nurse drops of this liquid gold that you produced for your baby. After a few days, your milk will come in and you'll be on your way.

From there we wish it were a simple matter of pumping and feeding, pumping and feeding. ("And she pumped happily ever after . . ."). But any mom, even those with full-term babies, may experience trouble pumping, whether it's sore, cracked nipples or painful blocked ducts or just unbelievable fatigue. Moreover, any mom who has flipped the switch on a breast pump or started squeezing a manual handle will tell you it ain't the most heartwarming experience. It can feel clinical and even embarrassing.

And because you don't have the immediate gratification of looking at your baby while you induce lactation, the prospect of pumping is incredibly odious (giving *let-down* a whole new meaning).

There are many ways to get through this, including drinking plenty of water, using nipple cream such as lanolin, and getting a nurse or lactation consultant to help you use the pump correctly. One mom we know also says that it was very helpful when she was pumping at home in the wee hours of the morning to call the NICU and talk to the nurses, asking how her little guy did at his last feeding and what he was doing right then. Anything that will help you bond—even long distance—with your baby may give you the push you need to plug in the pump again.

If, however, there are physical or emotional reasons making you feel that you just can't do it, then you just can't do it. Huh? Did you read that right? Yep, we said that perhaps you just can't do it. And while we don't say this lightly, we won't hesitate to add fuel to the controversial fire by adding that it doesn't make you a bad mother if you stop, nor will it impede your ability to bond with your baby. You know what you can handle, and if you are pushed beyond exhaustion or find yourself pulling away from your baby because you are so frustrated, or fatigued, or in physical pain, then you probably aren't in the best shape to bond with your baby anyway. As we've said—ad nauseam by this chapter—if you don't take care of yourself, you won't be able to take care of your baby.

However, when you have a preemie, we understand that the guilt accompanying your choice may be particularly wrenching, because you are hyperaware of your baby's health. Every time they weigh the contents of your baby's diaper, you might wonder if your breast milk could have made it heavier. But this is just another instance of maternal guilt making you feel like crap, and once again this stinkin' thinkin' won't help you—and it won't help your baby.

What will help is you being there for your baby, speaking to him, caressing him, holding him, and kissing him (the forehead, the belly, the toes, be sure to ask!). Indeed, however you nourish your baby, you both will benefit from this hands-on contact. Ask the NICU doctor or nurses when you can do this and how often. Holding your baby may take some practice, however. Even if the medical staff gave you carte blanche to reach in and pick him up whenever you wanted, and you were sterilized from head to toe, you still might not know how to safely go about it. In addition to all the wires and tubes, the mattress might have a rolled blanket to keep the baby in a certain position, or he might be swaddled just so. Depending on the baby, it can take some effort to get a preemie set up in his crib so he is safe and comfortable (no wonder there are times when some staff may not be thrilled to mess up the bed), but try to find the courage to ask for close contact. For some, that will mean reaching into an isolette; for others, "kangaroo care"— holding your baby skin-to-skin, which has been shown to benefit both mother and child (and father and child, too!). Chances are the NICU staff knows about kangaroo care, and may even bring it up with you. But if not, be sure to ask. If you would like to learn more, go to prematurity.org/baby/kangaroo.html.

If it happens that you are discharged from the hospital weeks or months before your baby (and that's often the case), it doesn't mean an end to the bonding that's begun. Many hospitals allow parents to spend as much time as they like in the NICU, day or night.

WHERE TO TURN FOR MORE HELP

- American Academy of Pediatrics, aap.org, 847-434-4000.
- Children's Neurobiological Solutions (CNS) Foundation, cnsfoundation.org, 866-267-5580.
- Pathways Awareness Foundation, pathwaysawareness.org.
- March of Dimes, marchofdimes.com, 888-663-4637.
- Easter Seals, easterseals.com, 800-221-6827.
- Genetics Home Reference, ghr.nlm.nih.gov, 888-346-3656.
- Centers for Disease Control and Prevention, cdc.gov, 800-311-3435.
- Zero to Three, zerotothree.org.
- National Institue of Child Health & Human Development (NICHD), nichd.nih.gov.
- Beech-Nut Nutrition Hotline, 800-523-6633.
- Gerber Nutrition hotline, gerber.com, 800-4-GERBER.
- La Leche League, lalecheleague.com.
- Medela, medela.com, 800-TELL-YOU.
- Johnson & Johnson Pediatric Institute, jjpi.com.
- Gotmom.org, a breastfeeding resource sponsored by Avent and the American College of Nurse-Midwives (ACNM).

Life at Home

The day you hug the nurses good-bye, wish luck to the other NICU parents, and head out for home, you can expect your endorphins to be firing on all cylinders. You and your baby are finally free! You can also expect some scary bursts of adrenaline, particularly that first night when you freak out that you don't have a trained staff watching over your baby every minute. You might have had some training before you left the hospital, with the nurses watching you feed and care for your baby without helping you, and making sure that you have the correct type of car seat for her. Some parents are also sent home with a hospital apnea monitor for safety's sake. But leaving behind the NICU, you won't leave behind all of the anxiety you felt there. During those first days and weeks you may even have to return—more than once—to the hospital to treat any complications or to monitor your baby's weight gain.

Even if all is well, you will be visiting your pediatrician for regular follow-ups. The first will be a couple of days after you leave the hospital, and if there are no outstanding medical complications the main objective will be to make sure that your baby is eating and gaining weight. Perhaps the best way to do this is to rent a baby scale to use at home, so you know exact numbers and have some peace of mind. (Get one from Medela, medela.com, 800-435-8316.) You'll also be told to hold off well-wishers until your baby's fledgling immune system can handle more germs. This may be months down the road, so be ready with a tactful rebuff for well-meaning neighbors and friends. No one says that you can't visit others— bringing a thick brag book of pictures along, of course. It's a nice way to keep friends involved and improve your mental health as well.

Common Preemie Problems

Problem: **Apnea**
What It Is: Brief cessation of breathing (apnea), sometimes accompanied by slowed heart rate (bradycardia).
Treatment: A massage may stimulate breathing, or compression of a handheld bag can temporarily administer air. If spells are repeated or prolonged, a doctor may attach a CPAP (continuous positive airway pressure) device to the baby's nose or insert a tube down her throat into the lungs for mechanical ventilation. An apnea monitor attached with electrodes may

be used at home. As the baby grows, her monitor will need to be adjusted, but it's usually no longer necessary after six months.

Problem: **Bronchopulmonary dysplasia (BPD)**
What It Is: Chronic lung disease due to damage to the immature lung development after premature birth.
Treatment: Increased oxygen, supplementation of breast milk or premature infant formula with extra calories, and, occasionally, restriction of fluid or using a bronchodilator to reduce buildup of fluid and maintain open breathing tubes in the lungs. As the lungs mature and the baby gains weight, her lungs heal; the condition resolves over months or occasionally years.

Problem: **Intraventricular hemorrhage**
What It Is: A rupture of still-developing blood vessels in the brain of premature infants, with blood going into the fluid spaces of the brain, which occurs within the first few days of life.
Treatment: The bleeding usually stops quickly without treatment. Cranial ultrasounds, CT scans, or MRIs (magnetic resonance imaging, a specialized brain scan) may be used to make this diagnosis. Occasionally, the bleeding may result in blockage of fluid drainage from the brain, which leads to hydrocephalus (a buildup of fluid surrounding the brain); a surgical procedure may be needed to place a shunt in the brain to relieve pressure. The prognosis depends on the extent of bleeding and amount of other brain injury noted on MRIs.

Problem: **Jaundice**
What It Is: An excess of bilirubin (the waste from normal red blood cell breakdown) in the blood due to the inability of a baby's immature liver to process it or to blood group incompatibility (Rh factor, ABO, and others).
Treatment: Phototherapy in which a baby is placed under blue spectrum lights called bililights. Extreme amounts of bilirubin in the blood may necessitate a partial or complete blood transfusion, called an exchange transfusion. For more on treating less serious jaundice, see pages 225–26.

Problem: **Respiratory syncytial virus (RSV)**
What It Is: A virus that causes what looks like a cold, with symptoms such as coughing and inflamed mucous membranes, but which may cause difficulty breathing or become a serious lung infection in very young infants. Premature infants are especially susceptible to this virus.
Treatment: Antiviral drugs or treatment of the symptoms. A preventive measure is the Synagis vaccine, which insurance should cover; it's recommended for premature infants during winter months. (For more information, go to synagis.com.)

Problem: **Respiratory distress syndrome (RDS)**
What It Is: A common condition in which a baby has difficulty breathing caused by a lack of elasticity in her lungs.
Treatment: Tubes inserted in the nose or mouth or extra oxygen via an oxygen hood administer continuous positive airway pressure (CPAP) and may be necessary to prevent the lungs from collapsing. Given time and treatment, most babies develop normal elasticity. In severe cases, a heart-lung machine may be used to provide support. Premature infants are much more vulnerable to RDS than full-term infants.

Problem: **Retinopathy of prematurity (ROP or retrolental fibroplasia)**
What It Is: Damage to the retina, perhaps caused by an imbalance in the blood's oxygen level or extreme prematurity.
Treatment: Examination by a pediatric ophthalmologist. If progression of ROP is observed, surgery by a pediatric ophthalmologist may be required to prevent blindness.

"WHAT NOBODY TOLD ME ABOUT HAVING A PREEMIE"

"My little Sophia Rose came into the world five weeks early at four pounds, six ounces. It was our first child and it was like weathering a hurricane when the weathermen only predicted a small chance of showers. It started with a partial placenta abruption at thirty-four weeks, and I spent my last week of pregnancy in the hospital listening to the heart monitor twenty-four hours a day and praying they would let me get up and take a shower. I'll never forget the sound of that monitor—it was like a horse galloping away. It would get louder and softer, faster and slower, and I couldn't tune it out except when I'd hear women in labor screaming. It always seemed I'd hear a screamer about the time my food would arrive and I couldn't eat because I would be crying for them (and for me since I was totally petrified about labor).

"When after a week in the hospital it was evident that the baby wasn't growing well inside me it was time to get her out. It took twenty hours of Pitocin-induced labor, two epidurals that didn't help much, and forty-five minutes of pushing before I was wheeled in for my C-section. Sophia, as small as she was, just wouldn't come out! When I first laid eyes on her I couldn't believe how small she was: like the size of my husband's hand. I tried to breastfeed her but my breast was twice (okay, three) times the size of her head. We had no idea when we'd be able to take her home and heard so many different responses from the staff—from 'any day' to 'probably by her actual due date.' She was jaundiced and spent lots of time under the lights with the little padded sunglasses on. She had wires coming out from all over, monitoring her heart rate, oxygen levels, and a host of other things I can't even remember.

"I'm happy to report she actually came home only one day after me. We had a few scares (funny discoloration of her skin below the diaper line and a weird squishy soft spot on the back of her head) and spent a few days in Boston getting advice from specialists who had multiple copies of the book *When Bad Things Happen to Good People* in their waiting room. We gladly accepted the services of an early-intervention program and they have been so helpful and supportive all along the way. Now we have an incredibly happy healthy toddler who went from not being even on the weight charts to nearing the 95th percentile in weight and height. And when I had her sister two years later, who was born a healthy eight pounds, fifteen ounces, at thirty-nine weeks, I realized for the first time what it's like to be nine months' pregnant!" —*Andrea, Byfield, Massachusetts*

"My son was born at thirty-five weeks. Not terribly premature, but he developed an infection (I was group B strep positive) and was transported several hundred miles away to a regional facility with more specialized equipment for preemies and hospitalized for three days. On top of this, I was sick. My son was premature because I had pre-eclampsia and HELLP Syndrome (hemolysis, elevated liver enzyme

(continued on next page)

levels, and a low platelet count). My blood pressure was sky-high, my liver was failing, and I was so anemic I was as white as the hospital bedsheets. As hard as it is to cope with a sick newborn when you're well, it's exponentially more frustrating to be unable to leave your hospital room without a wheelchair and adult escort.

"Prematurity is not what I expected. It changes everything—all bets are off. Everything that I thought I had in my power to control was no longer within my reach, and this loss of control was frightening. Some of the doctors and nurses who cared for our baby didn't have many people skills in relating to grown-ups, so sometimes I felt shut out and isolated. Plus, all of my friends who had 'normal' experiences didn't know how to relate to my experience.

"Here's what I'd tell any mom who has a preemie: Get help anywhere you can. The hospital should have informational packets with the resources they have available to help you—read them. You won't be able to go through this alone, especially if you are sick, too. Learn as much as you can about your baby's condition and treatment options. That will give you a feeling of control you really need to have. If your doctor/healthcare team doesn't seem to be communicating well, ask to see the hospital ombudsman or patient representative. If there is a support group, you should definitely take part. Just to be around other parents who understand is comforting, even if you don't participate much. You can do it!"   —*Denise, Hugo, Colorado*

"After having a perfectly uneventful first pregnancy we planned our second to be exactly two years apart from our first, but at twenty-nine weeks I was out on a walk with my son and my water broke (but no labor). I had to stay in the hospital for five weeks on all kinds of medicines to delay labor, steroids to strengthen the baby's organs in case he did come early, and antibiotics to prevent infection in my uterus because there was now a hole in the amniotic sac. Then one morning during a routine sonogram reading I started having contractions—I was in labor at thirty-four weeks.

"When the delivery was over, instead of getting to hold my son, he was brought to me very quickly with a very tiny oxygen mask on because he was having trouble breathing and they needed to get him to the NICU. I had to stay in the hospital an extra three days because of an infection, and I wasn't able to go see my son because I had a low-grade fever.

"Finally, I was able to visit him just before I left the hospital. It is the most horrible thing to see your baby hooked up to machines with tubes coming out everywhere. He was born with pneumonia because the infected amniotic fluid got into his lungs so he stayed in the hospital for two weeks (which is not that long for a preemie). It's the hardest thing in the world to leave a hospital without your baby, but it did give me some much-needed time to prepare for him coming home, and to bond with my older son.

"I went to the hospital every day to breastfeed and hold him. But it still wasn't enough, because I had to leave knowing that while I wasn't there a nurse was taking care of my son, feeding him, changing him, bathing him, during an important bonding time for a mother and baby! When the day came that I got to bring him home, it was like all was right in the world again . . . except that he was now used to quiet and lack of movement from being in an incubator! Every time I moved him to change his diaper or his clothes or flip him over he screamed like I was hurting him! Now my son is a healthy fourteen-month-old who started walking last month. He is doing things late, but they are right on time for his gestational age (if he had been born when he was supposed to be!)."

—*Melody, Deer Park, Texas*

"I went into preterm labor at twenty-five weeks. After arriving at the hospital, I defiantly announced to the staff that I was *not* having this baby tonight. Two hours later, my second child, Lex, arrived, weighing just under two pounds. It was a bumpy twelve weeks in the NICU. At six days old, he perforated his bowel and had to be rushed to surgery. He was given an ostomy (hard to look at, even harder to smell). Every day we were told that it was 'touch and go' and that we should be prepared for that. At home, I diligently pumped breast milk every few hours, day and night, to freeze for him at home and at the hospital for the day when he would actually be allowed to eat. I was a zombie . . . and thankfully, my husband was my rock. He would remind me that we should cherish every minute, every day that Lex was with us—that it was a gift. My two-year-old Lauren kept me going forward. She had to eat, get a bath, go to bed . . . I could never get too wrapped up in 'what if he doesn't make it?' That was how I coped.

"Today, Lex is fourteen months and doing well. Developmentally he falls between his corrected and adjusted ages. To me, he's just my little miracle. There are great things in store for him—he has already made such a journey to get this far!"

—*Amy, Virginia Beach, Virginia*

CHAPTER 12

Different Births
Bringing Home Multiples and
Adopted Babies

Walking through the Museum of Parenting—if such a place existed—you would be fascinated by the Rare and Strange Families exhibition. There you would see oddities like a photograph of the one woman on earth who experienced a completely uneventful pregnancy, delivery, and postpartum recovery. Or you might hear weird and wonderful things, like a recently discovered recording of a husband volunteering to take over all 2 AM feedings. What you would *not* find among these rarities are families who gave birth to twins, triplets, or more. Nor would there be anything showing families bringing home adopted babies. Yes, they used to be part of this imaginary exhibition, but they were moved years and years ago. Now they're down the hall in the Everyday People exhibit.

Considering the statistics, it's not difficult to understand the switch: Although the number of parents having three or more babies has dipped slightly in the last few years—perhaps due to selective reduction or improvements in implantation procedures that are less likely to result in high-order multiples—the numbers are still hovering at record levels, in part because they rose an astonishing 404 percent between 1980 and 1997.

As for adoptions, while the annual number of adopted children in the United States has remained relatively steady (anywhere between 118,000 and 127,000), the interest in adoption has made significant gains. A 2002 survey reported that four in ten American adults considered adoption for their families and 90 percent of Americans have a favorable opinion about adoption, which is a gain of 7 percentage points since 1997. In addition, according to the U.S. Census Bureau, the number of immigrant visas granted to orphans coming to the United States for adoption increased from seven thousand in 1990 to nearly eighteen thousand in 2000. Between 1992 and 2001, in fact, the number of foreign-born adoptees rose from 5 to 15 percent of all adoptions. And while new restrictions in countries such as China and Romania have precipitated a drop in international adoptions in very recent years, the residual effect is that many Americans no longer view adoption—by either regular folk or celebrities—as something rare and exotic.

This is all great news, because the more visible these types of families are, the better chance they have to find the support and information necessary to meet their unique needs. And as a parent of multiples or an adopted baby, you already know that you *do* have very specific needs, whether it's how to go about feeding your baby, how to deal with insensitive or uneducated comments from others, or where to find other families like yours. In this chapter, we'll address these issues, along with tips from parents who have already walked a mile in your shoes. And hopefully by the end of our Everyday People tour, you'll have a much better grip on how to take in the chaos, confusion, and amazing beauty that you will experience. Every day.

Multiples

Let us guess: There you were, at the twenty-week mark of your pregnancy, lying on the table for a sonogram, and wondering if you should find out whether you had a boy or girl, when the doctor looked up and told you: It wasn't *one* of either. Or maybe after months of fertility treatments, you had the news sprung on you that—surprise!—more than one fertilized egg "took," and multiple fetuses were now happily embedded in your womb. However you made the discovery, your reaction was probably the same as other moms of multiples. Something along the lines of "Holy ____!" No doubt it took awhile for your stunned brain to compute the fact that you were not only Mom, you were Mom^2 (squared) or Mom^3 (cubed), or even more. And it was then that you realized your pregnancy, your delivery, and, let's be honest, your future would be vastly different than you had planned. Everything from the birth plan to the shower gifts was out the window, and you started reassessing what you need to handle being a mom of multiples.

The good news is that having more than one baby doesn't make you *completely* different from parents of singletons. During the first year, you will confront many of the same issues as they do: You may have a C-section scar that needs tending, a lactating body that needs hydrating, a fatigued brain that needs sleeping, or a husband that needs kicking (just kidding . . . or are we?). Likewise, your babies are not totally unique in their needs: Each of them requires adequate nutrition, periodic cleanings, plenty of rest, plenty of play, and of course lots and lots of love. As other moms of multiples will tell you, the difference isn't necessarily what needs to be done for you or your babies; it's how to go about doing it. As the saying goes—you know, the one that you'll be repeating to your kids their entire lives—*I only have two hands!* And when you are trying to keep more than one baby clean, fed, and happy, two hands just ain't enough. Truth be told, even a parent with only one baby sometimes feels woefully deficient in her anatomy, especially when her kid multitasks (such as pooping and puking at the same time, or eating food while simultaneously throwing it at the wall). But until there is a medical miracle that allows you to split like an amoeba into two or more mommies, you'll have to cope with twins, triplets, or more the old-fashioned way: with a whole lotta help and a whole lotta humor.

Postpartum Daze

Whether you delivered vaginally or by C-section, went early or made it the full thirty-eight weeks (considered full term for multiples), you'll soon realize that there is no easing into your new life. In part, because with two or more there is virtually no downtime between feedings, burpings, changings, and cuddlings. And if you are one of the many multiples' moms who have premature or low-birth-weight babies—both more common with multiple births—you may have much more to think about and less time to figure out which way is up. That's why it's important during your stay in the hospital to take advantage of more than just the room service and extra-large sanitary pads (stuff a bunch into your going-home bag). While you are there, you'll have more hands on deck than you'll ever enjoy at home, so don't be shy about asking for their help. For example, have your babies brought to you and taken back to the nursery rather than trying to do it yourself. Or, if they are in the NICU and you spend more time sitting by their beds than lying in your own, ask your husband or a family member to take some shifts. (We know. You'll ask them, then you won't agree to leave or you'll return in five minutes racked with guilt. But please try to take breaks when you can.)

Sometimes, one baby will gain weight and thrive while the other has a difficult fight, and you may find yourself bringing one baby home while another stays in the hospital. This is the best and worst of both worlds, and can be difficult to handle without others to take over some of your daily duties. Get help from neighbors or friends with hot meals so you don't subsist on pretzels or peanut butter—most people are happy to help. If you feel funny asking, get one good friend to spread the word. Also, ask the hospital staff if one baby can "visit" his sibling in his isolette, as this contact by a familiar person may be beneficial to both babies, or at least enter the NICU with your husband holding the one child. It may be easier on you, as well, because having both babies near you relieves the feeling that you are abandoning one to tend to the other(s)—not to mention that it can be difficult to find a friend to watch your other newborn for the couple of hours you may have between feedings. The bottom line is, ask for and accept help. You've probably already had plenty of people say, "If there's anything we can do . . ." The next time the offer is made, summon your inner executive and tell them exactly what you need. For instance, "Maybe you could stop at the deli and pick up a roast chicken and some salad—we'll pay, of course." They probably won't let you pay, and you shouldn't press the matter—might as well start saving now!

Mouths to Feed

One of the first tasks that might prod you to reach for the red help button on your adjustable bed is feeding your babies. Whether they receive nutrition from pumped breast milk, directly from your breasts, or from bottles of formula, you'll want some advice on how to get the food from starting point A into tummies B and C (and D and E, if you have multiple multiples). Believe us, practically everyone can use some advice on this subject. Feeding your baby seems like it should be intuitive (he cries, you nurse) and easy to understand (he opens his mouth, you insert breast or bottle). And it is. Until it's not. As you may have already discovered, it's not always easy to tell if a baby is hungry just because he's crying—a baby might cry an hour *after* he eats ("do I feed him again or does he have gas?"). And just because you tickle your baby's cheek with a nipple doesn't mean he will be enticed to turn his head and open wide. Added to that, you may experience very early on the whole "twins have individual personalities" conundrum, which gives you one baby who is a ravenous breastfeeder and another who screams at the very sight of an areola as big as his head.

The good news is that whatever your predicament, there is a workable solution. First off, since preemies will usually have weak sucking reflexes, you may have no choice but to begin by pumping and tube or bottlefeeding (see chapter 11, page 409). If you can hold your babies while you feed them, you may want to get your partner to feed one while you feed the other, or take shifts, feeding one then another (you don't have to worry about getting them in sync until you're at home without extra help). Preemies often fall asleep while eating and may not take very much at any one time. So while you may not have marathon sucking sessions, you may have to feed more often around the clock. Either way, it's common to feel that all you are doing is pumping or nursing or bottlefeeding. Sometimes it will infuse you with a glowing pride that your babies are thriving because of your efforts. Other times you'll just feel bone-crushing exhaustion and boredom from providing never-ending grist for the feeding mills that are your babies. And as many moms would tell you, both feelings are normal and usually temporary.

Once your babies have reached term or an acceptable weight and can nurse, the question is whether or not you choose to breastfeed. If you go this route, ask a lactation consultant, a trained doula, or a nurse for help achieving the proper latch. Your first question if you have twins might be whether you can feed both at the same time. *Two breasts, two mouths,* you might reason. But it can take a bit of effort to actually get both on at once. That said, it most certainly is possible, but in the beginning you may want to give both you and your babies time to adjust and get it right, because two poor latches equal two sore nipples and one seriously sore and unhappy mommy. So to start, you may be better off feeding one at a time and learning how each baby nurses. If you discover, for example, that one baby always tucks under his bottom lip or the other doesn't like to open very wide, you'll be ready to make corrections. Also, be sure to alternate the side that each baby feeds on, as one may be a more efficient feeder than another. You want both breasts to receive the same stimulation and be emptied well. (Tip: Take notes about who was where, because we can guarantee you will not remember. If your mom or partner happens to be around, they can keep notes, too, with you doing the dictating.) Once you believe you are ready to double up for the first time, grab a couple of pillows (good ones include the EZ-2-Nurse or Anna Double Nursing Pillow), and enlist your partner to be on standby as you attach one and then the other.

There are a number of tandem nursing positions to make both you and your babies comfortable, but it will likely take some experimentation to figure out what works. The first you may try—because it's the most instinctual—has both babies facing each other with bodies crossing in front of yours. If this has the babies hitting your C-section scar, however, add another pillow or try a different position. The second type puts the two heads together with their feet flanking either side of your body. You will be cradling your babies in your forearms, but will want pillows underneath their bodies for support. Finally, you could try the head-to-feet baby chain in which both babies are facing the same direction, one with his legs going across your tummy, the second with his legs tucked under your arm. It will take practice to keep babies and boobs in place, but you'll have plenty of opportunities to hone your skills every day.

Figure 12.1a The cradle hold is probably the most commonly used position when nursing one baby, so mothers of twins may find the double cradle hold, with the babies facing each other, the most natural as well.

Figure 12.1b The double football hold is ideal if you delivered by cesarean because it doesn't put as much pressure on your tender abdominal incision in the early weeks. In this position, the two babies' heads are aligned in front of your breasts, and their bodies with the feet at the rear.

Figure 12.1c A third option is to position one baby in the cradle hold and the other in the football hold.

Bottlefeeding can actually be a bit more difficult to coordinate, as your hands are occupied, but again, with the help of pillows and a friend, you might be able to find a position that works. Newborns may be small enough to face each other in your arms while you crisscross bottles, while older babies with neck control might enjoy facing out on your lap while you hold the bottles in front. While experts usually advise that you not make a habit of propping up your baby's bottle and going about your life while she suckles alone—because the nurturing interaction during feeding is nourishing, too—with multiples you may find there are times when you simply have to go this route to get everyone fed. Do what you must and ditch the guilt trip, please. (Frankly, occasional bottle propping of single-tons is certainly A-okay with us as well.) In fact, a mom of twins we know recently told us about a clever invention called the Milk Maid Baby Bottle Holder (greatbabyproducts.com), a soft, lightweight, inexpensive, foam like device that sits on the baby's lap and holds the bottle securely in position at the perfect angle. And don't forget the easiest way of all to hold and bottlefeed your babies: Have your spouse take half the feeding duty. This is also a great way for Dad to start bonding with his kids.

Now, for the times when practice doesn't make perfect, listen up: If you are breastfeeding and experiencing chronic problems, be it sore, cracked nipples, clogged milk ducts, or a fatigue that no mortal could handle, or if your pediatrician is concerned that your babies are not gaining enough weight, then you should consider supplementing with a bottle of pumped milk or formula. Get Dad involved, particularly at night so you can get some extra sleep, or perhaps during the dinner hour if you have older children whining for food. You may recover enough to continue exclusive nursing or pumping, but if you don't, do your best to swallow your unnecessary guilt and get on with bonding and bulking up your babies.

Speaking of bonding, you may wonder whether all of your babies are getting the face time they crave during meals. And unless you move your head back and forth as if you're watching a tennis match, you are sure to shortchange one of your charges. But guess what? You'll probably shortchange the other one at the next feeding. In other words, don't stress about it, because it will even out over time (even over the course of one day). If you're still worried, try to talk a bit while you're feeding. Tell each one how much you love her, or tell them the story of how you watched stretch marks travel from your back to your belly. Don't worry about content: Almost anything in a soft soothing voice will benefit all the patrons at your restaurant.

Ready, Set, Sleep!

Next to feeding multiples, the biggest obstacle the first year is getting your babies (and you!) to sleep at the same time. It's hard enough to get one baby on a somewhat predictable sleep schedule, but when you have multiples, it can seem impossible. Maybe your hungry girl has an internal dinner bell that wakes her up every couple of hours without fail, while her roommate(s) would rather snooze or fuss. Because each newborn will react differently to her environment, not to mention her gastrointestinal development, you are bound to have sleep issues. Moms and experts with multiples have a few suggestions to get everyone in sync. First, consider your sleeping arrangements. While your babies may feel soothed by having their familiar womb-buddies nearby, experts warn that co-sleeping—yes, including two babies sleeping together in one crib—increases the risk of sudden infant death syndrome (SIDS). You never know, for example, when one infant will start rolling or will have her face buried in her sibling's sleeper. Bottom line, it's not the safest option. If you want the babies in your room, consider putting one in a bassinet or co-sleeper crib and another in the regular crib so they're next to each other, but not on the same mattress. If you can't sleep hearing every whimper and sneeze, try one baby in the crib and one in a portable bassinet in the nursery. Generally, babies don't care where they are, as long as they are warm, comfortable, and in the same zip code as a boob or bottle. We don't mean you should play musical beds, which would be confusing for everyone; simply try an arrangement for a few nights in a row to see how folks settle in.

Another way to get everyone on the same page is to have group feeding times. So if one baby wakes up and another is still sleeping, gently wake the latter to eat. We know that waking a sleeping baby goes against all maternal instinct, but it's worth trying; otherwise you might find yourself feeding one after another after another, with absolutely no downtime. And if there is no downtime, guess, who loses sleep? Not your babies. If you go the group-meal route, take shifts with your partner, so that each of you is guaranteed a few hours off in a row. (Another tip: Wear earplugs and shove a pillow over your head during his shift or it will be tough to tune out what's going on in the other room, especially when one baby starts crying.)

Whenever you can get your babies to sleep, eat, and poop in tandem (because it probably won't happen with precision every single day), take that opportunity to zonk out. Dishes can wait (paper plates are wonderful inventions), as can every other household task if you have delegated them out of your otherwise occupied hands (direct bill payment plans are another wonderful invention). Buy a sleeping mask, unplug the phone, put a sign on your door that tells visitors they risk dismemberment if they so much as breathe on the doorbell—or a more diplomatic version of this sentiment. Then curl up and rest. Don't stress out if you don't actually fall asleep. Just rest. When your darlings tell you it's time for a feeding, wake up, pour a huge glass of water for yourself, and feel good that you are treating yourself to the rest you earned.

Helpmates for Everyday Life

Okay, now that you've lined up helping hands and your babies are eating and sleeping at regular intervals (feel free to laugh out loud), let's talk about the gear that will help you get through each day and maybe even out the front door. First up, stowage. Even the strongest among us needs to hit the john or make a sandwich, and you can't do either (very well) while holding a couple of babies. Enter the bouncy seat, or in your case seats. We don't know who concocted the first one—it was probably a cavemom trying out a knot in a jungle tree limb long ago—but that person was a genius. Bouncy seats are light, portable, relatively cheap, and a safe place to put your babies practically from birth. If you received one for a shower gift, get your husband to pick up another or go online and place an order. When your kids get a bit older and stronger (after about five months), you may want to consider a stationary activity center. This handy, albeit space-eating apparatus has toys and a swiveling seat to keep curious minds engaged and your hands free. Depending on your baby's personalities, however, you may only want one. Some don't care for them, while others love to spin and jump.

Next comes gear for going places. You'll have two car safety seats, of course, but you'll want the convenience of a stroller (lugging an infant car seat/carrier on each arm is just way too bulky and heavy). One type of stroller frame allows you to snap on two car seats (Snap N Go by Baby Trend, babytrend.com), which can be a lifesaver if you have twins who have fallen asleep in the car. For standard strollers, you'll obviously want a model with enough seats for everyone, but also be sure that all the seats recline—at first they'll have to lie down, and later they will want to at times. Other than that, the extra features are up to your kids' personalities and your budget. In addition to side-by-side models, there are stroller designs with seats that let the kids face each other or sit stadium-style, one higher than the other, but some moms feel these are better suited to older/ younger rather than same-age siblings. These models don't always recline as easily, and think of the hair pulling that could go on! If you live in a metro area, you may also want to look for a narrower design for fitting through tight spaces. Try out stroller models in the store, if possible, testing how easy or difficult it is to fold and unfold or steer when fully loaded. And if you'd rather keep your hands free, MaxiMom (doubleblessings. com) makes a carrier you can strap on to hold twins and even triplets.

Other than these items, the main thing is to buy in bulk (diapers, wipes, bodysuits, laundry detergent), set up changing stations around the house so you don't have to mobilize an army to fight the battle, and try not to worry about your "decor" too much. All toys and chairs and play stations really are just passing through. Later, you'll be able to sell them on eBay or set fire to them—whatever makes you feel better.

To Each His or Her Own (That Includes You)

It doesn't matter if you have identical or fraternal twins, triplets, or quads, each of your babies is an individual human being, which among other things means that they will develop in their own time. So while one may just love to roll and reach, another may like to sit and watch the show. You may already be aware of some developmental delays if your babies were born premature or had difficulties during their first weeks of life. But while you remain vigilant to significant differences in your babies' cognitive and physical growth, keep in mind that there is nothing wrong with milestones passing at different times. No siblings chart the same course and hit their milestones on the same days, but certainly bring up any concerns you may have with your pediatrician. (For a list of developmental red flags at different points during the first year, see chapter 5.)

Despite the differences, you'll have it in your head that it's important to treat them the same. But try as you might, you won't be able to. Why? Because they are not the same. The good news is that this very fact should alleviate your guilt on those days when one newborn is having gas attacks and refuses any perch but your arms while the other is looking at you like *What am I? Chopped liver?* The not-so-good-news, of course, is that there may not be one toy, food, or baby gadget that will soothe all your little people all the time. Later, when your babies' personalities really start blooming, you may start to see a pattern to their behaviors. One always smiles at strangers, the other cries hysterically, or one likes to hit her sibling on the head for fun and the other cries hysterically. Experts will tell you not to label your babies (the cranky one, the sweet one, the devil-incarnate), and we concur, with one caveat. You should not label them *out loud*. Otherwise, feel free. Seriously, even singleton moms can't help doing this. So instead of yelling at yourself to treat everyone the same, remind yourself that you *love* all of your babies equally. And it's not for all the ways that they're similar, but all the ways they are different. (FYI: Someday soon, those differences will come in handy when they start entertaining each other. Hurrah!)

As for your own personality, you've already kissed it good-bye. At least the one you had before bringing home babies. But that doesn't mean you are devoid of *any* identity. You are a multifaceted person with many different personas, from Mom to Wife to Mom to Daughter to Mom to . . . Mom. Okay, during the first year, you are mostly Mom. And until you emerge from the round-the-clock feedings, burpings, and diaper changes, you can't expect your other selves (the vivacious friend, the loving wife, the indefatigable shoe shopper) to come out to play. But don't worry, they are still there waiting to emerge, and when they do you may be surprised to find how your twelve-month stint as the über-mom has made you a more sympathetic friend, more in-love wife, and even more efficient shoe shopper.

In the meantime, whenever you go out in public with your babies, you're not just a mom, you're a celebrity mom with an inquisitive public. "Are those twins?" "Feeding them sure must be a trick!" "How can you tell them apart?" "I'd hate to see your laundry pile!" "Did you conceive natu-

WHERE TO TURN FOR MORE HELP

- National Organization of Mothers of Twins Clubs, nomotc.org, 248-231-4480.
- Twins Magazine, twinsmagazine.com, 888-55-TWINS.
- Twinsetmoms.com (one mom is *Babytalk* contributing editor Christina Boyle).
- Mothers of Supertwins (MOST), mostonline.org, 631-859-1110.

rally?" From the well meaning to the rude to the mean-spirited, you'll hear it all. No matter how common multiples are, they still manage to draw a crowd, but instead of barricading your door and refusing to come out, it helps if you expect this response. The upside is that your multiple magnets may actually attract other moms like yourself, and you'll make connections you may have missed otherwise. (By the way, here are some pat answers. Feel free to use: "Let me check: Hmm, one, two. Yup. They're twins!" "Feeding is no problem. My husband loves doing it." "We put bar codes on their feet, so telling them apart is easy." "Yes, they were conceived naturally. Were you?")

It doesn't take other people to remind you that you are a mom with multiples, however. Every minute of every day, your babies will remind you. So take this piece of advice from moms who have experienced that first-year identity crisis, even if they can't remember much of it: Take time whenever you have the opportunity to be alone and don't waste that time by feeling guilty. (They would tell you that your guilt will be there to welcome you with open arms when you return.) And as we've said before, reach out to other moms with multiples, whether through community chapters of mothers' groups or online chat rooms, because these women have the wisdom to talk you through the tough spots (see "Where to Turn" on page 429). Finally, try to take a moment each day to remind yourself that while you only have two hands, you only need one heart to hold more than enough love for everyone in your family. And that's all that counts.

Supertwins

Supertwins (three or more babies) take superhuman strength and patience. Unfortunately, none of us can fly through the air or see through lead, much less change three diapers at once. So here are some tips from moms who have survived the first year with more than two infants. The first is not just to ask for help, but to pick up the phone and line it up. Work with your partner to draft a list of chores, then match them with friends or family who might be able to get them done each week. That's right. This is not a onetime "Could you do this for me?" It's more like "Could you take in my mail for a couple of weeks?" Maybe a neighbor who likes cooking wouldn't mind making more than usual and sharing a portion with your family (offer to pay for some groceries, of course). Or perhaps you have a friend who would agree to stop over and take the 3 PM feeding every other day? Also consider your husband as part of your help posse. Why not send him off to work with a kiss and a huge bag of laundry? Most Laundromats offer a wash, dry, and fold service—some even same-day— for a reasonable price. And if your partner forgets to pick up the clothes on the way home, that's okay. Chances are you'll need him to pick up more diapers anyway, so send him back out. (Or *you* might want to take advantage of a moment out of the house.) One more thing: If it's difficult to keep identical babies straight—and it would be difficult even if you were operating on all cylinders—consider color-coding your babies' clothes to help you know who's who. In time, you'll even be able to tell which baby is hitting another without turning your head, but for now, make things as easy to see as possible.

"WHAT NOBODY TOLD ME ABOUT MULTIPLES"

"What surprised me the most was that my identical twin boys have bowel movements at about the same time. It makes perfect sense if you think about it—after all, don't they eat at about the same time? Also, how they interact is something to see—their complete under-standing of each other, their wants, needs, games known only to them. I can now understand why people think there's a psychic connection. Last but not least, the amount of sheer chaos they can create in such a short amount of time shocked me. Often they find it great fun to split up and do the exact same 'no-no' in two different rooms. Do they plan it this way? Perhaps not, but watching their mom run from room to room to try stop the unwanted behavior amuses them immensely! I have so many stories I could tell you, from trying to get them both to bed to bathtime antics to watching them both strip down to their socks (yes, the diaper was gone, too!) at the dinner table. The only advice I have for new moms of multiples is this: Rest when you can, say yes when anyone offers to help, and most of all revel in the insan-ity as they, like all children, grow up far too quickly!"

—*Janeane, Northglenn, Colorado*

(continued on next page)

"Surviving the first year with my twins is the most rewarding experience of my life to date. My husband and I learned the 'assembly line' way of doing things to keep up with bathtime, diapers, feeding, et cetera. It is frustrating when strangers make comments like 'double trouble' when really they are truly a 'double blessing.'"
—*Angelice, Baton Rouge, Louisiana*

"I had twin boys nineteen months after my daughter was born. The weekend I brought the boys home, my daughter decided it was time to use the potty. So I was trying to nurse two babies at once, while sitting on the edge of the tub for hours waiting for my daughter to tinkle. The laundry and dishes piled up. My husband returned one day from work to find me still in my pajamas, in the same recliner I was in when he left that morning, nursing one of the boys. His comment was, 'Weren't you in that same spot ten hours ago? Aren't you feeding the same baby? Have you left the chair?' No! For three months my life consisted of this: Change a diaper, nurse a twin, put the sleeping twin in the crib, grab the other twin and change his diaper, nurse him, and lay him back down. Go to the bathroom, get a drink of water, and start all over again because the other twin is now awake. Looking back I have no idea how I did it—you just do it! Once twins start acknowledging each other—playing on the floor or in the crib together—it starts to get easier. Yes, it is crazy at bath time! Yes, we eat a lot of cereal for dinner. Yes, I do laundry every night but I still find a pile somewhere that needs to be washed. Yes, my house is clean once the kids go to bed, but total chaos ten seconds after they wake up in the morning. And I wouldn't have it any other way!"
—*Emma, Berrien Springs, Michigan*

"What annoys me (and my husband and my oldest two kids) is the number of people who think they can just walk up and touch my ten-month-old twins. It is just weird because few people did this with my first two children but everyone thinks they can touch our twins. The other annoying thing is the comments about how identical they are. Here's a news flash, people: Boy and girl twins are not identical! They never were and never will be. He is a boy and she is a girl.

"The best moment was seeing them together for the very first time.

Our son had to have surgery and was in the NICU for twenty-six days, but our daughter was able to come home. We almost lost him early in the pregnancy, right after I found out I was expecting twins, and it kept going through my mind that if I hadn't known I was expecting twins and I lost one maybe it wouldn't hurt as much. I also heard comments like, 'If you lose one, you'll still have the other baby.' People do not realize how cold that sounds to the expecting mother. If a mother loses her baby—whether a singleton or a multiple—it is a baby she is losing that she will never get to know. Sometimes technology is a blessing so things can be fixed ahead of time, and sometimes technology can play with your mind if you are told something is wrong and no one can fix it.

"My husband and I have learned to brush aside people's comments, but we try to make sure we do not offend people in public. We praise all parents who have multiples, premature, or special-needs children because marriage is hard enough and extra stress does not help."

—*Erin, Batavia, New York*

"Biggest surprise: I do not have a favorite. Biggest annoyance: Other people and their inability to grasp the obvious. Example: 'Are those triplets?' Best moment: When they hug and kiss each other. Worst: The first year. I don't remember much of it, but I must have been in a time machine because I looked about fifteen years older during it. Best advice: Keep them on a schedule, don't worry about cleaning your house, and yes, you will need three thousand diapers the first year."

—*Jennifer, Indianapolis, Indiana*

Adopted Babies

In theory, bringing home an adopted baby isn't much different from stepping over the threshold with a biological offspring. Both types of parents love their babies, both are desperate to bond with them, and both are facing a future of sleep deprivation and sublime revelations. Likewise, both types of babies crave food and warmth, and thrive on unconditional affection. In practice, however, there can be a world of difference, and as an adoptive parent you may find out very early that your family is dealing with a set of problems biological moms and dads just don't have. Whether it's a dearth of medical records or family history for your baby, a disappointing reaction from your family, or a deep, nagging fear that you aren't bonding as quickly as other parents, you may feel more than slightly removed from your new-parent peers.

Fortunately, unlike previous generations of adoptive parents, you have many more options to close the perceived gap, in part because adoption is no longer considered something discussed behind closed doors. This new acceptance has opened lines of communication and fostered support groups among parents across the country who have taken your same path to parenthood. Indeed, you may have already taken advantage of local resources or checked out Internet sites to help answer any questions or just enjoy a chance to vent (and if you haven't done this, we highly recommend it!). Hurdles remain, of course, because as with all new parents, a good portion of the first year is spent trying to figure out just what your baby needs to thrive and then running to catch up whenever she jumps to the next phase of her development. But with guidance from your pediatrician, the adoption community, and a bit from us, you'll know the most common issues that may crop up, which might help you spend less time running to catch up and more time just being there and being able to enjoy your baby.

History Lessons

All babies enter the world with secrets. Some are written on their genetic code, some are embedded in their temperament, and it may take much of the first year and beyond for their parents to discover them—if they ever do—because Lord knows the kids aren't talkin'. But with adoptive babies there are often more enigmas to solve, because the many keys used to unlock the mysteries—family history, medical history, or, if you've adopted an older baby, environmental history—may be missing. Even if you have met the birth mother, seen the orphanage, or received medical records, you will always find gaps in your knowledge. And, depending on how large they are, you may feel like you and your partner are always stumbling. Unfortunately, there are no Magic 8 Balls for babies. ("Is she wailing because her tummy hurts?" "My sources say yes.") However, moms and dads with adopted kids can tell you that you're no more clumsy than other parents and, more importantly, there are things you can do to pick yourself up and move forward.

As with all parents, the most immediate concern when you first bring your baby into your family is her health. Is her body functioning as it should? Is she eating enough? Is anything causing her pain? If you are at the hospital when your baby is born, you will know (and should ask) about the newborn screenings and tests that are routine. You may also have some idea about the birth mother's medical history, which you should pass along to your pediatrician for future reference. If you know your baby was exposed to dangerous substances in utero, you should obviously bring this to your doctor's attention and start whatever medical interventions or therapies may be necessary to cleanse your baby of the toxins or temper their effects. Even without an adequate knowledge of what may have happened during gestation, you and your doctor should be vigilant, particularly if your baby was born premature, has a low birthweight, or is extremely fussy or lethargic. If you weren't present at your baby's birth but she was born in the United States, you should still have access to her medical records from the agency that arranged the adoption, including her immunization chart and background on any anomalies that were noticed or treated.

As for babies born in another country, their medical histories may be a bit more difficult to decipher, if they're available at all. You may have only a sketch of the birth mother's history and none of the father's. In addition, different countries have different newborn screening tests and immunization schedules. That's why if you haven't already, you should ask your pediatrician if he has any experience treating babies of foreign birth or can recommend someone who does. He should evaluate your baby to see if she is up to date with vaccinations, and should screen her for hepatitis B and C, HIV, parasites, syphilis, and tuberculosis. If your baby has any documented gaps in her vaccinations, if the shots were given at different intervals, or if you just can't be sure whether she received all the immunizations recommended by the Centers for Disease Control, you should talk to your doctor about doubling back and giving your baby the shots she needs. According to the American Academy of Pediatrics, it is safer to double up on a vaccination than to miss some. Even if your baby is in tip-top shape, you can expect her to contract more than the usual number of colds during her first year, as her body is being exposed to all sorts of new germs in her new environment. These will lessen over time as her immune system builds up its defenses, but for those first months at home, expect to grow quite familiar with your pediatrician's office

One word of advice: You may feel slightly inhibited about asking "too many" questions, because—like everyone else who decides to adopt kids—you may have the mistaken notion that the minute someone gives birth she is imbued with a maternal instinct that is practically omnipotent. Because *your* baby didn't exit *your* body, you're afraid you missed that transformative moment. But listen to us and every other adoptive parent: You didn't miss it, because it didn't exist! Maternal instinct is real, but it comes from spending time with your baby, not physically giving birth. If you ask a ton of questions, it won't reveal you as a fraud. Doctors and nurses won't suddenly say, *We knew it! You aren't a* real *parent.* So ask questions, be involved with your baby, pay attention to her behavior, and rest assured that everyone populating the maternity ward is just as clueless as you are.

Getting to Know You

No matter how you met your baby—if you were present at the birth, arranged a visit through a private or state agency, or traveled thousands of miles around the globe—you may have known the minute you laid eyes on him, or even on his photo, that he was your baby. Indeed, many adoptive parents we spoke with said that the feeling was unmistakable, something akin to love at first sight. At the same time, however, many also say they did not feel they immediately bonded. Can you have deep, unconditional love without bonding? Absolutely. And that's not just a fact for adoptive parents. No one can predict how she'll feel holding her baby for the first time, and many a birth parent is disappointed to discover that a lightning bolt of bonding didn't strike her the moment she held her baby for the first time. And so it goes for parents who adopt.

WHERE TO TURN FOR MORE HELP

- Adoption Online, adoptiononline.com.
- Adoption.com.
- Child Welfare Information Gateway, childwelfare.gov/adoption/postadoption.
- Center for Family Connections, kinnect.org.
- Dave Thomas Foundation for Adoption, davethomasfoundationforadoption.org.
- National Adoption Center, adopt.org.
- International Adoption Resource, iaradopt.com.

The biggest difference for you is how suddenly you arrived at that moment. We know it may have taken you years to meet your baby, but that doesn't negate the fact that when you finally "got the call" to get to the hospital or to hop a plane across the country or around the world, you were knocked sideways by the thought that you were about to become a parent. From what other adoptive parents tell us, that's completely normal. Without a definite due date marked on your calendar or an ever-swelling belly to get your mind used to the idea that you are beholden to a little being, jumping the divide between childless and with child is no easy task. So it's no surprise that while you may have waited and hoped and wanted this baby more than anything else in the world, you may discover that even after the joyous moment you bring your baby home, you still feel a strange sense that she is a bit beyond your reach. In other words, you don't feel the so-called maternal instinct. Fortunately, no matter how big you perceive the chasm, time as well as a few age-old parenting tools can help you build a bridge to span it. The best way to feel closer to your baby is, well, by being closer to your baby. Holding her often (no, you can't spoil a newborn) will get him accustomed to your feel and smell, and soon he will equate your loving arms with the maternal comfort zone he craves. And while breastfeeding doesn't guarantee bonding, if you were thinking that you wish you could nurse your baby, you should know that it is possible for an adoptive parent to breastfeed. However, it requires a bit of time (and luck) to get the message to your brain so it can ready your body for lactation. You should ask your doctor for guidance or contact a lactation consultant, but in general what you need to get started is a breast pump, which you would use every couple of hours to stimulate the release of milk-producing hormones. It also helps if you can be present for as many feedings following your baby's birth as possible. On the other hand, if you, like most adoptive moms, think trying to breastfeed on top of everything else you're doing is looney-tunes, don't for a second let anybody guilt-trip you. Bonding is about emotional closeness, which both feeding methods provide. For moms both biological and adoptive, bonding with your baby isn't an overnight phenomenon, but with patience, practice, and time, it will happen.

It Takes a Village

You probably have a pretty good idea at this point how your family feels about your decision to adopt, and we hope everyone gave you a wholehearted hooray! If, however, you've received lukewarm responses or even outright rejection, you and your husband may feel isolated and more than a bit hurt. It's difficult enough to care for yourself and your baby without having to worry about others' opinions. So here's our advice: Try not to worry about others' opinions. We don't mean you should lash out at people who are less than enthusiastic ("Oh yeah, Dad? Talk to the hand!"). We mean you shouldn't let the negative responses overwhelm your joy and daily efforts to bond with your baby, particularly since your obvious commitment to your child is the best way to show your family how right you were in your decision. In time, they may come around to see your child as a legitimate branch on the family tree. Meanwhile, do what you can to bring them closer to your baby, from frequent visits or perhaps even little gifts from your baby (#1 Grandma, anyone?). These are not cheap ploys. This is what most families do to widen the circle of support for their child. Sadly, there are people who never come around, and that is truly their loss. You just need to remember that you can only offer to share the love that comes with knowing your baby. It's up to each person to accept it.

As for friends who may not have been privy to your adoption plans, you may wonder how to broach the subject gracefully. The best way is to follow the footsteps of every other new parent and send out birth announcements trumpeting your new arrival. Instead of vital stats, however, you may simply want to say that you are overjoyed to welcome your baby into your family, and include his name and birthday. And of course you'll want to show off your baby with tons of pictures, which you can share online or via e-mail. After that, you don't have to introduce your baby as an adopted child. He's your baby and that's all that anyone else who isn't very close to your family needs to know.

Open Adoption

One of the many differences between today's adoptive families and those of previous generations is the option to pursue an "open adoption," meaning that the adopted child will know one or both of his birth parents. If you went this route—whether you made the choice or simply agreed to these terms based on the birth mother's preferences—you and your baby will reap some unique benefits (greater knowledge of medical history, closer connection with your baby's heritage, and the elimination of curiosity about a birth parent). However, you may also come up against unique difficulties that can be stressful on your new family.

Because having an open adoption means bringing another relative into your family, you can expect a degree of misunderstanding, hurt feelings, or resentments at any given time. As adoptive parents, you may feel a need to accommodate a birth mother's requests for visitation or parenting input, even if it goes beyond your original agreement. Or your original desire to allow her to stay involved may wane as you become more involved in the day-in, day-out job of raising your baby. The birth parent, on the other hand, may start to feel that she is being shut out and fear that she did not "choose" the right parents. Or she may start to pull away from her biological child because she realizes that staying involved only prolongs her grief or may prevent her from moving on.

However your relationship with the birth parent evolves, the best way to prevent it from becoming disruptive or troublesome is to try to keep lines of communication open. This may mean calling the birth mother directly when you have a concern, or making it a priority to return her calls. But as with any family relationship, talking alone isn't the answer. It has to come with understanding as well. And according to experts, perhaps the best way to facilitate understanding is through an intermediary, such as your adoption attorney or agency. Through a third party—preferably before you bring your baby home—you can outline when and how you will remain in contact and mediate any disagreements that occur.

Foreign Adoptions, Special Concerns

Most parents who adopt children from another country are not bringing home newborns, but older babies who have already developed routines and expectations of the adults caring for them. And while they're too little to have old habits, the habits they do have are hard to break. As parents who have been through intercountry adoption have told us (including some parents on our *Babytalk* staff), babies are tenacious when it comes to holding on to the only routines they've ever known. It's not difficult to understand that although they are arriving into a loving household and may receive more one-on-one attention than ever before in their lives, this may do little to soothe their anxiety at being removed from all that is familiar, from their diet to their sleeping arrangements. This adjustment can cause some harrowing behaviors, from hunger strikes to wailing all night.

To ease the transition, experts and parents advise you to take note of your baby's daily routine in her home country. Stock up on the same type of formula, for example, so you can bring it with you, and ask her caretakers if they've noticed any specific problems or preferences with her diet. In addition, observe where your baby sleeps. Is it in a large room with lots of other children or perhaps even in one crib with other babies? Are the lights kept on, but dim? If so, the utter silence and darkness of her cozy nursery may be frightening. If your baby seems to have trouble sleeping, you may want to try a bassinet in your room or a bedside sleeper that will reassure her that she isn't completely alone. What you should avoid, particularly in the first few months, is letting your baby cry it out until she falls asleep, which would undermine your efforts to provide her a feeling of security in your family. If you're concerned that your baby seems unhappy and unable to adjust to her daily schedule, you may want to get in touch with a therapist trained to counsel adoptive parents. (For tips on finding a good therapist, check out the article "Selecting and Working with an Adoption Therapist," published by the Child Welfare Information Gateway, childwelfare.gov/pubs/r_tips.cfm.) And by all means reach out to parents who've adopted from the same country—as they may provide tips that helped them through the first months home. (Ask your adoption agency for leads, or Google international adoption parent groups online.)

"WHAT NOBODY TOLD ME ABOUT ADOPTION"

"We're an adoptive family and I was fortunate to be in the delivery room when our son was born. I think the most amazing, although I'm not sure I'd say 'surprising,' thing is how very much he fits us. We often marvel that we could never have envisioned a child more like us even if we'd had a biological child.

"For me, it's been helpful to talk about us as an 'adoptive family' as opposed to saying 'our son is adopted.' It took me a long time to figure out what language felt best when talking about our family. To me, saying 'he's adopted' singles him out, but adoption really affects the whole family.

"Some of the best advice we received was to be selective in what we told people about the circumstances around the birth mom's adoption decision. In a sense, by telling the whole story before the child can understand it, you're telling the child's story without their permission. So, we decided early on what information we'd give out and what parts of the story will be for him to choose to tell.

"*You grew in your birth mom's belly, but grew in our hearts,* is a such a wonderful statement. I knew it was true for us when the birth mom was convinced that he would be a girl. Yet we'd always thought in our minds of a baby boy. His arrival confirmed to me that he had indeed grown in our hearts!" —*Gloria, Davis, California*

"The road to adoption was a long one for us—years of infertility treatments and a lot of sadness. That longing for a child is powerful stuff. But on the day we became parents for the first time and held our beautiful six-month-old baby girl we knew we had taken the right road. We now have two adopted children.

"It was never important to us that our children look like us; we just wanted to be parents. We are fortunate to live in a diverse community, one that celebrates and respects other cultures. This has given our kids a chance to be proud of their heritage in a safe and nurturing environment. When we travel to other places, however, our family is sometimes met with inquisitive stares or whispers—thankfully we have not encountered anything worse than that!

"We once traveled to China with five other families, all of whom adopted babies from the same orphanage in Yue Yang, Hunan province. Since then, each year we gather the "Yue Yang Gang" at a hotel to celebrate our girls' adoption day. It has been such fun watching our daughter's "Yue Yang Sisters" and their siblings grow up! The girls have an important bond, one they perhaps aren't able to articulate yet, but I think they understand that this is a connection that will be important throughout their lives. We traveled back to China a couple of years ago so Lea could see her native country and that was a great experience.

"Though our son is also adopted, we didn't travel halfway around the world to find him. He came to us as a result of work I was doing for the family court in St. Louis County. My project entailed helping the various child welfare systems work together to find permanent homes for children in foster care. During one of our meetings a social worker kept referring to an African American baby in the system they

(continued on next page)

were struggling to place. My husband and I decided to learn more about this child, and within a few months he was in our home and subsequently adopted six months later. Although Brandon was not born in Africa we do plan to take him there one day when he's a little older. I think that sometimes adoptive parents are so concerned that their kids fit in, or not be seen as different from other kids, that they are reluctant to embrace their child's culture. I would urge them to be open to learning about their children's heritage and taking part in their cultural community. It tells our kids that we value every part of who they are."   —*Donna, St. Louis, Missouri*

"After two years of unsuccessful infertility treatments, the last of which landed me in the ER, my husband and I made the decision to adopt. I contacted a placement agency to inquire about one baby boy we saw on the Web site. I will never forget the social worker saying to me, 'Well, you know, he's in Kazakhstan.' She could have said, *Well, you know, he's on the moon.* I didn't care. This was our baby. And so began seven months of paperwork, waiting, more paperwork, more waiting . . . and a surprise pregnancy!

"After receiving word that everything had been approved, we traveled halfway around the world to a little town in Kazakhstan called Taraz to meet our son. I was also five months' pregnant at the time with baby number two. The Kazakhstan government requires two weeks of bonding with your child prior to the court hearing. A day or two before court, our coordinator had picked up little Alexander at the orphanage to take him to get a passport photo taken. Once they got into the van and were on their way, he started crying and could not be consoled. My husband and I were resting in our hotel room when we got the call that our baby was downstairs! This was quite unusual. We raced down to the parking lot to see our coordinator holding a sobbing Alex. As soon as he saw us, he reached out to be held. This was the moment we knew that he knew.

"And now three years later, we have two beautiful boys: Alex who is four years old and Connor who is three. As a book we have says it best, 'Big brother, Alexander, adopted from the start. Although we are not blood brothers, we are brothers of the heart.'"

—*Annmarie, Cantonment, Florida*

Where to Turn for More Insight and Advice

The following organizations, books, Web sites, and manufacturers can provide further assistance for whatever unique needs you and your child may have.

Adoption

Adoption.com
459 North Gilbert Road, Suite C-100
Gilbert, AZ 85234
480-446-0500
adoption.com
Information on international, special-needs, independent, and private adoptions. Other features include message boards, news, and a directory of adoption professionals.

The National Adoption Center
1500 Walnut Street, Suite 701
Philadelphia, PA 19102
800-TO-ADOPT
adopt.org
Browse though a database of children looking for homes. To narrow the search, you can state preferences of age, race, and gender.

Adoption Online
6030 Daybreak Circle
#A-150, Department 211
Clarksville, MD 21029-1638

301-854-1501
adoptiononline.com
A Web site dedicated to helping prospective adoptive parents and prospective birth parents meet.

U.S. Department of State Office of Children's Issues
SA-29
U.S. Department of State
2201 C Street, NW
Washington, DC 20520-2818
888-407-4747
travel.state.gov/family
A federal agency that provides information and assistance on international adoptions.

Child Welfare Information Gateway
Children's Bureau/ACYF
1250 Maryland Avenue, SW, Eighth Floor
Washington, DC 20024
800-394-3366
childwelfare.gov
A national adoption directory search of state-by-state contact information for a variety of adoption-related organizations and services, including public and licensed private adoption agencies, support groups, state reunion registries, and more.

National Adoption Day
1010 Wisconsin Avenue, NW, Suite 800
Washington, DC 20007
202-572-2993
nationaladoptionday.com
A national effort to raise awareness of the children in foster care waiting to find permanent families.

Childcare and Working Mothers

National Association of Child Care Resource and Referral Agencies *and* Child Care Aware
3101 Wilson Boulevard, Suite 350
Arlington, VA 22201
703-341-4100 or 800-424-2246
naccrra.org or childcareaware.org
Provides referrals to local caregiver resources.

Sittercity.com
   213 West Institute Place, Suite 504
   Chicago, IL 60610
   888-SIT-CITY (748-2489)
   sittercity.com
   A national database for babysitters and nannies.

International Nanny Association
   2020 Southwest Freeway, Suite 208
   Houston, TX 77098
   888-878-1477
   nanny.org
   A nonprofit, educational association for nannies that also provides links to
nanny placement agencies, and hiring advice.

Au Pair Care
   600 California Street, FL 10
   San Francisco, CA 94108
   800-428-7247
   aupaircare.com
   A placement agency for in-home childcare.

Families and Work Institute
   267 Fifth Avenue, Floor 2
   New York, NY 10016
   212-465-2044
   familiesandwork.org
   A nonprofit research organization that provides information on families,
childcare, early-childhood development, and work.

The National Partnership for Women & Families
   1875 Connecticut Avenue, NW, Suite 650
   Washington, DC 20009
   202-986-2600
   nationalpartnership.org
   A nonprofit organization that uses public education and advocacy to promote fairness in the workplace, quality healthcare, and policies that help
women and men meet the dual demands of work and family.

National Association of Working Women
   207 East Buffalo Street, #211
   Milwaukee, WI 53202

800-522-0925
9to5.org
A hotline with information on labor laws, tips for handling a workplace problem, and legal referrals.

U.S. Department of Labor
    Frances Perkins Building
    200 Constitution Avenue, NW
    Washington, DC 20210
    866-4-USWAGE
    dol.gov
A federal agency that provides information on the Family and Medical Leave Act.

Bluesuitmom.com
    This site for working moms provides a support network, plus tips on balancing work and family and getting organized.

Colic and Soothing

Colichelp.com
    Maintained by a mother of two former colicky infants, it features colic-related message boards, chat rooms, and parent reviews of an array of colic remedies.

Pediatric Adolescent Gastroesophageal Reflux Association, Inc.
    PO Box 486
    Buckeystown, MD 21717-0486
    301-601-9541
    reflux.org
A nonprofit organization that provides information and support to parents and children dealing with gastroesophageal reflux (GER).

The Happiest Baby on the Block: The New Way to Calm Crying and Help Your Newborn Sleep Longer
    by Dr. Harvey Karp (Bantam, 2002)

The Out-of-Sync Child: Recognizing and Coping with Sensory Processing Disorder
    by Carol Stock Kranowitz (Perigee, 2005)

Sensory Processing Disorder Network
    5655 South Yosemite, Suite 305

Greenwood Village, CO 80111
303-794-1182
kidfoundation.org
An organization that focuses on research, education, and advocacy related to Sensory Processing Disorder (SPD).

Dunstan Baby Language System DVD
$59.99 plus shipping; to order call 888-386-7826, or go to dunstanbaby.com.
A new method that helps parents better understand and respond to their newborns' cries.

Disorders and Disabilities

National Institute of Child Health & Human Development
PO Box 3006
Rockville, MD 20847
800-370-2943
nichd.nih.gov
The institute conducts and supports research on all stages of human development, from preconception to adulthood, to better understand the health of children, adults, families, and communities.

National Dissemination Center for Children with Disabilities
PO Box 1492
Washington, DC 20013
800-695-0285
nichcy.org
This Web site can help you locate disability-related resources in each state.

Easter Seals
230 West Monroe Street, Suite 1800
Chicago, IL 60606
800-221-6827
easterseals.com
A nonprofit, community-based health agency dedicated to helping children and adults with disabilities attain greater independence.

Genetics Home Reference
888-FIND-NLM (346-3656)
ghr.nlm.nih.gov
A service of the U.S. National Library of Medicine that provides free access to consumer-friendly information on medical genetics.

Children's Neurobiological Solutions
   1826 State Street
   Santa Barbara, CA 93101-2420
   866-267-5580
   cnsfoundation.org
   A nonprofit organization dedicated to accelerating medical research for
pediatric brain repair and regeneration.

Interdisciplinary Council on Developmental and Learning Disorders
   4938 Hampden Lane, Suite 800
   Bethesda, MD 20814
   301-656-2667
   icdl.com
   An organization whose mission is to advance the identification, prevention, and treatment of developmental and learning disorders.

National Center on Birth Defects and Developmental Disabilities
   1600 Clifton Road
   Atlanta, GA 30333
   800-311-3435
   cd.gov/ncbddd
   A government agency that provides information on identifying the causes
of and preventing birth defects and developmental disabilities.

National Birth Defects Prevention Network
   nbdpn.org
   A national network of programs for birth defects surveillance, research,
and prevention

National Newborn Screening and Genetics Resource Center
   1912 West Anderson Lane, Suite 210
   Austin, TX 78757
   512-454-6419
   genes-r-us.uthscsa.edu
   A large collection of resources on birth defects and on genetic/metabolic
screening of infants.

Save Babies Through Screening Foundation
   4 Manor View Circle
   Malvern, PA 19355-1622
   888-454-3383
   savebabies.org

Information about screening choices and state requirements, plus a resource library and links to testing facilities.

The Autism Society of America
7910 Woodmont Avenue, Suite 300
Bethesda, MD 20814-3067
800-3-AUTISM (328-8476)
autism-society.org
A group that funds biomedical research into autism's causes and treatments, offers advice on early detection and treatment, and sponsors events for families.

Autism Speaks
2 Park Avenue, 11th Floor
New York, NY 10016
212-252-8584
autismspeaks.org
An organization dedicated to increasing awareness of autism spectrum disorders, to funding research into the causes, prevention, and treatments of and cure for autism, and to advocating for the needs of affected families.

First Signs
PO Box 358
Merrimac, MA 01860
978-346-4380
firstsigns.org
Includes information on healthy development, early identification of, and intervention for children with developmental delays and disorders, and even insurance coverage.

Cleft Palate Foundation
1504 East Franklin Street, Suite 102
Chapel Hill, NC 27514-2820
800-24-CLEFT
cleftline.org
A nonprofit organization dedicated to optimizing the quality of life for individuals affected by facial birth defects.

United Cerebral Palsy
1660 L Street, NW, Suite 700
Washington, DC 20036
800-872-5827
ucp.org

A leading source of information on cerebral palsy, and an advocate for the rights of those with any disability.

Pathways Awareness Foundation
    150 North Michigan Avenue, Suite 2100
    Chicago, IL 60601
    800-955-CHILD (2445)
    pathwaysawareness.org
    A nonprofit organization dedicated to raising awareness about the benefit of early detection and early therapy for children with early motor delays.

Spina Bifida Association of America
    4590 MacArthur Boulevard, NW, Suite 250
    Washington, DC 20007-4226
    800-621-3141
    sbaa.org
    Start here if your child has spina bifida, or call for information on multiple-marker screening and ultrasound.

American Speech-Language-Hearing Association
    10801 Rockville Pike
    Rockville, MD 20852
    800-638-8255
    asha.org
    Professional, scientific, and credentialing association for audiologists, speech-language pathologists, and speech, language, and hearing scientists. Also provides informative publications, a help line, and referral to audiologists and speech-language pathologists.

American Society for Deaf Children
    3820 Hartzdale Drive
    Camp Hill, PA 17011
    800-42-ASDC (2732)
    deafchildren.org
    An organization advocating for rights and education for deaf children.

Alexander Graham Bell Association for the Deaf and Hard of Hearing
    3417 Volta Place, NW
    Washington, DC 20007
    202-337-5220
    agbell.org
    An international organization and resource center on hearing loss.

National Down Syndrome Society
  666 Broadway
  New York, NY 10012
  800-221-4602
  ndss.org
  Provides help for people with Down syndrome and their families through national leadership in education, research, and advocacy.

National Association for Down Syndrome
  PO Box 206
  Wilmette, IL 60091
  630-325-9112
  nads.org
  The oldest organization in the country serving individuals with Down syndrome and their families.

National Down Syndrome Congress
  1370 Center Drive, Suite 102
  Atlanta, GA 30338
  800-232-NDSC (6372)
  ndsccenter.org
  A network of local and regional groups across the country aiming to reach out and embrace people with Down syndrome, their families, their friends, and the professionals who support them.

Fatherhood

National Fatherhood Initiative
  101 Lake Forest Boulevard, Suite 360
  Gaithersburg, MD 20877
  301-948-0599
  fatherhood.org
  Improves the well-being of children by increasing the proportion of those growing up with involved, responsible, and committed fathers.

Dadsadventure.com
  Run by Boot Camp for New Dads, a nonprofit group offering classes for rookie fathers across the country. The site includes articles on caring for your postpartum wife and bonding with your infant, a guide to a baby's cries, safety tips, basic babycare instructions, and a veteran dads' advice corner.

Fathersforum.com

An online meeting place for reflective dads provided by Bruce Linton, PhD, a psychotherapist in Berkeley, California. You'll find articles on how having children changes men, how marriage is altered by adding a child to the equation, and how the myths of fatherhood affect us all.

Fathersworld.com

A one-stop resource for advice, regular columnists, health news, bulletin boards, and a store. Founded by James McLaughlin, editor of *Full-Time Dads* magazine, the site also offers tips to anxious dads-to-be on how to prepare for fatherhood and how to choose a pediatrician.

Fathersonline.com

Lots of dad-to-dad interaction with lively chats, online mentors, and links.

Feeding

La Leche League
    800-LA-LECHE
    lalecheleague.org
    For answers to breastfeeding questions and contact numbers for local support groups.

International Lactation Consultant Association
    1500 Sunday Drive, Suite 102
    Raleigh, NC 27607
    919-861-5577
    ilca.org
    To find a lactation consultant.

The National Conference of State Legislatures
    ncsl.org/programs/health/breast50.htm
    A state-by-state list of breastfeeding laws.

American Dietetic Association
    120 South Riverside Plaza, Suite 2000
    Chicago, IL 60606-6995
    800-877-1600
    eatright.org
    The premier professional nutrition organization maintains this easy-to-navigate site, which affects information on women and children's nutrition, plus a dietitian referral system.

Gerber Nutrition Hotline
  800-4-GERBER
  gerber.com
  Useful advice on infant feeding in a personalized format.

Beech-Nut Nutrition Hotline
  800-523-6633
  beechnut.com
  Answers to your questions about feeding infants and toddlers.

Child of Mine: Feeding with Love and Good Sense
  by Ellyn Satter (Bull Publishing Company, 2000)

Guide to Your Child's Nutrition: Making Peace at the Table and Building Healthy Eating Habits for Life
  from the American Academy of Pediatrics (Villard, 1999)

Dr. Mom's Guide to Breastfeeding
  by Marianne Neifert, MD (Plume, 1998)

Lansinoh Lanolin Topical Treatment
  $9. For availability, call 800-292-4794 or visit lansinoh.com.

Medela Pump In Style Advanced breast pump
  $350. For availability, call 800-435-8316 or go to medela.com.

Playtex Embrace breast pump
  $249. For availability, contact 800-249-0832 or go to playtexbaby.com.

Ameda Purely Yours breast pump
  $200 and up, depending on bag style. For availability, contact 800-323-4060 or see ameda.com.

Lansinoh Double Electric Pump
  $150. For availability, call 800-292-4794 or visit lansinoh.com.

Avent ISIS iQ UNO handheld electric breast pump
  $150. For availability, call 800-542-8368 or see aventamerica.com.

Medela Single Deluxe Electric breast pump
  $65. For availability, call 800-435-8316 or go to medela.com.

Avent ISIS breast pump
$45. For availability, contact 800-542-8368 or go to aventamerica.com.

Easy Expression Hands-Free Pumping Bra or Bustier
$34. For availability, call 866-522-7177or visit easyexpressionproducts.
com.

Second Nature Nurser and Nipples
Prices range $12–20. For availability, contact 800-593-5522 or second naturefeeding.com.

Gear

Juvenile Products Manufacturers Association (JPMA)
15000 Commerce Parkway, Suite C
Mount Laurel, NJ 08054
856-638-0420
jpma.org
JPMA is a national trade organization of companies that manufacture and/ or import infant products such as cribs, car seats, strollers, bedding, and a wide range of accessories and decorative items. Its respected certification program helps guide parents on safe purchases; look for the seal on product packaging. The Web site also includes helpful safety advice.

Baby Must-Haves: The Essential Guide to Everything from Cribs to Bibs
by the editors of *Parenting* magazine (Time Inc. Home Entertainment, 2007)

General Health and Development

Babytalk magazine
Parenting.com/babytalk
Straight talk for new moms—of course!

Parenting magazine
Parenting.com
What matters to moms.

American Academy of Pediatrics
PO Box 927
141 Northwest Point Boulevard
Elk Grove Village, IL 60007

847-434-4000

aap.org

A nonprofit national organization of pediatricians dedicated to furthering children's health. The Web site includes robust health and development advice for parents. The AAP also contributes a column in every issue of *Babytalk*.

March of Dimes
  1275 Mamaroneck Avenue
  White Plains, NY 10605
  888-663-4637
  marchofdimes.com
The March of Dimes provides a wealth of research and advice for expectant moms and mothers of preemies or infants with other health issues.

Zero to Three
  2000 M Street, NW, Suite 200
  Washington, DC 20036
  202-638-1144
  zerotothree.org
A comprehensive interactive resource that supports the healthy development of children ages zero to three.

KidsHealth.org
  Doctor-approved, up-to-date news and information on children's health created by The Nemours Foundation's Center for Children's Health Media.

Kaiser Family Foundation
  1330 G Street, NW
  Washington, DC 20005
  202-347-5270
  kff.org
  Provides in-depth information on key health policy issues.

Johnson & Johnson Pediatric Institute
  jjpi.com
  Dedicated to saving mothers and babies by addressing critical health priorities around the world.

What to Expect the First Year
  by Arlene Eisenberg, Heidi E. Murkoff, and Sandee E. Hathaway (Simon & Schuster, 2004)

Whattoexpect.com is the perfect online companion to this classic book series, which also includes *What to Expect When You're Expecting, What to Expect the Toddler Years,* and a series of What to Expect children's books.

Webmd.com
   Smart, up-to-date health advice from doctors for the whole family.

Mayo Clinic
   mayoclinic.com
   A reliable source of health information.

Heading Home with Your Newborn: From Birth to Reality
   by Laura A. Jana, MD, FAAP, and Jennifer Shu, MD, FAAP (AAP, 2005)

The Experts' Guide to the Baby Years: 100 Things Every Parent Should Know
   by Samantha Ettus (Clarkson Potter, 2006)

The Baby Book
   by William Sears, MD, and Martha Sears, RN (Harper Thorsons, 2005)
   Solid health and development advice from *Babytalk* contributing editors.

Mom Care and Marriage

American College of Obstetricians and Gynecologists
   409 Twelfth Street, SW
   PO Box 96920
   Washington, DC 20090-6920
   202-638-5577
   acog.org
   A nonprofit organization of women's healthcare physicians advocating the highest standards of practice in the fields of obstetrics and gynecology.

Postpartum Support International
   PO Box 60931
   Santa Barbara, CA 93160
   805-967-7636
   postpartum.net
   A national education and referral resource for postpartum disorders.

Multiples

Twinsetmoms.com
A blog written by two moms of multiples, *Babytalk* contributing editor Christina Boyle and Cathleen Stahl.

The National Organization of Mothers of Twins Clubs
PO Box 700860
Plymouth, MI 48170-0955
248-231-4480
nomotc.org
A national support group for parents of twins, triplets, and beyond.

Twins Magazine
11211 East Arapahoe Road, Suite 101
Centennial, CO 80112-3851
888-55-TWINS (558-9467)
twinsmagazine.com
A paper and online magazine that provides product information, research, and advice for parents of multiples, plus message boards and periodic surveys.

Mothers of Supertwins
PO Box 306
East Islip, NY 11730
631-859-1110
mostonline.org
A network of families with triplets, quadruplets, and more.

The Triplet Connection
PO Box 429
Spring City, UT 84662
435-851-1105
tripletconnection.org
An international network for families of triplets and higher-order births.

Twin Services Consulting
PO Box 10066
Berkeley, CA 94709
510-524-0863
twinservices.org
Started by Patricia Malmstrom, an authority and advocate on multiple-birth development, to help parents cope with the twinshock that comes with

the diagnosis of a twin (or higher) pregnancy and with the care of multiple-birth children.

Double Blessings
 13876 Honnell Way
 Jamul, CA 91935
 800-584-TWIN
 doubleblessings.com
 Twin and multiple themes on shirts, caps, mugs, and gifts, along with accessories including nursing pillows, slings, strollers, backpacks, crib dividers, and other products for multiples.

Just 4 Twins
 269-763-9039
 just4twins.com
 An online store that specializes in creative and trendy gifts for twins, triplets, and higher multiples.

Mothering Twins: From Hearing the News to Beyond the Terrible Twos
 by Linda Albi, Deborah Johnson, Debra Catlin, Donna Florien Deurloo, and Sheryll Greatwood (Fireside, 1993)

The Joy of Twins and Other Multiple Births: Having, Raising, and Loving Babies Who Arrive in Groups
 by Pamela Patrick Novotny (Three Rivers Press, 1994)

Twins! Pregnancy, Birth, and the First Year of Life
 by Connie L. Agnew, MD Alan H. Klein, MD, and Jill Alison Ganon (Collins, 2006)

Entwined Lives: Twins and What They Tell Us about Human Behavior
 by Nancy Segal, PhD (Plume, 2000)

Prematurity

Prematurity.org
 A parent support site on preemie care.

March of Dimes
 1275 Mamaroneck Avenue
 White Plains, NY 10605

888-663-4637
marchofdimes.com
The March of Dimes provides a wealth of research and advice for expectant moms and mothers of preemies or infants with other health issues.

Safety

National Highway Traffic Safety Administration
400 Seventh Street, SW
Washington, DC 20590
888-327-4236
nhtsa.gov
A government agency dedicated to achieving the highest standards of excellence in motor vehicle and highway safety to save lives, prevent injuries, and reduce vehicle-related crashes.

Consumer Reports
101 Truman Avenue
Yonkers, NY 10703-1057
consumerreports.org
A national publication that features ratings and recommendations on thousands of products, including baby products. *Consumer Reports* also contributes a column in every issue of *Babytalk*.

Chrysler Seat Check
866-SEAT-CHECK
seatcheck.org
A national campaign to help parents properly secure their children in motor vehicles.

Safe Kids Worldwide
1301 Pennsylvania Avenue, NW, Suite 1000
Washington, DC 20004-1707
202-662-0600
safekids.org
A global network whose mission is to prevent accidental childhood injury. They offer lots of good safety advice online.

U.S. Consumer Product Safety Commission
4330 East West Highway
Bethesda, MD 20814

800-638-2772

cpsc.gov

The U.S. Consumer Product Safety Commission protects the public from unreasonable risks of serious injury or death from more than fifteen thousand types of consumer products under its jurisdiction.

Get on Board with Child Safety

getonboardwithsafety.com

A national child injury prevention initiative that educates parents, caregivers, and consumers about the changes they can make to prevent unintentional injuries in and around the home and on the road.

International Association for Child Safety

144 North Beverwyck Road, #202

Lake Hiawatha, NJ 07034

888-677-4227

iafcs.org

A nonprofit organization that promotes safety awareness and injury prevention for children. Contact this group to locate a childproofer in your area.

Home Safety Council

1250 Eye Street, NW, Suite 1000

Washington, DC 20005

202-330-4900

homesafetycouncil.org

Educates people to be safer in and around their homes, through national programs, partnerships, and the support of volunteers.

One Step Ahead

800-274-8440

onestepahead.com

A collection of home safety and childproofing products.

Safety 1st

800-544-1108

safety1st.com

Search for home safety products by age and room.

Perfectly Safe

800-837-5437

kidsstuff.com

Find child safety products to childproof every room in your home, as well as your car, outdoors, and on the go.

KidCo
    1013 Technology Way
    Libertyville, IL 60048
    800-553-5529
    kidcoinc.com
    Premier source of safety gates.

Safety Belt Safe
    PO Box 553
    Altadena, CA 91003
    310-222-6860
    carseat.org
    A child passenger safety advocacy group that provides information on selecting and properly using car seats and boosters.

SIDS

First Candle/SIDS Alliance
    1314 Bedford Avenue, Suite 210
    Baltimore, MD 21208
    800-221-7437
    sidsalliance.org
    A national nonprofit health organization that works to increase public participation and support in the fight against infant mortality.

National SIDS/Infant Death Resource Center
    8280 Greensboro Drive, Suite 300
    McLean, VA 22102
    703-821-8955
    sidscenter.org
    Provides information and resources about SIDS and other unexpected infant death, stillbirth, and miscarriage.

Single Parenting

Making Lemonade: The Single Parent Network
    makinglemonade.com
    A Web site for single parents with everything from legal resources to dating advice.

Parents without Partners, Inc.
 1650 South Dixie Highway, Suite 510
 Boca Raton, FL 33432
 800-637-7974
 parentswithoutpartners.org
 A nonprofit educational organization devoted to the interests of single parents and their children.

Single Mothers by Choice
 PO Box 1642
 Gracie Square Station
 New York, NY 10028
 212-988-0993
 singlemothersbychoice.com
 Provides support and information to single women who are considering, or who have chosen, single motherhood.

Single Parent Resource Center
 31 East Twenty-eight Street
 New York, NY 10016
 212-951-7030
 singleparentusa.com
 A clearinghouse for information on single-parent organizations in the United States and around the world.

National Organization of Single Mothers, Inc.
 PO Box 68
 Midland, NC 28107
 704-888-5437
 singlemothers.org
 Helps single moms meet the challenges of daily life with wisdom, wit, dignity, confidence, and courage.

Solo Parents Network
 soloparentsnetwork.com
 A social networking Web site for single parents by single parents to meet single parents.

In Praise of Single Parents: Mothers and Fathers Embracing the Challenge
 by Shoshana Alexander (Houghton Mifflin, 1994)

365 Positive Strategies for Single Parenting
 by Susan B. Brown and Monica Simmons (Smyth and Hewlys Publishing, 1998)

The Single Parent Resource
 by Brook Noel with Arthur C. Klein (Champion Press, 1998)

Solo Parenting: Raising Strong and Happy Families
 by Diane Chambers (Fairview Press, 1997)

Adopting on Your Own: The Complete Guide to Adopting as a Single Parent
 by Lee Varon (Farrar, Straus & Giroux, 2000)

Sleep

Sleeping through the Night: How Infants, Toddlers, and Their Parents Can get a Good Night's Sleep
 by Jodi Mindell, PhD (Collins, 1997)

The Baby Sleep Book: The Complete Guide to a Good Night's Rest for the Whole Family
 by William Sears, MD, Robert Sears, MD, James Sears, MD, and Martha Sears, RN (Little, Brown, 2005)

Solve Your Child's Sleep Problems
 by Richard Ferber, MD (Fireside, 2006)
 The classic sleep training book, updated, says crying it out is not right for sensitive babies.

Sleeplady.com and *Good Night, Sleep Tight: The Sleep Lady's Gentle Guide to Helping Your Child Go to Sleep, Stay Asleep, and Wake Up Happy*
 by Kim West and Joanne Kenen (CDS Books, 2006)
 Good information if you want to change your baby's sleep habits.

Travel

Baby's Away
 800-984-9030
 babysaway.com
 The largest baby and child supply rental service, providing quality equipment such as cribs, strollers, car seats, and high chairs.

Family Travel Forum
  891 Amsterdam Avenue
  New York, NY 10025
  212-665-6124
  familytravelforum.com
  The best family travel site on the Web, including everything from car trip survival tips to reader reviews of destinations and gear. You'll also find inside scoop on special deals, how-tos on subjects like house swapping and cruising with kids, and a free monthly e-mail bulletin. Join the site for $48 a year to receive members-only bargains, a print newsletter, and access to additional articles.

Travel with Kids
  travelwithkids.about.com
  Clean, easy-to-navigate design, lots of links, and tips on topics ranging from getting around Disney to traveling with a special-needs child. Free newsletter, weekly bargains, recommended destinations, and printable packing lists are all included.

Family Travel Guides
  familytravelguides.com
  A searchable database of lodging, attractions, and activities for families planning travel vacations.

GORP
  gorp.com
  This site is a resource for adventure travel and outdoor recreation, with information on top destinations, national parks, outdoor gear, hiking, and kayaking.

Baby Maneuvers: For Parents On-the-Go Anywhere and Everywhere with Babies and Tots
  by Ericka Lutz (Alpha Books, 1997)

Have Kid, Will Travel: 101 Survival Strategies for Vacationing with Babies and Young Children
  by Claire Tristram and Lucille Tristram (Andrews McMeel, 1997)

Trouble-Free Travel with Children: Helpful Hints for Parents on the Go
  by Vicki Lansky (Book Peddlers, 1996)

About the Authors

KITTY O'CALLAGHAN is a freelance writer and a columnist for and former senior editor of *Babytalk* magazine. She is the winner of a National Magazine Award for Personal Service for her article "You Can Breastfeed!" which appeared in the August 2005 issue of *Babytalk*. Her work has appeared in numerous national publications, including *Parenting*; *O, the Oprah Magazine*; *Self*; and *Nick Jr. Magazine*, as well as the *New York Times*. She has three children and lives in White Plains, New York.

STEPHANIE WOOD is a contributing editor at *Babytalk* and a freelance journalist who has been covering the subject of parenting and family life for twenty years. Her work has appeared in many national publications in addition to *Babytalk*, including *Parenting, Family Life, Child, Parents, Working Mother, Redbook, Woman's Day, McCalls, Nick Jr.*, and *Sesame Street Parents*. She is a former executive editor of *Child* and editor-in-chief of *Reader's Digest Your Family*. Wood is the co-author, with Robert Shaw, MD, of *The Epidemic: The Rot of American Culture, Absentee and Permissive Parenting, and the Resulting Plague of Joyless, Selfish Children* (Regan Books, 2003). She lives with her husband and three children in Blauvelt, New York.

SUSAN KANE has been editor-in-chief of *Babytalk* magazine since October 1998. Since then, she has increased the magazine's reach to nearly 5.5 million readers, helping women navigate the emotional roller coaster and practical realities of being a new mom.

With a greater focus on a confidence-building mix of news and advice from experts and moms who "tell it like it is," Susan recently spearheaded the successful repositioning of all three publications in the *Babytalk* franchise—*Babytalk*, *Babytalk Mom-to-Be*, and *Babytalk First Months*. *Babytalk* also added another award to its growing list of industry accolades in 2005—the National Magazine Award for Personal Service.

Prior to joining *Babytalk*, Susan held positions as executive editor at *YM*, executive editor at *New Woman*, and senior editor at *Woman*.

Susan frequently appears on national television on behalf of *Babytalk*, providing lively commentary on issues ranging from affordable daycare to new trends in baby gear on programs including *Today*, *Good Morning America*, and *The Early Show*.

A Phi Beta Kappa graduate of Vassar College, Susan lives in Chappaqua, New York, with her husband and two children.

Index

Index